Phrases Make History Here

To Cathy, Michael, Joan,
Patrick and Emer

Phrases Make History Here

A CENTURY OF
IRISH POLITICAL QUOTATIONS
1886-1986

CONOR O'CLERY

B

THE O'BRIEN PRESS
DUBLIN

First published 1986 by The O'Brien Press Ltd.
20 Victoria Road, Dublin 6, Ireland

British Library Cataloguing in Publication Data
O'Clery, Conor
Phrases make history here: a century
of Irish political quotations.
1. Ireland — History — 1837-1901
2. Ireland — History — 20th century
I. Title
941.508 DA950
ISBN 0-86278-108-6

10 9 8 7 6 5 4 3 2 1

Production editing: Íde ní Laoghaire
Book design: Michael O'Brien
Typesetting: Phototype-Set Ltd.
Set in Plantin
Printing: Billings Ltd.

Contents

✎ Introduction ✎

THE title of this book, 'Phrases Make History Here', is taken from a letter written on May 21, 1945, by the British Ambassador in Dublin, Sir John Maffey, to the Dominions Office in London.[1] Sir John was referring to two radio broadcasts made a few days before, one on May 13 by the British Prime Minister, Winston Churchill, announcing victory in Europe in the Second World War;[2] the other by the Taoiseach, Eamon de Valera, three days later.[3] In his radio address, Churchill had made a strong personal attack on his old adversary in Ireland. Because of de Valera's policy of Irish neutrality in the war, he said, Britain, standing alone, had been denied the use of Irish ports in fighting for its survival while the Taoiseach 'frolicked' with the Germans. De Valera had gone on Irish radio to reply. Churchill, he said, had been proud of Britain's stand alone. Could he not find in his heart the generosity to acknowledge a small nation that had stood against aggression for several hundred years? The Ambassador, listening to his radio in the Irish capital, had no doubt who had got the better of the argument. De Valera had emerged with dignity, adopting the pose of an elder statesman. Maffey wrote in despair of Churchill: 'How are you to control Ministerial incursions into your china shop? Phrases make history here.'

Sir John Maffey had touched upon a unique feature of Irish politics in his conclusion that phrases make history in Ireland. Irish history has been dominated for centuries by the struggle with Britain which, in the way of constitutional epics everywhere, has produced heroic words and resounding phrases from both sides. Words have often come to be charged with as much significance as the events which inspired them. As British Prime Minister, Lloyd George had to caution MPs in Commons on December 14, 1921, when they were debating the Anglo-Irish Treaty, with the words: 'You do not settle great complicated problems the moment you utter a good phrase about them.'[4] The 'good phrase' has nevertheless inspired, inflamed and

7

bedevilled Irish politics and has become part of the intellectual and emotional baggage of every generation of politicians, North and South.

Nationhood in Ireland is measured still by the words of Robert Emmet, spoken in the dock before his execution in September 1803 for leading a rebellion against the English: 'When my country takes her place among the nations of the earth, then, and not till then, let my epitaph be written.'[5] The concept of the ideal Irish Republic is to this day defined by politicians and editorial writers in the phrases of Wolfe Tone, leader of the 1798 rebellion, who aspired to 'substitute the common name of Irishman in place of the denominations of Protestant, Catholic and dissenter.'[6] In Ireland the perception of the English is still coloured by the folk-memory of the contemptuous words of Oliver Cromwell when he crushed the Irish Catholics in the seventeenth century. They could, he said, 'go to hell or Connaught',[7] Connaught being the most barren and westerly of the four Irish provinces. In the same century, in 1689, the loyalist cry of 'No surrender!' was first heard when the Protestants of Derry held out against the Catholic army of King James.

This phrase has become part of the permanent vocabulary of Unionism, as has the saying 'Ulster will fight; Ulster will be right',[8] one of the first phrases quoted in this book. These words, uttered in 1886 by the English Conservative politician, Lord Randolph Churchill, were a response to the prospect of Home Rule being granted to Ireland mainly because of the agitation of the Irish Party MPs at Westminster, led by Charles Stewart Parnell, who in our opening quote claimed to have Home Rule within the hollow of his hand[9], and who the year before had inspired his followers with the declaration: 'No man has the right to fix the boundary to the march of a nation. No man has the right to say to his country "Thus far shalt thou go and no further".'[10] In that critical year of 1886, the British Prime Minister, William Gladstone, who had said his mission was to pacify Ireland,[11] introduced the first of three Home Rule Bills, thus setting in motion a sequence of events which over the next hundred years would result in recurring warfare, the partitioning of the country and the creation of two political entities, the Irish Free State, which would eventually become the Republic of Ireland, and Northern Ireland, still part of the United Kingdom. As the issue of Home Rule became the subject of great debates in the House of Commons in the years after 1886, 'Ulster' fought, as Randolph Churchill predicted, mainly with words and phrases, developing, under the Unionist leader, Edward Carson, a grammar of anarchy to threaten rebellion if Home Rule, or rule from Dublin, were imposed upon them. They imported arms and drilled, and by playing the 'Orange card' got their way in destroying the Home Rule Bills.

Nationalist Ireland drew the conclusion that only force would have any effect on Britain and the debate about Home Rule was replaced with the rhetoric of rebellion. The Nationalist leader, Padraic Pearse, proclaimed, only a few months before his execution for leading the 1916 Rising in Dublin, in words used today by Sinn Féin: 'Ireland unfree shall never be at peace.'[12] After the rebellion and the ensuing War of Independence, Lloyd George tried again to 'pacify' Ireland, this time by a treaty with the Nationalist leaders which accepted Irish partition and gave limited independence to a Free State of twenty-six counties. It was agreed to by Irish representatives, elected as members of an embryo Irish Republic, but only with the words of Lloyd George, threatening renewed 'war, and war in three days',[13] ringing in their ears, and in the hope that, as the IRA leader, Michael Collins, promised, it meant 'freedom to achieve freedom.'[14] The romantic and ringing phrases of the fight against the traditional enemy then gave way to the bitter words of civil war and the defeat of the Republicans by Free State forces. 'We had fed the heart on fantasies,' wrote the poet W. B. Yeats, 'The heart's grown brutal from the fare.'[15] He wondered if words of his had sent young men out to be shot. The great political arguments gave way to debates within the two states on how to come to terms with the societies they had inherited and the constitutional tensions which remained. In the North, this meant the consolidation of a 'Protestant Parliament and a Protestant State' as the Northern Ireland Prime Minister, James Craig, described it in 1934.[16] In the South, Eamon de Valera, his Republican cause defeated, abandoned violence and founded Fianna Fáil, a 'slightly constitutional' party.[17] He and the emerging force in British politics, Winston Churchill, both outstanding phrase-makers, dominated Anglo-Irish exchanges for three decades. As British wartime leader, Churchill bitterly opposed Irish neutrality, but de Valera, who had become leader of the Irish Government in 1932, never deviated from a policy of refusal to cooperate with England in waging war while Britain kept Ireland partitioned. All his public statements reflected his concept of Irish independence and his refusal to compromise, even when Churchill tempted him with eventual Irish unity in return for wartime cooperation. De Valera's vision of Ireland was of a nation which would decide its own international policies and which would, as he said in a famous St Patrick's Day broadcast in 1943, become a land 'whose countryside would be bright with cosy homesteads, whose fields and villages would be joyous with the sounds of . . . the contests of athletic youths and the laughter of comely maidens.'[18] It would be a land where people devoted their leisure to the things of the spirit and were satisfied with frugal comfort.

This vision was by and large shared by the Catholic Church. In Ireland, politicians come and go, but as a body, the Irish Catholic bishops have been a constant voice. The hundred years with which this book is concerned open with their influential support for Home Rule and close with their successful opposition to social changes in the South. The Catholic Hierarchy became a powerful force in shaping the state which emerged after the Treaty. The bishops spoke out against the Republicans in the civil war, forbade Catholics to enter the Protestant Trinity College in Dublin (until recently), described as sinners politicians who supported the Sunday opening of public houses (until forced to accept that they could not prevent it happening), and, in a celebrated intervention in 1951, succeeded in stopping the Coalition Government of John A. Costello from introducing a 'Mother and Child' welfare scheme because it offended the anti-socialist principles of the Catholic Church, precipitating the resignation of the Health Minister, Noel Browne.[19] The bitterness of that debate still finds echoes in the rhetoric of Church-State relations today.

The other constant in Irish political argument for a hundred years has been the debate about physical force, embodied on the Nationalist side by the IRA, which emerged with renewed strength after years of defeat and disillusion in 1970 when the Catholic population of the North came into open conflict with the Unionist Government over civil rights. The Provisional IRA was set up in that year with some help from elements in the Fianna Fáil Government, resulting in the arrest of ministers and an arms trial which shook the foundations of the state, and led to a painful re-wording of the language of nationalism in the Republic, as politicians came to terms with the passions unleashed North and South and the reality of the Northern situation. The verbal Republicanism of decades of comparative peace was challenged. In the seventeen years of the present 'troubles' in the North, new phrase-makers have emerged, defining and re-defining the concepts of nationalism and the union: Jack Lynch, Conor Cruise O'Brien, Garret FitzGerald, Charles Haughey, John Hume, Gerry Adams, Enoch Powell, Ian Paisley, Andy Tyrie, James Molyneaux, Harold McCusker, and, on the part of successive British Governments, Harold Wilson, Jim Callaghan, Edward Heath, Margaret Thatcher and Tom King, all trying again to pacify Ireland.

The quotations in this book have been selected to give a chronology of the remembered and the telling phrases of the last hundred years, touching on the great issues and arguments of the day, the political and social preoccupations and the passing distractions. The selection is subject to my own judgement, ignorance and prejudices as to what is apt, controversial, interesting, or worthy of inclusion. It is not quite correct to say, as Dr Johnson once did, that the Irish are a fair-minded people as 'they never speak well of each other.'[20] The common abuse of political debate in the Irish parliament is no more vindictive than in the House of Commons or any other legislature; most is not worth recording. Where possible, the quotations have been obtained from primary sources such as newspapers, parliamentary records or original writings. Many of the earlier quotations have, by necessity, been taken from the dozens of history books written about Ireland in the last hundred years. Practically every quotation since 1968 has been obtained from the volumes of *The Irish Times* in the British Newspaper Library in London. Each quotation is placed in context and the source identified.

Phrases Make History Here will, I hope, be delved into for interest, amusement or reference, or read from beginning to end as an oral history of Ireland during its most turbulent years, a sort of historical transcript, with plot, dialogue and a multitude of characters, all in their different ways using words and phrases to shape the society and the destiny of the communities that coexist on the island of Ireland.

I would like to thank all those who helped me find quotations, including the staff of *The Irish Times* and the House of Commons Libraries, and to express my particular thanks to Íde O'Leary of The O'Brien Press for her help, patience and encouragement.

FOOTNOTES

1 See page 108.
2 See page 108.
3 See page 108.
4 *HC Debates:* Vol. 149: Col. 31.
5 T.D., A.M. & D.B. Sullivan, *Speeches from the Dock,* Gill and Macmillan, 1968, pp. 42-43.
6 McMahon, Sean, *A Book of Irish Quotations,* O'Brien, 1984, p. 155.
7 O'Farrell, Patrick, *Ireland's English Question,* Batsford, 1971, p. 37.
8 See page 26.
9 See page 25.
10 Lyons, F. S. L., *Ireland Since the Famine,* Fontana, 1985, p. 186.
11 McMahon, Sean, *A Book of Irish Quotations,* O'Brien, 1984, p. 65.
12 See page 49.
13 See page 68.
14 See page 71.
15 Yeats, W. B., 'The Stare's Nest by My Window', from 'The Tower', 1928; *Collected Poems,* Macmillan, 1965, p. 230.
16 See page 95.
17 See page 89.
18 See page 106.
19 See page 112.
20 Ervine, St John, *Bernard Shaw,* Constable, 1956, p. 273.

HOW TO USE THIS BOOK

The quotations are arranged in chronological order, and may be read straight through as an oral history.

There is an index to speakers on page 220. Speakers are arranged here in alphabetical order and the page reference for each quotation is given.

There is a subject index on page 226. Subjects are arranged in alphabetical order and quotations are indexed by page number. Where a person occurs in a quotation as the subject of that quotation they are indexed in this subject index.

There is a historical summary on page 13. This gives an account of the political developments in Ireland from 1886-1986, thus providing general background information for the quotations.

Running heads list the most significant topics on each page.

When a quotation is taken from 'This Week They Said' (*The Irish Times*), the date attributed is the same as the date of publication unless the original date has been established.

❧ *Historical Summary* ❧
1886-1986

1886

By 1886, the island of Ireland is being ruled direct from London. It is an integral part of the United Kingdom, and has been for eighty-five years, since the Act of Union in 1800 which abolished an independent Irish Parliament and amalgamated it with the British Parliament. The majority Catholic population in Ireland had once supported the Act of Union; the old Irish Parliament had been controlled by the mainly Protestant British settlers who had come across the Irish Sea in the sixteenth and seventeenth centuries, seizing most of the land, depriving the Catholics of property and civil rights. But direct rule had not substantially improved the Catholics' lot. Now, Catholics and Nationalist-minded Protestants are demanding the creation of a new Irish Parliament which the reform of the francise would allow them to dominate. This in turn has led most Irish Protestants to see the continuance of the Union as their main protection against expropriation and religious discrimination. By 1886, attitudes towards the Union have in fact become almost the only issue in Irish politics, which now has three main groupings: (1) Protestant Unionists living mainly in the North and forming 25 per cent of the population, and who regularly return about twenty of the 105 Irish MPs to the British Parliament; (2) Constitutional Nationalists, overwhelmingly Catholic, though now led by a Protestant landowner, Charles Stewart Parnell, who want local self-government, or Home Rule, and who hold almost all the remainder of the Irish seats, and (3), separatist Nationalists prepared to use violence to achieve freedom, many of whom belong to the secret Irish Republican Brotherhood (IRB), but who attract little support, partly because constitutional nationalism looks like succeeding. Parnell has won national leadership by linking the demand for Home Rule with the campaign by the long-suffering tenant farmers of Ireland for lower rents. He now leads an eighty-five strong Irish Party in the Commons, large enough to make or break a British Government, and therefore able to dictate terms for Home Rule. In February 1886, the Liberal leader, William Gladstone, comes to power. Within weeks he introduces a Home Rule Bill. The Unionist and Conservative MPs, and a section of the Liberal Party, combine to defeat the Bill. There is violence on the streets of Belfast, where loyalists opposed to Home Rule clash with Catholics and police.

1887-1900

In the aftermath of the defeat of the first Home Rule Bill, Parnell is attacked by the London *Times*, which accuses him of associating with violent elements in

Ireland. His name is not vindicated until two years later, when a special Commission, set up to examine the evidence, discovers that letters printed by *The Times* to prove its cases are forgeries. Then in 1890, Parnell is named as co-respondent in the O'Shea divorce case. The Irish leader has been living with Kitty O'Shea for several years. Gladstone tells the Irish Party to find a new leader: he cannot deal with Parnell after such a scandal. In a welter of bitter arguments, the Party splits; most members desert Parnell.

1891-1900

Conservative Governments, in this decade, try to kill Home Rule 'with kindness', passing laws to allow Irish tenants to buy out their holdings with British Government money, known as annuities. In a brief return to office, Gladstone introduces a second Home Rule Bill. Again, there is rioting in Belfast. The Bill gets through the Commons but is this time blocked by the House of Lords. Resurgent Irish nationalism, encouraged by the prospect of some independence, leads to a renewal of cultural nationalism: Douglas Hyde sets up the Gaelic League in 1893 to revive the Irish language. W. B. Yeats leads a literary revival, resulting in the foundation in 1899 of the Irish Literary (later the Abbey) Theatre. The Gaelic Athletic Association, established in 1884, is now the most popular sporting body, and a recruiting ground for the IRB. Socialist movements emerge to mobilise the working class, led by James Connolly and James Larkin. In 1900, the Irish Party ends its split by selecting John Redmond as its leader.

1901-1910

Continuing Irish trust in constitutional nationalism is reflected in cheering crowds which turn out for King Edward VIII when he visits Dublin in 1903. There is a limited pogrom against Jews in Limerick in 1904. In 1905, Arthur Griffith founds Sinn Féin (ourselves alone), to work for full Irish autonomy under a dual monarchy, as in Austria-Hungary. In 1907, Larkin organises a dock strike in Belfast which temporarily unites Protestant and Catholic workers.

1911-1914

A new Liberal Government under Herbert Asquith abolishes the veto power of the Lords in 1911 and prepares to introduce a third Home Rule Bill. Unionists hold mass demonstrations and threaten civil war. Led by Edward Carson and James Craig, they get backing from prominent Conservatives. In 1912 the Bill is debated in the Commons; Ulster Unionists sign a solemn league and covenant to resist Dublin rule. In Dublin, the Irish Women's Suffrage Federation is formed. In 1913, an Ulster Volunteer Force starts drilling. In the South, a corresponding nationalist force, the Irish Volunteers, is formed, under Eoin MacNeill. The Home Rule Bill is passed by the Commons. The Lords uses its now limited powers to delay it. A strike of tramway workers in Dublin, led by Larkin, becomes a lockout of Irish Transport and General Workers Union members. This results in hardship, street disturbances and the imprisonment of Larkin. The strike ends in failure in early 1914. In March that year the British Government capitulates to the Curragh mutiny — a refusal by army officers to move North to guard armories against possible Unionist raids. They act in solidarity with the anti-Home Rule cause. In April, German guns are run into Larne by Ulster Volunteers. In July, Irish Volunteers do the same in Howth; this time British soldiers open fire, killing four people. Asquith and

Redmond fail to agree on a partition clause in the Home Rule Bill just as the First World War begins. The Bill passes through the Commons again in September, with a provision that it is suspended until after the war. Both Redmond, who has taken over the Irish Volunteers, and Carson urge their followers to join the British Army to fight Germany.

1915-1916

Carson joins the wartime Coalition Government in London. Redmond refuses. He begins to lose support in Ireland because of his enthusiasm for the British side in the war. On the basis that England's misfortune is Ireland's opportunity, the IRB, which has taken control of a section of the Irish Volunteers, plans a rising. This takes place on April 24, 1916, despite a countermanding order from Eoin MacNeill and the arrest of Roger Casement, who was trying to organise a new shipment of German arms. The rebels, led by Padraic Pearse and James Connolly, are crushed by British forces within five days. Public opinion, opposed to the Rising, changes when the leaders are executed over a period of weeks.

1917-1918

Britain attempts again to find a solution in Ireland. Irish prisoners, including Eamon de Valera and Michael Collins, are released. A Convention is held but is boycotted by Sinn Féin, which is daily growing stronger. Conscription is threatened, and is opposed by the Irish Volunteers, now led by Eamon de Valera. Most of the Ulster Volunteers of 1914 have been killed in the war. In a general election in December 1918, Sinn Féin wins seventy-three of the 105 Irish seats.

1919-1921

Sinn Féin members set up their own parliament, Dáil Éireann, in Dublin and declare an Irish Republic, headed by de Valera. In January 1919, a War of Independence begins with the killing of two Royal Irish Constabulary (RIC) men at Soloheadbeg. It develops into guerrilla attacks on RIC barracks and military convoys. By 1920, RIC recruitment has dried up and ex-soldiers are recruited from Britain. They are called 'Black and Tans' because of their makeshift uniforms. By 1920, Republican courts are in operation in many rural areas. Britain adopts a ruthless policy of reprisals. The post-war Liberal Prime Minister, David Lloyd George, has talks with Unionist leaders; a parliament is created in Belfast, and Northern Ireland is established as part of the United Kingdom, comprising Armagh, Down, Derry, Antrim, Fermanagh and Tyrone. In November 1920, on 'Bloody Sunday', the War of Independence reaches a climax with the killing by Michael Collins's men of fourteen British agents. The Black and Tans retaliate by shooting dead twelve spectators at a match in Croke Park. In Belfast, during 1920 and 1921 dozens are killed in sectarian disturbances. On July 9, 1921, a truce is signed in Dublin. De Valera and Lloyd George agree to Anglo-Irish negotiations. Delegates are appointed to discuss how best to reconcile Irish national aspirations with association with the British Empire. On December 6, a Treaty is signed in London. It sets up an Irish Free State with Dominion status — more than Home Rule but less than a Republic. Dáil members must take an oath of loyalty to the British Crown and agree to a Boundary Commission to adjust the Border according to the interests of the local inhabitants. A rejection of the Treaty means renewed war.

1922-1923

The Dáil divides on the Treaty, after lengthy argument, on January 7, 1922. There are sixty-three votes for and fifty-seven against (including Eamon de Valera). Anti-Treaty TDs refuse to betray the Republic; pro-Treaty members led by Arthur Griffith and Michael Collins argue that nothing more can be gained and that the Treaty gives freedom to achieve freedom. The country is war-weary. British forces begin to withdraw. Collins takes over Dublin Castle, the heart of British rule in Ireland. Collins and James Craig, the NI Prime Minister, meet and agree on a (short-lived) peace pact. Collins and de Valera agree on an equally short-lived pact that new Dáil elections in June should be fought with panels of existing members. Pro-Treaty candidates win a majority. Anti-Treaty forces meanwhile seize the Four Courts building in Dublin. Civil war begins when pro-Treaty forces, now the Free State Army, move against them, partly under pressure from a British Government infuriated by the IRA murder in London of Sir Henry Wilson. Republican resistance in the Four Courts collapses and the two sides fight for control of the countryside. In August 1922, Michael Collins is killed in an ambush in Co. Cork. In September 1922, the new Dáil approves the use of the death penalty. One of the first Republicans to be shot is Erskine Childers, on November 24. The pro-Treaty forces gradually win territorial control. The Catholic Church gives its backing, condemning the Republicans. By 1923, the Republicans are beaten. The civil war ends when de Valera, on May 24, asks his followers to lay down their arms.

1924-1931

In this period, the pro-Treaty government, which becomes the Cumann na nGaedheal Party under William Cosgrave, consolidates the machinery of the new State. They follow a conservative social and economic policy. The Irish language is made compulsory in schools and Catholic morality is entrenched in legislation, with the outlawing of divorce and the introduction of censorship. In Northern Ireland, where border clashes between the IRA and the UVF took place in 1920 and 1921 and where sectarian violence claimed many lives up to 1923, order is imposed by a new police force, the Royal Ulster Constabulary, aided by 'A' and 'B' special constabularies. Initially the one-third Catholic population refuses to co-operate with the Unionist Government, which adopts a policy of discrimination against Catholics on the grounds that they are potentially disloyal. Local government is gerrymandered to ensure Unionist control and proportional representation is abolished. By the early 1930s, Unionist leaders are openly boasting of a Protestant State for a Protestant people. Meanwhile in the Free State, stability is threatened in 1924 by an abortive mutiny of army officers disenchanted with the non-Republican character of the Government. The Defence Minister, Richard Mulcahy, resigns. In 1925, the Boundary Commission is disbanded after recommending only minimal changes to the Border. The Free State had hoped for large areas of Fermanagh, Tyrone and South Down, as well as Derry city. The Dublin, London and Belfast Governments sign a new agreement whereby the Border is ratified as it stands, the idea of a Council of Ireland is dropped, and the Free State, in compensation, is released from having to pay any more of the public debt of the pre-1921 United Kingdom. Opposition in the Dáil to the Free State Government in the early 1920s comes only from the Labour Party and independents, but in 1926, de Valera leaves Sinn Féin and forms a new party, Fianna Fáil, which, in June 1927, wins forty-four of the 153 Dáil seats. Fianna Fáil members at first refuse to enter the Dáil because of their objections to the oath, but after a leading minister, Kevin O'Higgins, is assassinated by unknown gunmen on July 10, 1927, the Government introduces emergency legislation which requires TDs to take the oath or forfeit their seats. On August 11, de Valera leads his party into the Dáil to become the Opposition. The oath is dismissed as a meaningless formula.

1932-1939

In February 1932, Fianna Fáil wins a general election and Eamon de Valera forms the first Fianna Fáil Government, which is to remain in office until after the Second World War. It does not conduct a purge of those who served the pro-Treaty Government, as many feared, but does set about dismantling the links with Britain and creating a Republic in all but name. General Eoin O'Duffy, Chief Commissioner of the Gardaí is dismissed for opposing Government policy. He becomes leader of the 'Blueshirts', a neo-fascist organisation created in reaction to the de Valera victory and events in Europe. It is declared illegal. The Blueshirts join with Cumann na nGaedheal to form a new United Ireland Party, later known as Fine Gael. In 1937, the Dáil approves a new Constitution which carries no reference to the Crown and gives the Catholic Church a special position. The following year, de Valera meets the British Prime Minister, Neville Chamberlain, and both sides agree to bring to an end the economic war caused by de Valera's decision to withhold land annuity payments and introduce protective tariffs. Britain also agrees to hand back the three Irish ports held under the Treaty. The last British units leave Free State territory on November 11, 1938, allowing de Valera to declare a policy of neutrality in the coming war. During this period, de Valera gradually severs his contacts with the IRA, now a small extremist organisation which in 1939 declares war on Britain over partition and starts a bombing campaign in England. An explosion in Coventry on August 25, 1939, kills five people.

1940-1945

De Valera acts to suppress the IRA, which threatens his Government's authority. Emergency measures are brought in. In April 1940, two IRA prisoners in the Free State are allowed to die on hunger strike. Northern Ireland is drawn into the Second World War by being part of the United Kingdom. In April 1940, Belfast is blitzed by German bombers and four hundred people are killed. James Craig dies in November and is succeeded by J. M. Andrews as Northern Ireland Prime Minister. He is in turn succeeded by Basil Brooke in 1943. The Chamberlain Government in Britain, then Winston Churchill, who became Prime Minister on May 10, 1940, make tentative approaches to de Valera to give up neutrality for Irish unity. They are not taken seriously in Dublin. The Fianna Fáil Government refuses a British request for the return of the Treaty ports and Churchill restricts the use of British shipping to bring foodstuffs to the Free State. At first, neutrality is strictly enforced, with both German and Allied servicemen who land in Ireland being detained; as the war proceeds, however, this becomes benevolent neutrality towards the Allies, whose servicemen are quietly sent to the North if they stray onto Free State territory. After the USA comes into the war, President Roosevelt attacks Irish neutrality and demands the closure of the German legation in Dublin. De Valera refuses and Irish-US relations plummet. When Hitler dies, de Valera makes a defiant gesture of independence by paying his respects at the German embassy. The Second World War ends with Churchill and de Valera engaging in recriminations through radio broadcasts.

1946-1951

In the post-war period there is hardship in the Free State and Fianna Fáil's popularity falls. A new left-of-centre Republican party, Clann na Poblachta, is formed by Sean MacBride. In the general election of 1948 it wins ten seats and forms a Coalition Government with Fine Gael. Partly under the influence of Clann na Poblachta, the Fine Gael Taoiseach, John A. Costello, declares a Republic and withdraws from the Commonwealth. In retaliation, the British Government passes an Act declaring that Northern Ireland shall remain part of the United Kingdom as long as the Parliament there so desires. The new Irish Government tries to bring in reforms but the Catholic Hierarchy intervenes in 1951 to force the withdrawal of a Mother and Child Welfare Bill, introduced by the Health Minister, Noel Browne, of Clann na Poblachta. He resigns and the correspondence between the Church and State is published in *The Irish Times*. The episode breaks up MacBride's party and eventually the Coalition Government. Fianna Fáil returns to office.

1952-1964

The early 1950s are a time of economic depression in both parts of Ireland, though in the North the effects are cushioned by a British subvention enabling the payment in full of social service rates set in London. In 1954 the IRA begins a campaign against police barracks in Northern Ireland, attracting some Nationalist sympathy but little support. There is little prospect of effecting change by violence and the campaign peters out in 1962, after a period of declining support during which many members are interned, North and South. National morale in the Republic is raised by Irish participation in a United Nations force in the Congo in 1960, the opening of RTE television the same year, and a visit by US President Kennedy in June 1963. Apart from one brief period, Fianna Fáil remains in office throughout this period. In 1959 Sean Lemass replaces de Valera as Taoiseach. He pushes through the first programme for economic development, encouraging free trade, foreign borrowing and investment. Economic issues begin to replace the national question in elections. The Vatican Council of 1962 encourages a move away from the old conservatism. Censorship laws are eased and many of the old assumptions are questioned publicly in the press and on television. In the North, Basil Brooke, now Lord Brookeborough, is replaced by Terence O'Neill in 1963. O'Neill also begins to question the nature of society in Northern Ireland and to preach reform.

1965-1968

Both Lemass and O'Neill feel the climate has thawed sufficiently to enable them to meet in Belfast in January 1965, the first meeting of Prime Ministers from North and South since the 1920s, to discuss cross-border economic co-operation. The Nationalist Party reacts by accepting the role of official Opposition at the Stormont Parliament. There are, however, signs of trouble ahead. The Rev. Ian Paisley emerges in demonstrations against O'Neill and the new spirit of ecumenism. Tension is raised when there are widespread celebrations of the fiftieth anniversary of the 1916 Rising. A Catholic barman is shot dead in Belfast by loyalist extremists, the first victim of the present troubles. Lemass retires and is replaced by Jack Lynch who continues the cross-border talks with O'Neill, meeting him at Stormont in December 1967, when Paisley supporters throw snowballs at his car. There are the first stirrings of unrest in Derry. Both communities there unite in 1965 to oppose a Government decision to site a second NI university in Coleraine rather than in

Derry; Coleraine is largely Protestant. John Hume emerges as a leader of the protest movement. The climate of reform and the Civil Rights movement in America encourages the formation of a Northern Ireland Civil Rights Association in 1967, to campaign for one man one vote in local elections, fair housing allocations and the end of the Special Powers Act. On October 5, 1968, a Civil Rights march in Derry is attacked by police and O'Neill warns, in a television address, that Ulster is at the crossroads.

1969

A student Civil Rights march is attacked by Loyalists at Burntollet. O'Neill calls an election in which Paisley does unexpectedly well. Nationalist politicians are replaced by Civil Rights figures like John Hume. O'Neill resigns in April. His successor, James Chichester-Clark, continues the reform programme under pressure from the Labour Government in Britain. Police lose control in Derry rioting in August. The British Army is called in. The British Home Secretary, James Callaghan, visits the North and further reforms are forced on the Unionist Government, including the abolition of the Protestant B Special police force. In December, the IRA, which has become more socialist after the failure of the Border campaign of the 1950s, splits and a more violent Provisional wing emerges.

1970-1972

The reforms continue in Northern Ireland with the Ulster Defence Regiment replacing the B Specials. On May 6, there is a Government crisis in Dublin when Lynch sacks two ministers, Charles Haughey and Neil Blaney. Charges brought against them of conspiring to import arms for the North fail in the courts. In the North, relations between the Catholic population and the British Army deteriorate. Six people are killed in arms searches on the Falls Road which is curfewed on July 3, 1970. A Conservative Government under Edward Heath is returned in Britain. The Social Democratic and Labour Party is formed in Northern Ireland under Gerry Fitt to replace the old Nationalist Party. Violence between the IRA and the British Army intensifies in 1971. Chichester-Clark resigns as NI Prime Minister and is replaced by Brian Faulkner. On August 9, 1971, Faulkner introduces internment. Violence continues to increase. On January 30, 1972, thirteen anti-internment protesters are shot dead in Derry in Ireland's second 'Bloody Sunday'. An angry crowd burns down the British embassy in Dublin. On March 30, the Stormont Parliament is abolished and the British Government imposes direct rule. The paramilitary Ulster Defence Regiment takes to the streets, and sectarian assassinations claim dozens of victims. The IRA calls a ceasefire in July and meets the NI Secretary, William Whitelaw. The talks come to nothing. The IRA kills eleven people in a series of bombings in Belfast on July 21, 1972 – 'Bloody Friday'. On July 31, in Operation Motorman, the British Army takes control of Catholic areas. Lynch and Heath meet in September and again in November, 1972. On November 24 Lynch sacks the RTE authority for an interview with a Provisional leader. On December 7 the Republic votes by a large majority to remove the special position of the Catholic Church from the Constitution, and on December 31 joins the EEC, along with the United Kingdom.

1973-1974

The year 1973 heralds a new era of prosperity for Ireland through EEC membership, but political events continue to be dominated by the North. IRA violence and sectarian assassinations continue at a high level. On February 28 Fianna Fáil loses a general election and a new Coalition Government is formed under the Fine Gael leader, Liam Cosgrave. The British Government announces new terms for a Northern settlement, and elections to a power-sharing assembly at Stormont are held on June 28, 1973. On October 2 the leaders of the SDLP, Unionists and the moderate Alliance Party, agree on forming a power-sharing Executive. They join the British and Irish Governments at a conference at Sunningdale in England at which they agree to set up a Council of Ireland. The Executive takes office on January 1, 1974. IRA violence increases and Unionist opposition to the Council of Ireland and power-sharing leads to a loyalist strike in May which paralyses much of the North. During the strike, car bombs planted by the UDA kill twenty-five people in Dublin and six in Monaghan. The Labour Government of Harold Wilson, who replaced Edward Heath in February, shows no stomach for a confrontation with the loyalists, and the power-sharing Executive collapses. The Labour Secretary of State, Merlyn Rees, reimposes direct rule. In December, Protestant clergymen meet the IRA and the first of a number of ceasefires is called. IRA bombs in Birmingham kill nineteen people and Britain introduces the Prevention of Terrorism Act under which suspected terrorists can be deported.

1975-1978

The Labour Government embarks on a policy of releasing internees, criminalising the IRA and replacing the British Army with the RUC in fighting paramilitary activity. It also calls an elected Convention of Northern Ireland politicians to try to agree on a future government of the North, but it is dominated by anti-power-sharing Unionists, and London refuses to accept its eventual recommendations. In the Republic the Coalition Government introduces a Criminal Law Bill to counter the IRA. It is referred to the Supreme Court by President Ó Dálaigh who is later called a 'thundering disgrace' by the Defence Minister, Paddy Donegan, and resigns, on October 18, 1976. The year 1976 is marked by the sectarian killings of five Catholics and ten Protestants in Co. Armagh in January, the assassination of the British Ambassador, Christopher Ewart-Biggs, in Dublin on July 21 and the formation of the Peace People in Belfast on August 10. Rees is replaced by Roy Mason as NI Secretary, heralding two years when no new initiatives are tried by the British Government. In 1977 Fianna Fáil wins an overwhelming victory in a general election in the Republic and Jack Lynch brings Charles Haughey into his Cabinet as Health Minister. Cosgrave resigns as Fine Gael leader and is replaced by Garret FitzGerald. The British Government is found guilty of torturing internees by the European Commission of Human Rights in Strasbourg. In 1978, twelve die when the IRA firebomb the La Mon restaurant in Co. Down. In the same year Irish troops join the United Nations peace-keeping forces in South Lebanon.

1979-1982

In 1979, Margaret Thatcher emerges as leader of a new Tory Government in Britain, and Charles Haughey becomes Taoiseach after Lynch resigns, following a backbench revolt by Fianna Fáil TDs opposed to his conciliatory attitude towards the North. The year is also marked by the development of the serious economic crisis which afflicts the Republic until the present day, and by two IRA attacks – the murder of Lord Mountbatten off the coast of Sligo and the killing of eighteen British soldiers near Warrenpoint, Co. Down. Pope John Paul II visits the Republic and begs the youth of Ireland to turn away from the paths of violence; he decides against visiting the North because of the heightened feelings over the IRA killings. Humphrey Atkins becomes the NI Secretary, the first in a succession of Conservative ministers at Stormont who include James Prior, Douglas Hurd and Tom King. In December 1980, Thatcher and Haughey meet and reach agreement to discuss institutional arrangements for inter-government co-operation on the North. Haughey calls an election in June 1981 but loses, and Garret FitzGerald forms a Coalition Government with Labour. He announces a constitutional crusade to reform the Republic and make it a more secular state. In January 1982 the Coalition falls when independent TD Jim Kemmy withdraws his support over the budget. Haughey returns to office with the support of the Workers Party and independent TD, Tony Gregory. The ten months of Fianna Fáil Government are marked by challenges to his leadership and a series of mishaps, including the finding of a double murderer in the apartment of the Attorney General. His Government falls in November 1982 and FitzGerald returns at the head of another Coalition. Haughey's former Justice Minister, Sean Doherty, is forced to resign as are the Commissioner and deputy Commissioner of the gardaí, over disclosures about telephone tapping and other surveillance. Meanwhile the IRA continues its campaign and Sinn Féin wins significant support in local elections after the British Government allows a series of hunger strikers, including MP Bobby Sands, to die rather than concede their demand for political status in Northern Ireland prisons. This, and the opposition of the Fianna Fáil Government to the British Falklands adventure, brings Anglo-Irish relations to a new low.

1983-1986

FitzGerald's constitutional crusade receives a setback with the anti-abortion referendum of September 1983, but good relations are re-established with Mrs Thatcher. The three main parties in the Republic and the SDLP meet in the New Ireland Forum to discuss the kind of Ireland they would offer Unionists. The Forum sits in Dublin from November 1983 to May 1984, eventually agreeing on a report which suggests a unitary state, federation or joint authority, or any other suggested way forward. President Reagan visits the Republic and gives the process his backing. The IRA tries to kill Mrs Thatcher by bombing the Grand Hotel in Brighton on October 11, during the Conservative Party Conference. After a summit meeting with FitzGerald on November 19, Mrs Thatcher makes her 'out, out, out' remarks about the three main Forum options, causing deep offence in the Republic and a temporary setback to negotiations between British and Irish officials on a new Anglo-Irish Agreement. In February 1985 FitzGerald succeeds in liberalising contraceptive legislation in a vote in the Dáil during which Des O'Malley of Fianna Fáil abstains, for which he is expelled from Fianna Fáil, a move which eventually leads to his setting up a new centre-right party, the Progressive Democrats. An Anglo-Irish Agreement is signed at Hillsborough on November 15, 1985, giving the Republic a say in Northern Ireland affairs, and giving the British Government the prospect of defeating the IRA through increased security co-operation from the Republic and a lessening of the alienation of Northern Catholics. Unionist politicians, with one or two exceptions, boycott the House of Commons and the Northern Ireland Office in protest, and loyalist street violence increases throughout 1986. FitzGerald receives a further serious setback in his attempts to reform the Republic when proposals to make divorce legal are heavily defeated in a referendum.

❧ Political Quotations ❧
1886–1986

February 10, 1886

Charles Stewart Parnell

I have a parliament for Ireland within the hollow of my hand.

Addressing by-election meeting in Galway, as leader of eighty-six-member Irish Party at Westminster, where William Gladstone had just become Liberal Prime Minister, promising Home Rule. Ervine, St John, *Parnell*, Penguin, 1944, p. 170.

February 16, 1886

Lord Randolph Churchill

I decided some time ago that if the GOM [the Grand Old Man i.e. William Gladstone, Liberal leader] went for Home Rule, the Orange card would be the one to play. Please God it may turn out the ace of trumps and not the two.

In letter, as leading Conservative to Lord Justice Fitzgibbon on tactics opponents of first Home Rule Bill, being prepared by Gladstone, might adopt. Churchill, Winston Spencer, *Lord Randolph Churchill*, Vol. 11, Macmillan, 1906, p. 65.

February 17, 1886

Dr Walsh, Archbishop of Dublin

As regards 'self-government' or Home Rule, it is our firm and conscientious conviction . . . that it alone can satisfy the wants, the wishes, as well as the legitimate aspirations of the Irish people.

In letter, as chairman of meeting of Irish Catholic bishops in Dublin, to British Prime Minister William Gladstone expressing support for Home Rule Bill Gladstone was about to introduce in Commons giving measure of independence to all-Ireland Parliament. *Freeman's Journal*, February 22, 1886.

February 22, 1886

Lord Randolph Churchill

Like Macbeth before the murder of Duncan, Mr Gladstone asks for time. Before he plunges the knife into the heart of the British Empire he reflects, he hesitates . . .

Diligence and vigilance ought to be your watchword; so that the blow, if it does come, may not come upon you as a thief in the night.

Addressing Unionist rally in Ulster Hall, Belfast, called to protest against plan by Liberal Prime Minister William Gladstone to introduce Home Rule Bill for Ireland. Churchill, Winston Spencer, *Lord Randolph Churchill*, Vol. II, Macmillan, 1906, p. 62.

April 8, 1886

William Gladstone

I cannot allow it to be said that a Protestant minority in Ulster, or elsewhere, is to rule the question at large for Ireland . . . Various schemes . . . have been proposed on behalf of Ulster. One scheme is that Ulster itself, or perhaps, with more appearance of reason, a portion of Ulster, should be excluded from the operation of the Bill . . . there is no one of them [these schemes] . . . so completely justified . . . as to warrant our including it in the Bill.

Introducing, as Liberal Prime Minister, first Home Rule Bill in Commons. *HC Debates:* Vol. 304: Cols. 1053-54.

April 8, 1886

Colonel T. Waring

The course foreshadowed [in the Home Rule Bill] was one which could not be adopted without dishonour to England and the nation at large, and that was to turn over those who had been England's faithful garrison in Ireland, bound hand and foot, to the tender mercies of their bitterest enemies.

Opposing, as North Down MP, introduction of Home Rule Bill in Commons. *HC Debates:* Vol. 304: Col. 1089.

April 9, 1886

Joseph Chamberlain

I am not prepared to take a risk in order to promote what is, in my judgement, a thinly-veiled scheme of separation . . . How do you propose to carry out this scheme without coercion . . . it is the difficulty, one of the great difficulties of this problem, that Ireland is not a homogeneous community – that it consists of two nations, that it is a nation which comprises two nations and two religions.

Speaking in Commons against Home Rule Bill, over which he resigned from Liberal Government. *HC Debates:* Vol. 304: Cols. 1194-1200.

April 9, 1886

Timothy Healy

I want to live at peace with my fellow countrymen; I want to give them all the securities and all the guarantees that man can give . . . and I say . . . that if in Ireland in the future time I thought there would continue those miserable wranglings, those horrible religious animosities, I would rather see my country perish forever from the face of the earth.

Speaking in support of Home Rule Bill in Commons as MP for Londonderry. *HC Debates:* Vol. 304: Cols. 1212-13.

April 26, 1886
Lord Randolph Churchill

Ulster at the proper moment will resort to the supreme arbitrament of force: Ulster will fight; Ulster will be right; Ulster will emerge from the struggle victorious.

Writing as leader of Conservative Party to prominent Unionist; the phrase 'Ulster will fight and Ulster will be right' was subsequently used for anti-Home Rule campaign. Churchill, William Spencer, *Lord Randolph Churchill*, Vol. II, Macmillan, 1906, p. 65.

May 25, 1886
Charles Russell

A great many of these Orange orators who were so loud-voiced about their Protestantism and about their loyalty ... allowed their so-called Protestantism and loyalty entirely to eclipse their Christianity ... A considerable and, I believe, a growing number among the Protestant Liberals in Ulster are in favour of this measure.

Introducing, as Liberal Attorney General, second reading of Home Rule Bill. *HC Debates:* Vol. 306: Cols. 63-64.

June 7, 1886
Charles Stewart Parnell

We [the Irish Party] look upon the provisions of the [Home Rule] Bill as a final settlement of this [the Irish] question, and ... I believe that the Irish people have accepted it as such a settlement.

Speaking in Commons, as leader of Irish Party, during closing stages of debate on Gladstone's Home Rule Bill setting up a devolved parliament in Dublin for whole of Ireland. *HC Debates:* Vol. 306: Col. 1173.

June 7, 1886
William Gladstone

You have power, you have wealth, you have rank, you have station, you have organisation. What have we? We think we have the [Irish] people's heart ... the ebbing tide is with you

and the flowing tide is with us. Ireland stands at your bar expectant, hopeful, almost suppliant.

Addressing opponents of Home Rule Bill in Commons. *HC Debates:* Vol. 306: Col. 1239.

June 13, 1886
Rev. Hugh ('Roaring') Hanna

We must see to it that the terrible massacre on Wednesday last, shall, if possible, be brought home to the perpetrators. At the door of the Government lies the guilt of bloodshed on that occasion, the guilt of seven innocent lives sacrificed to avenge the resistance of a loyal people to a perfidious and traitorous policy.

As loyalist leader, preaching at St Enoch's Church, Belfast, during period of rioting which followed defeat of Home Rule Bill and claimed some fifty lives. Bardon, Jonathan, *Belfast,* Blackstaff, 1983, pp. 148-49.

June 20, 1886
Lord Randolph Churchill

Mr Gladstone has reserved for his closing days a conspiracy against the honour of Britain and the welfare of Ireland more startlingly base and nefarious than any of those numerous designs and plots which, during the last quarter of a century, have occupied his imagination.

Commenting on Gladstone's support for Home Rule. Mansergh, Nicholas, *The Irish Question,* Unwin University Books, 1968, p. 114.

April 18, 1887
Richard Piggot

May 15th, 1882
Dear Sir
I am not surprised at your friend's anger, but he and you should know that to denounce the murders was the only course open to us. To do that promptly was plainly our best policy. But you can tell him and all others concerned that, though I regret the accident of Lord F. Cavendish's death, I cannot refuse to admit that Burke got no more than his deserts. You are at liberty to show him this, and others whom you can trust also, but let not my address be known. He can write to the House of Commons.
Yours very truly,
Charles S. Parnell.

Letter forged by Richard Piggot to show Parnell privately supported Phoenix Park murders of 1882, in which Chief Secretary Lord Frederick Cavendish and Under-Secretary Thomas H. Burke were assassinated, and bought and published as authentic by *The Times*. Ervine, St John, *Parnell*, Penguin, 1944, pp. 179-80.

April 18, 1887
Kitty O'Shea
The Times is unusually stodgy. Do eat your breakfast first.

Attempting to delay Parnell, with whom she lived, seeing forged letter (above) in *The Times*. Ervine, St John, *Parnell*, Penguin, 1944, p. 180.

April 20, 1887
Lord Salisbury
[Gladstone] mixed on terms of intimacy with those whose advocacy of assassination was well known.

Speaking, as Conservative Prime Minister, at meeting in Swansea after *The Times* had published forged letter about Parnell as authentic. Ervine, St John, *Parnell*, Penguin, 1944, p. 181.

September 10, 1887
Arthur Balfour
Don't hesitate to shoot.

Order given as Irish Secretary to police at Mitchelstown where they shot dead three men at public meeting called to demonstrate against evictions. Gwynn, Denis, *The Life of John Redmond*, Harrap, 1932, p. 89.

March 15, 1888
John O'Brien
In hard times like the present, workmen, whether in the east end of London or the east end of Cork, feel it hard to have, as they think, the bread taken out of their mouths by the forced immigration of so many refugees who have been forced out of their own land by the oppression of the Hebrews abroad. But allow me to say ... there is and has not been in the city of Cork any feeling, adverse or otherwise than kindly towards the men of the Jewish faith.

In letter to *The Times* as Mayor of Cork after allegations of anti-Jewish sentiments expressed by Cork trade unions. Hyman, Louis, *The Jews of Ireland*, Keter, 1972, p. 220.

May 7, 1888
John Dillon
We owe it to our Protestant fellow-countrymen, who expect they are about to share with us a free Ireland, that it will not be an Ireland that will conduct its affairs at the bidding of any body of cardinals ... were we to exchange for servitude in Westminster servitude to ... any body of cardinals in Rome, then I would say good-bye for ever to the struggle for Irish freedom.

Speaking, as Irish Party MP, in response to papal rescript of April 20, 1888 condemning as illegal the boycott and Plan of Campaign under which tenants combined to withhold excessive rents from landlords. Lyons, F. S. L., *Ireland Since the Famine*, Fontana, 1985, pp. 190-91.

May 8, 1888
Charles Stewart Parnell
I should have advised against it ... I considered, and still consider, that there were features in the Plan of Campaign, and in the way in which it was necessary it should be carried out, which would have had a bad effect upon the general political situation – in other words, upon the national question.

In speech to Eighty Club in London opposing William O'Brien's Plan of Campaign, whereby tenants offered only 'fair' rents to landlords, resulting in some violence and evictions. Ervine, St John, *Parnell*, Penguin, 1944, p. 179.

May 17, 1888
Catholic MPs in Irish Party
While unreservedly acknowledging as Catholics the spiritual jurisdiction of the Holy See, we ... feel bound solemnly to reassert that Irish Catholics can recognise no right in the Holy See to interfere with the Irish people in the management of their political affairs.

In statement issued after meeting to discuss papal rescript of April 1888 condemning Plan of Campaign. Lyons, F. S. L., *Charles Stewart Parnell*, Collins, 1977, pp. 386-87.

June, 1888
Dr O'Dwyer, Bishop of Limerick
There has never been in Ireland since St Patrick planted the Faith here a greater scandal or more injury done to religion than this most deplorable agitation.

Condemning Plan of Campaign. O'Farrell, Patrick, *Ireland's English Question*, Batsford, 1971, p. 195.

July 6, 1888
Richard Piggot
January 9th, 1882
Dear E,
What are these fellows waiting for? This inaction is inexcusable; our best men are in prison, and nothing is being done. Let there be an end to this hesitency [sic]. Prompt action is called for. You undertook to make it hot for old Foster and Co. Let us have some evidence of your power to do so. My health is good, thanks.
Yours very truly,
Charles Stewart Parnell.

Letter produced by *The Times* in evidence against Parnell in London court. Misspelling of word 'hesitancy' proved it had been forged by Richard Piggot, who sold it to *The Times* for a profit. Ervine, St John, *Parnell*, Penguin, 1944, p. 184.

October 26, 1888
Thomas Shillington
The Protestant Home Rule Association [has] rescued [Protestants] from the obloquy and shame with which posterity would inevitably have covered the Protestants of Ireland if [they] had disassociated themselves from their fellow countrymen in the endeavour to obtain the right of political freedom ... Protestants [are] not afraid to take their stand by the side of their fellow countrymen of other denominations ... We will live, I hope, to settle our differences among ourselves.

Speaking, as leading member of Irish Party, as Portadown representative and President of the Protestant Home Rule Association, at public meeting in Dublin. *The Irish Times,* January 18, 1978.

April 12, 1889
Charles Russell
This inquiry, intended as a curse, has proved a blessing. Designed, prominently designed, to ruin one man, it has been his vindication. In opening this case I said that we represented the accused. My Lords, I claim leave to say, that today the positions are reversed. We are the accusers; the accused are there [pointing to representatives of *The Times*].

At end of eight-day closing speech for defence in Parnell Commission during which it was revealed *The Times* had used forged letters to incriminate

leader of Irish Party. Russell, Sir Charles, *The Parnell Commission: The Opening Speech for the Defence,* Macmillan, 1889, p. 602.

November 20, 1890
Timothy Healy
For Ireland and for Irishmen, Parnell is less a man than an institution. We have under the shadow of his name secured a power and authority in the councils of Great Britain and the world such as we never possessed before; and when I see a demand made for retirement and resignation [because of his involvement in divorce case] I ask you to remember the futility thereof ... if we join with this howling pack, would that be a noble spectacle before the nations?

Speaking, as leading member of Irish Party, at meeting in Mansion House, Dublin, three days after Captain O'Shea obtained his divorce because of his wife's association with Parnell. Ervine, St John, *Parnell*, Penguin, 1944, pp. 203-4.

November 24, 1890
William Gladstone
Notwithstanding the splendid services rendered by Mr Parnell to his country, his continuance at the present moment in the leadership would be productive of consequences disastrous in the highest degree to the cause of Ireland ... the continuance I speak of would not only place many hearty and effective friends of the Irish cause in a position of great embarrassment, but would render my retention of the leadership of the Liberal Party, based as it has been mainly upon the presentation of the Irish cause, almost a nullity.

Writing, as Prime Minister, to Irish Party members following Captain O'Shea's divorce action in which Parnell was named. Ervine, St John, *Parnell*, Penguin, 1944, p. 207.

November 27, 1890
William Gladstone
It was odd that the man who was a rock to all the world was like a bit of wax in the hands of a woman.

Commenting, as Prime Minister, to Irish Party MP Timothy Healy about Parnell's relationship with Kitty O'Shea. Carty, James, *Ireland 1851-1921*, Fallon, 1951, p. 62.

November 28, 1890
Charles Stewart Parnell

The integrity and independence of a section of the Irish Parliamentary Party has been sapped and destroyed by the wire-pullers of the English Liberal Party ... The English wolves are now howling for my destruction ... I do not believe that any action of the Irish people in supporting me will endanger the Home Rule cause.

From 'Manifesto to the People of Ireland' issued to press after Gladstone published letter stating that Parnell's continued leadership of Irish Party, after O'Shea divorce case, would be 'disastrous' for Home Rule. Ervine, St John, *Parnell*, Penguin, 1944, pp. 212-13.

November 30, 1890
William Gladstone

Since the month of December, 1885, my whole political life has been governed by a supreme regard to the Irish question. For every day, I may say, of these five years, we have been engaged in laboriously rolling up-hill the stone of Sisyphus. Mr Parnell's decision of yesterday means that the stone is to break away from us and roll down again to the bottom of the hill.

From memorandum written as Prime Minister on day after Parnell had refused to stand down as leader of Irish Party at request of Gladstone because of political damage arising from O'Shea divorce action in which Parnell was named. Ervine, St John, *Parnell*, Penguin, 1944, p. 211.

December 4, 1890
Charles Stewart Parnell

Gentlemen, it is for you to act in this matter. You are dealing with a man [Gladstone] who is an unrivalled sophist ... if I surrender to him, if I give up my position to him, if you throw me to him, I say, gentlemen, that it is your bounden duty to see that you secure value for the sacrifice.

Speaking at meeting of Irish Parliamentary Party in House of Commons committee room called to consider Parnell's leadership because of his involvement in O'Shea divorce case. Ervine, St John, *Parnell*, Penguin, 1944, p. 220.

December 4, 1890
Timothy Healy

It perished in the stench of the divorce courts.

Referring to break-up of Liberal-Irish Party alliance at Westminster, in exchange with Parnell at meeting of Irish Parliamentary Party called to discuss Parnell's leadership. Ervine, St John, *Parnell*, Penguin, 1944, p. 221.

December 6, 1890
John Redmond

He [Gladstone] is the master of the [Irish] party.
Timothy Healy

Who is to be the mistress of the party?

Exchange at meeting of Irish Parliamentary Party called to discuss Parnell's leadership. Ervine, St John, *Parnell*, Penguin, 1944, p. 223.

December 10, 1890
Charles Stewart Parnell

I don't pretend to be immaculate, I don't pretend that I have not had my moments of trial and of temptation, but I do claim that never in thought, in word or deed have I been false to the trust that Irishmen have confided in me.

Speaking to supporters in Dublin after majority of Irish Parliamentary Party had rejected his leadership following Gladstone's assertion that Parnell could not win Home Rule after being named in the O'Shea divorce case. Ervine, St John, *Parnell*, Penguin, 1944, p. 227.

June 1, 1891
Timothy Healy

For years he has been stealing the money entrusted to his charge.

Attack on Parnell in national press under heading 'Stop Thief'. Lyons, F. S. L., *Charles Stewart Parnell*, Collins, 1977, p. 589.

November 5, 1891
John Redmond and Patrick O'Brien

BRAVO! WE CONGRATULATE YOU ON HAVING WHIPPED THAT COWARDLY CUR WHO ATTACKED A DEFENCELESS, SORROWING WOMAN.

Telegram to Alfred Tudor MacDermott, nephew of Parnell, who horsewhipped Timothy Healy in Four Courts, Dublin, after Healy referred to Parnell's widow, Kitty O'Shea, in a speech, as 'convicted British prostitute'. Ervine, St John, *Parnell*, Penguin, 1944, p. 242.

June 17, 1892
Duke of Abercorn
Great danger is hanging over our heads. This plot of Home Rule is being hatched in darkness. It will not bear the light.

Speaking at anti-Home Rule rally in Belfast as Gladstone prepared second Home Rule Bill. Bardon, Jonathan, *Belfast*, Blackstaff, 1983, p. 151.

June 17, 1892
Thomas Sinclair
We will have nothing to do with a Dublin parliament. If it is ever set up we shall simply ignore its existence. Its acts will be but as waste paper; the police will find their barracks preoccupied with their own constabulary; its judges will sit in empty courthouses.

Speaking, as Liberal Unionist, at anti-Home Rule rally in Belfast as Gladstone prepared second Home Rule Bill. Bardon, Jonathan, *Belfast*, Blackstaff, 1983, p. 151.

November 25, 1892
Douglas Hyde
[The] failure of the Irish people in recent times [to prosper] has been largely brought about by the race diverging during this century from the right path and ceasing to be Irish without becoming English ... In order to de-anglicise ourselves, we must at once arrest the decay of the language.

In lecture to Irish National Literary Society which foreshadowed his foundation of Gaelic League in 1893. Carty, James, *Ireland 1851-1921*, Fallon, 1951, p. 103.

May 9, 1894
M. L. Cohen
Our people here were bitterly attacked by the mob here. On last Sunday houses and windows were broken and lots of damage done, notwithstanding the loyal support our chief treasurer, Mr S. Montagu and his colleagues are giving to Ireland in the House of Commons.

Writing as vice-commander of Zion Society Cork branch to London headquarters about attacks on Jews in Cork after one was mistakenly identified as anti-Catholic preacher and beaten up. Hyman, Louis, *The Jews of Ireland*, Keter, 1972, p. 223.

May 9, 1894
Justin McCarthy
The Irish people are in strong political sympathy with the Jews. Our Irish national poet, Thomas Moore, has again and again drawn comparison between the persecution of the Irish race and that of the 'Sad One of Zion'. You may be sure that the ill-treatment of any of your co-religionists is regarded with utter detestation by every Irish nationalist.

In letter as leading member of Irish Party to Samuel Montagu MP about attacks on Jews in Cork. Hyman, Louis, *The Jews of Ireland*, Keter, 1972, p. 222.

February 11, 1895
Dr Croke, Archbishop of Cashel
The hope of attaining a legislature for our country within measurable time is no longer entertained by reasoning men.

In letter to *Freeman's Journal* after defeat at Westminster of two Home Rule Bills since 1886. Moody, Martin, Byrne (Eds.), *A New History of Ireland*, Vol. VIII, Oxford, 1982, p. 370.

November 17, 1895
John Redmond
Ireland for the Irish is our motto, and the consummation of all our hopes and aspirations is, in one word, to drive English rule, sooner or later, bag and baggage from the country.

Speaking at Kanturk as leader of pro-Parnell members of Irish Parliamentary Party after defeat of second Home Rule Bill. Escouflaire, R. G., *Ireland, an Enemy of the Allies?*, Murray, 1919, p. 230.

May 29, 1896
James Connolly
The great appear great because we are on our knees: let us arise.

From manifesto of Irish Socialist Revolutionary Party founded in Dublin by Connolly (who read this Desmoulins aphorism in *Labour Chronicle* two years earlier and used it frequently throughout his political career). Dudley Edwards, Ruth, *James Connolly*, Gill and Macmillan, 1981, p. 19.

1899
James Connolly
After Ireland is free, says the patriot who won't touch socialism, we will protect all classes, and if you won't pay your rent, you will be evicted same as now. But the evicting

party ... will wear green uniforms and the harp without the Crown ... Now isn't that worth fighting for?

Writing, as labour organiser, in *Workers' Republic*. Dudley Edwards, Ruth, *James Connolly*, Gill and Macmillan, 1981, p. 31.

March 4, 1899
Arthur Griffith
Lest there might be a doubt in any mind, we will say that we accept the nationalism of [17]98, [18]48 and [18]67 as the true nationalism and Grattan's cry 'Live Ireland – perish the Empire!' as the watchword of patriotism.

Writing, as emerging leader of separatist movement in Ireland, in *United Irishman*. Lyons, F. S. L., *Ireland Since the Famine*, Fontana, 1985, p. 248.

1900
Hanna Sheehy Skeffington
I ... was amazed and disgusted to learn that I was classed among criminals, infants and lunatics – in fact, that my status as a woman was worse than any of these.

On being initiated into women's suffrage movement. Owens, Rosemary Cullen, *Smashing Times*, Attic, 1984, p. 39.

1900
John Ingram
I have no sympathy with those who preach sedition in our own day, when all the circumstances are radically altered. In my opinion no real popular interest can now be furthered by violence.

Note written by author of the popular poem 'Who Fears to Speak of '98', written in 1843, which praises the violent rising of 1798. Robinson, Lennox, *Lady Gregory's Journal*, Putnam, 1946, p. 243.

February 9, 1900
Irish Parliamentary Party
In the name of Ireland, we declare at an end the divisions which hitherto separated the Irish Nationalist representatives, and we hereby form ourselves into one united party.

Resolution bringing about end of Parnellite split in Irish Parliamentary Party and election of John Redmond as leader. Gwynn, Denis, *The Life of John Redmond*, Harrap, 1932, p. 94.

July 7, 1900
James Connolly
Ireland without her people is nothing to me, and the man who is bubbling over with love and enthusiasm for 'Ireland' and yet can pass unmoved through our streets and witness all the wrong and suffering, the shame and degradation wrought upon the people of Ireland, aye, wrought by Irishmen upon Irish men and women, without burning to end it, is in my opinion a fraud and a liar in his heart.

Writing, as labour organiser, against romantic nationalism, in *Workers' Republic*. Carty, James, *Ireland 1851-1921*, Fallon, 1951, p. 168.

January 7, 1901
Douglas Hyde
We cannot turn our back on the Davis ideal of every person in Ireland being an Irishman, no matter what their blood and politics, for the moment we cease to profess that, we land ourselves in an intolerable position. It is equally true, though, that the Gaelic League [aims] at stimulating the old peasant, Papist, aboriginal population.

In letter to Lady Gregory, referring to his own organisation, the Gaelic League, which he founded in 1893. Hepburn, A.C., *The Conflict of Nationality in Modern Ireland*, Arnold, 1980, p. 65.

May 12, 1902
John Morley
Dublin Castle [is] the best machine that has ever been invented for governing a country against its will.

Speaking at Manchester as leading member of Liberal Party. Macardle, Dorothy, *The Irish Republic*, Irish Press, 1951, p. 53.

September 3, 1902
Captain John Shawe-Taylor
The land war in this country has raged fiercely and continuously ... producing hatred and bitterness ... [at] a conference to be held in Dublin within one month from this date ... an honest, simple and practical suggestion will be submitted.

Letter from Galway landowner inviting selected politicians and landlords to conference from which emerged proposal whereby Treasury provided money to allow tenants buy land and repay by annuities under Land Act of 1904. Gwynn, Denis, *The Life of John Redmond*, Harrap, 1932, p. 99.

October 26, 1902
Arthur Griffith

We call upon our countrymen abroad to withdraw all assistance from the promoters of a useless, degrading and demoralising policy [seeking Home Rule within the Empire] until such time as the members of the Irish Parliamentary Party substitute for it the policy of the Hungarian deputies of 1861, and refusing to attend the British parliament or to recognise its right to legislate for Ireland remain at home to help in promoting Ireland's interests.

Resolution proposed to convention of Cumann na nGaedheal, forerunner of Sinn Féin. Lyons, F. S. L., *Ireland Since the Famine*, Fontana, 1985, p. 251.

July 21, 1903
George Wyndham

For three miles to Trinity one roar of cheers and frenzy of handkerchiefs . . . they lift their hands to Heaven to imprecate 'God bless the King' as if adjuring the Deity to fulfil their most ardent desire . . . the people became nearly delirious. They worked themselves into an ecstasy.

Describing, as Chief Secretary for Ireland, reception given to King Edward on visit to Dublin. Robinson, Lennox, *Lady Gregory's Journals*, Putnam, 1946, p. 239.

January, 1904
Rev. Fr Creagh

Have no dealings of any kind with them [Jews].

Preaching as Redemptorist in Limerick in sermon which resulted in attacks on and boycott of Jews. From account by Redemptorists in *The Irish Times*, April 13, 1904.

January 18, 1904
Michael Davitt

I protest, as an Irishman and a Christian, against this spirit of barbarous malignity [anti-semitism] being introduced into Ireland, under the pretended form of a material regard for the welfare of our workers. The Jews have never done any injury to Ireland. Like our own race, they have endured a persecution, the records of which will forever remain a reproach to the 'Christian' nations of Europe. Ireland has no share in this black record.

Writing in *Freeman's Journal*, as founder of United Irish League, about anti-semitism in Limerick. Hyman, Louis, *The Jews in Ireland*, Keter, 1972, p. 213.

April 10, 1904
Marcus Joseph Blond

All of a sudden, like a thunderstorm [they] spoke hatred and animosity against the Jews, how they crucified Lord Jesus, how they martyred St Simon, and gradually in one month's time I have none of my previous customers . . . I defy anyone in this city to say whom I have wronged, what did I overcharge?

Writing to *The Times*, as Limerick shopkeeper, originally from Lithuania, who was victim of anti-Jewish boycott which drove 80 of 140 Jews out of city. Hyman, Louis, *The Jews in Ireland*, Keter, 1972, p. 217.

May 7, 1904
Standish O'Grady

If there were no Jews in Ireland, our own Irish Christian usurers . . . would be at just the same bad work, only without competitors.

Replying in *All-Ireland Review* of which he was editor to attacks on Limerick Jews for money-lending practices. Hyman, Louis, *The Jews in Ireland*, Keter, 1972, p. 213.

August 25, 1904
Irish Reform Association

We believe that [the] Union is compatible with the devolution to Ireland of a larger measure of self-government than she now possesses.

Manifesto from body which included leading Irish landlords. Gwynn, Denis, *The Life of John Redmond*, Harrap, 1932, p. 105.

August 25, 1904
John Dillon

[It is an attempt] to kill home rule with kindness.

Reacting, as Irish Party MP, to manifesto from Irish Reform Association suggesting limited devolution. Gwynn, Denis, *The Life of John Redmond*, Harrap, 1932, p. 106.

September, 1904
John Redmond

The announcement is of the utmost importance. It is simply a declaration for Home Rule and is quite a wonderful thing.

Reacting, from America, to manifesto from Irish Reform Association. Gwynn, Denis, *The Life of John Redmond*, Harrap, 1932, p. 106.

March 3, 1905
George Wyndham

I must insist on resigning . . . because my policy – which is not the policy of the Reform Association – cannot proceed now.

In comment to friend on day after resigning as Irish Secretary under pressure from Unionist MPs who believed he was behind manifesto from Irish Reform Association suggesting limited devolution. Gwynn, Denis, *The Life of John Redmond*, Harrap, 1932, p. 109.

April 27, 1905
Pope Pius X

To my beloved son, John Redmond . . . with a wish that he, together with his equally beloved colleagues, using all legal and peaceful means, may win that liberty which makes for the welfare of the whole country.

Inscription on photograph of himself presented to Redmond after audience in Rome which signalled end of period of strained relations between Vatican and Irish Party over papal rescript of 1888. Gwynn, Denis, *The Life of John Redmond*, Harrap, 1932, p. 113.

July 13, 1905
Lindsay Crawford

The Anniversary of the Battle of the Boyne seems to us a fitting opportunity to address our countrymen – both Protestant and Catholic . . . [standing] once more on the banks of the Boyne, not as victors in the fight, nor to applaud the noble deeds of our ancestors, but to bridge the gulf that has so long divided Ireland into hostile camps, and to hold out the right hand of fellowship to those who, while worshipping at other shrines, are yet our countrymen, bone of our bone, flesh of our flesh.

From 'Magheramourne Manifesto', drawn up by Crawford as Grand Master of Independent Orange Order. Gray, John, *City in Revolt*, Blackstaff, 1985, p. 48.

September 11, 1905
William Walker

Protestantism means protesting against superstition and hence true Protestantism is synonymous with Labour.

In reply published in *Northern Whig* to question from Belfast Protestant Association asking if he put Protestantism before Labour Party, which he was representing in election. Gray, John, *City in Revolt*, Blackstaff, 1985, p. 37.

September 11, 1905
Ramsay MacDonald

I was never more sick of an election than that at North Belfast, and the religious replies at the back of it knocked everything out of me.

As British Labour leader, acting as election agent for Labour candidate William Walker who was publicly questioned about his Protestantism by Belfast Protestant Association. Gray, John, *City in Revolt*, Blackstaff, 1985, p. 37.

September 23, 1906
John Redmond

The Irish Party and I have no responsibility whatever, direct or indirect, for the proposal of any such makeshift . . . nothing short of a complete scheme of Home Rule can ever be accepted as a settlement of the Irish question.

Speaking at Limerick on new Government proposal for form of administrative Home Rule. Gwynn, Denis, *The Life of John Redmond*, Harrap, 1932, p. 133.

January 28, 1907
Lady Gregory

AUDIENCE BROKE UP IN DISORDER AT THE WORD SHIFT.

Telegram to W. B. Yeats, in Scotland, after disturbances at first-night performance at Abbey Theatre, Dublin, of *The Playboy of the Western World* by J. M. Synge, during which word 'shift' was used to indicate female attire. Hogan & Kilroy, *The Abbey Theatre: The Years of Synge*, Dolmen, 1978, p. 126.

January 29, 1907
William Butler Yeats

I ask you to remain seated in your places, and to listen to a play by a most distinguished countryman of yours (cheers and a few hisses). It deserves your hearing. If it is a play that is bad it will die without your help (hear, hear). If the play is good your hindrance cannot mar it. What you can mar very greatly is the reputation of the country for fair play. (boohs and hear, hear).

Report in Dublin's *Daily Express* of appeal from stage before second-night performance at Abbey Theatre of *The Playboy of the Western World* by J.

M. Synge. There were disturbances on both evenings at mention of word 'shift'. Hogan & Kilroy, *The Abbey Theatre: The Years of Synge*, Dolmen, 1978, p. 128.

May 18, 1907
James Larkin

Although St Patrick was credited with banishing the snakes, there was one he forgot and that was Gallagher – a man who valued neither country, God nor creed.

Comment quoted in *Northern Whig* about Thomas Gallagher of Gallagher's Tobacco during industrial dispute in Belfast organised by Larkin. Gray, John, *City in Revolt*, Blackstaff, 1985, p. 63.

July 17, 1907
Alex Boyd

He [Alex Boyd] was proud of the fact that he could come to Clonard Gardens and address a meeting in his official capacity as the representative of Sandy Row (cheers) ... his friend Lindsay Crawford [Grand Master of Independent Orange Order] (cheers) and a few others had set about to unite the people of Ireland in one strong bond of friendship.

Speaking as Protestant leader of Municipal Employees' Association at strike meeting in Catholic area of Belfast. Gray, John, *City in Revolt*, Blackstaff, 1985, p. 92.

July 27, 1907
James Sexton

We do not recognise any distinction in the labour movement between the man who works with a baton and the man who works with a spade.

Speaking as docker's leader at meeting in Belfast in support of striking RIC men. Gray, John, *City in Revolt*, Blackstaff, 1985, p. 126.

August 3, 1907
Constable William Barrett

Down with blacklegs and cheap labour, say I, whether in civilian or constabulary life. All men are entitled to a living wage. Complaints are made that we demand the redress of our grievances at the wrong time. I quite agree that we should have struck out for more pay at the time of the Boer War when there was no military force available in this country.

Addressing strikers, including RIC men, at meeting at Belfast's Customs House called to support police

strike for more pay. Gray, John, *City in Revolt*, Blackstaff, 1985, p. 132.

August 4, 1907
Assistant Inspector General Alexander Gambell

General [Dawson] and I think that for the good of the city and for the purposes of showing the turbulent classes how easily we can cover the city with military pickets, it would be very advisable to put the scheme into operation.

In message, as senior RIC officer, to Dublin Castle from Belfast during dock strike, agreeing with use of troops to restore order. Gray, John, *City in Revolt*, Blackstaff, 1985, p. 144.

August 12, 1907
James Larkin

It was a scandalous thing that they should disgrace a broken bottle by using it on an officer of the British Army.

Comment after troops brought into Belfast to break dock strike organised by Larkin. Gray, John, *City in Revolt*, Blackstaff, 1985, p. 149.

August 12, 1907
James Larkin

Not as Catholics or Protestants, as Nationalists or Unionists, but as Belfastmen and workers, stand together and don't be misled by the employers' game of dividing Catholic and Protestant.

In handbill, after rioting during lockout and strike in Belfast. Berresford Ellis, Peter, *A History of the Irish Working Class*, Pluto, 1985, p. 180.

August 18, 1907
Rev. Fr P. Convery

It was a scandal and a shame that the police should have been attacked in such an outrageous way ... They [the police] were the best Catholics in the city; they were steady, respectable, and sober men ... When he [Rev. Convery] was in financial difficulties in regard to the completion of the church, the men in Cullingtree Road and Roden Street barracks had responded nobly.

Preaching at St Paul's Church, Belfast, after riots in Falls Road area when police helped to break dock strike. Gray, John, *City in Revolt*, Blackstaff, 1985, pp. 165-66.

January 4, 1909
Sean O'Casey
In a room in a tenement in Townsend Street, with a candle in a bottle for a torch, and a billycan of tea, with a few buns for a banquet, the Church militant here on earth, called the Irish Transport and General Workers' Union, was founded.

On occasion of formation by James Larkin of ITGWU in Dublin. Curriculum Development Unit, *Dublin 1913*, O'Brien, 1984, p. 62.

July 1909
Countess Markievicz
As our country has had her Freedom and her Nationhood taken from her by England, so also our sex is denied emancipation and citizenship by the same enemy. So therefore, the first step on the road to freedom is to realise ourselves as Irishwomen – not as Irish or merely as women, but as Irishwomen doubly enslaved and with a double battle to fight.

Writing in *Bean na hÉireann* on suffrage issue. Owens, Rosemary Cullen, *Smashing Times*, Attic, 1984, p. 104.

November 27, 1909
John Redmond
The political conditions in Ireland are such that, unless an official declaration on the question of Home Rule be made, not only will it be impossible for us to support Liberal candidates in England, but we will most unquestionably have to ask our friends to vote against them.

In letter to Lord Morley of Liberal Party. Gwynn, Denis, *The Life of John Redmond*, Harrap, 1932, pp. 166-67.

December 10, 1909
Herbert Asquith
The solution of the [Irish] problem can be found only in one way, by a policy which, while explicitly safeguarding the supremacy and indefectible authority of the Imperial Parliament, will set up in Ireland a system of full self-government in regard to purely Irish affairs.

In election speech, as Prime Minister, in Albert Hall, London, committing Liberal Party again to Home Rule. Gwynn, Denis, *The Life of John Redmond*, Harrap, 1932, p. 169.

January, 1910
Arthur Griffith
Ireland has maintained a representation of 103 men in the English parliament for 108 years ... The 103 Irishmen are faced with 567 foreigners ... Ten years hence, the majority of Irishmen will marvel they once believed that the proper battleground for Ireland was one chosen and filled by Ireland's enemies.

Arguing, as Sinn Féin leader, case for separation, in *The United Irishman*. Mansergh, Nicholas, *The Irish Question*, Unwin University Books, 1968, p. 226.

July 1, 1910
James Connolly
Only the Irish working class remain as the incorruptible inheritors of the fight for freedom in Ireland.

From *Labour in Irish History*, Dudley Edwards, Ruth, *James Connolly*, Gill and Macmillan, 1981, p. 78.

January 9, 1911
James Craig
There is a spirit spreading abroad which I can testify to from my personal knowledge that Germany and the German Emperor would be preferred to the rule of John Redmond, Patrick Ford, and the Molly Maguires [i.e. the Ancient Order of Hibernians].

As Ulster Unionist MP, speaking against Home Rule. Reported in *Morning Post*. Horgan, J. J., *The Complete Grammar of Anarchy*, Nisbet, 1919, p. 19.

July 1, 1911
Irish Parliamentary Party
Our people will receive the King on his coming visit to Ireland with the generosity and hospitality which are traditional with the Irish race; and when the day comes that the King will enter the Irish capital to reopen the ancient Parliament of Ireland we believe he will obtain from the Irish people a reception as enthusiastic as ever welcomed a British monarch in any of his dominions.

In statement after coronation of King George V. Gwynn, Denis, *The Life of John Redmond*, Harrap, 1932, p. 189.

July 12, 1911
King George V
Wherever we have gone, we and our children have been welcomed with a spontaneous and hearty loyalty that has greatly touched our hearts and made a permanent impression upon us. Without effort and without restraint, and in obedience to what seemed a natural impulse of goodwill, the entire populace, men, women and children, came out into the streets and parks to give us a true Irish welcome.

From letter to the Irish people after visit to Dublin. Curriculum Development Unit, *Dublin 1913,* O'Brien, 1984, p. 18.

September 25, 1911
Council of Unionist Clubs and Orange Lodges
It is resolved ... to take immediate steps in consultation with Sir Edward Carson to frame and submit a constitution for a Provisional Government for Ulster ... to come into operation on the day of the passage of any Home Rule bill.

At meeting in Belfast as Asquith prepared to introduce third Home Rule Bill. Horgan, J. J., *The Complete Grammar of Anarchy,* Nisbet, 1919, pp. 20-21.

September 30, 1911
Éamonn Ceannt
You appear to see Larkin at the bottom of all trouble. Sufficient for you is that Larkin is the agitator causing troubles between employer and employed. In similar manner the English Tory and his Irish allies described Irish politicians as vile agitators who caused trouble between the good and kind landlords and their willing slaves, the tenant farmers of Ireland.

In letter, published in *Sinn Féin,* attacking Arthur Griffith for his opposition to James Larkin. Berresford Ellis, Peter, *A History of the Irish Working Class,* Pluto, 1985, p. 191.

October, 1911
Winston Churchill
We must not attach too much importance to these frothings of Sir Edward Carson. I daresay when the worst comes to the worst, we shall find that civil war evaporates in uncivil words.

Commenting on Carson's threats, as leader of Ulster Unionists, about Unionist reaction to Home Rule. Bardon, Jonathan, *Belfast,* Blackstaff, 1983, p. 178.

October 7, 1911
Arthur Griffith
The fight of the Irish people for the land was the fight of a nation for reconquest of a soil that had been theirs and had been confiscated. The landlord did not make the soil – the industrialists made the industry ... In Dublin the wives of some men that Larkin has led out on strike are begging in the streets. The consequences of Larkinism are workless fathers, mourning mothers, hungry children and broken homes.

Replying in *Sinn Féin* to Éamonn Ceannt, who had written on September 30, 1911, defending Larkin. Berresford Ellis, Peter, *A History of the Irish Working Class,* Pluto, 1985, p. 191.

1912
Rev. J. B. Armour
Under the reign of terrorising prejudice it is not easy to indicate the number of those, especially in the Presbyterian Church who refuse to make anti-Home Rule an article of a standing, or falling, Church. But the drastic methods used to repress free speech and the right of private judgement in a political question are indications that the secret disciples of Home Rule are not only a large but an increasing number ... the belief that democracy in Ireland would become a persecutor of Protestants ... can only arise in the minds of those who hate democracy and all its works.

Writing on case for Home Rule from Presbyterian viewpoint. Armour, J. B., *The New Irish Constitution,* Hodder and Stoughton. (Quoted in *The Irish Times,* September 9, 1969.)

1912
John Dillon
Women's suffrage will, I believe, be the ruin of our western civilisation. It will destroy the home, challenging the headship of man, laid down by God. It may come in your time, I hope not in mine.

In conversation with suffragettes, as recalled by Hanna Sheehy Skeffington. Owens, Rosemary Cullen, *Smashing Times,* Attic, 1984, p. 48.

1912
Rudyard Kipling
Before an Empire's eyes,
the traitor claims his price.
What need for further lies?
We are the sacrifice ...

From poem published in *Morning Post* in London to express Unionist opposition to Home Rule, and adopted by opponents of Anglo-Irish Agreement in 1985-86.

January 8, 1912
Jennie Wyse Power
As an Irish Nationalist I cannot see why there should be any antagonism between the Irish women's demand for citizenship and the demand for a native parliament. Our claim is that we shall not be debarred merely by sex from the rights of citizens.

Writing as Vice-President of Sinn Féin in *Irish Citizen* on agitation for female suffrage. Owens, Rosemary Cullen, *Smashing Times*, Attic, 1984, p. 52.

January 15, 1912
Augustine Birrell
I don't see how I could remain in a Cabinet which has adopted en bloc Female Suffrage, married and single – and if I couldn't, how could Asquith [the Prime Minister]? I believe the wire-pullers are satisfied that no such Amendment [to allow female suffrage] can pass.

In letter from Chief Secretary for Ireland to John Dillon of Irish Party. Owens, Rosemary Cullen, *Smashing Times*, Attic, 1984, p. 47.

January 22, 1912
Frederick Smith
There was no length to which Ulster would not be entitled to go, however desperate or unconditional, in carrying the quarrel if the quarrel was wickedly fixed upon them.

Speaking in Liverpool, as Conservative MP, on anti-Home Rule platform. Gwynn, Denis, *The Life of John Redmond*, Harrap, 1932, p. 200.

January 22, 1912
Edward Carson
If they [Ulster Unionists] did anything else, they would have been false to the position in which they were placed. If that is inciting to riot, here I am.

Speaking in Liverpool about action taken by Ulster Unionists' Standing Committee to physically prevent Winston Churchill speaking in favour of Home Rule in Ulster Hall. Gwynn, Denis, *The Life of John Redmond*, Harrap, 1932, p. 200.

February 8, 1912
Winston Churchill
What harm could Irish ideas and sentiment, and Irish dreams, if given free play in an Irish parliament, do to the strong structure of British power? The separation of Ireland from Great Britain was absolutely impossible ... The two nations were bound together till the end of time. Was it not worthwhile for the English statesmen to try to make their life-long partner happy and contented and free? Let [Protestant Ulster] fight for the spread of charity, tolerance and enlightenment among men. Then indeed, gentlemen, Ulster will fight, and Ulster will be right.

Speaking, as First Lord of Admiralty, at Home Rule rally to mostly Catholic crowd in Belfast's Celtic Park, after Unionist council had refused use of Ulster Hall. *The Irish Times*, February 9, 1912.

March 31, 1912
Padraic Pearse
The [Home Rule] bill which we support today will be for the good of Ireland ... But if we are tricked this time, there is a party in Ireland, and I am one of them, that will advise the Gael to have no counsel or dealings with the Gall [foreigner] for ever again, but to answer them henceforward with the strong hand and the sword's edge. Let the Gall understand that if we are cheated once more there will be red war in Ireland.

Speaking in Dublin at meeting, also addressed by Redmond, on eve of introduction of Home Rule Bill. Macardle, Dorothy, *The Irish Republic*, Irish Press, 1955, p. 82.

April 9, 1912
Andrew Bonar Law
You [Ulster Unionists] hold the pass, the pass for the Empire ... The Government by their Parliament Act have erected a boom against you, a boom to cut you off from the help of the British people. You will burst that boom.

As leader of Conservative Party, addressing hundred-thousand-strong anti-Home Rule demonstration at Balmoral, near Belfast, two days before introduction of third Home Rule Bill. Lyons, F.S.L., *Ireland Since the Famine*, Fontana, 1982, p. 301.

April 16, 1912
John Redmond
Ireland today is peaceful beyond record. She has almost entirely, I believe, cast aside her suspicions and her rancour toward this country; and England, on her side, is, I believe, today more willing that ever she was in her past history to admit Ireland on terms of equality, liberty and loyalty into that great sisterhood of nations that makes up the British Empire.

Speaking in Commons, as leader of Irish Party, on first reading of Home Rule Bill. Gwynn, Denis, *The Life of John Redmond*, Harrap, 1932, p. 203.

April 29, 1912
Major Fred Crawford
If they [Ulster Unionists] were put out of the Union ... he [Major Crawford] would infinitely prefer to change his allegiance right over to the Emperor of Germany.

Speaking at Bangor as Director of Ordnance for Ulster Unionists – i.e., responsible for Ulster gun-running. Horgan, J. J., *The Complete Grammar of Anarchy*, Nisbet, 1919, p. 23.

May 10, 1912
Edward Carson
Assuming ... that the people of this country [Britain] would allow the coercion of their kith and kin [Ulster Unionists] – what would be the effect upon the army? Many officers would resign; no army could stand such a strain upon them.

Speaking in London, as Unionist leader, after second reading of Home Rule Bill. Horgan, J. J., *The Complete Grammar of Anarchy*, Nisbet, 1919, p. 24.

June 11, 1912
T. G. Agar-Robartes
I have never heard that Orange bitters will mix with Irish whiskey.

Speaking in Commons as Liberal MP on his amendment to Home Rule Bill to exclude Antrim, Armagh, Down and Londonderry. Coogan, Tim Pat, *The IRA*, Fontana, 1980, p. 27.

June 14, 1912
Edward Carson
The Government last night declared war against Ulster and have announced that the only solution to this question is to drive them out of a community in which they are satisfied into a community which they loathe, hate and detest. We will accept the declaration of war. We are not altogether unprepared.

Speaking in London as Unionist leader after defeat of Home Rule Bill amendment to exclude Antrim, Armagh, Down and Londonderry. Horgan, J. J., *The Complete Grammar of Anarchy*, Nisbet, 1919, p. 25.

June 18, 1912
Andrew Bonar Law
If Ulster does resist [Home Rule] by force ... no Government would dare to use their troops to drive them out ... the Government which gave the order to employ troops for that purpose would run a greater risk of being lynched in London than the Loyalists of Ulster would run of being shot in Belfast.

Speaking in Commons as Conservative leader. Gwynn, Denis, *The Life of John Redmond*, Harrap, 1932, p. 208.

July 20, 1912
Katherine Tynan
The women were hunted like rats in the city.

In recollection, as Dublin poet and novelist, of mob violence in Dublin against women after English suffragettes had thrown a hatchet into a carriage carrying British Prime Minister Herbert Asquith and Irish Party leader John Redmond through Dublin. Owens, Rosemary Cullen, *Smashing Times*, Attic, 1984, p. 60.

July 27, 1912
Frederick Smith
Should it happen that Ulster is threatened with a violent attempt to incorporate her in an Irish parliament with no appeal to the English electors, I say to Sir Edward Carson, appeal to the young men of England.

Speaking, as Liverpool Conservative MP, at anti-Home Rule rally in Blenheim Palace. Horgan, J. J., *The Complete Grammar of Anarchy*, Nisbet, 1919, p. 27.

July 27, 1912

Andrew Bonar Law

If an attempt were made to deprive these men [Ulster Protestants] of their birthright – as part of a corrupt parliamentary bargain – they would be justified in resisting such an attempt by all means in their power, including force ... I can imagine no length of resistance to which Ulster can go in which I would not be prepared to support them.

In address as Conservative Party leader to anti-Home Rule rally at Blenheim Palace. Lyons, F. S. L., *Ireland Since the Famine*, Fontana, 1982, p. 303.

July 31, 1912

Herbert Asquith

Has the right honourable gentleman [Andrew Bonar Law] considered ... what might be the attitude of the people of Ireland ... if a subsequent parliament should refuse to grant them their constitutional demand ... What answer are you going to make to the vast majority of the Irish people when they resist the considered determination of Parliament, and appeal to the language of the right honourable gentleman to justify their action?

Speaking in Commons, as Prime Minister, in response to Conservative leader's speech at Blenheim on July 27, 1912. Horgan, J. J., *The Complete Grammar of Anarchy*, Nisbet, 1919, pp. 27-28.

August 14, 1912

Hanna Sheehy Skeffington

Hunger-strike was then a new weapon – we were the first to try it out in Ireland – had we but known we were the pioneers in a long line.

Recalling hunger strikes by English and Irish suffragettes in prison in Dublin after being refused political prisoner status. Women on hunger strike were released and later re-arrested. Owens, Rosemary Cullen, *Smashing Times*, Attic, 1984, p. 63.

August 15, 1912

Augustine Birrell

Personally I am dead against Forcible Feeding which always ends with the release of the prisoner long before her time. I want to keep these ladies under lock and key for five years and I am willing to feed them with Priests' [*sic*] Champagne and Michaelmas Geese all the time, if it can be done but ... these

wretched hags ... are obstinate to the point of death.

In letter as Chief Secretary of Ireland to John Dillon, member of Irish Party. Owens, Rosemary Cullen, *Smashing Times*, Attic, 1984, p. 64.

September 21, 1912

Edward Carson

In the event of this proposed parliament being thrust upon us, we solemnly and mutually pledge ourselves not to recognise its authority ... I do not care twopence whether it is treason or not.

Speaking against Home Rule in Coleraine. Horgan, J. J., *The Complete Grammar of Anarchy*, Nisbet, 1919, p. 29.

September 24, 1912

Lord Willoughby de Broke

The Unionists of England were going to help Unionists over here, not only by making speeches. Peaceable methods would be tried first, but if the last resort was forced on them by the radical Government, the latter would find that they had not only Orangemen against them, but that every white man in the British Empire would be giving support, either moral or active, to one of the most loyal populations that ever fought under the Union Jack.

Press report of speech at anti-Home Rule rally in Dromore, Co. Down. Horgan, J. J., *The Complete Grammar of Anarchy*, Nisbet, 1919, p. 29.

September 28, 1912

Ulster Covenant

We ... do hereby pledge ourselves in Solemn Covenant throughout this our time of threatened calamity to stand by one another in defending for ourselves and our children our cherished position of equal citizenship in the United Kingdom, and in using all means which may be found necessary to defeat the present conspiracy to set up a Home Rule Parliament in Ireland.

From Ulster Covenant, signed at Belfast and other centres, as demonstration against Home Rule, by 474,414 people. Harbinson, John F., *The Ulster Unionist Party*, Blackstaff, 1973, p. 28.

October 1, 1912
Edward Carson

The Attorney General has been reading me a lecture upon what is a serious matter, because I myself once or twice had the honour of being a law officer of the Crown. He says that my doctrines and the course I am taking [against Home Rule] lead to anarchy. Does he not think I know that?

Speaking in Glasgow. Horgan, J. J., *The Complete Grammar of Anarchy*, Nisbet, 1919, p. 32.

October 5, 1912
Herbert Asquith

The reckless rodomontade at Blenheim [against Home Rule] in the early summer as developed and amplified in this Ulster campaign, furnishes for the future a complete grammar of anarchy ... This new dogma, countersigned as it now is by all the leading men of the Tory party, will be invoked, and rightly invoked, cited and rightly cited, called in aid and rightly called in aid, whenever the spirit of lawlessness, fed and fostered by a sense whether of real or imagined injustice, takes body and shape and claims to stop the ordered machinery of a self-governing society ... A more deadly blow has never been dealt in our time by any body of responsible politicians at the very foundations on which democratic government rests.

Speaking, as Prime Minister, in Ladybank. Horgan, J. J., *The Complete Grammar of Anarchy*, Nisbet, 1919, p. 33.

February 22, 1913
Sean O'Casey

The delivery of Ireland is not in the Labour Manifesto, good and salutary as it may be, but in the strength, beauty, nobility and imagination of the Gaelic ideal.

Irish Worker, February 22, 1913.

June 22, 1913
Padraic Pearse

We pledge ourselves to follow in the steps of [Wolfe] Tone, never to rest, either by day or by night, until his work be accomplished, deeming it the proudest of all privileges to fight for freedom, to fight, not in despondency, but in great joy, hoping for the victory in our day, but fighting on whether victory seem far or near, never lowering our ideal, never bartering one jot or tittle of our birthright, holding faith to the memory and the inspiration of Tone, and accounting ourselves base as long as we endure the evil thing against which he testified with his blood.

From address at grave of Wolfe Tone in Bodenstown churchyard. Pearse, Padraic H., *Political Writings and Speeches*, Talbot, 1952, p. 63.

July 12, 1913
Edward Carson

The Government know perfectly well that they could not tomorrow rely upon the army to shoot down the people of Ulster ... The other day – I know of it myself – a British officer was asked to send in his papers and resign because he had joined us ... He did not send them in and they did not turn him out, but they ordered him to rejoin his regiment. They did that because they knew that if they once commenced that sort of thing, there would be no end. The army are with us.

Speaking in Belfast on prospect of army being used to enforce Home Rule. Horgan, J. J., *The Complete Grammar of Anarchy*, Nisbet, 1919, p. 40.

July 19, 1913
William Martin Murphy

I would think there is talent enough amongst the men in the [tramways] service to form a union of their own, without allying themselves to a disreputable organisation, and placing themselves under the feet of an unscrupulous man who claims the right to give you the word of command and to issue his orders to you and to use you as tools to make him the labour dictator of Dublin.

In address, as leader of Dublin employers, to Tramways Company employees to persuade them not to join ITGWU at urging of James Larkin. Curriculum Development Unit, *Dublin 1913*, O'Brien, 1984, pp. 74-75.

July 29, 1913
James Connolly

I don't think I can stand Larkin as a boss much longer ... He is consumed with jealousy and hatred of anyone who will not cringe to him and beslaver all over him.

In letter to friend, William O'Brien, about bad relations between Connolly and Larkin. Dudley Edwards, Ruth, *James Connolly*, Gill and Macmillan, 1981, p. 101.

August 4, 1913
James Craig

According to the Government programme, we may look for Home Rule in May, Civil War in June, the Union Jack being hauled down and being tramped upon in July and the smash up of the Empire in August.

Writing, as Unionist MP and organiser of Ulster Volunteers, about effect of enforcing Home Rule. Macardle, Dorothy, *The Irish Republic*, Irish Press, 1951, p. 89.

August 26, 1913
James Larkin

This is not a strike, it is a lockout ... We will demonstrate in O'Connell Street. It is our street as well as William Martin Murphy's. We are fighting for bread and butter. We will hold our meetings in the street and if any one of our men fall, there must be justice. By the living God, if they want war they can have it.

In address to striking tramway workers on first day of the Dublin lockout. Curriculum Development Unit, *Dublin 1913*, O'Brien, 1984, p. 78.

August 31, 1913
Winston Churchill

Something should be done to afford the characteristically Protestant and Orange counties the option of a moratorium of several years before acceding to the Irish parliament ... Much is to be apprehended from a combination of the rancour of a party in the ascendant and the fanaticism of these stubborn and determined Orangemen.

In letter to John Redmond. Hepburn, A. C., *The Conflict of Nationality in Modern Ireland*, Arnold, 1980, p. 77.

September 7, 1913
Edward Carson

We will set up a government [in Belfast]. I am told it will be illegal. Of course it will. Drilling is illegal. I was reading an Act of Parliament forbidding it. The Volunteers are illegal, and the Government know they are illegal, and the Government dare not interfere with them. Don't be afraid of illegalities.

Speaking in Newry on consequences of Home Rule. Horgan, J. J., *The Complete Grammar of Anarchy*, Nisbet, 1919, pp. 41-42.

September 11, 1913
Lenin

The police have gone positively wild; drunken policemen assault peaceful workers, break into homes, torment the aged, women and children ... People are thrown into prison for making the most peaceful speeches. The city is like an armed camp.

Writing in *Severnaya Pravda* on 1913's 'Bloody Sunday' when police attacked a crowd after Larkin appeared on balcony of Imperial Hotel, O'Connell Street, Dublin. Berresford Ellis, Peter, *A History of the Irish Working Class*, Pluto, 1985, pp. 195-96.

September 20, 1913
Frederick Smith

[British Conservatives] would say to their followers in England: 'To your tents, Oh Israel!' and would stand side by side with loyal Ulster refusing to recognise any law, and prepared with them to risk the collapse of the whole body politic to prevent this monstrous crime.

Speaking, as Liverpool Conservative MP, at anti-Home Rule rally in Ballyclare. (Frederick Smith, some three years later, acted as prosecuting counsel at trial of Roger Casement on charge of high treason.) Horgan J. J., *The Complete Grammar of Anarchy*, Nisbet, 1919, p. 43.

October 7, 1913
George Russell (AE)

I address this warning to you, the aristocracy of industry in this city ... you determined deliberately, in cold anger, to starve out one third of the population of this city, to break the manhood of the men by the sight of the sufferings of their wives and the hunger of their children. We read in the Dark Ages of the rack and thumbscrew. But these iniquities were hidden and concealed from the knowledge of men in dungeons and torture chambers ... It remained for the twentieth century and the capital city of Ireland to see an oligarchy of four hundred masters deciding openly upon starving one hundred thousand people ... You may succeed in your policy and ensure your own damnation by your victory. The men whose manhood you have broken will loathe you, and will always be brooding and scheming to strike a fresh blow. The children will be taught to curse you ... your class will be cut off from humanity as the surgeon cuts the cancer and alien growth from the body. Be warned ere it is too late.

From open letter, as author and poet, to Dublin employers during 1913 lockout of workers. *The Irish Times,* October 7, 1913.

October 9, 1913
Dr O'Donnell, Bishop of Raphoe
There is no length to which any of us would refuse to go to satisfy the Orangemen at the start of our new Government [in Dublin], provided Ireland did not suffer seriously.

In letter to Redmond as rumours of partition gained ground. Gwynn, Denis, *The Life of John Redmond,* Harrap, 1932, p. 231.

October 12, 1913
John Redmond
Ireland is a unit. It is true that within the bosom of a nation there is room for diversities of the treatment of government and of administration but ... The two-nation theory is to us an abomination and a blasphemy.

Speaking in Limerick, as leader of Irish Party. Gwynn, Denis, *The Life of John Redmond,* Harrap, 1932, p. 232.

October 20, 1913
Dr Walsh, Archbishop of Dublin
They can be no longer held worthy of the name of Catholic mothers if they so far forget that duty as to send away their little children to be cared for in a strange land, without security of any kind that those to whom the poor children are to be handed over are Catholics, or indeed any persons of any faith at all.

In letter to press about proposal to send children of impoverished strikers to homes in England. Curriculum Development Unit, *Dublin 1913,* O'Brien, 1984, p. 94.

November, 1913
Augustine Birrell
It certainly was an outrage. For in the first place, there are no starving children in Dublin, and in the second place, the place swarms with homes for them.

Report from Chief Secretary's Office to Prime Minister on proposal to send children of impoverished strikers to homes in England. Curriculum Development Unit, *Dublin 1913,* O'Brien, 1984, p. 96.

November, 1913
Padraic Pearse
I am glad that the Orangemen have armed, for it is a goodly thing to see arms in Irish hands. I should like to see the AOH armed. I should like to see the Transport Workers armed. I should like to see any and every body of Irish citizens armed. We must accustom ourselves to the thought of arms, to the sight of arms, to the use of arms. We may make mistakes in the beginning and shoot the wrong people; but bloodshed is a cleansing and a sanctifying thing, and the nation which regards it as the final horror has lost its manhood. There are many things more horrible than bloodshed; and slavery is one of them.

From pamphlet *The Coming Revolution.* Pearse, Padraic H., *Political Writings and Speeches,* Talbot, 1952, pp. 98-99.

November, 1913
Padraic Pearse
I think the Orangeman with a rifle a much less ridiculous figure than a Nationalist without a rifle.

From article in *Irish Freedom.* Pearse, Padraic H., *Political Writings and Speeches,* Talbot, 1952, p. 185.

November 13, 1913
James Connolly
I am going to talk sedition. The next time we are out for a march I want to be accompanied by four battalions of trained men with their corporals and sergeants. Why should we not drill and train men as they are doing in Ulster?

Speaking at Dublin meeting to celebrate release of Larkin from prison. Boyle, John W., *The Making of 1916: Studies in the History of the Rising,* Stationery Office, 1969, p. 55.

November 14, 1913
Irish Churchman
We have the offer of aid from a powerful continental monarch [German Kaiser] ... should our King sign the Home Rule Bill, the Protestants of Ireland will welcome this

continental deliverer as their forefathers under similar circumstances did once before.

Protestant journal's comment on meeting in Hamburg between Edward Carson and the German Kaiser. Berresford Ellis, Peter, *A History of the Irish Working Class,* Pluto, 1985, p. 205.

November 25, 1913
Eoin MacNeill
We do not contemplate any hostility to the Volunteer movement that has already been initiated in parts of Ulster ... The more genuine and successful the local Volunteer movement in Ulster becomes, the more completely does it establish the principle that Irishmen have the right to decide and govern their own national affairs.

Speaking as chairman at inaugural meeting of Irish Volunteers (set up in response to creation of Ulster Volunteers) at Rotunda, Dublin. Macardle, Dorothy, *The Irish Republic,* Irish Press, 1951, p. 96.

November 28, 1913
Andrew Bonar Law
King James had behind him the letter of the law just as completely as Mr Asquith ... the King had the largest army which had ever been seen in England. What happened? There was no civil war. There was a revolution, and the King disappeared. Why? Because his own army refused to fight for him.

In speech in Dublin, as Conservative leader, widely regarded as incitement to British Army to mutiny if ordered against Unionists. Gwynn, Denis, *The Life of John Redmond,* Harrap, 1932, p. 239.

December, 1913
Padraic Pearse
A citizen without arms is like a priest without religion, like a woman without chastity, like a man without manhood ... I say to each one of you who read this that it is your duty to arm ... if you cannot arm otherwise than by joining Carson's Volunteers, join Carson's Volunteers. But you can, for instance, start Volunteers of your own.

From article in *Irish Freedom* promoting Irish Volunteer force. Pearse, Padraic H., *Political Writings and Speeches,* Talbot, 1952, pp. 196-97.

December 5, 1913
Lieutenant-Colonel Pretyman Newman
If Mr Asquith [the British Prime Minister] did employ the British Army [to impose Home Rule], he would break the back of the Army, and if by any chance he should bring bloodshed in Ulster by means of Imperial troops, then ... any man would be justified in shooting Mr Asquith in the streets of London.

Speaking, as Conservative MP, at anti-Home Rule meeting in Potter's Bar, England. Horgan, J. J., *The Complete Grammar of Anarchy,* Nisbet, 1919, p. 46.

January 30, 1914
James Larkin
We are beaten. We make no bones about it; but we are not too badly beaten still to fight.

In speech in Dublin on workers' defeat in Dublin lockout. Curriculum Development Unit, *Dublin 1913,* O'Brien, 1984, p. 102.

February 7, 1914
Padraic Pearse
The Gaelic League will be recognised in history as the most revolutionary influence that has ever come into Ireland. The Irish revolution really began when the seven proto-Gaelic Leaguers met in O'Connell Street ... The germ of all future Irish history was in that back room.

Writing in *The Irish Volunteer.* Macardle, Dorothy, *The Irish Republic,* Irish Press, 1951, p. 61.

February 9, 1914
James Connolly
And so we Irish workers must again go down into hell, bow our backs to the lash of the slave driver, let our hearts be seared by the iron of his hatred, and instead of the sacramental wafer of brotherhood and common sacrifice, eat the dust of defeat and betrayal. Dublin is isolated.

Writing in *Forward* on workers' defeat in Dublin lockout. Dudley Edwards, Ruth, *James Connolly,* Gill and Macmillan, 1981, p. 110.

February 25, 1914

Edward Carson

Crawford, I'll see you through this business, if I should have to go to prison for it.

Major Fred Crawford

Sir Edward, that is all I want. I leave tonight; good-bye.

Exchange in London after Crawford asked if he had Carson's backing for his plans to run guns to Unionist Volunteers. Gwynn, Denis, *The Life of John Redmond*, Harrap, 1932, p. 303.

March 1, 1914

John Redmond

The rights and interests of the Nationalists of Ulster will not be neglected or betrayed by us.

In letter to Bishop McHugh of Derry after he had persuaded Dr McHugh to call off Home Rule rally in Derry because of possible disorder. Gwynn, Denis, *The Life of John Redmond*, Harrap, 1932, p. 267.

March 2, 1914

John Redmond

We are ready to give our acquiescence to the solution of the standing out for three years by option of the counties of Ulster as the price of peace.

In memorandum to Asquith offering compromise on Home Rule Bill. Gwynn, Denis, *The Life of John Redmond*, Harrap, 1932, p. 269.

March 9, 1914

Edward Carson

We do not want sentence of death, with a stay of execution for six years.

Responding to publication of Asquith's proposal to allow individual counties to opt out of Home Rule for six years. Gwynn, Denis, *The Life of John Redmond*, Harrap, 1932, p. 274.

March 12, 1914

Lenin

The British Conservatives, led by that Black Hundred landlord, Purishkevich – that is to say Carson – have raised a frightful howl against the Irish autonomy. That means, they say, subjecting Ulsterites to alien people of alien faith! Lord Carson has threatened rebellion, and has organised armed Black Hundred gangs for this purpose.

This is an empty threat of course. There can be no question of rebellion by a handful of hooligans.

Writing on Ireland in *Put Pravdy*. Berresford Ellis, Peter, *A History of the Irish Working Class*, Pluto, 1985, p. 205.

March 14, 1914

Winston Churchill

They [Unionists] denounce all violence except their own ... if all the loose, wanton and reckless chatter is in the end to disclose a sinister and revolutionary purpose then ... put these grave matters to the proof.

In speech at Bradford. Gwynn, Denis, *The Life of John Redmond*, Harrap, 1932, p. 275.

March 14, 1914

War Office, London

I am commanded by the Army Council to inform you that in consequence of reports which have been received by His Majesty's Government that attempts may be made in various parts of Ireland by evil-disposed persons to obtain possession of arms, ammunition and other Government stores, it is considered advisable that you should at once take special precautions for safeguarding depots and other places where arms or stores are kept, as you may think advisable. It appears from the information received that Armagh, Omagh, Carrickfergus and Enniskillen are insufficiently guarded, being specially liable to attack. You will, therefore, please to take the necessary steps, and report to this office.

Order to General Sir Arthur Paget, General Officer Commanding in Chief for Ireland, to move British troops at Curragh to North in anticipation of Unionist revolt against Home Rule. Horgan, J. J., *The Complete Grammar of Anarchy*, Nisbet, 1919, p. 48.

March 17, 1914

General Sir Arthur Paget

Any such move of troops [as ordered by War Office] would create intense excitement in Ulster, and possibly precipitate a crisis. For these reasons I do not consider myself justified in moving troops.

Reply sent, as British Army Commander-in-Chief in Ireland, to War Office after being ordered to send troops to North. Gwynn, Denis, *The Life of John Redmond,* Harrap, 1932, p. 288.

March 19, 1914
Colonel J. E. B. Seely
Officers actually domiciled in Ulster would be exempted from taking part in any operations that might take place. They would be permitted to 'disappear' and when all was over would be allowed to resume their place without their career or their position being affected.

Agreeing, as War Minister, to concession to try to prevent Curragh mutiny. Gwynn, Denis, *The Life of John Redmond,* Harrap, 1932, p. 289.

March 20, 1914
General Sir Arthur Paget
OFFICER COMMANDING 5TH LANCERS STATES THAT ALL OFFICERS, EXCEPT TWO AND ONE DOUBTFUL, ARE RESIGNING THEIR COMMISSIONS TODAY. I MUCH FEAR SAME CONDITIONS IN THE 16TH LANCERS. FEAR MEN WILL REFUSE TO MOVE.

REGRET TO REPORT BRIGADIER-GENERAL GOUGH AND FIFTY-SEVEN OFFICERS 3RD CAVALRY BRIGADE PREFER TO ACCEPT DISMISSAL IF ORDERED NORTH.

Telegrams sent to War Office after further orders received to move army units from Curragh to North. Horgan, J. J., *The Complete Grammar of Anarchy,* Nisbet, 1919, p. 48.

March 23, 1914
Colonel J. E. B. Seely
The Army Council are satisfied that the incident which has arisen ... has been due to a misunderstanding ... His Majesty's Government must retain the right to use all the forces of the Crown in Ireland to maintain law and order and to support the civil power in the ordinary execution of its duty. But they have no intention whatever of taking advantage of this right to crush political opposition to the policy or principles of the Home Rule Bill.

Paragraph added by War Minister to Cabinet document, and given to Brigadier General Gough enabling reinstatement of officers who rebelled at Curragh. Gwynn, Denis, *The Life of John Redmond,* Harrap, 1932, pp. 296-97.

March 25, 1914
Brigadier-General Hubert Gough
I got a signed guarantee [from the Government] that in no circumstances shall we be used to force Home Rule on the Ulster people. If it came to civil war, I would fight for Ulster rather than against her.

In statement issued after consultations with War Office over his refusal to obey order to move north against Ulster Unionists. *Daily Telegraph,* March 25, 1914.

March 26, 1914
Morning Post
The Army has killed the Home Rule Bill.

Commenting on Curragh mutiny. Gwynn, Denis, *The Life of John Redmond,* Harrap, 1932, p. 297.

March 27, 1914
Roger Casement
Irishmen should be grateful to the English Unionist leaders, their press organs, and, above all, their military junta for the striking revelation we have had, once and for all, of the true meaning of the words 'Union', 'Unionist', and 'Unionism', in British politics. Not that any Irishman of average intelligence has ever been in doubt about the realities ... the 'Union' means the military occupation of Ireland as a conquered country, that the real headquarters of Irish Government, on the Unionist principle, is the Curragh Camp ... the cat is out of the Irish bag.

In letter to *Irish Independent* on Curragh mutiny. Casement, Roger, *The Crime Against Europe: The Writings and Poetry of Roger Casement,* Fallon, 1958, pp. 110-111.

April 24, 1914
Ulster Volunteers
'Gough'

Password used by Ulster Volunteers during gun-running at Larne. Brigadier-General Hubert Gough was leader of Curragh mutiny. *Daily Mail,* April 28, 1914.

May 6, 1914
Hanna Sheehy Skeffington
The proposed 'Ladies Auxiliary Committee' [Cumann na mBan] has apparently no function beyond that of a conduit pipe to pour a stream of gold into the coffers of the male organisation [the Irish Volunteers], to be

turned off automatically as soon as it had served this mean and subordinate purpose.

Writing as representative of women's suffrage movement in *Freeman's Journal* following formation of Cumann na mBan. Owens, Rosemary Cullen, *Smashing Times,* Attic, 1984, p. 110.

May 8, 1914
Mary Colum and Louise Gavan Duffy

We consider at the moment that helping to equip the Irish Volunteers is the most necessary national work. We may mention that many of the members of our Society [Cumann na mBan] are keen suffragists, but as an organisation we must confine ourselves within the four walls of our constitution.

Writing in *Irish Independent* as joint honorary secretaries of Cumann na mBan in response to criticism of its formation by members of the women's suffrage movement. Owens, Rosemary Cullen, *Smashing Times,* Attic, 1984, p. 111.

May 25, 1914
William O'Brien

This Act will be born with a rope around its neck. It is not even intended to be enforced ... We regard this Bill as no longer a Home Rule Bill but as a Bill for the murder of Home Rule.

Speaking in Commons, as Irish Party MP for Cork, after Government announced plans to amend Home Rule Bill to exclude part of Ulster. Macardle, Dorothy, *The Irish Republic,* Irish Press, 1951, p. 107.

June 9, 1914
John Redmond

The effect of Sir Edward Carson's threats upon public opinion in England, the House of Commons and the Government, the occurrences at the Curragh Camp, and the successful gun-running in Ulster vitally altered the position, and the Irish Party took steps about six weeks ago to inform their friends ... it was desirable to support the [Irish] Volunteer movement.

In letter to Irish newspapers announcing that Irish Party would join governing committee of Irish Volunteers. Gwynn, Denis, *The Life of John Redmond,* Harrap, 1932, p. 317.

June 16, 1914
John Dillon

You do not put down Irishmen by coercion. You simply embitter them and stiffen their backs.

Explaining why Irish Party leaders did not demand the prosecution of Unionists for incitement or treason. Gwynn, Denis, *The Life of John Redmond,* Harrap, 1932, p. 225.

July 12, 1914
Edward Carson

Give us a clean cut.

As Unionist leader, after House of Lords on July 8 voted to make exclusion of six counties from Home Rule permanent. Dudley Edwards, Ruth, *The Making of 1916: Studies in the History of the Rising,* Stationery Office, 1969, p. 130.

July 21, 1914
King George V

We have watched with deep misgivings the course of events in Ireland ... today the cry of civil war is on the lips of the most responsible and sober-minded of my people. We have in the past endeavoured to act as a civilising example to the world, and to me it is unthinkable, as it must be to you, that we should be brought to the brink of fratricidal strife upon issues apparently so capable of adjustment as those you are now asked to consider.

In speech at first meeting of conference called by king at Buckingham Palace to try to reach settlement over Ulster. Gwynn, Denis, *The Life of John Redmond,* Harrap, 1932, p. 337.

July 24, 1914
John Redmond

[Let's] have a good shake-hands for the sake of the old days together on circuit.

To Carson, as Buckingham Palace conference on Ulster broke up in disagreement. Gwynn, Denis, *The Life of John Redmond,* Harrap, 1932, p. 343.

July 24, 1914
Herbert Asquith

Nothing could have been more amicable in tone or more desperately fruitless in result.

Commenting on Buckingham Palace conference on Ulster. Gwynn, Denis, *The Life of John Redmond,* Harrap, 1932, p. 343.

July 25, 1914
James Larkin
Oh Irishmen, dear countrymen, take heed of what we say, for if you do England's dirty work, you will surely rue the day.

In article in *Irish Worker* opposing Irish recruitment to the British Army at outbreak of war.

August 1, 1914
James Connolly
I know of no foreign enemy in this country except the British Government. Should a German army land in Ireland tomorrow, we should be perfectly justified in joining it, if by doing so we could rid this country once and for all from its connection with the Brigand Empire that drags us unwillingly to war.

Writing in *Irish Worker* on outbreak of war in Europe. Greaves, Desmond, C., *The Life and Times of James Connolly,* Lawrence and Wishart, 1961, p. 284.

August 3, 1914
John Redmond
I say to the Government that they may tomorrow withdraw every one of their troops from Ireland. I say that the coast of Ireland will be defended from foreign invasion by her armed sons, and for this purpose armed Nationalist Catholics in the South will be only too glad to join arms with the armed Protestant Ulstermen in the North. Is it too much to hope that out of this situation there may spring a result which will be good, not merely for the Empire, but good for the future welfare and integrity of the Irish nation?

Speaking in Commons, as leader of Irish Party, on outbreak of war. Hepburn, A. C., *The Conflict of Nationality in Modern Ireland,* Arnold, 1980, p. 84.

August 5, 1914
Winston Churchill
I have called the new battleship 'Erin' on account of your memorable speech, the echoes of which will long linger in British ears.

In letter to John Redmond referring to Redmond's promise of August 3 of support in war. Gwynn, Denis, *The Life of John Redmond,* Harrap, 1932, p. 362.

August 7, 1914
Lord Kitchener
Give me five thousand men and I will say thank you. Give me ten thousand and I will take off my hat to you.

Remarks to Redmond in turning down, as new War Secretary, Redmond's offer to use Irish Volunteers as home guard. Gwynn, Denis, *The Life of John Redmond,* Harrap, 1932, p. 366.

August 8, 1914
Arthur Griffith
Ireland is not at war with Germany . . . we are Irish nationalists and the only duty we can have is to stand for Ireland's interests . . . If Irishmen are to defend Ireland they must defend it for Ireland, under Ireland's flag, and under Irish officers.

Commenting, as Sinn Féin leader, at outbreak of war. *Sinn Féin,* August 8, 1914.

August 21, 1914
Herbert Asquith
The old bother about Tyrone and those infernal snippets of Fermanagh and Derry etc. popped up again.

Commenting, as Prime Minister, on further negotiations over Home Rule Bill. Gwynn, Denis, *The Life of John Redmond,* Harrap, 1932, p. 373.

September 3, 1914
Edward Carson
Our country and our Empire are in danger. I say to our [Ulster] Volunteers without hesitation, go and help to save your country.

In speech at meeting of Ulster Unionist Council following which Ulster Volunteers joined the British Army 36th (Ulster) Division en masse. Bardon, Jonathan, *Belfast,* Blackstaff, 1983, p. 184.

September 12, 1914
Herbert Asquith
We must all recognise . . . that employment of force, any kind of force, for what you call the coercion of Ulster is an absolutely unthinkable thing . . . the Home Rule Bill will not, and cannot, come into operation until Parliament has had the fullest opportunity, by an Amending Bill, of altering, modifying or qualifying its provisions in such a way as to secure the general consent both of Ireland and of the United Kingdom.

Announcing to Commons, as Prime Minister, that
Home Rule Bill would be put on Statute Book but
suspended until end of war. Gwynn, Denis, *The
Life of John Redmond*, Harrap, 1932, p. 380-81.

September 15, 1914
John Redmond

Just as Botha and Smuts have been able to say
... that the concession of free institutions to
South Africa has changed the men who but
ten or a little more years ago were your bitter
enemies in the field into your loyal comrades
and fellow citizens in the Empire, just as
truthfully can I say to you that ... Ireland has
been transformed from what George
Meredith described a short time ago as 'the
broken arm of England' into one of the
strongest bulwarks of the Empire.

Speaking in Commons, as leader of Irish Party, on
passing of Home Rule Act. *HC Debates:* Vol. 66:
Col. 912.

September 20, 1914
John Redmond

The war is undertaken in defence of the
highest principles of religion and morality and
right, and it would be a disgrace for ever to
our country, and a reproach to her manhood,
and a denial of the lessons of her history, if
young Ireland confined their efforts to
remaining at home to defend the shores of
Ireland from an unlikely invasion, and shrunk
from the duty of proving on the field of battle
that gallantry and courage which has
distinguished our race all through its history.

Speaking, as Irish Party leader, at parade of Irish
Volunteers at Woodenbridge, Co. Wicklow.
Hepburn, A. C., *Conflict of Nationality in Modern
Ireland*, Arnold, 1980, p. 84.

September 24, 1914
Provisional Committee of Irish Volunteers

Mr Redmond [is] no longer entitled, through
his nominees, to any place in the
administration and guidance of the Irish
Volunteer organisation.

Statement signed by majority of committee,
including Pearse, repudiating Redmond's
Woodenbridge speech of September 20 promoting
recruitment to British Army. Gwynn, Denis, *The
Life of John Redmond*, Harrap, 1932, p. 392.

September 28, 1914
Edward Carson

When the War is over and we have beaten the
Germans, as we are going to do, I tell you
what we will do; we will call our Provisional
Government together, and we will repeal the
Home Rule Bill, so far as it concerns us, in ten
minutes.

Speaking at Ulster Day rally in Belfast. Gwynn,
Denis, *The Life of John Redmond*, Harrap, 1932,
p. 395.

October, 1914
Louie Bennett

I suppose when the necessity of knitting socks
is over, the order will be 'Bear Sons'. And
those of us who can't will feel we had better
get out of the way as quickly as we can.

In letter about war from co-founder of Irish
Women's Suffrage Federation to Hanna Sheehy
Skeffington. Owens, Rosemary Cullen, *Smashing
Times*, Attic, 1984, p. 98.

October 5, 1914
Roger Casement

Ireland has no blood to give to any land, to
any cause, but that of Ireland.

Letter published in Ireland and United States. *Irish
Independent*, October 5, 1914.

October 29, 1914
General Sir Lawrence Parsons

To establish special recruiting centres where
Mr Crilly suggests would mean filling us with
Liverpool and Glasgow and Cardiff Irish who
are slum-birds that we don't want. I want to
see the clean, fine, strong, temperate, hurley-
playing country fellows such as we used to get
in the Munsters, Royal Irish, Connaught
Rangers.

As officer in charge of recruitment to Irish Division,
rejecting request from F. L. Crilly, secretary of the
United Irish League of Great Britain, to open
recruiting centres in Britain for Irish division.
Gwynn, Denis, *The Life of John Redmond*, Harrap,
1932, p. 400.

1915
Padraic Pearse

O wise men, riddle me this: what if the dream
  come true?
What if the dream come true? and if millions
  unborn shall dwell

In the house that I shaped in my heart, the
noble house of my thought?

From 'The Fool', a poem about a dream of an
independent Ireland. *Collected Works of Padraic H.
Pearse*, Phoenix, p. 336.

February 1, 1915
General Sir Lawrence Parsons
Politicians are apt to forget that I alone am
responsible that I get my division fit to take its
place in the field, and that when it gets there it
will not disgrace the British Army and its
country, and that I therefore cannot go on
sacrificing military to political interests.

Letter refusing John Redmond's request for a
commission for his son in Irish division and
considered by Irish Party leader to be extremely
offensive. Gwynn, Denis, *The Life of John Redmond*,
Harrap, 1932, p. 411.

February 3, 1915
Hugh Lane
This is a Codicil to my last Will to the effect
that the group of pictures now at the London
National Gallery, which I had bequeathed to
that institution, I now bequeath to the city of
Dublin, providing that a suitable building is
provided for them within 5 years of my death.

As art collector, in disputed amendment to will, not
recognised by British Government because it was
not witnessed. Robinson, Lennox, *Lady Gregory's
Journals*, Putnam, 1946, p. 285.

May 18, 1915
Herbert Asquith
The Ministry is about to be reconstructed on a
broad national basis ... I am most anxious you
should join. The Opposition are anxious that
Carson, whose administrative gifts they value,
should be included.

Message to Redmond inviting him to join wartime
Coalition Government. Gwynn, Denis, *The Life of
John Redmond*, Harrap, 1932, p. 423.

May 19, 1915
John Redmond
The principles and history of the party I
represent make the acceptance of your offer
impossible ... I think most strongly Carson
should not be included.

Reply to Asquith refusing offer of inclusion as
leader of Irish Party in wartime Coalition
Government, in which Carson was made Attorney

General. Gwynn, Denis, *The Life of John Redmond*,
Harrap, 1932, p. 423.

June 7, 1915
John Redmond
This step was taken without any consultation
whatever with ... your Irish allies: and the
first intimation received by me included the
statement that Sir Edward Carson, the leader
of the small Unionist Party in Ireland, who
had constituted himself the apostle of physical
force against law, was to be included in the
new Cabinet. I was offered ... by you a place
in the cabinet ... I was not offered a place in
the government of my own country.

In letter to Asquith opposing wartime Coalition
Government. Gwynn, Denis, *The Life of John
Redmond*, Harrap, 1932, pp. 430-31.

August 1, 1915
Padraic Pearse
They think that they have pacified Ireland.
They think that they have purchased half of us
and intimidated the other half. They think
that they have foreseen everything, think that
they have provided against everything; but the
fools, the fools, the fools! – they have left us
our Fenian dead, and while Ireland holds
these graves, Ireland unfree shall never be at
peace.

From oration at funeral in Glasnevin of Fenian
Jeremiah O'Donovan Rossa. Pearse, Padraic H.,
Political Writings and Speeches, Talbot, 1952, p. 137.

November 15, 1915
Roger Casement
If conscription is applied to Ireland, it will be
met, and instead of recruits for the British
Army in Flanders, England will have to
greatly increase her garrison in Ireland.
Already we have kept 200,000 Irishmen out of
the ranks of the British Army in this war ...
no Act of Parliament will convert them into
English soldiers to assail a friendly land, and a
friendly people who have never wronged
Ireland. This act of mine is termed treason in
England. In Ireland men call it by another
name.

Casement, Roger, *The Crime Against Europe: The
Writings and Poetry of Roger Casement*, Fallon, 1958,
p. 137.

November 23, 1915
John Redmond
Ireland would for ever be disgraced in the history of the world if, having sent these men to the front, she did not raise the necessary reserves to fill every gap that may arise in their ranks.

In speech, as leader of Irish Party, on return from visit to Irish regiments on Continent. Gwynn, Denis, *The Life of John Redmond,* Harrap, 1932, p. 453.

December, 1915
Padraic Pearse
War is a terrible thing but war is not an evil thing. It is the things that make war necessary that are evil ... Many people in Ireland dread war because they do not know it. Ireland has not known the exhilaration of war for over a hundred years. Yet who will say that she has known the blessings of peace? When war comes to Ireland, she must welcome it as she would welcome the Angel of God. And she will ... we must not faint at the sight of blood. Winning through it, we (or those of us who survive) shall come unto great joy.

From pamphlet *Peace and the Gael.* Pearse, Padraic H., *Political Writings and Speeches,* Talbot, 1952, pp. 217-18.

December 18, 1915
James Connolly
We cannot conceive of a free Ireland with a subject working class; we cannot conceive of a subject Ireland with a free working class.

Writing in *Workers' Republic.* Berresford Ellis, Peter, *A History of the Irish Working Class,* Pluto, 1985, p. 192.

January 1, 1916
Padraic Pearse
I have spent the greater part of my life in immediate contemplation of the most grotesque and horrible of the English inventions for the debasement of Ireland. I mean their education system ... They have planned and established an education system which more wickedly does violence to the elementary human rights of Irish children than would an edict for the general castration of Irish males. The system has aimed at the substitution for men and women of mere

Things ... these Things have no allegiance. Like other Things, they are for sale.

From pamphlet *The Murder Machine.* Pearse, Padraic H., *Political Writings and Speeches,* Talbot, 1952, pp. 6-7.

February 1, 1916
Eoin MacNeill
I do not know at this moment whether the time and circumstances will yet justify distinct revolutionary action, but of this I am certain, that the only possible basis for successful revolutionary action is deep and widespread popular discontent. We have only to look around us in the streets to realise that no such condition exists in Ireland.

Writing, as leader of Irish Volunteers, in response to arguments put forward by Pearse and Connolly about revolutionary nature of Irish people. Wall, Maureen, *The Making of 1916: Studies in the History of the Rising,* Stationery Office, 1969, p. 160.

April 8, 1916
James Connolly
We are out for Ireland for the Irish. But who are the Irish? Not the rack-renting, slum-owning landlord; not the sweating, profit-grinding capitalist; not the sleek and oily lawyer; not the prostitute pressmen – the hired liars of the enemy ... but the Irish working class ...

The cause of labour is the cause of Ireland. The cause of Ireland is the cause of labour. They cannot be dissevered ... Therefore, on Sunday, April 16th, the Green Flag of Ireland will be solemnly hoisted over Liberty Hall.

Writing in *Workers' Republic.* Berresford Ellis, Peter, *A History of the Irish Working Class,* Pluto, 1985, pp. 191, 226.

April 17, 1916
James Connolly
In the event of victory, hold on to your rifles, as those with whom we are fighting may stop before our goal is reached. We are out for economic as well as political liberty.

In message to the Citizen Army as its commander. Dudley Edwards, Ruth, *James Connolly,* Gill and Macmillan, 1981, p. 145.

April 22, 1916
Irish Volunteer Executive
Arrangements are now nearing completion in all the more important brigade areas for the holding of a very interesting series of manoeuvres at Easter ... the Dublin programme may well stand as a model for other areas.

Announcement carried in *Irish Volunteer*. Wall, Maureen, *The Making of 1916: Studies in the History of the Rising*, Stationery Office, 1969, p. 203.

April 22, 1916
Eoin MacNeill
Owing to the very critical position, all orders given to Irish Volunteers for tomorrow, Easter Sunday, are hereby rescinded, and no parades, marches or other movements of Irish Volunteers will take place. Each individual Volunteer will obey this order strictly in every particular.

Notice, calling off Easter Rising, issued by MacNeill as Chief of Staff of the Volunteers on hearing of failure to land German arms in Kerry. It was inserted in *Sunday Independent* of April 23, 1916.

April 23, 1916
Eoin MacNeill
As Chief of Staff I have ordered and hereby order that no movement whatsoever of Irish Volunteers is to be made today. You will carry out this order in your own command and make it known to other commands.

Message sent to Eamon de Valera, Adjutant of Dublin Brigade. Macardle, Dorothy, *The Irish Republic*, Irish Press, 1951, p. 163.

April 24, 1916
Thomas MacDonagh
The four City Battalions will parade for inspection and route march at 10 am today.

Message, coutersigned by Padraic Pearse, signalling start of Rising, against wishes of Volunteer leader, Eoin Mac Neill. Macardle, Dorothy, *The Irish Republic*, Irish Press, 1951, p. 165.

April 24, 1916
James Connolly
We are going out to be slaughtered.

On leaving Liberty Hall to participate in Rising. Hayes-McCoy, G. A., *The Making of 1916: Studies in the History of the Rising*, Stationery Office, 1969, p. 263.

April 24, 1916
James Connolly
Thanks be to God, Pearse, we have lived to see this day.

Remark made when taking Pearse's hand after tricolour had been hoisted over General Post Office. Dudley Edwards, Ruth, *James Connolly*, Gill and Macmillan, 1981, p. 139.

April 24, 1916
The Provisional Government of the Irish Republic
Irishmen and Irishwomen: In the name of God and of the dead generations from which she receives her old tradition of nationhood, Ireland, through us, summons her children to her flag and strikes for her freedom ... We declare the right of the people of Ireland to the ownership of Ireland ... Standing on that fundamental right and again asserting it in arms in the face of the world, we hereby proclaim the Irish Republic as a sovereign independent state.

From Easter Rising Proclamation, signed by Thomas J. Clarke, Sean MacDiarmada, Thomas MacDonagh, P. H. Pearse, Éamonn Ceannt, James Connolly, Joseph Plunkett. Hepburn, A. C., *The Conflict of Nationality in Modern Ireland*, Arnold, 1980, pp. 94-95.

April 25, 1916
Padraic Pearse
The Republican forces hold the lines taken up at Twelve noon on Easter Monday, and nowhere, despite fierce and almost continuous attacks of the British troops, have the lines been broken through. The country is rising in answer to Dublin's call and the final achievement of Ireland's freedom is now, with God's help, only a matter of days ... Such looting as has already occurred has been done by hangers-on of the British Army. Ireland must keep her new honour unsmirched.

From war communiqué circulated in Dublin. Macardle, Dorothy, *The Irish Republic*, Irish Press, 1951, pp. 171-72.

April 27, 1916
James Connolly
Courage, boys, we are winning, and in the hour of our victory let us not forget the splendid women who have everywhere stood by us and cheered us on. Never had man or

woman a grander cause, never was a cause more grandly served.

Message dictated to his secretary, Winifred Carney, after he had been wounded by rifle fire. Dudley Edwards, Ruth, *James Connolly*, Gill and Macmillan, 1981, p. 140.

April 28, 1916
Padraic Pearse
If they [Volunteers] do not win this fight, they will at least have deserved to win it. But win it they will, although they may win it in death. Already they have won a great thing. They have redeemed Dublin from many shames, and made her name splendid among the names of cities.

Manifesto paying tribute to Volunteers and issued as British troops besieged General Post Office. Macardle, Dorothy, *The Irish Republic*, Irish Press, 1951, p. 174.

April 28, 1916
General Sir John Maxwell
If necessary, I shall not hesitate to destroy all buildings within any area occupied by the rebels.

In proclamation on arrival from Dublin to take over supreme command of British Army in Ireland. Macardle, Dorothy, *The Irish Republic*, Irish Press, 1951, pp. 173-74.

April 28, 1916
Joseph Plunkett
It is the first time it has happened since Moscow, the first time that a capital has been burnt since then.

Comment made in General Post Office, as one of leaders of Easter Rising, as O'Connell Street was on fire. Hayes-McCoy, G. A., *The Making of 1916: Studies in the History of the Rising*, Stationery Office, 1969, p. 325.

April 28, 1916
Padraic Pearse
I am satisfied that we should have accomplished more ... had our arrangements for a simultaneous rising of the whole country, with a combined plan as sound as the Dublin plan has proved to be, been allowed to go through on Easter Sunday. Of the fatal countermanding order which prevented those plans from being carried out I shall not speak further.

In final bulletin from General Post Office. Wall, Maureen, *The Making of 1916: Studies in the History of the Rising*, Stationery Office, 1969, p. 188.

April 28, 1916
Louis Botha
ACCEPT MY HEARTFELT SYMPATHY. REGRET THAT SMALL SECTION IN IRELAND ARE JEOPARDISING THE GREAT CAUSE.

Telegram to John Redmond from South African leader in Cape Town. Gwynn, Denis, *The Life of John Redmond*, Harrap, 1932, p. 474.

April 29, 1916
Padraic Pearse and James Connolly
In order to prevent further slaughter of Dublin citizens, and in the hope of saving the lives of our followers now surrounded and hopelessly outnumbered, the members of the Provisional Government present at Headquarters have agreed to an unconditional surrender, and the Commandants of the various districts in the City and Country will order their commands to lay down arms.

Order signed at 3.45 pm after Pearse had surrendered his sword to Brigadier-General Lowe of the British Army. Macardle, Dorothy, *The Irish Republic*, Irish Press, 1951, pp. 176-77.

May 1, 1916
The Irish Times
The State has struck but its work is not yet finished. The surgeon's knife has been put to the corruption in the body of Ireland and its course must not be stayed until the whole malignant growth has been removed ... The rapine and bloodshed of the past week must be finished with a severity which will make any repetition of them impossible for generations to come.

In editorial calling for executions after Easter Rising. *The Irish Times*, edition dated April 28 and 29 and May 1.

May 2, 1916
Padraic Pearse
We seem to have lost. We have not lost. To refuse to fight would have been to lose; to fight is to win. We have kept faith with the past, and handed on a tradition to the future.

At court-martial on day before his execution. Dudley Edwards, Ruth, *Patrick Pearse – The Triumph of Failure*, Gollancz, 1977, p. 318.

May 2, 1916
General Sir John Maxwell

I am going to punish the offenders, four of them are to be shot tomorrow morning. I am going to ensure that there will be no treason whispered, even whispered, in Ireland for a hundred years.

In comment to John Dillon of Irish Party who was pleading that executions should not take place. Robinson, Lennox, *Lady Gregory's Journals,* Putnam, 1946, p. 170.

May 3, 1916
German Army

IRISHMEN! HEAVY UPROAR IN IRELAND. ENGLISH GUNS ARE FIRING ON YOUR WIVES AND CHILDREN!

Message on board erected on German lines facing Royal Irish Regiment in France. Gwynn, Denis, *The Life of John Redmond,* Harrap, 1932, p. 495.

May 3, 1916
John Redmond

I would most earnestly beg of you to prevent any wholesale trials of this kind – wholesale executions would destroy our last hope. The precedent of Botha's [South African leader] treatment of the rebels in S. Africa is the only wise and safe one to follow.

Private letter sent to Asquith after first reports of executions of leaders of Rising. Gwynn, Denis, *The Life of John Redmond,* Harrap, 1932, p. 482.

May 3, 1916
Thomas MacDonagh

We do not profess to represent the mass of the people of Ireland. We stand for the intellect and the soul of Ireland. To Ireland's soul and intellect the inert mass, drugged and degenerate by ages of servitude, must, in the distant day of resurrection, render homage and free service.

In address, taken in shorthand by British officer, at court-martial at which MacDonagh was sentenced to death for being a signatory to Easter Proclamation. Sullivan, T. D., A. M. and D. B., *Speeches from the Dock,* Gill and Macmillan, 1968, p. 339.

May 9, 1916
Herbert Asquith

I sent a strong telegram to [General] Maxwell yesterday, and I hope that the shootings –

unless in some quite exceptional case – will cease.

In response, as Prime Minister, to Redmond's pleas that execution of leaders of Rising should cease. Gwynn, Denis, *The Life of John Redmond,* Harrap, 1932, p. 488.

May 9, 1916
James Connolly

Irishmen are ready to die endeavouring to win for Ireland those national rights which the British Government has been asking them to die to win for Belgium. As long as that remains the case, the cause of Irish freedom is safe.

From statement at court-martial which sentenced him to death for his part in Easter Rising. Dudley Edwards, Ruth, *James Connolly,* Gill and Macmillan, 1981, p. 142.

May 10, 1916
John Dillon

It is not murderers who are being executed. It is insurgents who fought a clean fight, a brave fight.

Speaking, as Irish Party MP, in Commons. Macardle, Dorothy, *The Irish Republic,* Irish Press, 1951, p. 188.

May 10, 1916
George Bernard Shaw

My own view is that the men who were shot in cold blood, after their capture or surrender, were prisoners of war, and that it was therefore entirely incorrect to slaughter them ... It is absolutely impossible to slaughter a man in this position without making him a martyr and a hero, even though the day before the rising he may have been only a minor poet.

From letter to *Daily News,* May 10, 1916. Macardle, Dorothy, *The Irish Republic,* Irish Press, 1951, pp. 185-87.

May 10, 1916
Herbert Asquith

So far as the great body of insurgents is concerned I have no hesitation in saying in public that they conducted themselves with great humanity ... They were young men; often lads. They were misled, almost unconsciously, I believe, into this terrible business. They fought very bravely and did not resort to outrage.

Speaking in Commons, as Prime Minister, about 1916 Rising. Macardle, Dorothy, *The Irish Republic*, Irish Press, 1951, pp. 187-88.

June 30, 1916
Roger Casement

Ireland has outlived the failure of all her hopes – and she still hopes. Ireland has seen her sons – aye, and her daughters, too! – suffer from generation to generation, always for the same cause, meeting always the same fate, and always at the hands of the same power. Still, always a fresh generation has passed on to withstand the same oppression.

... when we had the doctrine of Unionist loyalty at last – 'Mausers and Kaisers, and any King you like' ... I felt that I needed no other warrant than that these words conveyed, to go forth and do likewise. The difference between us was that the Unionist champions chose a path which they felt would lead to the woolsack[House of Lords], while I went a road I knew must lead to the dock and the event proved we were both right.

In speech from dock on fourth day of his trial in London for 'High Treason Without the Realm of England', for which Casement was executed on August 3, 1916. Casement, Roger, *The Crime Against Europe: The Writings and Poetry of Roger Casement*, Fallon, 1958, pp. 152-56.

July 4, 1916
Trotsky

The experiment of an Irish national rebellion ... is over. But the historical role of the Irish proletariat is only beginning. Already it has brought into this revolt, even though under an archaic flag, its class indignation against militarism and imperialism. This indignation will not now subside.

Writing on implications of 1916 Rising in journal *Nashe Slovo*. Berresford Ellis, Peter, *A History of the Irish Working Class*, Pluto, 1985, p. 233.

July 20, 1916
Dr O'Dwyer, Bishop of Limerick

I have very little pity for you or yours. You have ceased to be men; your leaders consequently think they can sell you like chattels.

In letter to Belfast Nationalists about Irish Party's acquiescence in scheme to exclude six counties from Home Rule. Macardle, Dorothy, *The Irish Republic*, Irish Press, 1951, p. 195.

July 20, 1916
Dr McHugh, Bishop of Derry

What seems to be the worst feature of all this wretched bargaining is that Irishmen, calling themselves representatives of the people, are prepared to sell their brother Irishmen into slavery to secure a nominal freedom for a section of the people ... Was coercion of a more objectionable or despicable type ever resorted to by England in its dealings with Ireland than that now sanctioned by the men whom we elected to win us freedom?

In letter read to meeting in Derry protesting against Irish Party's acquiescence in scheme to exclude six counties from Home Rule. Macardle, Dorothy, *The Irish Republic*, Irish Press, 1951, p. 195.

July 22, 1916
G. B. Shaw

Casement should be treated as a prisoner of war ... In Ireland he will be regarded as a national hero if he is executed, and quite possibly as a spy if he is not. For that reason it may well be that he would object very strongly to my attempt to prevent his canonisation. But Ireland has enough heroes and martyrs already, and if England has not by this time had enough of manufacturing them in fits of temper, experience is thrown away on her and she will continue to be governed, as she is at present to so great an extent unconsciously, by Casement's contemporaries.

In letter from Irish playwright to *Times* which was rejected but published by *Manchester Guardian*, on why Roger Casement should not be executed for his part in events surrounding Easter Rising. *The Manchester Guardian*, July 22, 1916.

September 14, 1916
Dr O'Dwyer, Bishop of Limerick

Ireland will never be content as a province. God has made her a nation, and while grass grows and water runs there will be men in Ireland to dare and die for her.

In acknowledging the conferral on him of freedom of city of Limerick. Sullivan, T. D., A. M. and D. B., *Speeches from the Dock*, Gill and Macmillan, 1968, p. 318.

September 25, 1916
William Butler Yeats
I write it out in a verse –
MacDonagh and MacBride
And Connolly and Pearse
Now and in time to be,
Wherever green is worn,
Are changed, changed utterly:
A terrible beauty is born.

From 'Easter 1916'. Yeats, W. B., *Collected Poems*, Macmillan, 1965, p. 205.

October 18, 1916
David Lloyd George
[These errors are] stupidities which sometimes almost look like malignancy.

Describing in Commons, as Liberal minister, mistakes made by British Government in recruitment policy in Ireland. Gwynn, Denis, *The Life of John Redmond*, Harrap, 1932, p. 531.

November 30, 1916
John Redmond
The condition of Ireland, though still far from satisfactory, has vastly improved within the last two months ... due, amongst other causes, to the release of over a thousand of the interned prisoners, and the confident expectation, which has been spread by us, that the Government contemplated ... the release of the remainder of the interned prisoners ... a refusal to release these men will be most dangerous to the position and influence of the National Party in Ireland.

In letter, as leader of Irish Party, to British Prime Minister Herbert Asquith. Hepburn, A. C., *The Conflict of Nationality in Modern Ireland*, Arnold, 1980, pp. 98-99.

March 7, 1917
Willie Redmond
In the name of God, we here who are about to die, perhaps, ask you to do that which largely induced us to leave our homes ... make our country happy and contented, and enable us when we meet the Canadians and the Australians and the New Zealanders ... to say to them 'Our country, just as yours, has self-government within the Empire.'

Son of Irish Party leader John Redmond, in Commons as MP before returning to the front as major in Royal Irish Regiment where he was killed some months later. Gwynn, Denis, *The Life of John Redmond*, Harrap, 1932, p. 541.

March 7, 1917
David Lloyd George
In the north-eastern portion of Ireland, you have a population as hostile to Irish rule as the rest of Ireland is to British rule, yea, and as ready to rebel against it as the rest of Ireland is against British rule – as alien in blood, in religious faith, in traditions, in outlook – as alien from the rest of Ireland in this respect as the inhabitants of Fife or Aberdeen.

Speaking in Commons, as Liberal Prime Minister. Macardle, Dorothy, *The Irish Republic*, Irish Press, 1951, p. 211.

April 13, 1917
Cecil Spring-Rice
The fact that the Irish question is still unsettled is continually quoted against us, as a proof that it is not wholly true that the fight is one for ... the independence of small nations.

Writing as British Ambassador in London to British Government on American arguments against coming into war. Macardle, Dorothy, *The Irish Republic*, Irish Press, 1951, p. 212.

May 6, 1917
Joe Devlin
The electors had to decide ... whether they were in favour of a self-governed Ireland or a hopeless fight for an Irish Republic.

Speaking, as Belfast MP, for Irish Party candidate in South Longford by-election, which resulted in Sinn Féin victory. Macardle, Dorothy, *The Irish Republic*, Irish Press, 1951, p. 214.

May 8, 1917
'Bishops' Manifesto'
To Irishmen of every creed and class and party the very thought of our country partitioned and torn as a new Poland must be one of heart-rending sorrow.

Protest against partition signed by three Catholic archbishops, fifteen Catholic bishops, three Church of Ireland bishops and county council chairmen. Macardle, Dorothy, *The Irish Republic*, Irish Press, 1951, p. 214.

June 2, 1917
Arthur Griffith
He [Lloyd George] summons a Convention and guarantees that a small minority of people will not be bound by its decision, and thus, having secured its failure, he is armed to

assure the world that England left the Irish to settle the question of government for themselves and that they could not agree.

Writing, as Sinn Féin leader, in *Nationality* about convention summoned by Lloyd George to discuss future government of Ireland. Macardle, Dorothy, *The Irish Republic,* Irish Press, 1951, p. 217.

July 5, 1917
Eamon de Valera
Let Ulster Unionists recognise the Sinn Féin position which has behind it justice and right. It is supported by nine tenths of the Irish people and if those Unionists do not come in on their side, they will have to go under.

Speaking in Killaloe, as Sinn Féin candidate in Clare by-election which he won from Irish Party. Macardle, Dorothy, *The Irish Republic,* Irish Press, 1951, p. 224.

July 9, 1917
T. P. O'Connor
I feel almost like James II – a new desertion every day.

In letter to John Redmond from United States where he had been sent to rally Irish American support for Irish Party, but found it slipping away to Sinn Féin. Hepburn, A. C., *The Conflict of Nationality in Modern Ireland,* Arnold, 1980, p. 103.

September 30, 1917
Michael Collins
Nothing additional remains to be said. That volley which we have just heard is the only speech which it is proper to make above the grave of a dead Fenian.

Oration at burial of Thomas Ashe who died on hunger strike, as reported in *Irish Independent,* October, 1917. Mitchell and Ó Snodaigh, *Irish Political Documents 1916-1949,* Irish Academic, 1985, p. 31.

October 23, 1917
David Lloyd George
I have read the speeches of the honourable member for East Clare [de Valera]. They are not excited, and so far as language is concerned they are not violent. They are plain, deliberate, and I might also say, cold-blooded incitements to rebellion.

Speaking, as Prime Minister, in Commons. Macardle, Dorothy, *The Irish Republic,* Irish Press, 1951, p. 236.

October 25, 1917
Eamon de Valera
England pretends it is not by the naked sword, but by the good will of the people of the country that she is here. We will draw the naked sword to make her bare her own naked sword.

In speech on election as President of Sinn Féin. Macardle, Dorothy, *The Irish Republic,* Irish Press, 1951, p. 917.

January 4, 1918
John Redmond
My modest ambition would be to serve in some quite humble capacity under the first Unionist Prime Minister of Ireland.

Addressing Irish Convention of Unionist and Nationalist Politicians in Dublin. Gwynn, Denis, *The Life of John Redmond,* Harrap, 1932, p. 582.

January 14, 1918
Dr O'Donnell, Bishop of Raphoe
A parliament in Dublin two months hence, without customs . . . will not bear examination. The principle is given away. If Ulster had come in, or had promised to come in, we could have given something away . . . The proposition would be drowned in scorn and ridicule before it was a week before the public.

In letter to John Redmond which signified end of Redmond's last attempt at compromise on Home Rule and collapse of Irish Convention. Gwynn, Denis, *The Life of John Redmond,* Harrap, 1932, pp. 584-85.

January 27, 1918
Eamon de Valera
[The Unionists are] a rock in the road . . . they [Nationalists] must make up their minds not to be peddling with this rock. They must if necessary blast it out of their path.

Account in *Belfast Newsletter,* January 28, 1918, of speech in South Armagh. Bowman, John, *De Valera and the Ulster Question,* Clarendon, 1982, p. 35.

April 16, 1918
Field-Marshal Lord French
Home Rule will be offered and declined, then conscription will be enforced. If they will leave me alone I can do what is necessary. I shall notify a date before which recruits must offer themselves in the various districts. If they do not come we will fetch them.

Commenting, as Lord Lieutenant of Ireland, on Bill passed by Commons on April 16 for conscription in Ireland. Macardle, Dorothy, *The Irish Republic,* Irish Press, 1951, p. 252.

April 18, 1918
Mansion House Conference
The passing of the Conscription Bill by the British House of Commons must be regarded as a declaration of war on the Irish nation.

From resolution passed at anti-conscription meeting presided over by Lord Mayor of Dublin and attended by de Valera, Griffith, Dillon and other Nationalist leaders. Mitchell and Ó Snodaigh, *Irish Political Documents 1916-1949,* Irish Academic, 1985, p. 42.

April 18, 1918
Catholic Hierarchy
We consider that conscription forced in this way upon Ireland is an oppressive and inhuman law which the Irish people have a right to resist by every means that are consonant with the law of God.

Manifesto issued after visit by deputation from Mansion House Conference opposing Conscription Bill. Mitchell and Ó Snodaigh, *Irish Political Documents 1916-1949,* Irish Academic, 1985, pp. 42-43.

May 1, 1918
Ernest Blythe
A Conscription campaign will be an unprovoked onslaught by an army upon the civilian population ... anyone, civilian or soldier, who assists directly or by connivance in this crime against us, merits no more consideration than wild beasts, and should be killed without mercy or hesitation as opportunity offers.

In statement, as member of Sinn Féin Executive, smuggled from prison and printed in *An t-Óglach,* Volunteer journal. Macardle, Dorothy, *The Irish Republic,* Irish Press, 1951, p. 260.

May 18, 1918
Field-Marshal Lord French
Certain subjects of His Majesty the King, domiciled in Ireland, have conspired to enter into and have entered into treasonable communication with the German enemy ... drastic measures must be taken to put down this German plot ... we shall cause still

further steps to be taken to facilitate and encourage voluntary enlistment.

Proclamation issued from Dublin Castle, signalling internment without trial, after uncovering of alleged 'German plot'. Mitchell and Ó Snodaigh, *Irish Political Documents 1916-1949,* Irish Academic, 1985, pp. 44-45.

June 25, 1918
Edward Shortt
Ireland – I mean the great, true heart of the Irish people – is not responsible for what the Germans do and is not responsible for what the two or three hundred extremists in Ireland do. Ireland, I believe, is sound at the core today.

Speaking in Commons after being appointed Chief Secretary for Ireland. Escouflaire, R. G., *Ireland, an Enemy of the Allies?,* Murray, 1919, p. 230.

August 1, 1918
An tÓglach
The Irish Volunteers are the Army of the Irish Republic.

Announcement in Volunteer magazine signifying the birth of the IRA. Coogan, Tim Pat, *The IRA,* Fontana, 1980, p. 42.

November 16, 1918
William O'Brien
It is because a degenerate parliamentarianism spent all its precious years of power in misrepresenting and thwarting the principles now clung to in desperation that opportunities such as never occurred before, and are not likely soon to occur again, were madly sacrificed.

In letter, as Irish Party MP for Cork, published in press regarded as prophecy of downfall of Irish Party. Macardle, Dorothy, *The Irish Republic,* Irish Press, 1951, p. 262.

November 25, 1918
Sinn Féin Election Manifesto
Sinn Féin gives Ireland the opportunity of vindicating her honour and pursuing with renewed confidence the path of national salvation by rallying to the flag of the Irish Republic. Sinn Féin aims at securing the establishment of that Republic (1) By withdrawing the Irish representation from the British Parliament ... (2) By making use of any and every means available to render

impotent the power of England to hold Ireland in subjection by military force or otherwise.

Issued after election called for December 14. Mitchell and Ó Snodaigh, *Irish Political Documents 1916-1949,* Irish Academic, 1985, p. 48.

December 1, 1918
Michael Collins

Any scheme of government which does not confer upon the people of Ireland the supreme, absolute and final control of all of this country, external as well as internal, is a mockery and will not be accepted.

In address for election of December 14 for which he was successful Sinn Féin candidate for South County Cork. Macardle, Dorothy, *The Irish Republic,* Irish Press, 1951, p. 264.

January 21, 1919
Dáil Éireann

We, the elected representatives of the ancient Irish people in National Parliament assembled, do, in the name of the Irish nation, ratify the establishment of the Irish Republic and pledge ourselves and our people to make this declaration effective by every means at our command.

From Declaration of Independence read at first meeting of Dáil after pro-Republic candidates won 73 of 105 Irish seats in general election. Mitchell and Ó Snodaigh, *Irish Political Documents 1916-1949,* Irish Academic, 1985, pp. 57-58.

January 21, 1919
Cathal Brugha

Deputies, you understand from what is asserted in this Declaration that we are now done with England. Let the world know it and those who are concerned bear it in mind.

Speaking, as Sinn Féin member, at first meeting of Dáil. Macardle, Dorothy, *The Irish Republic,* Irish Press, 1951, p. 274.

January 21, 1919
Dan Breen

Our only regret was that the police escort had consisted of only two peelers instead of six. If there had to be dead peelers at all, six would have created a better impression than a mere two.

On the killing of two RIC men in the Soloheadbeg ambush which signalled start of War of

Independence. Breen, Dan, *My Fight for Irish Freedom,* Anvil, 1981, p. 32.

January 23, 1919
Dr Fogharty, Bishop of Killaloe

The fight for Irish freedom has passed into the hands of the young men of Ireland ... and when the young men of Ireland hit back at their oppressors it is not for an old man like me to cry 'foul'.

In statement seen as justifying armed action against British forces. Macardle, Dorothy, *The Irish Republic,* Irish Press, 1951, pp. 289-90.

March 4, 1919
United States Congress

It is the earnest hope of the Congress of the United States of America that the Peace Conference now sitting in Paris and passing upon the rights of the various people will favourably consider the claims of Ireland to self-determination.

Resolution moved by Thomas Gallagher of Illinois and passed by House of Representatives by 261 to 41. Macardle, Dorothy, *The Irish Republic,* Irish Press, 1951, p. 280.

June 6, 1919
United States Senate

The Senate of the United States earnestly requests the American Peace Commission at Versailles to endeavour to secure for Eamon de Valera, Arthur Griffith and George Noble Count Plunkett, a hearing before the Peace Conference ... and further the Senate of the United States expresses its sympathy with the aspirations of the Irish people for a government of their own choice.

Resolution passed with only one vote against. Macardle, Dorothy, *The Irish Republic,* Irish Press, 1951, pp. 296-97.

July 17, 1919
General Smuts

The most pressing of all constitutional problems is the Irish question. It has become a chronic wound, the septic effects of which are spreading to our whole system.

Speaking in Paris on occasion of post-war Peace Conference which he was attending as South African representative. Macardle, Dorothy, *The Irish Republic,* Irish Press, 1951, p. 299.

August 30, 1919
President Wilson, USA
When I gave utterance to those words [that every nation had a right to self determination] I said them without the knowledge that nationalities existed which are coming to us day after day. Of course, Ireland's case, from the point of view of population, from the point of view of the struggle it has made, from the point of interest it has excited in the world, and especially among our own people, whom I am anxious to serve, is the outstanding case of a small nationality. You do not know and cannot appreciate the anxieties I have experienced as the result of these many millions of peoples having their hopes raised by what I said.

In interview with Frank Walsh of American Friends of Irish Freedom making clear that President Wilson was unable to secure voice for Ireland at Paris post-war Peace Conference because of English opposition. Macardle, Dorothy, *The Irish Republic,* Irish Press, 1951, p. 297.

December 8, 1919
Herbert Samuel
If what is now going on in Ireland had been going on in the Austrian Empire, all England would be ringing with denunciation of the tyranny of the Hapsburgs and of denying people the right to rule themselves.

Speaking at St Albans as former British Cabinet Minister. Macardle, Dorothy, *The Irish Republic,* Irish Press, 1951, p. 319.

December 22, 1919
David Lloyd George
I think it is right to say here, in the face of the demands which have been put forward from Ireland, with apparent authority, that any attempt at secession will be fought, with the same determination, with the same resources, with the same resolve, as the Northern States of America put into the fight against the Southern States. It is important that this should be known not merely throughout the world, but in Ireland itself.

Speaking, as Prime Minister, in Commons. Mitchell and Ó Snodaigh, *Irish Political Documents 1916-1949,* Irish Academic, 1985, p. 68.

January 23, 1920
Field-Marshal Lord French
The principal cause of the trouble is that for five years emigration has practically stopped. In this country there are from one hundred thousand to two hundred thousand young men from eighteen to twenty-five years of age who in normal times would have emigrated.

In interview with *Le Journal* of Paris, as Lord Lieutenant of Ireland. Macardle, Dorothy, *The Irish Republic,* Irish Press, 1951, p. 333.

February 3, 1920
Walter Long
The people in the inner circles hold the view that the new province [to be excluded from Home Rule] should consist of the six counties, the idea being that the inclusion of Donegal, Cavan and Monaghan would provide such an access of strength to the Roman Catholic party that the supremacy of the Unionists would be seriously threatened.

Reporting, as First Lord of the Admiralty, to British Cabinet Committee on Ireland. Arthur, Paul, *Government and Politics of Northern Ireland,* Longman, 1980, p. 14.

February 6, 1920
Eamon de Valera
The United States safeguarded itself from the possible use of the island of Cuba as a base for an attack by a foreign power by stipulating that the Government of Cuba shall never ... permit any foreign power or powers to obtain ... for military or naval purposes ... control over any portion of said island. Why doesn't Britain do with Ireland as the United States did with Cuba?

In interview with *New York Globe.* Mitchell and Ó Snodaigh, *Irish Political Documents 1916-1949,* Irish Academic, 1985, p. 69.

February 14, 1920
John Devoy
If the present movement should be metamorphosed into a demand for a free Ireland under an English Protectorate [rather than an independent Republic], there would be a sudden waning, if not complete collapse, of the present enthusiasm in America.

Responding as Irish American leader to de Valera proposal of February 6 for Cuba-type association of

Ireland with Britain. Mitchell and Ó Snodaigh, *Irish Political Documents 1916-1949*, Irish Academic, 1985, p. 69.

February 15, 1920
Dr Browne, Bishop of Cloyne

The policy [law and order] of the British Government seems to be to make use of every means and every opportunity to exasperate the people and drive them to acts of desperation.

In Lenten pastoral after widespread arrests throughout Ireland. Macardle, Dorothy, *The Irish Republic*, Irish Press, 1951, p. 330.

March 4, 1920
Erskine Childers

We do not attempt secession. Nations cannot secede from a rule they have never accepted. We have never accepted yours and never will. Lincoln's reputation is safe from your comparison. He fought to abolish slavery, you fight to maintain it.

Replying, in *Irish Bulletin*, to Lloyd George's Commons speech of December 22, 1919, in which he said Ireland was attempting to secede just as southern states fought to secede from United States of America. Macardle, Dorothy, *The Irish Republic*, Irish Press, 1951, p. 322.

March 18, 1920
United States Senate

When self-government is attained by Ireland, a consummation it is hoped is at hand, it should promptly be admitted as a member of the League of Nations.

Resolution passed during debate on Treaty of Versailles. Macardle, Dorothy, *The Irish Republic*, Irish Press, 1951, pp. 366-67.

March 18, 1920
Edward Carson

The truth is that we came to the conclusion after many anxious hours and anxious days of going into the whole matter almost parish by parish and townland by townland that you would have no chance of successfully starting a parliament in Belfast which was to be responsible for the government of Donegal, Cavan and Monaghan ... We should like to have the very largest area possible, naturally ... The figures will at once show where the difficulties come in. We have to refer in these matters to Protestant and Catholic because

these are really the burning questions over there ... while you would leave out seventy thousand [Protestants] who are in these three counties, you would bring from these three counties into the Northern province an additional two hundred and sixty thousand Roman Catholics.

Explaining to Commons, in debate on Bill setting up Northern Ireland Parliament, why Unionists demanded only six counties of Ulster. Macardle, Dorothy, *The Irish Republic*, Irish Press, 1951, pp. 338-39.

March 20, 1920
Cork Coroner's Jury

[Tomás Mac Curtáin] was wilfully murdered under circumstances of most callous brutality ... the murder was organised and carried out by the Royal Constabulary, officially directed by the British Government.

In returning verdict of wilful murder against Lloyd George and others on Lord Mayor of Cork, shot dead at his home by armed men. Macardle, Dorothy, *The Irish Republic*, Irish Press, 1951, p. 334.

March 30, 1920
Terence MacSwiney

This contest of ours is not, on our side, a rivalry of vengeance, but one of endurance – it is not they who can inflict most, but they who can suffer most, will conquer – though we do not abrogate our function to demand and see that evil-doers and murderers are punished for their crimes.

In address on election as Lord Mayor of Cork in succession to Tomás Mac Curtáin, assassinated by Crown forces on March 19. Sullivan, T. D., A. M. and D. B., *Speeches from the Dock*, Gill and Macmillan, 1968, p. 327.

June 17, 1920
Colonel Smyth

Now, men, Sinn Féin has had all the sport up to the present, and we are going to have the sport now ... you may make mistakes occasionally, and innocent persons may be shot, but that cannot be helped, and you are bound to get the right parties sometime. The more you shoot, the better I will like you, and I assure you, no policeman will get into trouble for shooting any man.

Addressing RIC men at Listowel, as RIC Divisional Police Commander, Munster. Macardle, Dorothy, *The Irish Republic,* Irish Press, 1951, p. 360.

June 17, 1920
Spokesman for Listowel RIC

By your accent I take it you are an Englishman and in your ignorance forget that you are addressing Irishmen. These too [cap, belt and bayonet] are English. Take them as a present from me and to hell with you – you are a murderer.

Responding to invitation from Colonel Smyth to shoot whoever they liked without fear of official retribution in war against IRA. Macardle, Dorothy, *The Irish Republic,* Irish Press, 1951, pp. 361-62.

June 28, 1920
Henry Wilson

I really believe that we shall be kicked out [of Ireland].

In private note written as Chief of Imperial Staff at British War Office. Macardle, Dorothy, *The Irish Republic,* Irish Press, 1951, p. 377.

July 5, 1920
Lord Monteagle

The Sinn Féin courts are steadily extending their jurisdiction and dispensing justice even-handed between man and man, Catholic and Protestant, farmer and shopkeeper, grazier and cattle driver, landlord and tenant.

Writing as landlord. *The Irish Times,* July 5, 1920.

July 5, 1920
Hugh Martin

Ireland is taking pleasure in law and order for the first time within the memory of man.

Reporting, as Irish correspondent, in *Daily News* on success and popularity of Sinn Féin courts. Macardle, Dorothy, *The Irish Republic,* Irish Press, 1951, p. 350.

July 12, 1920
Edward Carson

If ... you [the British Government] are yourselves unable to protect us from the machinations of Sinn Féin, and you won't take our help; well then, we tell you that we will take the matter into our own hands ... I am sick of words without action.

Speaking, as Unionist leader, at Orange demonstration in Belfast. Some days later Catholic

workers were expelled from shipyards following meeting of workers at which Carson's words were repeated. Bardon, Jonathan, *Belfast,* Blackstaff, 1983, p. 190.

August 11, 1920
Henry Grattan Bellew

I hope my colleagues will follow my example so that the wrecking of Irish towns and the ruin of Irish industry [by Crown forces] may be proceeded with without any camouflage or appearance of approval by Irishmen of the sabotage of their country.

In letter to Lord Chancellor resigning as magistrate in Cork. Macardle, Dorothy, *The Irish Republic,* Irish Press, 1951, p. 363.

August 13, 1920
Dr Harty, Archbishop of Cashel

It seems futile to demand justice from the British Government in Ireland ... They speak of outrages attributed to Sinn Féin, but they do not call attention to the murder of a nation, or the depopulation of the country ... or the protection afforded to the criminal [Edward Carson] who taught the grammar of anarchy.

In open letter addressed to British authorities after killing in his diocese of James Mulcahy by military. Sullivan, T. D., A. M. and D. B., *Speeches from the Dock,* Gill and Macmillan, 1968, pp. 335-36.

August 17, 1920
Terence MacSwiney

I will put a limit to any term of imprisonment you may impose as a result of the action I will take. I have taken no food since Thursday, therefore ... I shall be free, alive or dead, within a month.

As Lord Mayor of Cork before being sentenced to two years' imprisonment at court-martial in Cork for possession of secret code, and embarking on hunger strike from which he died. Sullivan, T. D., A. M. and D. B., *Speeches from the Dock,* Gill and Macmillan, 1968, pp. 331-32.

September 24, 1920
General Macready

Punishment for such acts [reprisals] is a delicate matter, inasmuch as it might be interpreted as setting at naught the hoped-for effect of the training the officers had given their men.

In interview with American correspondents after sacking by military of Balbriggan and similar attacks

in Carrick-on-Shannon, Tuam, Galway and
Drumshanbo and several murders of civilians.
Macardle, Dorothy, *The Irish Republic,* Irish Press,
1951, p. 389.

October 4, 1920
Herbert Asquith

Its only logical sequence is to take in hand the
task of reconquering Ireland and holding her
by force – a task which, though not perhaps
beyond the powers, will never be sanctioned
by the will or the conscience of the British
people.

As former Liberal Prime Minister in letter about
Lloyd George's policy of repression and reprisal in
Ireland. *The Times,* October 4, 1920.

October 9, 1920
David Lloyd George

A small body of assassins, a real murder gang,
dominate the country and terrorise it . . . it is
essential in the interests of Ireland that that
gang should be broken up . . . we have murder
by the throat.

Speaking, as British Prime Minister, at Carnarvon,
and quoted in Commons debate. *HC Debates:* Vol.
147: Cols. 1373-74.

October 14, 1920
James Craig

Do I approve of the action you boys have
taken in the past? I say yes.

Speaking, as Unionist MP, in Belfast shipyard
about expulsion of Catholics. Farrell, Michael,
Northern Ireland: The Orange State, Pluto, 1983,
p. 34.

October 20, 1920
Hammar Greenwood

I found that from 100 to 150 men went to
Balbriggan determined to avenge the death of
a popular comrade shot at and murdered in
cold blood. I find it is impossible out of that
150 to find the men who did the deed, who
did the burning. I have had the most
searching inquiry made . . . But I cannot in my
heart of hearts . . . condemn in the same way
those policemen who lost their heads as I
condemn the assassins who provoked this
outrage.

Giving account in Commons, as Chief Secretary of
Ireland, of sacking of Balbriggan and killing of two
inhabitants by Crown forces. *HC Debates:* Vol. 133:
Col. 947.

October 20, 1920
Lord Curzon

It is not guerrilla warfare. It is the warfare of
the red Indian, of the Apache. It is the
warfare, which nearly a hundred years ago the
Government of India had to suppress, and
which was known as 'Thuggee' – the
manoeuvres of the thugs of that country . . .
this is not rebellion by rising; this is not
freedom by fighting; this is rebellion by
murder.

Speaking in Lords as Foreign Secretary about IRA
campaign in Ireland. Mitchell and Ó Snodaigh,
Irish Political Documents 1916-1949, Irish Academic,
1985, p. 85.

October 25, 1920
Joe Devlin

The Chief Secretary is going to arm
pogromists to murder the Catholics . . . The
Protestants are to be armed, for we [Catholics]
would not touch your special constabulary
with a forty-foot pole. Their pogrom is to be
made less difficult. Instead of paving stones
and sticks, they are to be given rifles.

Speaking as Belfast Nationalist MP in Commons
debate on setting up of Ulster Special Constabulary.
Farrell, Michael, *Arming the Protestants,* Brandon,
1983, pp. 48-49.

October 29, 1920
Colonel Wilfrid Spender

The Government plans [for NI police force]
are a great advance on all previous proposals.
The Government has definitely recognised
that there are two distinct elements among the
population – those who are loyal to the British
Crown and Empire and those who are not . . .
There is no reason why the UVF should not
furnish all the numbers required.

In memorandum sent as commander of Ulster
Volunteer Force to all members urging them to join
newly-formed 'A', 'B', and 'C' Specials as reserves
to Royal Ulster Constabulary. Mitchell and
Ó Snodaigh, *Irish Political Documents 1916-1949,*
Irish Academic, 1985, pp. 86-89.

November 4, 1920
Hamar Greenwood

I have never associated the majority of the
Irish people with this campaign of murder. I
believe they loathe it. I believe that if they
could be made articulate and could speak their

minds they would help us not only to condemn it but to put it down. We have every information that they welcome the increasing energy of the soldiers and the police in stamping out this campaign.

Replying, as Chief Secretary for Ireland, in Commons debate on reprisals by Crown forces in Ireland. *HC Debates:* Vol. 134: Col. 722.

November 11, 1920
David Lloyd George
Neither for the sake of Britain nor for the sake of Ireland can we contemplate anything which would set up in Ireland an independent sovereign state ... We cannot consent to anything which will enable Ireland to organise an army and a navy of her own.

Speaking, as Prime Minister, in Commons. Mitchell and Ó Snodaigh, *Irish Political Documents 1916-1949*, Irish Academic, 1985, p. 89.

November 11, 1920
Edward Carson
I hope with all my heart that in the long run it [Government of Ireland Bill] will lead to unity and peace in Ireland, and that in the long run it will lead the Honourable Gentleman opposite [Joe Devlin] and myself to see Ireland one and undivided, loyal to this country and loyal to the Empire.

In Commons, speaking, as Unionist leader, in support of Bill partitioning Ireland. *HC Debates:* Vol. 134: Col. 1442.

November 11, 1920
Joe Devlin
They take the Catholic minority ... and place that minority at the mercy of the Protestant majority, and they plead in the most tender way, almost with tears in their voice, for the acceptance of this Bill, that it may end religious rancour ... my friends and myself, 340,000 Catholics ... are to be left permanently and enduringly at the mercy of the Protestant Parliament in the North of Ireland.

In Commons, opposing, as Belfast Nationalist MP, third reading of Government of Ireland Bill partitioning Ireland. *HC Debates:* Vol. 134: Col. 1447.

November 21, 1920
Michael Collins
I found out that those fellows [British agents] we put on the spot were going to put a lot of us on the spot, so I got in first.

In conversation with General Crozier of British Army after Truce, and referring to Bloody Sunday, November 21, 1920, when fourteen British agents were shot dead in Dublin. Lyons, F. S. L., *Ireland Since the Famine*, Fontana, 1985, p. 419.

November 24, 1920
Hamar Greenwood
I will admit it here at once – some creameries have been destroyed by the forces of the Crown. In some cases they were justified in the destruction ... They are not always innocent institutions, allied with gaily caparisoned dairy maids, spreading beneficent light and humour in the neighbourhood. They are sometimes the headquarters of the assassins.

Justifying in Commons, as Chief Secretary for Ireland, official reprisals against creameries. *HC Debates:* 5th Series: Vol. 135: Cols. 499-500.

November 24, 1920
Oswald Mosley
A village is partially burned, and houses and creameries by the forces of the Crown, but what do the murder gang care, they are men with no fixed habitation ... Is not the object of the system of reprisals to render the population more frightened of the Government of this country than they are of the murder gang of Sinn Féin so that they may be forced to surrender the murderers?

Speaking in Commons on policy of reprisals over which Mosley, who later became Britain's fascist leader, left Government benches and crossed the floor of the House in protest. *HC Debates:* 5th Series: Vol. 135: Cols. 520-21.

November 24, 1920
Joe Devlin
I will tell the House when high treason started. It was when [Edward Carson] made a speech in which he said 'I am not sorry for the armed drilling of those who are opposed to me in Ireland. I have certainly no right to complain of it. I started it myself. I was told at the time that I was looking for revolution two and a half or three years ahead. I was very glad. I did not

mind that' ... There is the root of it. There is where treason started.

Speaking in Commons, as Belfast Nationalist MP, in debate on 'murders and reprisals' in Ireland. *HC Debates:* 5th Series: Vol. 135: Col. 534.

November 29, 1920
Tom Barry
Close quarter fighting did not suit them. It does not suit the Essex [Regiment] or the [Black and] Tans. Keep close to them should be our motto, for generally they must be better shots than us because of their opportunity for practice and their war experience. There are no good or bad shots at ten yards' range.

As IRA leader in Co. Cork, in reflections recorded on day after he led ambush on British convoy at Kilmichael, in which seventeen Auxiliaries and three Volunteers were killed. Barry, Tom, *Guerilla Days in Ireland,* Irish Press, 1949, p. 47.

November 29, 1920
Kevin Barry
During the twisting of my arm, the first officer continued to question me as to the names and addresses of my companions, and also asked me for the name of my company commander and any other officer I knew ... He informed me that if I gave all the information I knew I could get off.

In sworn statement before his execution for taking part in ambush in Dublin – read at later date to Commons by J. H. Thomas, MP. *HC Debates:* Vol. 1341. Col. 708.

January, 1921
Eamon de Valera
You are going too fast. This odd shooting of a policeman here and there is having a bad effect, from the propaganda point of view, on us in America. What we want is one good battle about once a month with about 500 men on each side.

Comment to Richard Mulcahy, IRA Chief of Staff. Valiulis, Maryann, *De Valera and His Times,* Cork University Press, 1983, p. 94.

March 1, 1921
Brigadier-General Hubert Gough
Law and order have given place to a bloody and brutal anarchy, in which the armed agents of the Crown violate every law in aimless and vindictive and insolent savagery. England has departed further from her own standards even of any nation in the world, not excepting the Turk and Zulu, than has ever been known in history before.

As British Army leader of Curragh mutiny in 1914, writing about situation in Ireland. Macardle, Dorothy, *The Irish Republic,* Irish Press, 1951, p. 432.

March 30, 1921
Eamon de Valera
From the Irish Volunteers we fashioned the Irish Republican Army to be the military arm of the Government. This army is therefore a regular State force, under the civil control of the elected representatives ... the Government is therefore responsible for the actions of this army ...

If they [the British] may use their tanks and steel-armoured cars, why should we hesitate to use stone walls and ditches? Why should the use of the element of surprise be denied to us?

Taking responsibility, in interview, as Sinn Féin President, for first time for actions of IRA, and justifying use of ambush tactics. Macardle, Dorothy, *The Irish Republic,* Irish Press, 1951, pp. 437-38.

April 2, 1921
Michael Collins
We have got them beaten, practically so, and it is only a question of time until we shall have Ireland cleared of Crown forces ... When I saw you before I said that the same effort that would get us Dominion Home Rule would get us a Republic. I am still of that opinion ... Compromises are difficult and settle nothing.

In interview in Dublin, as IRA Director of Organisation, with American reporter. Mitchell and Ó Snodaigh, *Irish Political Documents 1916-1949,* Irish Academic, 1985, pp. 102-3.

May 4, 1921
David Lloyd George
I will meet Mr de Valera, or any of the Irish leaders, without condition on my part.

Remark conveyed to de Valera on May 11 by American journalist. Macardle, Dorothy, *The Irish Republic,* Irish Press, 1951, p. 450.

May 4, 1921
Eamon de Valera
The blossoms are not the fruit but the precursors of the fruit – beware how you pluck them.

Warning that any settlement must be on 'the basis of right', in election address. Macardle, Dorothy, *The Irish Republic,* Irish Press, 1951, p. 933.

May 11, 1921
Henry Wilson
We are having more success than usual in killing rebels and now is the time to reinforce and not to parley.

Reporting as Chief of Imperial Staff to Lloyd George advising against negotiations. Macardle, Dorothy, *The Irish Republic,* Irish Press, 1951, p. 450.

June 22, 1921
King George V
I speak from a full heart when I pray that my coming to Ireland today may prove to be the first step towards an end of strife among her people, whatever their race or creed. In that hope I appeal to all Irishmen to pause, to stretch out the hand of forbearance and conciliation, to forgive and forget, and to join in making for the land which they love a new era of peace, contentment and goodwill ... May this historic gathering be the prelude of a day in which the Irish people, North and South, under one parliament or two, as those parliaments may themselves decide, shall work together in common love for Ireland upon the sure foundation of mutual justice and respect.

At opening of Northern Ireland Parliament, in speech widely regarded as prelude to Anglo-Irish negotiations though written largely without help of Government. Mitchell and Ó Snodaigh, *Irish Political Documents 1916-1949,* Irish Academic, 1985, p. 112.

June 24, 1921
David Lloyd George
The British Government are deeply anxious that, as far as they can assure it, the King's appeal for reconciliation in Ireland shall not have been made in vain. Rather than allow yet another opportunity of settlement in Ireland to be cast aside, they feel it incumbent on them to make a final appeal, in the spirit of the King's words, for a conference between themselves and the representatives of Southern and Northern Ireland.

In letter to De Valera which led to truce on July 11 and initiated Anglo-Irish negotiations. Mitchell and Ó Snodaigh, *Irish Political Documents 1916-1949,* Irish Academic, 1985, p. 112.

June 28, 1921
Eamon de Valera
We most earnestly desire to help in bringing about a lasting peace between the peoples of these two islands, but see no avenue by which it can be reached if you deny Ireland's essential unity and set aside the principle of national self-determination.

In reply to invitation from Lloyd George to begin negotiations. Mitchell and Ó Snodaigh, *Irish Political Documents 1916-1949,* Irish Academic, 1985, p. 113.

July 12, 1921
Orangeman
Ye never heard of the Twelfth? Away home, man, and read your bible.

Remark to foreigner asking about July 12 Orange celebrations, as recounted in diaries of Lady Spender. Buckland, Patrick, *The Factory of Grievances,* Gill and Macmillan, 1979, p. 185.

August 4, 1921
General Smuts
I believe that ... the force of community of interests will, over a period of years, prove so great and compelling that Ulster will herself decide to join the Irish State.

As unofficial South African mediator, in letter to de Valera. Macardle, Dorothy, *The Irish Republic,* Irish Press, 1951, p. 488.

August 10, 1921
Eamon de Valera
We cannot admit the right of the British Government to mutilate our country, either in its own interest or at the call of any section of our population; we do not contemplate the use of force. If your Government stands aside, we can effect a complete reconciliation.

In letter to Lloyd George, rejecting initial British proposals for settlement. Moynihan, Maurice, *Speeches and Statements by Eamon de Valera, 1917-1973,* Gill and Macmillan, 1980, p. 52.

August 13, 1921
David Lloyd George
We are profoundly glad to have your agreement that Northern Ireland cannot be coerced.

Replying to de Valera's rejection of initial settlement proposals. Macardle, Dorothy, *The Irish Republic,* Irish Press, 1951, p. 494.

August 19, 1921
David Lloyd George
The Government ... are sincerely desirous that peace should ensue, that the mischievous, long misunderstandings, sometimes sulking, sometimes, I am sorry to say, savage ... should be brought to an end. I hope that ... Irish leaders will not reject the largest measure of freedom ever offered to their country, and will not take the responsibility of renewing a conflict which would be robbed of all its glory and of all gratitude by its overshadowing calamity.

Speaking in Commons on attempt to begin Anglo-Irish negotiations. *HC Debates:* Vol. 146: Col. 1877.

August 22, 1921
Eamon de Valera
Dáil Éireann had not the power and some of them had not the inclination to use force with Ulster ... He [de Valera] did not think that policy would be successful. They would be making the same mistake with that section as England had made with Ireland. He would not be responsible for such a policy. For his part, if the Republic were recognised, he would be in favour of giving each county power to vote itself out of the Republic if it so wished.

Speaking in Dáil during private session. Quoted by Conor Cruise O'Brien in *The Irish Times,* October 3, 1972.

August 26, 1921
Seán Mac Eóin
Eamon de Valera first met the English as a soldier and beat them as a soldier. He has been meeting them now as a statesman and he will beat them as a statesman.

Proposing de Valera as President of Irish Republic at Dáil meeting in Mansion House. Macardle, Dorothy, *The Irish Republic,* Irish Press, 1951, p. 502.

August 30, 1921
Eamon de Valera
Great Britain ... acts as though Ireland were bound to her by a contract of union that forbade separation. The circumstances of the supposed contract are notorious, yet on the theory of its validity the British Government and Parliament claim to rule and legislate for Ireland, even to the point of partitioning Irish territory against the will of the Irish people, and killing or casting into prison every Irish citizen who refuses allegiance.... We have proposed the principle of government by consent of the governed ... on this basis we are ready at once to appoint plenipotentiaries.

Reply to Lloyd George agreeing to begin negotiations. Macardle, Dorothy, *The Irish Republic,* Irish Press, 1951, pp. 509-11.

September 4, 1921
Eoin O'Duffy
They [Sinn Féin] would have to put on the screw – the boycott. They would have to tighten that screw and, if necessary, they would have to use the lead against them [Unionists].

Remark used, as Sinn Féin speaker, at Armagh rally after which he became known among Unionists as 'Give them the lead' O'Duffy. Farrell, Michael, *Northern Ireland: The Orange State,* Pluto, 1983, p. 43.

September 7, 1921
David Lloyd George
We cannot accept as a basis of practical conference an interpretation of that principle [Government by consent of the governed] which would commit us to any demands which you might present – even to the extent of setting up a republic and repudiating the Crown ... Her Majesty's Government must therefore ask ... whether you are prepared to enter a conference to ascertain how the association of Ireland with the community of nations known as the British Empire can best be reconciled with Irish national aspirations.

In letter to de Valera. Macardle, Dorothy, *The Irish Republic,* Irish Press, 1951, pp. 512-13.

September 12, 1921
Eamon de Valera
We have no hesitation in declaring our willingness 'to enter a conference to ascertain

how the association of Ireland with the
community of nations known as the British
Empire can best be reconciled with Irish
national aspirations' ... Our nation has
formally declared its independence and
recognises itself as a sovereign State. It is only
as the representatives of that State ... that we
have any authority or powers to act on behalf
of our people.

In letter to Lloyd George. Macardle, Dorothy, *The
Irish Republic,* Irish Press, 1951, pp. 513-14.

September 15, 1921
David Lloyd George
Your claim to negotiate with His Majesty's
Government as the representatives of an
independent and sovereign State would make
conference between us impossible ... I must
accordingly cancel the arrangements for
conference.

In letter to de Valera. Macardle, Dorothy, *The Irish
Republic,* Irish Press, 1951, pp. 515-16.

September 23, 1921
Winston Churchill
A lasting settlement with Ireland would not
only be a blessing in itself but with it would
also be removed the greatest obstacle which
has ever existed to Anglo-American unity and
... far across the Atlantic Ocean we should
reap a harvest sown in the Emerald Isle.

Speaking, as War Secretary, in Dundee. Macardle,
Dorothy, *The Irish Republic,* Irish Press, 1951,
p. 522.

September 29, 1921
David Lloyd George
Conference not correspondence is the most
practical and hopeful way to an understanding
... We, therefore, send you herewith a fresh
invitation to a conference in London on
October 11th where we can meet your
delegates as spokesmen of the people whom
you represent.

In letter to de Valera stating terms, agreed
beforehand by both sides, under which Anglo-Irish
negotiations could begin. Mitchell and Ó Snodaigh,
Irish Political Documents 1916-1949, Irish Academic,
1985, p. 115.

September 30, 1921
Eamon de Valera
We accept the invitation, and our delegates
will meet you in London on the date
mentioned to explore every possibility of
settlement by personal discussion.

In letter to Lloyd George. Macardle, Dorothy, *The
Irish Republic,* Irish Press, 1951, p. 524.

October 7, 1921
Eamon de Valera
It is understood before decisions are finally
reached on the main question, that a despatch
notifying the intention to make these decisions
will be sent to members of the Cabinet in
Dublin, and that a reply will be awaited by the
plenipotentiaries before final decision is made.

From instructions given to Griffith, Collins, Barton,
Duggan, and Gavan Duffy before travelling to
London to negotiate Anglo-Irish Treaty. Mitchell
and Ó Snodaigh, *Irish Political Documents 1916-
1949,* Irish Academic, 1985, p. 116.

October 19, 1921
Pope Benedict XV
We rejoice at the resumption of the Anglo-
Irish negotiations and pray to the Lord, with
all our heart that He may bless them and grant
to your Majesty the great joy and imperishable
glory of bringing to an end the age-old
dissension.

In telegram to King George V. Macardle, Dorothy,
The Irish Republic, Irish Press, 1951, p. 535.

October 21, 1921
Arthur Griffith
The Truce does not mean that your military
forces should prepare during the period of the
Truce for the end of it and that we should not.

Replying to British allegations of breaches of Truce
in importing arms and drilling. Macardle, Dorothy,
The Irish Republic, Irish Press, 1951, p. 540.

October 31, 1921
Lieutenant-Colonel Croft
[A member] asks us whether the British
conscience is free, I would remind him of the
liquor legislation in Ireland, where preference
has always been given; the land legislation for
which this country poured out its millions for
the peasants of Ireland; conscription, from
which Ireland was exempt; the rationing of

food which did not apply to Ireland, and when we were tightening our belts Ireland got fat ... Far from being oppressed or downtrodden, Ireland seems to have been the spoilt darling of the Empire.

Speaking in Commons on Anglo-Irish negotiations. *HC Debates:* Vol. 147: Cols. 1434-35.

October 31, 1921
Lieutenant-Colonel Sir Samuel Hoare

The Irish administration of the last 12 months has been deplorable ... policies adopted one day and abandoned the next ... a war that has not been a war, peace that has not been peace.

Speaking in Commons on Anglo-Irish negotiations. *HC Debates:* Vol. 147: Cols. 1393-94.

October 31, 1921
Colonel Gretton

If we have a British Government terrorised, and a British Government submitting to negotiations with a gang of gunmen, what a vista is opened! A British Government brought to heel here may be brought to heel elsewhere than in Ireland by methods of this kind. They are beginning in India. We hear of something in Egypt.

Introducing, in Commons, as leader of Conservative Unionists, censure motion on Anglo-Irish negotiations. *HC Debates:* Vol. 147: Col. 1378.

November, 1921
Winston Churchill

It was a good price – £5,000. Look at me: £25 dead or alive. How would you like that?

In conversation in his London home during Treaty negotiations with Michael Collins for whose capture a £5,000 reward had been offered in Dublin. The Boers had offered £25 for Churchill. Pelling, Henry, *Winston Churchill,* Pan, 1977 p. 169.

November 29, 1921
James Craig

By Thursday next either [the Anglo-Irish] negotiations will have broken down or the Prime Minister will send me new proposals for consideration by the Cabinet. In the meantime the rights of Ulster will be in no way sacrificed or compromised.

Speaking in Belfast, as NI Prime Minister. Macardle, Dorothy, *The Irish Republic,* Irish Press, 1951, p. 574.

December 5, 1921
David Lloyd George

I have to communicate with Sir James Craig [NI Prime Minister] tonight: here are the alternative letters I have prepared, one enclosing the Articles of Agreement reached by His Majesty's Government and yourselves, the other saying that the Sinn Féin representatives refuse the oath of allegiance and refuse to come within the Empire. If I send this letter it is war – and war in three days! Which letter am I to send?

... we must know your answer by 10pm tonight. You can have until then but no longer to decide whether you will give peace or war to your country.

Addressing Irish delegation, as British Prime Minister, at end of Treaty negotiations in London. Owen, Frank, *Tempestuous Journey: Lloyd George, His Life and Times,* Hutchinson, 1954, p. 587.

December 5, 1921
Arthur Griffith

I personally will sign this Agreement and recommend it to my countrymen.

Responding, before final conference of Irish delegates, to Lloyd George request that Treaty be signed almost immediately. Owen, Frank, *Tempestuous Journey: Lloyd George, His Life and Times,* Hutchinson, 1954, p. 587.

December 6, 1921
Anglo-Irish Treaty, Paragraph 4

The oath to be taken by Members of the Parliament of the Irish Free State shall be in the following form:
I ... do solemnly swear true faith and allegiance to the Constitution of the Irish Free State as by law established and that I will be faithful to H. M. King George V, his heirs and successors by law, in virtue of the common citizenship of Ireland with Great Britain and her adherence to and membership of the group of nations forming the British Commonwealth of Nations.

From 'Articles of Agreement' as signed by British and Irish delegations. Macardle, Dorothy, *The Irish Republic,* Irish Press, 1951, p. 953.

December 6, 1921
Lord Birkenhead (Frederick Smith)

I have signed my political death warrant.

Remark made after signing Treaty as member of the British team. *Eamon de Valera,* The Irish Times Ltd., 1976, p. 100.

December 6, 1921
Michael Collins

Think – what have I got for Ireland? Something which she has wanted these past seven hundred years. Will anyone be satisfied at the bargain? Will anyone? I tell you this – early this morning I signed my death warrant.

From letter written immediately after signing Treaty. Ó Broin, Leon, *Michael Collins,* Gill and Macmillan, 1980, p. 113.

December 6, 1921
Winston Churchill

Michael Collins looked for all the world as if he was signing his death warrant.

Observation on Treaty signing. Owen, Frank, *Tempestuous Journey: Lloyd George, His Life and Times,* Hutchinson, 1954, p. 588.

December 10, 1921
James Larkin

It was born in dishonour and shame. It was drafted and signed by creatures [who] for their own aggrandisement – or because of ambition and due to their lack of courage, signed this unholy compact under duress. We pledge ourselves now and in the future, to destroy this plan of a nation's destruction. We propose carrying on the fight until we make the land of Erin a land fit for men and women – a Workers' Republic or death.

Writing about the Treaty. Berresford Ellis, Peter, *A History of the Irish Working Class,* Pluto, 1985, p. 263.

December 14, 1921
Edward Carson

At that time [of anti-Home Rule agitation], I did not know, as I know now, that I was a mere puppet in a political game ... I was fighting with others whose friendship and comradeship I hope I will lose from tonight, because I do not value any friendship that is not founded upon confidence and trust. I was in earnest. What a fool I was! I was only a puppet, and so was Ulster, and so was Ireland, in the political game that was to get the Conservative Party into power ... The

Conservatives never yet took up a cause without betraying it in the end ... Ulster is not for sale. Her loyalty does not depend upon taxes.

In attack, as Unionist leader, on Government and Conservative Party for signing Treaty with Sinn Féin, in first speech to House of Lords during which phrase 'Ulster is not for sale', referring to lower tax rates promised if Six Counties joined Free State, was used for first time. House of Lords: Vol. 48: Deb. 5: Cols. 44-50.

December 15, 1921
Winston Churchill

Whence does this mysterious power of Ireland come? It is a small, poor, sparsely-populated island, lapped about by British sea power, accessible on every side, without iron or coal. How is it that she sways our councils, shakes our parties and infects us with her bitterness, convulses our passions and deranges our action. How is it that she has forced generation after generation to stop the whole traffic of the British Empire in order to debate her domestic affairs? Ireland is not a daughter race. She is a parent nation.

Speaking in Commons on Treaty. *HC Debates:* Vol. 149: Col. 182.

December 15, 1921
R. S. Gwynn

What effect must this surrender, or Treaty, or whatever you like to call it, have on other parts of our Empire? It is a direct inducement to the rebels in India to go on and shoot more. The Prime Minister eats his words, he eats his Bills, he even eats his Acts, and that is from fear, no doubt, of the gunmen.

Speaking in Commons on Treaty. *HC Debates:* Vol. 149: Cols. 165-66.

December 15, 1921
Colonel Gretton

When the Danes began to ravage the Saxon shores, the feeble Saxon kings tried to buy them off by this, that and the other concession. They did not succeed. The Danes came looking for more, and the institution of Danegeld led to the downfall and destruction of the Saxon kingdom. We are repeating that process. We are inviting everybody throughout the world to come to the British

Government with sufficient violence and persistence in outrage to insist on getting what they want, and we shall be told of another great act of statesmanship.

Speaking in Commons on Treaty. *HC Debates:* Vol. 149: Col. 155.

December 15, 1921
Herbert Asquith

There is a nearer approach to unanimity over a long and embittered subject of party and political dispute than I have ever witnessed ... Are we or are we not prepared to welcome ... this new compact between two peoples, giving as it does to Ireland complete local autonomy, and at the same time, what is equally important, preserving for Irishmen a full share of free citizenship throughout the British Empire?

Speaking in Commons on Treaty. *HC Debates:* Vol. 149: Col. 138.

December 15, 1921
William Davison

Is not the bitterness of Ulster as the bitterness of gall?
You have:
Jeered at her loyalty
Trod on her pride,
Scorned her, repulsed her –
Great-hearted Ulster –
Flung her aside.
That is the feeling of Ulster today.

Speaking as pro-Unionist MP in Commons debate on Treaty. *The Irish Times,* November 26, 1985.

December 17, 1921
David Lloyd George

WE CANNOT CONSENT TO ANY ABANDONMENT ... OF THE PRINCIPLE OF ALLEGIANCE TO THE KING.

In telegram to de Valera turning down request for further Anglo-Irish conference. Macardle, Dorothy, *The Irish Republic,* Irish Press, 1951, p. 519.

December 19, 1921
Arthur Griffith

We have come back from London with that treaty – Saorstát na hÉireann recognised – the Free State of Ireland. We have brought back the flag; we have brought back the evacuation of Ireland after 700 years by British troops

and the formation of an Irish army. We have brought back to Ireland her full rights and powers of fiscal control. We have brought back to Ireland equality with England ... in any contest that would follow the rejection of this offer, Ireland would be fighting with the sympathy of the world against her ... If the Irish people say 'We have got everything else but the name Republic and we will fight for it' I would say to them that they are fools.

Moving motion, as signatory to Treaty, that Dáil Éireann 'approves of the Treaty between Great Britain and Ireland, signed in London on December 6, 1921.' *DÉ*, pp. 21-23.

December 19, 1921
Seán Mac Eóin

To me this Treaty gives me what I and my comrades fought for; it gives us for the first time in 700 years the evacuation of Britain's armed forces out of Ireland.

Seconding the motion that Dáil Éireann approve the Treaty. *DÉ*, p. 23.

December 19, 1921
Eamon de Valera

We were elected by the Irish people, and did the Irish people think we were liars when we said that we meant to uphold the Republic ... I am against this Treaty because it does not reconcile Irish national aspirations with association with the British Government. I am against this Treaty, not because I am a man of war, but a man of peace. I am against this Treaty because it will not end the centuries of conflict between the two nations of Great Britain and Ireland.

A war-weary people will take things which are not in accordance with their aspirations ... immediate war was threatened upon our people ... are we in this generation which has made Irishmen famous throughout the world to sign our names to the most ignoble document that could be signed?

Opposing, as President of Irish Republic, the motion that Dáil Éireann approve the Treaty. *DÉ*, p. 24.

December 19, 1921
Austin Stack

Has any man here the hardihood to stand up and say that it was for this our fathers suffered, that it was for this our comrades have died in the field and in the barrack yard?

Speaking, as member of Republic 'Cabinet' for Home Affairs, in Dáil debate on Treaty. *DÉ*, p. 28.

December 19, 1921
Michael Collins
We, as negotiators, were not in the position of conquerors dictating terms of peace to a vanquished foe. We had not beaten the enemy out of our country by force of arms. To return to the Treaty, hardly anyone, even those who support it, really understands it ... the immense powers and liberties it secures ... the power to hold and to make secure and to increase what we have gained. I say that rejection of the Treaty is a declaration of war until you have beaten the British Empire ... The Treaty was signed by me, not because they held up the alternative of immediate war. I signed it because I would not be one of those to commit the Irish people to war without the Irish people committing themselves to war ... It offers freedom to achieve freedom.

Speaking, as signatory to Treaty and member of Republic 'Cabinet' for Finance, in Dáil debate on Treaty. *DÉ*, pp. 32-34.

December 19, 1921
Erskine Childers
Irish Ministers will be King's Ministers; the Irish Provisional Government that under this Treaty is going to be set up, within a month would be the King's Provisional Government. Every executive Act in Ireland, every administrative function in Ireland would be performed – you cannot get away from it – in the name of the King.

From Treaty debates. *DÉ*, p. 40.

December 19, 1921
Kevin O'Higgins
We sent these men to London, trusting them, and they have brought back a document which they believe represents the utmost that can be got for the country, short of the resumption of war against fearful odds ... you are not entitled to reject it without being able to show them you have a reasonable prospect of achieving more ...

What remains between the Treaty and the fullness of your rights? It gives to Ireland complete control over her internal affairs. It removes all English control or interference within the shores of Ireland. Ireland is liable to no taxation from England ... She has the right to maintain an army.

Speaking, as 'Minister' of Republic, in Dáil debate on Treaty. *DÉ*, pp. 42-45.

December 19, 1921
Sean MacSwiney
I have sworn an oath to the Republic, and for that reason I could not vote for the Treaty.

From Treaty debates. *DÉ*, p. 49.

December 19, 1921
Robert Barton
The English Prime Minister [Lloyd George] with all the solemnity and the power of conviction that he alone, of all men I met, can impart by word and gesture ... declared that the signature and recommendation of every member of our delegation was necessary, or war would follow immediately.

Speaking, as signatory to Treaty, in Dáil debate on Treaty. *DÉ*, p. 49.

December 20, 1921
Sean Etchingham
I say to you, finally, if you do vote for this thing ... it will be a renunciation of your principles ... Nay, it is more, it is the burial service over the grave of the Irish nation, and there is to be no firing party.

Speaking, as 'Minister' of Republic, in Dáil debate on Treaty. *DÉ*, p. 57.

December 20, 1921
Finian Lynch
The bones of the dead have been rattled indecently in the face of this assembly ... I stand for this Treaty ... if this Treaty is rejected ... you are going to bring the people back to war, and make no mistake about it.

From Treaty debates. *DÉ*, pp. 57-59.

December 20, 1921
Sean T. O'Kelly
She [England] must laugh to think that while we play with words she gets adopted the system of government she ever wished to impose upon us. Let me remind you that we

have not got Irish unity in return for this oath. The two great principles for which so many have died, and for which they would still gladly die – no partition of Ireland and no subjugation of Ireland to any foreign power – have gone by the board in this Treaty.

From Treaty debates. *DÉ*, p. 65.

December 20, 1921
Sean Milroy
Reject this Treaty, you bring confusion and chaos throughout the whole of Ireland, and the sign to the bigots in Ulster to start with renewed vigour pogroms on the helpless minority.

From Treaty debates. *DÉ*, p. 74.

December 20, 1921
Patrick McCartan
It would take five years' fighting at the very least on the part of the Irish Republican Army, with all their gallantry, to get back to the position we were in two or three months ago. Therefore, I submit, as a political factor the Republic is dead ... We are presented with a fait accompli and asked to endorse it. I as a republican will not endorse it, but I will not vote for chaos.

From Treaty debates. *DÉ*, p. 81.

December 20, 1921
Sean Hayes
If we owe a duty to the dead, we also owe a duty to the living, and I, for one, cannot see how I could cast a vote that would expose the Irish people to the risk of war.

From Treaty debates. *DÉ*, p. 82.

December 21, 1921
George Gavan Duffy
I am going to recommend this Treaty to you very reluctantly, but very sincerely, because I see no alternative ... it inflicts a grievous wound upon the dignity of this nation by thrusting the King of England upon us ... It will be the duty of those who frame the Constitution ... to relegate the King of England to the exterior darkness as far as they can.

The complaint is ... that the alternative to our signing that particular Treaty was

immediate war; that we who were sent to London as the apostles of peace ... were suddenly to be transformed into the unqualified arbiters of war; that we had to make this choice within three hours ... And that monstrous iniquity was perpetrated by the man [Lloyd George] who had invited us under his roof in order, moryah, to make a friendly settlement.

Speaking, as signatory to Treaty, in Dáil debate on Treaty. *DÉ*, pp. 85-87.

December 21, 1921
David Ceannt
There will be shadows haunting the men of this assembly who will try to filch away the nation's rights.

From Treaty debates. *DÉ*, p. 95.

December 21, 1921
William T. Cosgrave
This instrument [the Treaty] gives us an opportunity of capturing the northern Unionists and that is the proposition worthy of our best consideration; and with a generous invitation to cultivate and recognise our national identity, and to help us in putting this country in its proper place, I believe that we would effect a united country in a way that was never done before. They are great citizens of this nation, even though they differ from us.

Speaking, as member of Republic 'Cabinet' for Local Government, in Dáil debate on Treaty. *DÉ*, pp. 106-7.

December 21, 1921
Mary MacSwiney
I stand here for the will of the people, and the will of the people of Ireland is for their freedom, which this so-called Treaty does not give them ... I ask any one of you voting for this Treaty what chance would you have if on the 24th of last May [polling day] you came out for Dominion Home Rule ... to many of the young men of this Dáil 'what is good enough for Michael Collins is good enough for me'. If Mick Collins went to hell in the morning would you follow him there?

Speaking, as one of five women members of Dáil, in debate on Treaty, which all five opposed. *DÉ*, pp. 109-14.

December 21, 1921
Richard Mulcahy
I personally see no alternative to the acceptance of this Treaty. I see no solid spot of ground upon which the Irish people can put its political feet but upon that Treaty. We are told that the alternative to the acceptance of the Treaty is war ... we have not been able to drive the enemy from anything but a fairly good-sized police barracks.

Speaking, as Chief-of-Staff of IRA, in Dáil debate on Treaty. *DÉ*, pp. 142-43.

December 21, 1921
Sean Moylan
If there is a war of extermination waged on us, that war will also exterminate British interests in Ireland; because if they want a war of extermination on us, I may not see it finished, but by God, no loyalist in North Cork will see its finish, and it is about time somebody told Lloyd George that.

From Treaty debates. *DÉ*, p. 146.

December 21, 1921
Sean MacEntee
I am opposed to this Treaty because it gives away our allegiance and perpetuates partition ... by the fact that it perpetuates partition it must fail utterly to do what it ostensibly intended to do – reconcile the aspirations of the Irish people to association with the British empire ... the provisions of this Treaty mean this: that in the North of Ireland, certain people differing from us somewhat in tradition, and differing in religion ... are going to be driven, in order to maintain their separate identity, to demarcate themselves from us, while we, in order to preserve ourselves against the encroachment of English culture, are going to be driven to demarcate ourselves as far as ever we can from them.

From Treaty debates. *DÉ*, pp. 152-56.

December 21, 1921
Fermanagh County Council
We ... do not recognise the partition parliament in Belfast and do hereby direct our secretary to hold no further communications with either Belfast or British local government

departments, and we pledge our allegiance to Dáil Éireann.

Motion passed on day local government powers were transferred from London to Belfast. The council was dissolved. Farrell, Michael, *Northern Ireland: The Orange State*, Pluto, 1983, p. 82.

December 25, 1921
Dr Fogharty, Bishop of Killaloe
Let the people have no mistake about it; the rejection of this Treaty must lead inevitably to war of such a destructive character as would lay Ireland out dead in a very short time.

Preaching at Ennis cathedral. Macardle, Dorothy, *The Irish Republic*, Irish Press, 1951, p. 624.

December 27, 1921
George Bernard Shaw
Any practical statesman will, under duress, swallow a dozen oaths to get his hand on the driving wheel.

Referring to Treaty. *Manchester Guardian*, December 27, 1921.

1922
David Lloyd George
Arguing with de Valera [is] like trying to catch a man on a merry-go-round or picking up mercury with a fork.

Remark attributed to British Prime Minister, Lloyd George. McMahon, Deirdre, *Republicans and Imperialists: Anglo-Irish Relations in the 1930s*, Yale University Press, 1984, p. 30.

January 3, 1922
Piaras Béaslaí
Think of the evacuation of Ireland by foreign troops. Why, it seems like a fairy vision. All the old Gaelic poets sang of the going of the foreign hosts out of Ireland as an unreal dream of far off happiness. They did not sing of a Republic.

Speaking in resumed Dáil debate on Treaty. *DÉ*, p. 178.

January 3, 1922
Countess Markievicz
These anti-Irish Irishmen [Southern Unionists] are to be given some select way of entering this House, some select privileges – privileges that they have earned by their cruelty to the Irish people and the working

classes of Ireland ... That is one of the biggest blots on this Treaty; this deliberate attempt to set up a privileged class in this, what they call a Free State, that is not free.

Speaking, as 'Minister' of Republic, in Dáil debate on Treaty. *DÉ*, pp. 181-82.

January 3, 1922
Ernest Blythe
I think we abandoned the possibility of getting an absolutely united Ireland – that is getting it immediately – when the President's [de Valera's] letter of the 10th August was sent. In it he stated he would not use coercion, and said we were agreeable to outside arbitration ... I am the only member of the Dáil who comes from the people [Ulster Protestants] who are going to exclude themselves, or may exclude themselves from the Free State. I know them. I have always believed that by suitable propaganda ... these people could eventually be brought to the side of the Irish nation ... I also believe that they might be coerced, and I would stand for it, that we have the right to coerce them, if we thought fit and if we have the power to do so.

Speaking, as 'Minister' of Republic, in Dáil debate on Treaty. *DÉ*, p. 194.

January 4, 1922
Alec McCabe
I am prepared to take the Treaty for what it is worth, and as a stepping stone to getting more.

From Treaty debates. *DÉ*, p. 215.

January 4, 1922
Margaret Pearse
It has been said here on several occasions that Padraic Pearse would have accepted the Treaty. I deny it. As his mother, I deny it ... Padraic Pearse would not have accepted a Treaty like this with only two-thirds of his country in it.

From Treaty debates. *DÉ*, pp. 221-23.

January 4, 1922
Eamon de Valera
One of the reasons why I did not go to London was that I wanted to keep that symbol of the Republic [its President] pure – even from insinuation – lest any word across the table

from me would, in any sense, give away the Republic.

Intervening in Dáil debate on Treaty. *DÉ*, p. 258.

January 4, 1922
Eoin O'Duffy
Let us consider for a moment what will happen our unfortunate people in the north-east if this Treaty is rejected. My opinion is that there will be callous, cold-blooded murder there again.

Speaking, as IRA leader in Ulster, in Dáil debate on Treaty. *DÉ*, p. 225.

January 4, 1922
Liam Mellowes
We would rather have this country poor and indigent, we would rather have the people of Ireland eking out a poor existence on the soil; as long as they possessed their souls, their minds and their honour. This fight has been for something more than the fleshpots of Empire.

Speaking, as IRA Director of Purchases, in Dáil debate on Treaty. *DÉ*, p. 231.

January 6, 1922
Eamon de Valera
I was reared in a labourer's cottage here in Ireland. I have not lived solely among the intellectuals. The first fifteen years of my life that formed my character were lived among the Irish people down in Limerick; therefore I know what I am talking about; and whenever I wanted to know what the Irish people wanted, I had only to examine my own heart and it told me straight off what the Irish people wanted.

In speech offering his resignation as President after emergence of divisions in Irish Cabinet over Treaty. *DÉ*, p. 274.

January 7, 1922
Harry Boland
The tragedy of all this is that, while the men who favour this Treaty have adopted a defeatist attitude ... they have not considered the weakness of that Empire. I respectfully suggest that this conference was called because England found it impossible to carry on her work in Ireland and to preserve and carry on her Empire; and having failed to force British

sovereignty on the Irish nation for 750 years, she has done it now by diplomacy.

Speaking, as Secretary to de Valera, in Dáil debate on Treaty. *DÉ*, p. 302.

January 7, 1922
P. J. Ward

Lloyd George is in the position of knowing that this country is absolutely disunited, and that ... the people of this country do not want to fight ... they are war-worn, they have come through a strenuous fight and they want peace, and they have not the smallest scruple about it; they are willing to take that prospect; and they at the same time are willing to take it as a stepping stone. I have no scruples about it either.

From Treaty debates. *DÉ*, p. 321.

January 7, 1922
Cathal Brugha

If ... our last cartridge had been fired, our last shilling had been spent, and our last man were lying on the ground and his enemies howling round him and their bayonets raised, ready to plunge them into his body, that man should say – true to the traditions handed down – if they said to him 'Now, will you come into our Empire?' – he should say, and he would say 'No! I will not'.

Speaking, as member of Republic 'Cabinet' for Defence, in Dáil debate on Treaty. *DÉ*, p. 330.

January 7, 1922
Arthur Griffith

We went there to London, not as republican doctrinaires, but looking for the substance of freedom and independence. If you think what we brought back is not the substance of independence, that is a legitimate ground for attack on us, but to attack us on the ground that we went there to get a Republic is to attack us on false and lying grounds ... 'We are ready,' said President de Valera – 'We are ready,' he said – 'to leave the whole question between Ireland and England to external arbitration' ... Is that saying you will have a Republic and nothing but a Republic? ... I say now to the people of Ireland that it is their right to see that this Treaty is carried into operation, when they get, for the first time in

seven centuries, a chance to live their lives in their own country and take their place among the nations of Europe.

Summing up in debate on Treaty which was approved by the Dáil by sixty-four votes to fifty-seven. *DÉ*, p. 340-44.

January 7, 1922
Michael Collins

Whether we are right or whether we are wrong in the view of future generations, there is this: that we now are entitled to a chance ... when countries change from peace to war or war to peace there are always elements that make for disorder and that make for chaos ... if we could form some kind of joint committee to carry on ... I think that is what we ought to do.

Speaking after Dáil had approved Treaty. *DÉ*, p. 346.

January 7, 1922
Eamon de Valera

We have had a glorious record for four years; it has been four years of magnificent discipline in our nation. The world is looking to us now –

Speaking after Dáil had approved Treaty. (The official report states 'The President here breaks down'.) *DÉ*, p. 347.

January 10, 1922
Michael Collins

Every Irishman here who has lived amongst them knows very well that the plain people of England are much more objectionable towards us than the upper classes ... they are always making jokes about Paddy and the pig and that sort of thing ... If we show that we are going to operate from the outset in a spirit of hostility ... that we are unable to carry on, England will say, and say with a certain amount of truth: 'I am afraid we will have to remain in Ireland to preserve law and order'.

Speaking in favour of election of Arthur Griffith as President of Dáil Éireann in place of Eamon de Valera. *DÉ*, p. 394.

January 10, 1922
Arthur Griffith

The Republic of Ireland remains in being until the Free State comes into operation.

Responding to questions before his election as President of Dáil Éireann. *DÉ*, p. 399.

January 10, 1922
Eamon de Valera

Mr Griffith ... is supposed with the right hand to maintain the Republic and, with the left, to knock it down. I say it is a mistake for any individual giving this support to become a Doctor Jekyll and Mr Hyde in the matter. He cannot do it. No matter what Mr Griffith says or undertakes to do, every Republican in the country will be suspicious of every act he is taking in the name of the Republic.

Opposing Griffith's election as President of Dáil Éireann. *DÉ*, p. 405.

January 10, 1922
Arthur Griffith

I will not reply to any damned Englishman in this Assembly.

Refusing, as President of Dáil Éireann, a question from Erskine Childers. *DÉ*, p. 416.

January 10, 1922
Richard Mulcahy

If any assurance is required – the Army [IRA] will remain the Army of the Irish Republic.

Concluding Treaty debates after Griffith elected President of Dáil Éireann. *DÉ*, p. 424.

January 16, 1922
Michael Collins

How could I ever have expected to see Dublin Castle itself – that dread Bastille of Ireland – formally surrendered into my hands by the Lord Lieutenant in the brocade-hung council chamber on my producing a copy of the London Treaty?

Describing his emotions as British surrendered Dublin Castle. Fanning, Ronan, *Independent Ireland*, Helicon, 1983, p. 1.

January 25, 1922
James Craig

I will never give in to any rearrangement of the boundary that leaves our Ulster area less than it is under the Government of Ireland Act [comprising total area of six counties].

Speaking in Belfast, as NI Prime Minister. Macardle, Dorothy, *The Irish Republic*, Irish Press, 1951, p. 658.

February 1, 1922
Michael Collins

Our claim [under the Boundary Commission] is clear; majorities must rule; in any map marked on that principle ... we secure immense anti-Partition areas [from Northern Ireland's six counties].

In statement issued in Dublin after meeting of Provisional Government. Macardle, Dorothy, *The Irish Republic*, Irish Press, 1951, p. 660.

February 15, 1922
Winston Churchill

If the Irish people accept his [Arthur Griffith's] advice and guidance and ratify the Treaty ... he will be able to disestablish the Irish Republic ... is it not a desirable thing that upon the authority of the Irish people recorded at an election, the Republican idea should be definitely, finally and completely put aside?

Speaking in Commons. Macardle, Dorothy, *The Irish Republic*, Irish Press, 1951, pp. 662-63.

February 16, 1922
Winston Churchill

[Since 1914], every institution, almost, in the world was strained. Great empires have been overturned. The whole map of Europe has been changed ... The modes of thought of men, the whole outlook on affairs, the grouping of parties, all have encountered violent and tremendous changes in the deluge of the world, but as the deluge subsides and the waters fall short we see the dreary steeples of Fermanagh and Tyrone emerging once again. The integrity of their quarrel is one of the few institutions that has been unaltered in the cataclysm which has swept the world.

Speaking in Commons during second reading of Irish Free State Bill. *HC Debates:* Vol. 150: Col. 1270.

February 16, 1922
Winston Churchill

Let us assume that the [Boundary] Commission ... were to reduce Ulster to its preponderatingly Orange areas ... would not that be a fatal and permanent obstacle to the unity and co-operation of Ireland?

Speaking in Commons. Macardle, Dorothy, *The Irish Republic*, Irish Press, 1951, p. 663.

March 3, 1922
Lord Birkenhead (Frederick Smith)
Northern Ireland ... is regarded as a creature already constituted, having its own Parliament and its own defined boundaries ... I have no doubt that the tribunal [Boundary Commission], not being presided over by a lunatic, will take a rational view of the limits of its own jurisdiction and will reach a rational conclusion.

In private letter, as British Government representative, to Conservative leader, Lord Balfour. Macardle, Dorothy, *The Irish Republic,* Irish Press, 1951, p. 685.

March 7, 1922
Winston Churchill
It is up to the Provisional Government not to allow themselves to be defied in public by lawless persons, and it is for me to see that they have the means for dealing with such acts of defiance ... I am supplying to them means to assert their authority.

Speaking in Commons after attacks on former RIC members in Tipperary by Republicans. *The Irish Times,* March 8, 1922.

March 14, 1922
James Craig
Come and see for yourselves. Come and ask the loyalists to go out of the Empire into the Free State ... When the Free Staters had got all they possibly could from the British Government, the Republicans would say: 'Thank you very much, and now we will take charge of the machine'.

Addressing British critics of Unionists, on occasion of opening of NI Parliament in Belfast, as first Unionist Prime Minister. *The Irish Times,* March 14, 1922.

March 16, 1922
Eamon de Valera
It was only by civil war after this that they [Republicans] could get their independence.

From report of speech at Dungarvan. Moynihan, Maurice, *Speeches and Statements by Eamon de Valera 1917-1973,* Gill and Macmillan, 1980, p. 98.

March 16, 1922
Lord Birkenhead (Frederick Smith)
If someone had presented Queen Elizabeth with this alternative ... 'Would you rather send Lord Essex and British troops to put down the turbulent population of the South of Ireland or would you rather deal with a man who is prepared, with Irish troops, to do it for you; who is prepared to acknowledge allegiance to yourself and who will relieve you of further anxiety and responsibility in the matter?' would [she] have hesitated? ... Mr Collins and Mr Griffith are attempting to place themselves, under great difficulties, at the head of such forces as are available in order that they may restore law and order ... I as an Englishman rejoice to see them making this effort.

Speaking for British Government in Lords. Macardle, Dorothy, *The Irish Republic,* Irish Press, 1951, p. 688.

March 17, 1922
Eamon de Valera
[Future Volunteers] would have to wade through Irish blood, through the blood of the soldiers of the Irish Government, and through, perhaps, the blood of some of the members of the Government in order to get Irish freedom.

Speaking at Thurles. Moynihan, Maurice, *Speeches and Statements by Eamon de Valera 1917-1973,* Gill and Macmillan, 1980, p. 98.

March 17, 1922
Eamon de Valera
If the Treaty was accepted [in an election], the fight for freedom would still go on, and the Irish people, instead of fighting foreign soldiers, would have to fight the Irish soldiers of an Irish Government set up by Irishmen.

Speaking at Carrick-on-Suir. Moynihan, Maurice, *Speeches and Statements by Eamon de Valera 1917-1973,* Gill and Macmillan, 1980, p. 98.

March 18, 1922
Eamon de Valera
In future, in order to achieve freedom, if our Volunteers continue, and I hope they will continue until the goal is reached – if we continue on that movement which was begun when the Volunteers were started, and we suppose this Treaty is ratified by your votes, then these men, in order to achieve freedom, will have ... to march over the dead bodies of their own brothers. They will have to wade

through Irish blood. If you don't want that, don't put up that barrier, because ... so long as Ireland remains unfree, there will be born the spirit to achieve complete freedom.

Speaking at Killarney. Moynihan, Maurice, *Speeches and Statements by Eamon de Valera 1917-1973*, Gill and Macmillan, 1980, pp. 103-4.

March 22, 1922
J. W. Dulanty

The [argument for the] abolition of the oath ... has been the cause of all the strife and dissension in the Irish Free State since the signing of the Treaty. The people ... regard it as an intolerable burden, a relic of mediaevalism, a test imposed from outside under threat of immediate and terrible war.

Writing as Irish High Commissioner in London to Dominion Secretary of British Government, J. H. Thomas. Mitchell and Ó Snodaigh, *Irish Political Documents 1916-1949*, Irish Academic, 1985, p. 195.

March 25, 1922
Joe Devlin

If Catholics have no revolvers to protect themselves they are murdered. If they have revolvers they are flogged and sentenced to death.

Speaking in Commons, as Belfast Nationalist MP, after murder of MacMahon family in Belfast on March 23 by men in uniform. Macardle, Dorothy, *The Irish Republic*, Irish Press, 1951, p. 683.

March 30, 1922
Michael Collins and James Craig

Peace is today declared.

From today the two Governments undertake to co-operate in every way in their power with a view to the restoration of peaceful conditions in the unsettled areas ...

The two Governments unite in appealing to all concerned to refrain from inflammatory speeches and to exercise restraint in the interests of peace.

From (short-lived) agreement signed in London by Collins and Craig. Mitchell and Ó Snodaigh, *Irish Political Documents 1916-1949*, Irish Academic, 1985, pp. 130-31.

April 5, 1922
David Lloyd George

A point might come when it would be necessary to tell Mr Collins that if he was

unable to deal with the situation the British Government would have to do so.

From Cabinet papers. Younger, Calton, *Ireland's Civil War*, Fontana, 1979, p. 265.

April 8, 1922
Winston Churchill

It is possible that things will get worse before they get better. It is possible that Irishmen will kill and murder each other, and destroy Irish property and cripple Irish prosperity.

Speaking at Dundee. Macardle, Dorothy, *The Irish Republic*, Irish Press, 1951, p. 702.

April 13, 1922
Rory O'Connor

I am safe in saying that if the [Republican] Army were ever to follow a political leader, Mr de Valera is the man.

In newspaper interview, as head of forces opposed to Treaty, after their occupation of Four Courts, Dublin. Macardle, Dorothy, *The Irish Republic*, Irish Press, 1951, p. 695.

April 26, 1922
Catholic Hierarchy

The best and wisest course for Ireland is to accept the Treaty and make the most of the freedom it undoubtedly brings us ... the young men connected with this military revolt ... when they shoot their brothers on the opposite side they are murderers.

In statement of full support for Free State, while seeking meeting of opposing sides as civil war loomed. Younger, Calton, *Ireland's Civil War*, Fontana, 1979, pp. 277-78.

May 20, 1922
Michael Collins and Eamon de Valera

We are agreed ... That a National Coalition panel for this Third Dáil, representing both parties in the Dáil and in the Sinn Féin Organisation be sent forward, on the ground that the national position requires the entrusting of the Government of the country into the joint hands of those who have been the strength of the national situation during the last few years, without prejudice to their present respective positions.

From agreement that election to new Dáil should not be fought on Treaty. Macardle, Dorothy, *The Irish Republic*, Irish Press, 1951, p. 712.

May 25, 1922
Henry Wilson

The surrender of the Provisional Government to de Valera [in agreeing to election pact with him, is] one of the most pitiful, miserable and cowardly stories in history ... the union must be re-established.

Speaking at Liverpool having been appointed military adviser to Northern Ireland Government. Macardle, Dorothy, *The Irish Republic,* Irish Press, 1951, p. 714.

June 2, 1922
Winston Churchill

The more the fear of renewed warfare is present in the minds of the electors, the more likely are they to get to the polls and support the Treaty [by voting for anti-de Valera candidates].

From Cabinet papers. Younger, Calton, *Ireland's Civil War,* Fontana, 1979, p. 305.

June 14, 1922
Michael Collins

I am not hampered now by being on a platform where there are coalitionists, and I can make a straight appeal to you to vote for the candidates you think best of.

From speech in Cork regarded as derogation from pact, with Eamon de Valera, that pro- and anti-Treaty candidates be returned as before in election to new Dáil on June 16. Younger, Calton, *Ireland's Civil War,* Fontana, 1979, p. 312.

June 16, 1922
Constitution of the Irish Free State (Article 17)

Such oath [as in the Treaty] shall be taken and subscribed by every member of the Parliament (Oireachtas) before taking his seat therein before the Representative of the Crown or some person authorised by him.

From Constitution of Free State, published on morning of polling day. Macardle, Dorothy, *The Irish Republic,* Irish Press, 1951, p. 723.

June 22, 1922
David Lloyd George

The ambiguous position of the Irish Republican Army can no longer be ignored by the British Government. Still less can Mr Rory O'Connor be permitted to remain with his followers and his arsenal in open rebellion in the heart of Dublin in possession of the Courts of Justice, organising and sending out from this centre enterprises of murder not only in the area of your Government but also in the six Northern counties and in Great Britain. His Majesty's Government cannot consent to a continuance of this state of things, and they feel entitled to ask you formally to bring it to an end forthwith ... His Majesty's Government are prepared to place at your disposal the necessary pieces of artillery.

From letter sent to Michael Collins following assassination in London of Henry Wilson. Mitchell and Ó Snodaigh, *Irish Political Documents 1916-1949,* Irish Academic Press, 1985, p. 137.

June 23, 1922
Eamon de Valera

The killing of any human being is an awful act, but as awful when the victim is the humble worker or peasant, unknown outside his own immediate neighbourhood, as when the victim is placed in the seats of the mighty and his name known in every corner of the earth. It is characteristic of our hypocritical civilisation that it is in the latter case only we are expected to cry out and express our horror and condemnation ... I know that life has been made a hell for the nationalist minority in Belfast ... I do not approve [the murder], but I must not pretend to misunderstand.

Commenting on assassination in London of Henry Wilson, who was military adviser to Northern Ireland Government. Moynihan, Maurice, *Speeches and Statements by Eamon de Valera 1917-1973,* Gill and Macmillan, 1980, pp. 105-6.

June 26, 1922
Winston Churchill

If it [the occupation of the Four Courts] does not come to an end, if through weakness, want of courage, or some other even less creditable reason it is not brought to an end, and a speedy end, then it is my duty to say ... that we shall regard the Treaty as having been formally violated ... we shall resume full liberty of action in any direction that may seem proper.

Speaking in Commons after assassination of Henry Wilson in London on June 22. Macardle, Dorothy, *The Irish Republic,* Irish Press, 1951, p. 741.

June 28, 1922
Eamon de Valera

At the bidding of the English, Irishmen are today shooting down, on the streets of our capital, brother-Irishmen, old comrades-in-arms, companions in the recent struggle for Ireland's independence and its embodiment – the Republic. English propaganda will strive to lay the blame for this war on Irishmen, but the world outside must not be deceived. England's threat of war – that, and that alone – is responsible for the present situation.

From press statement issued after Provisional Government forces attacked Four Courts. Moynihan, Maurice, *Speeches and Statements by Eamon de Valera 1917-1973,* Gill and Macmillan, 1980, p. 107.

June 28, 1922
Liam Lynch

The fateful hour has come. At the dictation of our hereditary enemy our rightful cause is being treacherously assailed by recreant Irishmen ... Gallant soldiers of the Irish Republic stand vigorously firm ... The sacred spirits of the Illustrious Dead are with us in this great struggle ... rally to the support of the Republic.

Issued on behalf of and signed by Irish Republican Army (anti-Treaty) Executive. Macardle, Dorothy, *The Irish Republic,* Irish Press, 1951, pp. 74, 46.

June 29, 1922
Richard Mulcahy

Today having driven the tyranny of the stranger from our land ... you are called upon to serve her still in arms to protect her from a madness from within ... In Dublin some of you will find yourselves today ranged in fighting against some who have been your comrades. The immediate reason for this is the seizure by them of your Assistant Chief of Staff, Lieutenant-General O'Connell ... The fundamental reason is that they systematically challenge 'those rights and liberties common to all the people of Ireland'.

In message to Free State Army, as Minister for Defence. Mitchell and Ó Snodaigh, *Irish Political Documents 1916-1949,* Irish Academic, 1985, p. 139.

June 30, 1922
Winston Churchill

The prolongation of the operations by the Free State troops against the Four Courts, coupled with the suggestion that has been put about that the Free State Government was acting at the behest of the British Government had ... reacted adversely on public opinion ... they [British ministers] should avoid any suggestion that the Free State Government was acting on British inspiration.

From Cabinet papers. Younger, Calton, *Ireland's Civil War,* Fontana, 1979, p. 325.

June 30, 1922
Oscar Traynor

To help me to carry on the fight outside you must surrender forthwith. I would be unable to fight my way through to you even at terrific sacrifice ... If the Republic is to be saved, your surrender is a necessity.

As OC Dublin Brigade, IRA, ordering surrender of Four Courts. Macardle, Dorothy, *The Irish Republic,* Irish Press, 1951, p. 751.

July 4, 1922
Frank Aiken

Boil down all this wrangling and fighting and however great the tactical mistakes of the anti-Treatyites may have been, you have the simple national abhorrence of swearing allegiance to a foreign king and allowing part of the Nation to be ruled by people who have sworn loyalty to that king ... Are you prepared to carry on a war with your own people to enforce that Oath of Allegiance to England, while you have a splendid opportunity of uniting the whole Nation to fight against it with success?

In letter to Richard Mulcahy, Minister for Defence, asking for removal of Article 17 from the Free State Constitution as possible way to avoid civil war. Macardle, Dorothy, *The Irish Republic,* Irish Press, 1951, pp. 761-62.

July 5, 1922
Winston Churchill

Better a State without archives than archives without a State.

Commenting in Commons on loss of Irish records in destruction of Four Courts. Younger, Calton, *Ireland's Civil War,* Fontana, 1979, p. 333.

July 6, 1922
Lord Birkenhead (Frederick Smith)
They [pro-Treaty forces] have destroyed in
the course of their necessary operations some
of the most beautiful and some of the most
historic districts of Dublin ... I, for one,
rejoice, as I have said before in this House,
that this task [defeating opponents of Treaty],
painful, costly, bloody as it must ultimately
prove, is being undertaken by those to whom
it properly falls.

Speaking for British Government in Lords.
Macardle, Dorothy, *The Irish Republic*, Irish Press,
1951, p. 757.

July 12, 1922
William Butler Yeats
A barricade of stone or wood;
Some fourteen days of civil war;
Last night they trundled down the road
That dead young soldier in his blood:
Come build in the empty house of the stare.

We had fed the heart on fantasies,
The heart's grown brutal from the fare;
More substance in our enmities
Than in our love; O honey-bees,
Come build in the empty house of the stare.

On outbreak of civil war, from 'Meditations in
Time of Civil War'. Yeats, W. B., *Collected Poems*,
Macmillan, 1965, pp. 230-31.

July 21, 1922
Reginald Dunne
The same principles for which we shed our
blood on the battle-field of Europe led us to
commit the act we are charged with ... what
we have done was necessary to preserve the
lives and the happiness of our countrymen in
Ireland.

From speech prepared for trial, with Joseph
O'Sullivan, for murder of Henry Wilson in London
on June 22. Both were former soldiers in British
Army. *Irish Independent*, July 21, 1922.

August, 1922
George Gavan Duffy
Ministers must feel some diffidence about
championing against their own justices the
judges of the old regime, most of whom, a year
or two ago, would have welcomed an

opportunity of lodging our present rulers in
jail.

On resigning from Provisional Government as
Minister for Foreign Affairs because of decision to
abolish Republican courts set up in 1920, retaining
only former British courts. Macardle, Dorothy, *The
Irish Republic*, Irish Press, 1951, p. 770.

August 20, 1922
Archdeacon Corbett of Mallow
The poor man is in a hurry to meet his death.

Comment made to member of Michael Collins's
convoy en route to Cork after brief conversation
between Archdeacon and Collins. Younger, Calton,
Ireland's Civil War, Fontana, 1979, p. 430.

August 23, 1922
Richard Mulcahy
To the men of the Army:
   Stand calmly by your posts. Bend bravely
and undaunted to your work. Let no cruel act
of reprisal blemish your bright honour.
   Every dark hour that Michael Collins met
since 1916 seemed but to steel that bright
strength of his and temper his gay bravery.
   You are left each inheritors of that strength
and of that bravery.
   To each of you falls his unfinished work.
No darkness in the hour – no loss of comrades
will daunt you at it.

In statement as Chief of General Staff of Free State
Army issued to newspapers after death of Michael
Collins in ambush at Béal na Bláth. *The Irish Times*
(reprinted), December 17, 1971.

September 9, 1922
William T. Cosgrave
If elected to this position [President of the
Dáil] it is my intention to implement the
Treaty ... to enact a Constitution, to assert the
authority and supremacy of Parliament ...

Speaking before election as President of first
National Government. Macardle, Dorothy, *The
Irish Republic*, Irish Press, 1951, pp. 782-83.

September 9, 1922
Kevin O'Higgins
Had we [pro-Treaty forces] not taken this step
[attacking the Four Courts] this Parliament
would not have met and the very existence of
the Parliament was at stake. We had very good
reasons to believe that we anticipated by a
couple of hours the creation of conditions ...

which would have brought back the British power – horse, foot, artillery and navy.

Speaking at first meeting of Dáil elected on June 16. Macardle, Dorothy, *The Irish Republic,* Irish Press, 1951, p. 785.

September 9, 1922
Cathal O'Shannon

There is not a county in the 26 Counties, there is not a barracks or jail out of which has not come information [about ill-treatment of prisoners] which is a disgrace to any Irish Government.

Speaking in Dáil as Labour Party Chairman. Macardle, Dorothy, *The Irish Republic,* Irish Press, 1951, p. 784.

September 12, 1922
Richard Mulcahy

If any young men in the [Free State] army brush up against individuals here and there in a rough or in an untactful way, well it is a very great credit to the army as a whole, and to the young men of this country who form it, that there is not a greater volume of complaint along that line.

Speaking in Dáil, as Minister for Defence, on allegations of ill-treatment of Republican prisoners. Macardle, Dorothy, *The Irish Republic,* Irish Press, 1951, p. 786.

September 24, 1922
Dr Cohalan, Bishop of Cork

The killing of National [Free State] soldiers is murder.

In pastoral letter to all Catholic churches in Cork diocese. Macardle, Dorothy, *The Irish Republic,* Irish Press, 1951, p. 801.

September 27, 1922
Kevin O'Higgins

I do know that the able Englishman [Erskine Childers] who is leading those who are opposed to this Government has his eye quite definitely on one objective, and that that is the complete breakdown of the economic and social fabric, so that this thing that is trying so hard to be an Irish nation will go down in chaos, anarchy and futility ... he keeps steadily, callously and ghoulishly at his career of striking at the heart of this nation ... and it is quite definitely our duty to face the fact, to

realise that there is a limit, to realise that it is very largely a question of time, and to take what we consider are the most effective steps to check this headlong race to ruin.

Speaking in Dáil, as Minister for Justice, in resolution to allow military authorities to set up military courts with powers to impose the death penalty. Macardle, Dorothy, *The Irish Republic,* Irish Press, 1951, pp. 802-3.

September 27, 1922
William T. Cosgrave

We are not going to treat rebels as prisoners of war.

Speaking in Dáil as President of National Government. Macardle, Dorothy, *The Irish Republic,* Irish Press, 1951, p. 804.

October 10, 1922
Catholic Hierarchy

A section of the community, refusing to acknowledge the Government set up by the Nation, have chosen to attack their own country as if she were a foreign power ... the guerrilla warfare now being carried on by the Irregulars [anti-Treaty forces] is without moral sanction, and, therefore, the killing of National soldiers in the course of it is murder before God.

From joint pastoral letter. Younger, Calton, *Ireland's Civil War,* Fontana, 1979, p. 482.

October 26, 1922
Liam Lynch

We, on behalf of the soldiers of the Republic ... have called upon the former President, Eamon de Valera, and the faithful members of Dáil Éireann, to form a Government, which they have done.

From proclamation signed also by twelve other IRA officers after secret meeting of Republican deputies in Dublin. Macardle, Dorothy, *The Irish Republic,* Irish Press, 1951, p. 808.

November 12, 1922
Winston Churchill

I have seen with satisfaction that the mischief-making murderous renegade, Erskine Childers, has been captured. No man has done more harm or shown more genuine malice, or endeavoured to bring a greater curse upon the common people of Ireland than this strange being, actuated by a deadly and malignant hatred for the land of his birth [England]. Such as he is, may all who hate us be.

Speaking at Dundee. Macardle, Dorothy, *The Irish Republic*, Irish Press, 1951, p. 811.

November 17, 1922
Kevin O'Higgins
If they took as their first case [for execution] some man who was outstandingly active and outstandingly wicked in his activities, the unfortunate dupes throughout the country might say that he was killed because he was a leader, because he was an Englishman, or because he combined with others to commit rape.

Speaking in Dáil after first four executions of Republican prisoners and taken as indication that Government planned execution of Erskine Childers, Republican leader, who was born in England. Younger, Calton, *Ireland's Civil War,* Fontana, 1979, p. 485.

November 19, 1922
Erskine Childers
The slow growth of moral and intellectual conviction had brought me where I stood, and it was, and is, impossible and unthinkable to go back. I was bound by honour, conscience and principle to oppose the Treaty by speech, writing and action, both in peace and, when it came to the disastrous point, in war ... Some day we shall be justified when the Nation forgets its weakness ... and may God hasten the day of reunion amongst us all under the honoured flag of the Republic.

Statement issued from prison and published after his execution, on November 24, for possession of a miniature pistol, a present from Michael Collins. *The Irish Times,* November 27, 1922.

November 23, 1922
Erskine Childers
I die full of love for Ireland. I die loving England and passionately praying that she may change completely and finally towards Ireland.

In letter to his wife, Mary, before his execution on November 24. Macardle, Dorothy, *The Irish Republic,* Irish Press, 1951, p. 814.

November 27, 1922
Liam Lynch
Every member of your body [the Dáil] who voted for this resolution by which you pretend to make legal the murder of soldiers, is equally guilty. We therefore give you and each member of your body due notice that unless your army recognises the rules of warfare in future, we shall adopt very drastic measures to protect our forces.

In letter, as leader of anti-Treaty forces, to Speaker of Dáil. Younger, Calton, *Ireland's Civil War,* Fontana, 1979, p. 491.

November 30, 1922
Richard Mulcahy
These men who were executed this morning were perhaps uneducated illiterate men ... We provided for these men all the spiritual assistance that we could to help them in their passage to eternity. We are people who realise that man is made in the image and likeness of God ... when a man is going to his death, he does get a priest.

Speaking, as Minister for Defence, in Dáil after execution of three IRA prisoners. Macardle, Dorothy, *The Irish Republic,* Irish Press, 1951, p. 816.

December 8, 1922
Free State Government
[This was] a reprisal for the assassination of Brig. Hales, TD, as a solemn warning to those associated with them who are engaged in the conspiracy of assassination against the Representatives of the Irish people.

In official proclamation issued after execution of Liam Mellows, Rory O'Connor, Joseph McKelvey and Richard Barrett in retaliation for IRA killing of Sean Hales. Macardle, Dorothy, *The Irish Republic,* Irish Press, 1951, p. 823.

December 8, 1922
Liam Mellows
Though unworthy of the greatest human honour that can be paid an Irishman or woman, I go to join Tone and Emmet, the Fenians, Tom Clarke, Connolly, Pearse, Kevin Barry and Childers. My last thoughts will be on God, and Ireland and on you.

In letter to his mother from Mountjoy Prison before his execution. Coogan, Tim Pat, *The IRA,* Fontana, 1980, p. 53.

December 8, 1922
William T. Cosgrave
Terror will be struck into them [IRA].

Speaking in Dáil, as President of Free State
Government, after execution of IRA prisoners.
Macardle, Dorothy, *The Irish Republic,* Irish Press,
1951, p. 823.

December 8, 1922
Kevin O'Higgins
Personal spite, great heavens! Vindictiveness!
One of these men was a friend of mine.

Speaking in Dáil about execution of four Republican
prisoners, one of whom, Rory O'Connor, had been
best man at O'Higgins's wedding the previous year.
Younger, Calton, *Ireland's Civil War,* Fontana,
1979, p. 494.

December 27, 1922
George Russell (AE)
Because of this warfare, those [pro-Treaty]
opposed to you who form a greater part of the
nation are led into a violence equal to your
own and a harshness of policy; and so the
whole national being is degraded in its
imagination of itself and in the regard of other
nations. No ideal, however noble in itself, can
remain for long lovable or desirable in the
minds of men while it is associated with deeds
such as have been done in recent years in
Ireland ... There is no dishonour in raising
the conflict from the physical to the
intellectual plane.

In letter to *The Irish Times,* December 27, 1922,
appealing to Republicans to lay down their arms.

December 31, 1922
Kevin O'Higgins
The Provisional Government was simply eight
young men in the City Hall standing amidst
the ruins of one administration, with the
foundations of another not yet laid and with
wild men screaming through the keyhole.

Reflecting, as Minister for Justice, on first months of
existence of Free State Government. Coogan, Tim
Pat, *The IRA,* Fontana, 1980, pp. 52-53.

February 7, 1923
Eamon de Valera
We can best serve the nation at this moment
by trying to get the constitutional way
adopted.

In letter to Liam Lynch suggesting end of armed
struggle. Moynihan, Maurice, *Speeches and
Statements by Eamon de Valera 1917-1973,* Gill and
Macmillan, 1980, p. 118.

May 13, 1923
James Larkin
I ask all Republicans to give up the armed
struggle and take up the political,
constitutional struggle. Give up your arms.
There is no disgrace in peace. There can never
be dishonour in peace.

Urging end to civil war as Labour leader at
Republican meeting in Dublin to honour James
Connolly. *The Irish Times,* January 20, 1976.

May 24, 1923
Eamon de Valera
Soldiers of the Republic, Legion of the
Rearguard: The Republic can no longer be
defended successfully by your arms. Further
sacrifice of life would now be vain, and
continuance of the struggle in arms unwise in
the national interest and prejudicial to the
future of our cause. Military victory must be
allowed to rest for the moment with those who
have destroyed the Republic. Other means
must be sought to safeguard the Nation's
right.

In message to anti-Treaty forces after defeat in civil
war accompanying order to cease fire and dump
arms. Moynihan, Maurice, *Speeches and Statements
by Eamon de Valera 1917-1973,* Gill and Macmillan,
1980, p. 114.

June 24, 1923
Major-General Liam Tobin and
Colonel Charles Dalton
The actions of the present GHQ staff since
the Commander-in-Chief's [Michael Collins]
death, their open and secret hostility to us, his
officers, have convinced us that they have not
the same outlook as he had ... we will expose
this treachery and take what steps we consider
necessary to bring about an honest, cleaner
and genuine effort to secure the Republic.

As leader of 'Old IRA' group in Free State Army in
statement to Government leader William Cosgrave
and Defence Minister Richard Mulcahy at meeting
to express dissatisfaction with progress towards
ideal of Republic. Valiulis, Maryann, *Almost a
Rebellion,* Tower Books, 1985, pp. 37-38.

June 25, 1923

Richard Mulcahy

I do not think that in any country in the world ... officers would come in uniform and sit down in front of the Commander-in-Chief of that country and read in his presence that document.

Responding, as Defence Minister and Commander-in-Chief of Free State Army, to demands from Major General Tobin, Colonel Dalton and other officers that Army should work more actively towards goal of Republic and reduce role of post-truce officers in deference to old IRA men. Valiulis, Maryann, *Almost a Rebellion,* Tower Books, 1985, p. 38.

March 3, 1924

Sean O'Casey

Sacred heart o' Jesus, take away our hearts o' stone, and give us hearts o' flesh! Take away this murdherin' hate an' give us Thine own eternal love!

Words spoken by Mrs Boyle, or Juno, on death of her son in the Troubles; first performance of *Juno and the Paycock* at Abbey Theatre, Dublin, on March 3, 1924. O'Casey, Sean, *Juno and the Paycock and The Plough and the Stars,* Macmillan, 1969, p. 72.

March 6, 1924

Major-General Liam Tobin and Colonel Charles Dalton

[The army will] take such action that will make clear to the Irish people that we are not renegades or traitors to the ideals that induced them to accept the Treaty. Our organisation fully realises the seriousness of the action we may be compelled to take, but we can no longer be party to the treachery that threatens to destroy the aspirations of the nation.

Ultimatum from Free State Army officers demanding that Government move towards setting up Republic, and threatening widespread mutiny. Valiulis, Maryann, *Almost a Rebellion,* Tower Books, 1985, p. 51.

March 10, 1924

Richard Mulcahy

Two army officers have attempted to involve the army in a challenge to the authority of the Government. This is an outrageous departure from the spirit of the Army. It will not be tolerated.

In statement, as Defence Minister, to newspapers on threatened mutiny of old IRA officers on grounds Government was not moving towards goal of Republic. Valiulis, Maryann, *Almost a Rebellion,* Tower Books, 1985, p. 53.

March 11, 1924

William T. Cosgrave

The attempt [by army officers to challenge Government], such as it is, is not against a particular Government, it is a challenge to the democratic foundations of the State, to the very basis of parliamentary representation and of responsible Government.

Responding in Dáil to threatened mutiny of old IRA officers on grounds Government was not moving towards goal of Republic. Valiulis, Maryann, *Almost a Rebellion,* Tower Books, 1985, p. 54.

March 12, 1924

Kevin O'Higgins

If the document [ultimatum from old IRA Army officers] were taken at its face value, it would be simply the Four Courts situation over again. It was represented to us that it need not be taken ... at its face value ... We were told that these men, while they might have written a foolish, an almost criminally foolish document, were not really taking up the position of challenging the fundamental right of the people to decide political issues.

Informing Dáil, as Minister for Home Affairs, that old IRA army officers had backed down in their threatened mutiny and that Government would not take severe punitive measures against them. Valiulis, Maryann, *Almost a Rebellion,* Tower Books, 1985, p. 54.

May 19, 1924

Joe McGrath

[I] would not be a party to taking action against a body of men who were responsible very largely for the birth of the Free State and for its life since.

Explaining in *Irish Independent* interview why he resigned as Minister for Industry and Commerce in sympathy with army officers who threatened mutiny on March 6 on grounds Government was not moving towards goal of Republic for which they had fought in old IRA. Valiulis, Maryann, *Almost a Rebellion,* Tower Books, 1985, p. 52.

August 15, 1924
Eamon de Valera
I would disappoint a number here if I were not to start by saying, 'Well, as I was saying to you when we were interrupted'.

Speaking at Ennis on first public appearance since arrested a year previously as he tried to address a crowd at same venue. Moynihan, Maurice, *Speeches and Statements by Eamon de Valera 1917-1973*, Gill and Macmillan 1980, p. 115.

October 15, 1924
William T. Cosgrave
Had those pronouncements been made at the time [of the Treaty negotiations], there would not have been Irish signatories to the Treaty.

Speaking as leader of Free State Government in Dáil debate, referring to British assurances to Unionists that Boundary Commission would not make significant changes to Border. Farrell, Michael, *Arming the Protestants*, Brandon, 1983, p. 225.

October 17, 1924
William Butler Yeats
I have no hope of seeing Ireland united in my time, or of seeing Ulster won in my time; but I believe it will be won in the end, and not because we fight it, but because we govern this country well. We can do that ... by creating a system of culture which will represent the whole of this country and which will draw the imagination of the young towards it.

Speaking in Seanad on relations with Northern Ireland. Pearce, Donald R., *The Senate Speeches of W. B. Yeats*, Faber and Faber, 1961, p. 87.

November 1, 1924
Justice Feetham
If the Commission were to make a change in the boundary ... simply in order to gratify 1,000 of such inhabitants at the cost of offending the other 999, such a proceeding would obviously be unreasonable.

As Chairman of Boundary Commission, in memorandum ruling on limitations of possible change. Cited by Dennis Kennedy in *The Irish Times*, January 29, 1970.

January 25, 1925
Eamon de Valera
No decent Republican should ever enter the present Dáil.

Comment, as Sinn Féin President. Browne, Vincent, *The Magill Book of Irish Politics*, Magill Publications, 1981, p. 56.

June 11, 1925
William Butler Yeats
I think it is tragic that within three years of this country gaining its independence we should be discussing a measure [the prohibition of divorce] which a minority of this nation considers to be grossly oppressive. I am proud to consider myself a typical man of that minority. We against whom you have done this thing are no petty people. We are one of the great stocks of Europe. We are the people of Burke; we are the people of Grattan; we are the people of Swift, the people of Emmet, the people of Parnell. We have created the most of the modern literature of this country. We have created the best of its political intelligence. Yet I do not altogether regret what has happened. I shall be able to find out, if not I, my children will be able to find out whether we have lost our stamina or not ... If we have not lost our stamina then your victory will be brief, and your defeat final, and when it comes this nation may be transformed.

Speaking in Seanad on Government measure to make it impossible to obtain a divorce in Free State. Pearce, Donald R., *The Senate Speeches of W. B. Yeats*, Faber and Faber, 1961, p. 99.

June 21, 1925
Eamon de Valera
For our part, we are content to rest for the moment, if it must be so, simply faithful. We know we have been true and have kept on the true road. We are no less confident of final victory than we were eight years ago. We are still able to fling back our old defiance at the ancient enemy of the nation. We recognise in that enemy the real enemy, and, as far as we can, we shall see to it that he will not divert against any section of our people the attacks that are meant for him.

In speech at grave of Wolfe Tone at Bodenstown. Moynihan, Maurice, *Speeches and Statements by Eamon de Valera 1917-1973*, Gill and Macmillan, 1980, p. 121.

October 1, 1925
James Craig
Not an inch!

Election slogan, referring to Border still to be ratified by British and Irish Governments. Younger, Calton, *A State of Disunion*, Muller, 1972, p. 212.

November 25, 1925
Sam Patterson
While the people of Belfast are starving, we have rogues, vagabonds, thieves and murderers in Sir James Craig and his Government ... by the aid of rifle, revolver and bomb we can blow the Government to hell.

In speech, as Northern Ireland Labour Party member, during outdoor relief agitation for which he was sentenced to six months hard labour for sedition. Farrell, Michael, *Northern Ireland: The Orange State*, Pluto, 1983, p. 123.

November 28, 1925
Kevin O'Higgins
The [Boundary] Commission took the line of least resistance; where the special police were thick in the North, the Commission sheered away ... the Commission has been influenced by specials standing with their fingers on the trigger.

As Minister for Justice, speaking at tripartite conference between Dublin, London and Belfast at Chequers, which ratified boundary of Northern Ireland. Farrell, Michael, *Arming the Protestants*, Brandon, 1983, p. 248.

December 4, 1925
William T. Cosgrave
I firmly believe that we have found the only solution in a very difficult situation ... It will remove obstacles which have ever been a source of bitter conflict between the peoples of Northern Ireland and the Irish Free State. I want you to put on record my belief that this situation will tend more surely and more speedily towards bringing about the ultimate political unity of the two sections of the country than any other course that could have been adopted.

In *Belfast Telegraph* interview, as leader of Free State Government, on Agreement of December 3, 1925, between Dublin, London and Belfast which ratified boundaries of Northern Ireland. Mitchell and Ó Snodaigh, *Irish Political Documents 1916-1949*, Irish Academic, 1985, p. 169.

December 5, 1925
Cahir Healy
The Nationalists of Fermanagh are overwhelmed with amazement that any men representing the country can sign such a document ... For what have the Nationalists been sold? ... Time will decide if the betrayal will not bring its retribution. John Redmond was driven from public life for even suggesting Partition for a period of five years. The new leaders agree to Partition forever.

In *Irish Independent* interview, as Nationalist MP for Fermanagh and Tyrone, on Agreement of December 3, 1925, between Dublin, London and Belfast which ratified boundaries of Northern Ireland. Mitchell and Ó Snodaigh, *Irish Political Documents 1916-1949*, Irish Academic, 1985, p. 170.

December 6, 1925
Eamon de Valera
In the long list of England's outrages against our people there is none greater than this outrage of partition ... there is not a nation on the earth, with any effective means at its disposal, but would have felt justified in shedding its best blood to prevent it. The Southern states of the American Union had a far better case for secession than our Northern Unionists have, and President Lincoln faced four years of terrible civil war rather than permit it ... But the worst of this bargain is the complexion that will be put upon it, for it will be said that we have sold our countrymen for the meanest of all considerations – a money consideration.

Speech delivered in Dublin protesting against the Boundary Agreement revoking the powers of the Boundary Commission, dispensing with the proposed Council of Ireland and releasing the Free State from any obligation to service the public debt of the former United Kingdom. Moynihan, Maurice, *Speeches and Statements by Eamon de Valera 1917-1973*, Gill and Macmillan, 1980, pp. 122-23.

December 9, 1925
James Craig
I rise with feelings of deep thankfulness and relief ... I am naturally cautious in the language that I use today ... injudicious statements or remarks may ... cause difficulty if not here in Ulster in other parts of Ireland ... I believe that a new era will be opened in Irish history and that there is a possibility that

not only may useful consultations take place between individual Ministers, but by meetings of the Executive much may be accomplished to smooth over those small but irritating difficulties that are bound to arise from time to time between two neighbouring States.

Speaking in Stormont, as NI Prime Minister, on Agreement of December 3, 1925, between Dublin, London and Belfast which ratified the boundaries of Northern Ireland. Mitchell and Ó Snodaigh, *Irish Political Documents 1916-1949,* Irish Academic, 1985, pp. 166-67.

January 22, 1926
Sean Lemass
Sinn Féin, for good or evil, is entering on another stage in its career . . . there are some who would have us sit by the roadside and debate abstruse points about a de jure this and a de facto that, but the reality we want is away in the distance – and we cannot get there unless we move.

Writing, as Sinn Féin member, in *An Phoblacht.* Farrell, Brian, *De Valera and His Times,* Cork University Press, 1983, p. 36.

February 11, 1926
William Butler Yeats
Fallon, I'm sending for the police; and this time it'll be their own police. (To audience) You have disgraced yourselves again.

Comment to actor Gabriel Fallon on fourth night at Abbey Theatre of Sean O'Casey's *The Plough and the Stars* when audience tried to rush stage in protest at scene where tricolour and plough and stars were carried into a pub. Tuohy, Frank, *Yeats,* Gill and Macmillan, 1976, p. 192.

March 3, 1926
Winston Churchill
Neither by threats or violence or by intrigues, nor yet by unfair economic pressure, shall the people of Ulster be compelled against their wishes to sever the ties which bind them to the United Kingdom, or be forced, unless by their own free and unfettered choice, to join another system of government.

Speaking as Chancellor of the Exchequer. (These words were engraved twelve years later on a silver cup presented to Churchill by James Craig, then Lord Craigavon.) *The Times,* March 3, 1926. Fisk, Robert, *In Time of War,* Paladin, 1985, pp. 61-62.

March 10, 1926
Eamon de Valera
That once the admission oaths of the 26-county and 6-county assemblies are removed, it becomes a question not of principle but of policy whether or not Republican representatives should attend these assemblies.

Motion proposed at Sinn Féin Árd Fheis but not put because of passing of amendment against attendance in Dáil. The following day de Valera resigned as President of Sinn Féin. Moynihan, Maurice, *Speeches and Statements by Eamon de Valera 1917-1973,* Gill and Macmillan, 1980, p. 127.

March 11, 1926
Eamon de Valera
[Lemass said to me] 'You are not going to leave us now, Dev, at this stage. You cannot leave us like that. We have to go on now. We must form a new organisation along the policy lines you suggested at the Árd Fheis . . . But we were only a few people and we hadn't a penny between us'.

De Valera's account to Michael McInerney of reaction of Lemass to his decision to leave public life after resigning as President of Sinn Féin. Farrell, Brian, *De Valera and His Times,* Cork University Press, 1983, p. 37.

May 16, 1926
Eamon de Valera
The question is raised whether this oath is really an oath at all in the theological sense . . . For me it is enough that it is called an oath officially and that it begins with 'I do solemnly swear' and that, whenever it suits, it will be held to be an oath by those who impose it and will be so understood by the world . . . if it is not an oath, why not away with the mockery?
. . . Another objection raised [to taking seats in the Dáil] is that entering a 26-county assembly would be an acceptance of partition. I deny that. To recognise the existence of facts, as we must, is not to acquiesce in them.

From speech at inaugural meeting of Fianna Fáil in La Scala Theatre, Dublin. Moynihan, Maurice. *Speeches and Statements of Eamon de Valera 1917-1973,* Gill and Macmillan, 1980, pp. 135-39.

1927
Catholic Hierarchy
Since there are within the Irish Free State three university colleges sufficiently safe in

regard to faith and morals, we, therefore, strictly inhibit, and under pain of grave sin, we forbid priests and all clerics by advice or otherwise, to recommend parents or others having charge of youth to send the young persons in their charge to Trinity College [Protestant University].

From statute passed by National Council of Bishops. Whyte, J. H., *Church & State in Modern Ireland,* Gill and Macmillan, 1980, p. 305.

June 27, 1927
Eamon de Valera

Unionists [who] have wilfully assisted in mutilating their motherland can justly be made to suffer for their crime.

In interview in *Manchester Guardian* which identified de Valera with a desire to 'punish Ulster'. Bowman, John, *De Valera and the Ulster Question,* Clarendon, 1982, p. 99.

August 10, 1927
Eamon de Valera

The required declaration is not an oath ... it is merely an empty political formula which deputies can conscientiously sign without becoming involved, or without involving their nation, in obligations of loyalty to the English Crown. The Fianna Fáil deputies would certainly not wish to have the feeling that they are allowing themselves to be debarred by nothing more than an empty formula from exercising their functions as public representatives, particularly at a moment like this.

Statement issued after Mr Cosgrave's Government announced, following the assassination of Kevin O'Higgins on July 10, proposals for legislation which would disqualify elected members of the Dáil who had not taken the Oath, forcing by-elections. The following day Fianna Fáil deputies entered the Dáil for the first time. Moynihan, Maurice, *Speeches and Statements by Eamon de Valera 1917-1973,* Gill and Macmillan, 1980, p. 150.

August 11, 1927
Eamon de Valera

I am prepared to put my name down on this book in order to get permission to go into the Dáil, but it has no other significance. You must remember I am taking no oath.

Addressing the clerk of the chamber in Dáil Éireann, after pushing aside the Bible. Coogan, Tim Pat, *The IRA,* Fontana, 1980, p. 80.

March 6, 1928
Colonel Howard Bury

Does he [Secretary to the Treasury] not consider that the recent flooding was a judgement of God upon the Trustees of the Tate Gallery. (Cries of Order, order).

Commenting, as MP, in Commons on flooding of Tate Gallery in London which threatened disputed Lane pictures claimed by Dublin. Robinson, Lennox, *Lord Gregory's Journals,* Putnam, 1946, p. 314.

March 14, 1928
Eamon de Valera

I still hold that [Dáil Éireann's] right to be regarded as the legitimate government of this country is faulty, that this House itself is faulty. You [Cosgrave Government] have secured a de facto position. Very well, there must be somebody in charge to keep order in the community, and by virtue of your de facto position you are the only people in a position to do it ... I say you have not come by that position legitimately. You brought off a coup d'état in the summer of 1922.

Speaking in Dáil on legitimacy of State. Coogan, Tim Pat, *The IRA,* Fontana, 1980, p. 81.

March 21, 1928
Sean Lemass

I think it would be right [to say] that Fianna Fáil is a slightly constitutional party. We are perhaps open to the definition of a constitutional party, but, before anything, we are a Republican party. We have adopted the method of political agitation to achieve our end because we believe, in the present circumstances, that method is the best in the interests of the nation and of the Republican movement, and for no other reason ... Five years ago we were on the defensive and perhaps in time we may recoup our strength sufficiently to go on the offensive. Our object is to establish a Republican Government in Ireland. If this can be done by the present methods we have, we would be very pleased. If not, we would not confine ourselves to them.

Intervening, as Fianna Fáil TD, in debate on prisoners. *DÉ Debates:* Vol. 22: Col. 1615.

November 17, 1928
George Bernard Shaw

If, having broken England's grip of her [Ireland], she slips back into the Atlantic as a little grass patch in which a few million moral cowards cannot call their souls their own ... then the world will let 'these Irish' go their own way into insignificance without the smallest concern.

Speaking from his home in England on Catholic influence on legislation in Free State. *Irish Statesman*, November 17, 1928, p. 208.

June 5, 1929
Sean T. O'Kelly

We of the Fianna Fáil party believe that we speak for the big body of Catholic opinion. I think I could say, without qualification of any kind, that we represent the big element of Catholicity.

Speaking in Dáil. Whyte, J. H., *Church & State in Modern Ireland*, Gill and Macmillan, 1980, p. 41.

1931
J. H. Thomas

... the Spanish onion in the Irish stew.

Description, as British Dominions Secretary, of de Valera, in private conversation. McMahon, Deirdre, *Republicans and Imperialists: Anglo-Irish Relations in the 1930s*, Yale University Press, 1984, p. 32.

January, 1931
Monsignor E. A. D'Alton, Dean of Tuam

We are not appointing a washerwoman or a mechanic, but an educated girl who ought to know what books to put into the hands of the Catholic boys and girls of this country ... is it safe to entrust a girl who is not a Catholic, and is not in sympathy with Catholic views, with their handling?

On decision of library committee of Mayo County Council not to approve appointment of Protestant librarian, Ms Dunbar-Harrison. Whyte, J. H., *Church & State in Modern Ireland*, Gill and Macmillan, 1980, pp. 44-45.

June 17, 1931
Eamon de Valera

If it is a mere passive position of handing down books that are asked for, then the librarian has no particular duty for which religion should be regarded as a qualification,

but if ... it is active work of a propagandist educational character – and I believe it to be such if it is to be of any value at all and worth the money spent on it – then I say the people of Mayo, in a county where, I think – I forget the figures – over 98 per cent of the population is Catholic, are justified in insisting upon a Catholic librarian.

If I had a vote on a local body, and if there were two qualified people who had to deal with a Catholic community, and if one was a Catholic and the other was a Protestant, I would unhesitatingly vote for the Catholic.

Speaking, in Dáil, as Fianna Fáil leader of Opposition, on decision of library committee of Mayo County Council not to approve appointment of Protestant librarian, Ms Dunbar-Harrison. Whyte, J. H., *Church & State in Modern Ireland*, Gill and Macmillan, 1980, pp. 45-46.

October 4, 1931
William T. Cosgrave

Foul murders have been committed, acknowledged and gloried in by certain organisations. Young men are being taught that murder is a legitimate instrument for the furtherance of Communist or political aims. They are being taught that the Christian Church around which our whole history and civilisation have been built up is an instrument of tyranny for the suppression of the people ... I believe, and my colleagues believe, that the future of this country is linked up with the traditions and teachings of the Christian religion which have governed the minds of its people for fifteen hundred years ... the new patriotism based on Muscovite teachings with a sugar coating of Irish extremism is completely alien to Irish tradition.

Speaking, as Government leader, in Dáil on need for special powers to combat Saor Éire (Socialist Republican Party). Mitchell and Ó Snodaigh, *Irish Political Documents 1916-1949*, Irish Academic, 1985, p. 186.

October 19, 1931
Catholic Hierarchy

We cannot remain silent in the face of the growing evidence of a campaign of revolution and communism, which if allowed to run its course unchecked must end in the ruin of Ireland, both soul and body ...

We appeal most earnestly and with deepest

anxiety to all our people and especially the young ... Surely the ranks of the communist revolution are no place for an Irish boy of Catholic instincts.

In statement on IRA and Saor Éire (Socialist Republican Party) and their policy of physical force to achieve all-Ireland Republic. Mitchell and Ó Snodaigh, *Irish Political Documents 1916-1949*, Irish Academic, 1985, pp. 187-88.

1932
Frank Ryan

While we have fists, hands and boots to use, and guns if necessary, we will not allow speech to traitors.

Speaking, as left-wing Republican leader, at public meeting in Dublin, about Cumann na nGaedheal and Blueshirts (neo-fascist National Guard). Coogan, Tim Pat, *The IRA*, Fontana, 1980, p. 91.

February 5, 1932
William T. Cosgrave

We won't stand these attacks against the liberties and rights of our people. Now, [the Government] having adopted a jury that will not be subject to their acts, they [the IRA] are whining. Gallant, patriotic Irishmen never whined in difficulties; they took their medicine like men, and if the cause were worthy of it, the means adopted to get what they want are not worthy of the people of this country: they are alien to us and to our religion, our nationality and our judgement.

Defending, as Government leader, setting up of military tribunals to deal with outbreak of IRA violence aimed at renewing struggle for all-Ireland Republic. Keogh, Dermot, in *De Valera and His Times*, Cork University Press, 1983, p. 154.

March 12, 1932
The IRA

Fianna Fáil declares its intention to chop off some of the imperial tentacles; every such achievement is of value and will be welcomed. Notwithstanding such concessions, the Irish Republican Army must continue its work, and cannot escape its role as the vanguard of the freedom movement.

Statement in *An Phoblacht* after Fianna Fáil victory in general election. Coogan, Tim Pat, *The IRA*, Fontana, 1980, p. 90.

March 23, 1932
J. H. Thomas

It is manifest that the oath is an integral part of the Treaty made ten years ago ... the Irish Free State Government propose to retain the land annuities accruing under the Irish Lands Acts, 1891-1909 ... the Free State Government are bound by the most formal and explicit undertaking to continue to pay the land annuities to the National Debt Commissioners, and the failure to do so would be a manifest violation of an engagement which is binding in law and honour on the Irish Free State.

As British Dominions Secretary, in despatch to Eamon de Valera who as head of first Fianna Fáil Government was pressing for abolition of oath of allegiance to Crown and withholding of land annuities. Mitchell and Ó Snodaigh, *Irish Political Documents 1916-1949*, Irish Academic, 1985, p. 196.

April 5, 1932
Eamon de Valera

The elimination of the oath is a measure required for the peace, order and good government of the State. The competence of the legislature of the Irish Free State to pass such a measure is not open to question.

With regard to the land annuities, my Government will be obliged if you will state what is the 'formal and explicit undertaking to continue to pay the land annuities to the National Debt Commissioners' ... The Government of the Irish Free State is not aware of any such undertaking.

Writing, as head of Fianna Fáil Government, to British Dominions Secretary J. H. Thomas. Mitchell and Ó Snodaigh, *Irish Political Documents 1916-1949*, Irish Academic, 1985, p. 198.

April 9, 1932
J. H. Thomas

What is actually raised is nothing less than a repudiation of the Settlement of 1921 as a whole ... relations cannot but be impaired by any failure in the complete fulfilment of obligations deliberately undertaken.

In further letter, as British Dominions Secretary, to de Valera on question of oath and land annuities. Mitchell and Ó Snodaigh, *Irish Political Documents 1916-1949*, Irish Academic, 1985, pp. 199-201.

April 27, 1932
William T. Cosgrave

The introduction of this Bill [to remove oath of allegiance] is not a matter upon which the Government should receive many congratulations. It appears to be one of the greatest pieces of political chicanery in history ... Two of the greatest Irishmen that ever lived ... signed that agreement [the Treaty] ... They never contemplated, never imagined, that this country would repudiate or make any attempt to repudiate the signatures appended to that instrument.

Speaking, in Dáil, as Opposition leader, in debate on removal of oath of allegiance to British Crown. Mitchell and Ó Snodaigh, *Irish Political Documents 1916-1949*, Irish Academic, 1985, p. 202.

April 29, 1932
Eamon de Valera

I never regarded freedom as an end in itself, but if I were asked what statement of Irish policy was most in accord with my view as to what human beings should struggle for, I would stand side by side with James Connolly. The thing that was most heartbreaking in this Dáil since I came into it was to find the two parties who should have stood side by side trying to secure freedom in order that they might have power to order their own policy, divided. I am speaking of the Fianna Fáil Party and the Labour Party.

Speaking, as Government leader, in Dáil debate on unemployment. Moynihan, Maurice, *Speeches and Statements by Eamon de Valera, 1917-1974*, Gill and Macmillan, 1980, p. 203.

July 7, 1932
James McNeill

I do not think I should resign any office because other office-holders think I am a suitable target for ill-conditioned bad manners.

Writing, as Governor General of Free State, to de Valera after series of snubs from Fianna Fáil ministers because he represented the Crown. The correspondence was published and McNeill forced to resign three months later. McMahon, Deirdre, *Republicans and Imperialists: Anglo-Irish Relations in the 1930s*, Yale University Press, 1984, p. 64

July 22, 1932
Ramsay MacDonald

So long as de Valera is there, there is no way out. He begins somewhere about the birth of Christ and wants a commission ... to explore the past centuries ... It makes one sick. Behind it all is the romance of force and of arms – shooting, murdering and being murdered. It is a gay adventure of a fool put into a china shop in hob nail boots and with liberty to smash.

In letter as British Prime Minister, after breakdown of talks with de Valera in Downing Street, London, over commission to settle dispute over land annuities. McMahon, Deirdre, *Republicans and Imperialists: Anglo-Irish Relations in the 1930s*, Yale University Press, 1984, p. 68.

August 5, 1932
Thomas Inskip

It is not money that stands in the way of peace. There is something bigger and deeper. Does Mr de Valera want to be a partner in the Empire, or is he pursuing the will-o'-the-wisp of a republic?

Speaking, as British Attorney General, about Fianna Fáil ending of annuity payments to Britain. *The Times*, August 5, 1932.

September 24, 1932
Sean MacEntee

I am sorry to say that while we have the support of every thinking Irishman, there are, unfortunately, reactionary and imperialist elements in the country, with the help of a reactionary and imperialist press, spreading the spirit of faction among us, and in this connection I recall the old saying: 'It never was the Sassenach that beat us; it was the Gael that beat us ... Knaves and traitors stand aside.'

In speech, as Minister for Finance in Fianna Fáil Government, about alleged collusion between Opposition and British Government. McMahon, Deirdre, *Republicans and Imperialists: Anglo-Irish Relations in the 1930s*, Yale University Press, 1984, pp. 79-80.

September 30, 1932
Tommy Henderson

We have not met for four months and we are going to adjourn for another two months; in the meantime the starving people of Northern

Ireland are to continue starving. The unemployed will have to beg in the streets. I condemn the way the Government have treated the unemployed. It is a disgrace to civilisation.

Speaking, as Shankill Unionist, during last sitting of Northern Ireland Parliament in Belfast City Hall before moving to Stormont. Bardon, Jonathan, *Belfast*, Blackstaff, 1983, p. 218.

September 30, 1932
Jack Beattie
I am going to put this out of action . . . The House indulges in hypocrisy while there are starving thousands outside.

Speaking, as Labour MP, before throwing mace on floor at last sitting of Northern Ireland Parliament in Belfast City Hall. Riots of unemployed against inadequate outdoor relief took place in October. Bardon, Jonathan, *Belfast*, Blackstaff, 1983, p. 218.

October 10, 1932
Tommy Geehan
For many years the workers of Belfast had been divided by artificial barriers of religion and politics but the past two months had witnessed a wonderful spectacle because the workers were now united on a common platform demanding the right to live.

Speaking, as Revolutionary Workers' Group organiser, during agitation uniting Protestants and Catholics in Belfast over low levels of outdoor relief pay. Farrell, Michael, *Northern Ireland: The Orange State*, Pluto, 1983, p. 127.

October 12, 1932
James Craig (Lord Craigavon)
If they [Nationalists] have any designs by the trouble they have created in our city, if they have it at the back of their minds that this is one step towards securing a Republic for all Ireland . . . I say they are doomed to bitter disappointment.

Speaking, as NI Prime Minister, after rioting in Protestant and Catholic areas of Belfast during agitation over low levels of outdoor relief pay. Farrell, Michael, *Northern Ireland: The Orange State*, Pluto, 1983, p. 130.

April 23, 1933
Eamon de Valera
Let it be made clear that we yield no willing assent to any form or symbol that is out of keeping with Ireland's right as a sovereign nation. Let us remove these forms one by one, so that this state that we control may be a Republic in fact and that, when the time comes, the proclaiming of the Republic may involve no more than a ceremony, the formal confirmation of a status already attained.

Speaking, as Government leader, at Arbour Hill, Dublin. Moynihan, Maurice, *Speeches and Statements by Eamon de Valera*, Gill and Macmillan, 1980, p. 237.

May 27, 1933
King Alfonso
I have just seen that rascal, de Valera. I cut him, of course. Wouldn't you have done the same?

Comment made by King of Spain to British Ambassador to Holy See after encountering de Valera in Rome. McMahon, Deirdre, *Republicans and Imperialists: Anglo-Irish Relations in the 1930s*, Yale University Press, 1984, p. 114n.

July 12, 1933
Basil Brooke
There was a great number of Protestants and Orangemen who employed Roman Catholics. He [Brooke] felt he could speak freely on this subject as he had not a Roman Catholic about his own place . . . Roman Catholics were endeavouring to get in everywhere and were out with all their force and might to destroy the power and constitution of Ulster. There was a definite plot to overpower the vote of Unionists in the North. He would appeal to loyalists therefore, wherever possible to employ good Protestant lads and lassies.

Mr Cahir Healy [Nationalist MP] complained that no appointments were given to Roman Catholics but in that he was quite wrong as . . . they had got too many appointments for men who were really out to cut their throats if opportunity arose.

From speech as reported in *Fermanagh Times*, July 13, 1933. Hepburn, A. C., *The Conflict of Nationality in Modern Ireland*, Arnold, 1980, p. 164.

July 12, 1933
J. M. Andrews
Another allegation made against the [Northern Ireland] Government, which is untrue, is that of 31 porters at Stormont 28 are Roman Catholic. I have investigated the matter and I have found that there are 30 Protestants and

only one Roman Catholic, there only
temporarily.

Speaking, as Stormont Minister of Labour, at
Orange demonstration. Farrell, Michael, *Northern
Ireland: The Orange State,* Pluto, 1983, p. 136.

July 12, 1933
Major McCormick
Too many Protestants were giving
employment to Roman Catholics . . . the
Protestant who did so was a traitor to his
country and his Protestantism was virtually
lost. Rome would be in power in twenty years
both inside Parliament and outside it.

As Belfast Unionist MP, speaking at Orange
demonstration at Newtownbutler, Co. Fermanagh.
The Irish Times, July 13, 1933.

July 12, 1933
Rev. W. J. Mitchell
Speakers [who urged Protestants not to
employ Catholics] seemed to have little or no
consideration for their Protestant brethren
across the Border [in the South] . . . where
many of their lads and lassies were depending
for their livelihood on Roman Catholic
employers . . . As an Orangeman [I feel] their
Six-County leaders should be more
considerate of their brethren across the
Border.

Writing to local newspaper, as Co. Cavan rector,
following call by Unionist MPs not to employ
Catholics. *The Irish Times,* August 14, 1933.

July 20, 1933
Eoin O'Duffy
While I am in charge [of the Blueshirts] I will
ensure that the organisation will keep within
the law and that illegalities will not be
tolerated. Physical drill will be practised only
as a means of promoting good health,
character and discipline. With the same object
a distinctive dress will be worn . . . Blue is
adopted as the organisation colour for flags,
shirts, ties, badges etc., just as sports clubs
adopt a distinctive blazer or jersey . . . One of
[our] principle objects . . . is to combat
communism.

Speaking on being chosen as leader of Army
Comrades, which became neo-fascist Blueshirts, at
meeting in Dublin hotel. *The Irish Times,* July 21,
1933.

August 13, 1933
Basil Brooke
Mr Mitchell was probably correct when he
said [July 12, 1933] that Protestants in the
Free State were getting a square deal . . . but
the question was an entirely different one in
the Free State to what it was in Northern
Ireland. In the Free State Protestants were in
a minority and the Roman Catholics could do
what they liked with them. Protestants in the
Free State were decreasing rapidly. On the
other hand, Roman Catholics were increasing
in the North . . . Ninety-seven per cent of the
Roman Catholics in Ireland politically were
disloyal and disruptive and if they in the
North would increase their power by
employing such people, in a very few years
Ulster would be voted into the Free State.
That was why he [Brooke] said: 'Do not
employ Roman Catholics where they could
get good Protestants to take their place'. If the
Roman Catholics in Northern Ireland were
prepared to back the Constitution and the
Empire he would not say a word.

Responding, as Unionist MP, at Enniskillen Orange
demonstration to criticisms by Rev. W. J. Mitchell
of effect his statement had south of Border. *The
Irish Times,* August 14, 1933.

September, 1933
Thomas O'Higgins
If the other side broke gobs, they [Blueshirts]
would also break gobs. They had the material
and they would use it.

Brother of assassinated Justice Minister Kevin
O'Higgins speaking, as founder and first President
of Army Comrades Association or National Guard,
known as Blueshirts, about Republican attempts to
break up their paramilitary meetings. Browne,
Vincent, *The Magill Book of Irish Politics,* Magill
Publications, 1981, p. 67.

September 8, 1933
Eoin O'Duffy
The people are being brought to beggary and
defrauded of all hope of getting rid of partition
by sham republicanism, which only uses the
name republic as a pretext for self-
glorification, for claiming a monopoly of
patriotism, and for perpetuating discord.

As former general and Blueshirt leader, in manifesto
as President of United Ireland Party, formed from
Cumann na nGaedheal, Centre Party and Army

Comrades Association. *The Irish Times,* September 9, 1933.

October 2, 1933
Joe McGarrity
They [the IRA] can do the things you will not care to do or cannot do in the face of public criticism, while the IRA pay no heed to public clamour so long as they feel they are doing a national duty ... [Get rid of] the old Free State or Cosgrave element ... They should all have gone with the rotten regime of which they were a part.

Writing, as Clan na Gael leader in USA, to Eamon de Valera on what he should do as leader of Irish Government. McMahon, Deirdre, *Republicans and Imperialists: Anglo-Irish Relations in the 1930s,* Yale University Press, 1984, p. 126.

November 11, 1933
United Ireland Party
[The party seeks] the voluntary reunion of all Ireland in a single independent state as a member, without any abnegation of Irish sovereignty, of the British Commonwealth in free and equal partnership.

In first policy statement of new party formed by coalition of Cumann na nGaedheal, National Centre Party and General O'Duffy's National Guard (Blueshirts). Browne, Vincent, *The Magill Book of Irish Politics,* Magill Publications, 1981, p. 47.

1934
Victor Fiorentini
We are the smallest Fascist club in the United Kingdom.
Benito Mussolini
Then grow.

Exchange in Rome between Italian-born secretary of Fascist Party in Derry and Italian Duce. Fisk, Robert, *In Time of War,* Paladin, 1985, p. 461.

January 31, 1934
Eamon de Valera
You talk about coming to an understanding with the IRA. You talk of the influence it would have both here and abroad. You talk as if we were fools and didn't realise this. My God! Do you know that ever since 1921 the main purpose in everything I have done has been to try and secure a base for national unity.

In letter to Joe McGarrity, Clan na Gael leader in USA, on need to repair damage of civil war, rather than reach agreement with IRA and get rid of 'Free State element' as suggested by McGarrity on October 2, 1933. McMahon, Deirdre, *Republicans and Imperialists: Anglo-Irish Relations in the 1930s,* Yale University Press, 1984, p. 126.

March 20, 1934
Basil Brooke
I recommend those people who are Loyalists not to employ Roman Catholics, 99 per cent of whom are disloyal ... I want you to realise that, having done your bit, you have got your Prime Minister behind you.

Speaking, as member of NI Government, to Derry Unionist Association. Farrell, Michael, *Northern Ireland: The Orange State,* Pluto, 1983, pp. 90-91.

March 21, 1934
James Craig (Lord Craigavon)
There is not one of my colleagues who does not entirely agree with him, and I would not ask him to withdraw one word he said.

Speaking at Stormont when asked to repudiate statement by Brooke recommending employers not to hire Catholics. Farrell, Michael, *Northern Ireland: The Orange State,* Pluto, 1983, p. 91.

April 8, 1934
The IRA
A Republic of an united Ireland will never be achieved except through a struggle which uproots capitalism on its way.

Resolution passed by IRA officers, meeting in Athlone. Moody, Martin, Byrne (Eds.), *A New History of Ireland,* Vol. VIII, Oxford, 1982, p. 418.

April 24, 1934
James Craig (Lord Craigavon)
I have always said that I am an Orangeman first and a politician and Member of this Parliament afterwards ... in the South they boasted of a Catholic State. They still boast of Southern Ireland being a Catholic State. All I boast of is that we are a Protestant Parliament and a Protestant State. It would be rather interesting for historians of the future to compare a Catholic State launched in the South with a Protestant State launched in the North and see which gets on the better and prospers the more.

Speaking at Stormont, as NI Prime Minister, in favour of motion condemning employment of 'disloyalists' entering Northern Ireland from Republic. Hepburn, A. C., *The Conflict of Nationality in Modern Ireland,* Arnold, 1980, p. 165.

August 25, 1934
Lord Granard

He [de Valera] is certainly not normal. He is on the border line between genius and insanity. I have met men of many countries and have been governor of a lunatic asylum, but I have never met anybody like the President ... before.

In private report to British Government as unofficial intermediary between de Valera and London, appointed because of his position as Irish senator while at the same time holding positions in royal household in London. McMahon, Deirdre, *Republicans and Imperialists: Anglo-Irish Relations in the 1930s,* Yale University Press, 1984, p. 143.

November 8, 1934
Wilfrid Spender

If the Prime Minister is dissatisfied with our present system [of recruitment], I think the only course would be for the Government to come out in the open and to say that only Protestants are admitted to our service.

From memo as permanent head of NI civil service to Cabinet Secretary after NI Prime Minister Lord Craigavon responded sympathetically to objections to Catholic worker being employed at Stormont. Buckland, Patrick, *James Craig,* Gill and Macmillan, 1980, p. 111.

November 21, 1934
James Craig (Lord Craigavon)

Regarding public appointments, these were given by the [NI] Government as far as possible to loyal men and women. We have our own means of finding out [their loyalty]. That was behind [the] whole idea of carrying on a Protestant Government for a Protestant people.

Replying, as Prime Minister, in NI Parliament to charge by Nationalist MP Cahir Healy that minority were denied their rights. *The Irish Times,* November 22, 1934.

December 19, 1934
Eamon de Valera

No longer shall our children, like our cattle, be brought up for export.

Speaking in Dáil on prospect of emigration ending under Fianna Fáil Government. Murphy, John A.,

in *De Valera and His Times,* Cork University Press, 1983, p. 10.

March 17, 1935
Eamon de Valera

Since the coming of St Patrick, fifteen hundred years ago, Ireland has been a Christian and a Catholic nation. All the ruthless attempts made through the centuries to force her from this allegiance have not shaken her faith. She remains a Catholic nation.

In radio broadcast to United States. *The Irish Press,* March 18, 1935.

March 22, 1935
The IRA

The Army Council offers the services of the Army to assist in mobilising the maximum support for the Dublin transport workers in their struggle, and is prepared to send representatives to meet the strike committee for this purpose.

Statement issued after Government used army lorries during transport strike. Police arrested forty-four IRA members the following day. Coogan, Tim Pat, *The IRA,* Fontana, 1980, p. 114.

1936
J. W. Dulanty

[I] felt like a whore at a christening.

Describing to Canadian High Commissioner his feelings as Irish High Commissioner in London at meetings with Commissioners from other Commonwealth countries. McMahon, Deirdre, *Republicans and Imperialists: Anglo-Irish Relations in the 1930s,* Yale University Press, 1984, p. 171.

June 18, 1936
Gerald Boland

We smashed them [Blueshirts] and we are going to smash the others [IRA].

Speaking in Dáil, as Fianna Fáil Minister for Justice, after IRA had been declared illegal following series of shootings. Coogan, Tim Pat, *The IRA,* Fontana, 1980, p. 123.

August 14, 1936
Sean Russell

Republican forces are awaiting an opportune moment to fight with all their might for the nation's freedom ... over in England, where we shall also take the offensive, we have another secret army of Irishmen, who meet quietly for drill and target practice. We have also quantities of ammunition and other war material in England. Our air force may be small, but it is reasonably efficient.

In interview, as IRA leader, in *Daily Mirror*. (The IRA had no air force; it did once hire a small aircraft in abortive attempt to rescue prisoners in British jail.) Coogan, Tim Pat, *The IRA*, Fontana, 1980, pp. 154-55.

November 27, 1936
William T. Cosgrave

[The Spanish Civil War] is for the victory or defeat of communism and all it stands for, with its denial of Christian principles, individual liberty and democracy.

Speaking in Dáil, as leader of Fine Gael. Moynihan, Maurice, *Speeches and Statements of Eamon de Valera 1917-1973*, Gill and Macmillan, 1980, p. 286.

December 11, 1936
Eamon de Valera

We propose to continue the King for the functions which he in fact directly exercises . . . from the King are being taken away any functions internal, either direct or indirect, in the administration of the Government and in the internal Executive of the country and we are retaining the King for those purposes for which he was used hitherto . . . because he is recognised as the symbol of . . . co-operation in the States of the Commonwealth. If the Irish people do not wish to continue him for these purposes they can end that by legislation.

Speaking in Dáil, as leader of Fianna Fáil Government, on External Relations Act, 1936. Chubb, Basil, *Source Book of Irish Government*, Institute of Public Administration, 1983, p. 14.

May 11, 1937
The Irish Constitution

Article 2. The National territory consists of the whole island of Ireland, its islands and the territorial seas.
Article 3. Pending the reintegration of the national territory, and without prejudice to the right of the Parliament and Government established by this Constitution to exercise jurisdiction over the whole of that territory, the laws enacted by that Parliament shall have the like area and extent of application as the laws of Saorstát Éireann and the like extra-territorial effect.

Territorial articles from revised Constitution presented to Dáil by de Valera for debate, and established by referendum. Mitchell and Ó Snodaigh, *Irish Political Documents*, Irish Academic, 1985, p. 216.

May 11, 1937
Eamon de Valera

If it [the Northern Ireland problem] was not there, in all probability there would be a flat, downright proclamation of the Republic in this.

Speaking in Dáil, as leader of Fianna Fáil Government, in debate on 1937 Constitution. Chubb, Basil, *Source Book of Irish Government*, Institute of Public Administration, 1983, p. 16.

August 29, 1937
German Foreign Ministry

The German Government will refrain from all hostile activity towards Irish territory and will respect Ireland's integrity provided that for her part, Ireland will observe strict neutrality towards Germany.

In letter to German Ambassador to Dublin, Eduard Hempel, after Hempel had informed Berlin that he had been told Irish Government would stay neutral in any war. Coogan, Tim Pat, *The IRA*, Fontana, 1980, p. 262.

May 5, 1938
Winston Churchill

These ports are in fact the sentinel towers of the western approaches, by which the forty-five million people in this island so enormously depend on foreign food for their daily bread . . . Now we are to give them up, unconditionally, to an Irish Government led by men – I do not want to use harsh words – whose rise to power has been proportionate to the animosity with which they have acted against this country . . .
The ports may be denied us in the hour of need . . . it will be no use saying 'then we will retake the ports' . . . To violate Irish neutrality should it be declared at the moment of a great war may put you out of court in the opinion of the world.

Speaking in Commons, as Conservative MP, about handing over of 'Treaty' ports of Cobh, Berehaven and Lough Swilly, retained up to then by Britain under 1921 Treaty. *HC Debates:* Vol. 355; Cols. 1094-1105.

May 5, 1938
Neville Chamberlain
We came to the conclusion that a friendly Ireland was worth far more to us both in peace and in war than those paper rights that could only be exercised at the risk of maintaining and perhaps increasing their sense of grievance.

Speaking, as Prime Minister, in Commons about end of economic war with Ireland and handing over of 'Treaty' ports to Free State. *HC Debates:* Vol. 355: Cols. 1072-78.

October 13, 1938
Eamon de Valera
We have definitely committed ourselves to the proposition that this island shall not be used as a base for enemy attacks upon Great Britain. It is possible to visualise a critical situation arising in the future in which a united free Ireland would be willing to co-operate with Britain to resist a common attack. Let me say clearly that the chances of such co-operation in the event of a European war are very, very slight while partition remains.

Interview, as leader of Irish Government, in *The Evening Standard.* Moynihan, Maurice, *Speeches and Statements by Eamon de Valera 1917-1973,* Gill and Macmillan, 1980, p. 361.

January 12, 1939
The IRA
I have the honour to inform you that the Government of the Irish Republic ... herewith demand the withdrawal of all British armed forces stationed in Ireland ... The Government of the Irish Republic believe that a period of four days is sufficient for your Government to signify its intention in the matter of the military evacuation ... Our Government reserve the right of appropriate action without further notice if on the expiration of the period of grace these conditions remain unfulfilled.

Letter issued to British Government, with copies to Hitler and Mussolini, preceding bombing campaign in England. Coogan, Tim Pat, *The IRA,* Fontana, 1980, pp. 164-65.

February 7, 1939
Eamon de Valera
If I were told tomorrow, 'You can have a united Ireland if you give up your idea of

restoring the national language to be the spoken language of the majority of the people,' I would for myself say no.

Speaking in Dáil. Moynihan, Maurice, *Speeches and Statements by Eamon de Valera 1917-1973,* Gill and Macmillan, 1980, p. 372.

April 28, 1939
Adolf Hitler
He [President Roosevelt] mentioned Ireland, for instance, and asks for a statement that Germany will not attack Ireland. Now I have just read a speech by de Valera, the Irish Taoiseach, in which, strangely enough, and contrary to Mr Roosevelt's opinion, he does not charge Germany with oppressing Ireland but he reproaches England with subjecting Ireland to continuous aggression.

In speech to Reichstag after Roosevelt had publicly asked Hitler for assurances he would not attack thirty-one specified countries, including Free State. Shirer, William L., *The Rise and Fall of the Third Reich,* Pan, 1960, p. 577.

September 2, 1939
Dáil Éireann
Arising out of the armed conflict now taking place in Europe, a national emergency exists affecting the vital interests of the State.

Declaration of emergency at outbreak of war. The declaration remained in effect until rescinded on August 31, 1976. Chubb, Basil, *Source Book of Irish Government,* Institute of Public Administration, 1983, p. 38.

October 28, 1939
The IRA
England's difficulty – Ireland's opportunity has ever been the watchword of the Gael ... Now is the time for Irishmen to take up arms and strike a blow for our Ulster people. By destroying the Orange ascendancy, by expelling the British Army, by abolishing the Border, we shall cut away the cancer that is gnawing away at the heart of Ireland.

In appeal in *War News,* journal issued sporadically by IRA after outbreak of war. Dwyer, Thomas Ryle, *Irish Neutrality and the USA 1939-1947,* Rowman and Littlefield & Gill and Macmillan, 1977, p. 21.

November 9, 1939
Eamon de Valera
There are no means by which the Government can secure the safety of the people here, except

the powers of arrest and detention of those [the IRA] who are in a position to bring this country to disaster ... the Government have been faced with the alternative of two evils. We have had to choose the lesser, and the lesser evil is to see men die, rather than that the safety of the whole community should be endangered.

Speaking in Dáil, as Taoiseach, on refusal to release IRA prisoners on hunger strike. Moynihan, Maurice, *Speeches and Statements by Eamon de Valera 1917-1973*, Gill and Macmillan, 1980, pp. 421-22.

1940
Nicholas Monsarrat

As they [British convoys] sailed past this smug coastline, past people who did not give a damn how the war went as long as they could live on in their fairy-tale world, they had time to ponder a new aspect of indecency. In the list of people you were prepared to like when the war was over, the man who stood by and watched while you were getting your throat cut could not figure very high.

From Monsarrat, N., *The Cruel Sea*, Cassell, 1951, p. 151.

January 23, 1940
Frank Aiken

Instead of earning the respect and goodwill of both belligerents it [neutrality] is regarded by both with hatred and contempt; 'he who is not with me is against me'. In the modern total warfare it is not a condition of peace with both belligerents, but rather, a condition of limited warfare.

In memorandum, as Minister for Co-ordination of Defence Measures, for Cabinet justifying strictures of Government censorship imposed on Irish newspapers during war. Fisk, Robert, *In Time of War*, Paladin, 1985, p. 165.

February 10, 1940
Paul Woermann

By reason of its militant attitude towards England, the IRA is a natural ally of Germany.

Writing, as Divisional Director, German Foreign Ministry, to von Ribbentrop after Sean Russell of IRA had made contact with German Government. Fisk, Robert, *In Time of War*, Paladin, 1985, p. 340.

May 28, 1940
Edward Warnock

I am no longer a member of the [Northern Ireland] Government. I have heard speeches about Ulster pulling her weight but they have never carried conviction.

On resigning as Parliamentary Secretary for Home Affairs at Stormont in protest at lack of urgency shown by Stormont Government in war effort. Kennedy, David, *Ireland in the War Years and After*, Gill and Macmillan, 1969, p. 55.

June 16, 1940
Jan Christiaan Smuts

The Irish Atlantic ports should be seized at once, even in the face of Irish opposition, to prevent them suffering the same fate as the Norwegian ports [seized by Germany].

In message as South African Prime Minister to British War Cabinet. Dwyer, Thomas Lyle, *Irish Neutrality and the USA 1939-1947*, Rowman and Littlefield & Gill and Macmillan, 1977, p. 73.

June 21, 1940
Malcolm MacDonald

That there should be a declaration of a United Ireland in principle, the constitutional and other practical details of the Union to be worked out in due course; Ulster to remain a belligerent, Éire to remain neutral at any rate for the time being; if both parties desired it, a Joint Defence Council to be set up at once; at the same time, in order to secure Éire's neutrality against violation by Germany, British naval ships to be allowed into Éire ports, British troops and aeroplanes to be stationed at certain agreed points in the territory, the British Government to provide additional equipment for Éire's forces, and the Éire Government to take effective action against the Fifth Column.

Offer on partition put to Taoiseach Eamon de Valera by British Government through MacDonald, Minister of Health, at meeting in Dublin. Fisk, Robert, *In Time of War*, Paladin, 1985, p. 197.

June 21, 1940
Eamon de Valera

That Éire and Ulster should be merged in a United Ireland, which should at once become neutral; its neutrality to be guaranteed by Great Britain and the United States of America; since Britain was a belligerent, its

military and naval forces should not take any
active part in guaranteeing that neutrality, but
American ships should come into the Irish
ports, and perhaps American troops into
Ireland, to effect this guarantee.

Counter-offer, as recorded in official report to
British War Cabinet from MacDonald, British
Health Minister, after Britain proposed united
Ireland in principle in return for use of Free State
territory. Fisk, Robert, *In Time of War*, Paladin,
1985, p. 198.

June 25, 1940
Neville Chamberlain
I do not believe that the Ulster Government
would refuse to play their part in bringing
about so favourable a development.

Comment, as Prime Minister, to War Cabinet on
British proposal to de Valera of United Ireland in
principle in return for use of Free State territory.
Fisk, Robert, *In Time of War*, Paladin, 1985, p. 201.

June 26, 1940
Malcolm MacDonald
If the authorities in Éire missed this
opportunity of reaching their great goal, the
opportunity might never present itself again
... on the assumption that Éire had carried out
its part of the plan and come into the war, it
was unthinkable that the promise [of a United
Ireland] should be broken.

As British Minister of Health, at meeting with de
Valera in Dublin. Fisk, Robert, *In Time of War*,
Paladin, 1985, p. 202.

June 26, 1940
Neville Chamberlain
You will observe that the document [outlining
British Government proposals on ending
partition] takes the form of an inquiry only,
because we have not felt it right to approach
you officially with a request for your assent
unless we had first a binding assurance from
Éire that they would, if the assent were given,
come into the war ... If therefore they refuse
the plan, you are in no way committed, and if
they accept you are still free to make your own
comments or objections as you may think fit.

From letter, as British Prime Minister, to Northern
Ireland Prime Minister Lord Craigavon on secret
negotiations with Taoiseach Eamon de Valera. Fisk,
Robert, *In Time of War*, Paladin, 1985, p. 207.

June 27, 1940
James Craig (Lord Craigavon)
AM PROFOUNDLY SHOCKED AND DISGUSTED
BY YOUR LETTER MAKING SUGGESTIONS SO
FAR REACHING BEHIND MY BACK AND
WITHOUT ANY PRECONSULTATION WITH ME.
TO SUCH TREACHERY TO LOYAL ULSTER I
WILL NEVER BE A PARTY.

Telegram, as NI Prime Minister, to British Prime
Minister Neville Chamberlain after being informed
of British proposal of agreeing to united Ireland in
principle in return for use of Free State territory
during war. Fisk, Robert, *In Time of War*, Paladin,
1985, p. 207.

June 27, 1940
Neville Chamberlain
REGRET YOU SHOULD MAKE SUCH UNFAIR
CHARGE ... LITTLE LIKELIHOOD OF PROGRESS
WITH ÉIRE BUT YOU CAN BE ASSURED THAT
YOU WILL HAVE EVERY OPPORTUNITY OF
MAKING YOUR VIEWS KNOWN BEFORE ANY
DECISION AFFECTING ULSTER IS TAKEN.
MEANWHILE PLEASE REMEMBER THE SERIOUS
NATURE OF THE SITUATION WHICH REQUIRES
THAT EVERY EFFORT BE MADE TO MEET IT.

Telegram to Craigavon in response to Craigavon's
telegram rejecting British Government proposals
put to Free State Government about partition. Fisk,
Robert, *In Time of War*, Paladin, 1985, pp. 207-8.

June 29, 1940
James Craig (Lord Craigavon)
YOUR TELEGRAM ONLY CONFIRMS MY
CONFIDENTIAL INFORMATION AND
CONVICTION DE VALERA IS UNDER GERMAN
DICTATION AND FAR PAST REASONING WITH
FULL STOP HE MAY PURPOSELY PROTRACT
NEGOTIATIONS TILL ENEMY HAS LANDED
FULL STOP STRONGLY ADVOCATE
IMMEDIATE NAVAL OCCUPATION OF
HARBOURS AND MILITARY ADVANCE SOUTH.

Telegram to Chamberlain in response to telegram
above. Fisk, Robert, *In Time of War*, Paladin, 1985,
p. 210.

July 1, 1940
Joachim von Ribbentrop
As long as Ireland conducts herself in a neutral
fashion it can be counted on with absolute
certainty that Germany will respect her
neutrality unconditionally.

As German Foreign Minister advising his
Government to promise to respect Irish neutrality,
after receiving message indirectly from de Valera
that this would help Free State resist pressure from
Britain to join Allies. Dwyer, Thomas Lyle, *Irish
Neutrality and the USA 1939-1947*, Rowman and
Littlefield & Gill and Macmillan, 1977, p. 73.

July 5, 1940

Eamon de Valera

We are unable to accept the plan outlined, which we note is purely tentative and has not been submitted to Lord Craigavon and his colleagues . . . The plan would commit us definitely to an immediate abandonment of our neutrality. On the other hand it gives no guarantee that in the end we would have a united Ireland, unless indeed concessions were made to Lord Craigavon opposed to the sentiments and aspirations of the great majority of the Irish people.

From message delivered to Chamberlain rejecting British Government proposals on partition and Irish involvement in war. Fisk, Robert, *In Time of War*, Paladin, 1985, p. 212.

July 11, 1940

Joachim von Ribbentrop

As long as Ireland conducts herself in a neutral fashion it can be counted on with absolute certainty that Germany will respect her neutrality unconditionally . . . it is an utterly unreasonable suspicion that we might have the intention to prepare to use Ireland as a military base against England through a so-called 'fifth column' which besides does not exist.

In message from German Foreign Minister to Eduard Hempel, German Minister to Éire. Fisk, Robert, *In Time of War*, Paladin, 1985, p. 333

August 15, 1940

President Roosevelt

[The Irish] must realise that in the end they will have to fish or cut bait.

In message to US Ambassador in Dublin on impatience of US President with Irish refusal to join Allies. Dwyer, Thomas Lyle, *Irish Neutrality and the USA 1939-1947*, Rowman and Littlefield & Gill and Macmillan, 1977, p. 81.

November 5, 1940

Winston Churchill

The fact that we cannot use the south and west coasts of Ireland to refuel our flotillas and aircraft, and thus protect the trade by which Ireland as well as Great Britain lives, is a most heavy and grievous burden and one which should never have been placed on our shoulders, broad though they may be.

Speaking, as British Prime Minister, in Commons. Fisk, Robert, *In Time of War*, Paladin, 1985, p. 287.

November 7, 1940

Eamon de Valera

There can be no question of the handing over of these ports so long as this State remains neutral . . . Any attempt to bring pressure to bear on us by any side – by any of the belligerents – by Britain – could only lead to bloodshed . . . we may be – I hope not – facing a grave crisis. If we are to face it, then we shall do it, anyhow, knowing that our cause is right and just and that, if we have to die for it, we shall be dying in that good cause.

In special statement to Dáil Éireann replying to Churchill's Commons speech complaining of Britain's inability to use Irish 'Treaty' ports. Moynihan, Maurice, *Speeches and Statements by Eamon de Valera 1917-1973*, Gill and Macmillan, 1980, pp. 451-52.

November 10, 1940

David Gray

[De Valera is] probably the most adroit politician in Europe and he honestly believes that all he does is for the good of the country. He has the qualities of martyr, fanatic and Machiavelli. No one can outwit him, frighten him or brandish him. Remember that he is not pro-German nor personally anti-British but only pro-de Valera. My view is that he will do business on his own terms or must be overcome by force.

In message, as US Ambassador in Dublin, to Roosevelt on futility of trying to pressurise de Valera into giving up Irish 'Treaty' ports to Britain. Dwyer, Thomas Lyle, *Irish Neutrality and the USA 1939-1947*, Rowman and Littlefield & Gill and Macmillan, 1977, pp. 90-91.

December 3, 1940

Adolf Hitler

A landing in Ireland can be attempted only if Ireland requests help . . . Ireland is important to the Commander in Chief, Air, as a base for attacks on the north west ports of Britain, although weather conditions must be investigated. The occupation of Ireland might lead to the end of the war.

At conference with German naval staff. Fisk, Robert, *In Time of War*, Paladin, 1985, p. 225.

December 12, 1940
George Bernard Shaw
The ['Treaty'] ports do not belong to Ireland, they belong to Europe, to the world, to civilisation ... and are only held in trust by your Government in Dublin. In their names we must borrow the ports from you for the duration.

Advice to Churchill on what to say to de Valera in controversy over Britain's inability to use 'Treaty' ports – returned to Free State in 1938 – while Atlantic losses mounted. *The Irish Press,* December 12, 1940.

December 13, 1940
Winston Churchill
Our merchant seamen ... take it much amiss that we should have to carry Irish supplies through air and U-boat attacks and subsidise them handsomely when de Valera is quite content to sit happy and see us strangle.

As British Prime Minister in message to Roosevelt explaining why Britain intended cutting down on shipments of feeding stuffs and fertilisers to Ireland. Dwyer, Thomas Lyle, *Irish Neutrality and the USA 1939-1947,* Rowman and Littlefield & Gill and Macmillan, 1977, p. 99.

January 1, 1941
Adolf Hitler
Éire's neutrality must be respected. A neutral Irish Free State is of greater value to us than a hostile Ireland.

In discussion with officer at Obersalzberg about possible invasion of Britain. Fisk, Robert, *In Time of War,* Paladin, 1985, p. 263.

January 20, 1941
John Maffey
Éire is a bog with a petty leader raking over old muck-heaps.

As British Ambassador in Dublin, in report to London. Fisk, Robert, *In Time of War,* Paladin, 1985, p. 297.

January 31, 1941
Winston Churchill
No attempt should be made to conceal from Mr de Valera the depth and intensity of feeling against the policy of Irish neutrality. We have tolerated and acquiesced in it, but juridically we have never recognised that southern Ireland is an independent sovereign state, and she herself has repudiated Dominion status. Her international status is undefined and anomalous. Should the present situation last till the end of the war, which is unlikely, a gulf will have opened between northern and southern Ireland, which it will be impossible to bridge in this generation.

In letter to Dominions Secretary Viscount Cranborne. Fisk, Robert, *In Time of War,* Paladin, 1985, pp. 298-99.

February 4, 1941
David Gray
The Dáil makes me think of the Supervisors meetings that I used to report in Monroe County when I worked on the *Rochester Union and Advertiser.*

In message to Roosevelt on quality of Irish politics. Dwyer, Thomas Lyle, *Irish Neutrality and the USA 1939-1947,* Rowman and Littlefield & Gill and Macmillan, 1977, p. 104.

February 10, 1941
James Dillon
We are living under a sword of Damocles that might fall to destroy freedom and man's right to adore God. All decent things are being assailed by the most formidable combination that ever existed to destroy worship of God. It may be policy of this Government to stand neutral, but I am not neutral. The issue at stake means whether I want to live or die. I pray Germany and its rulers may be smashed by the Anglo-American alliance.

In address, as deputy Fine Gael leader, to Fine Gael Árd Fheis. Fisk, Robert, *In Time of War,* Paladin, 1985, p. 303.

March 17, 1941
Eamon de Valera
A small country like ours that had for centuries resisted imperial absorption, and that still wished to preserve its separate national identity, was bound to choose the course of neutrality in this war ... The continued existence of partition, that unnatural separation of six of our counties from the rest of Ireland, added, in our case, a further decisive reason.

In St Patrick's Day radio broadcast to United States. Moynihan, Maurice, *Speeches and Statements by Eamon de Valera 1917-1973,* Gill and Macmillan, 1980, p. 454.

April 7, 1941
President Roosevelt
What you [Ireland] have to fear is German aggression.
Frank Aiken
Or British aggression.
President Roosevelt
I have never heard anything so preposterous in all my life.

Exchange in White House, between US President and Irish Minister for Co-ordination of Defensive Measures, which ended with Roosevelt pulling tablecloth from table and scattering cutlery around room in fury. Dwyer, Thomas Lyle, *Irish Neutrality and the USA 1939-1947*, Rowman and Littlefield & Gill and Macmillan, 1977, p. 113.

May 5, 1941
Ernst von Kuhren
When we approached the target at half past two we stared silently into a sea of flames such as none of us had seen before ... in Belfast there was not just a large number of conflagrations, but just one enormous conflagration which spread over the entire harbour and industrial area.

Radio reporter's broadcast on German Home Service as eye-witness to blitz on Belfast. Fisk, Robert, *In Time of War*, Paladin, 1985, p. 500.

May 5, 1941
Tommy Henderson
Will the right honourable member come with me to the hills and to Divis mountain? Will he go to the barns and sheughs throughout Northern Ireland to see the people of Belfast, some of them lying on damp ground? Will he come to Hannahstown and the Falls Road? The Catholics and Protestants are going up there mixed and they are talking to one another. They are sleeping in the same sheugh, below the same tree or in the same barn. They all say the same thing, that the Government is no good.

Speaking in Stormont as Shankill MP about flight of Belfast's population from German air raids. Fisk, Robert, *In Time of War*, Paladin, 1985, p. 508.

May 15, 1941
Dawson Bates
There are in the country [Northern Ireland] probably about 5,000 unbilletable persons.

They are unbilletable owing to personal habits which are sub-human.

As Home Affairs Minister in NI Government, in memorandum about refugees from German bombing. Fisk, Robert, *In Time of War*, Paladin, 1985, p. 507.

May 21, 1941
Robert (Bertie) Smyllie
It is damnably difficult for a newspaperman to deal with our friends in the Castle. It must be equally difficult for public representatives who have the moral courage to be critical ... Whenever I have appealed to Caesar [de Valera] – and I have done so more than once – I have found the long fellow more than anxious to be fair.

From letter, as editor of *Irish Times*, to Richard Mulcahy, of Fine Gael party, after censor deleted much of Mulcahy speech. UCD Archives, Mulcahy Papers; quoted in Fisk, Robert, *In Time of War*, Paladin, 1985, pp. 167-68.

May 24, 1941
Cardinal MacRory
That the people of all creeds and classes in Belfast have recently suffered heavily at the hands of the Germans, however regrettable it may be, does not touch the essence of the question which is that an ancient land, made one by God, was partitioned by a foreign power against the vehement protests of its people, and that conscription would now seek to compel those who still writhe under this grievous wrong to fight on the side of its perpetrators.

In statement, as leader of Catholic Church, on growing prospect of conscription in Northern Ireland. Fisk, Robert, *In Time of War*, Paladin, 1985, p. 513.

May 25, 1941
Eamon de Valera
The imposition of conscription [in Northern Ireland] in any form would provoke the bitterest resentment among Irishmen and would have the most disastrous consequences for our two peoples ... The conscription of the people of one nation by another revolts the human conscience ... The Six Counties have towards the rest of Ireland a status and a relationship which no act of parliament can change. They are part of Ireland, they have

always been part of Ireland, and their people, Catholic and Protestant, are our people.

In message to Winston Churchill after Unionist Government recommended conscription in Northern Ireland. Moynihan, Maurice, *Speeches and Statements by Eamon de Valera 1917-1973*, Gill and Macmillan, 1980, p. 459.

May 25, 1941
Frank Aiken

[Britain has] no right to occupy six counties of Ireland and then go on to commit the monstrous outrage of conscripting men into an army they allege is fighting for freedom and democracy.

Interviewed in *New York Times*, as visiting member of Irish Government to USA, over growing prospect of conscription in Northern Ireland. Dwyer, Thomas Lyle, *Irish Neutrality and the USA 1939-1947*, Rowman and Littlefield & Gill and Macmillan, 1977, p. 119.

May 25, 1941
Captain Denis Ireland

After one hundred and fifty years, Catholics and Protestants are once more united on the fundamental issue.

Speaking, as leader of Protestant Ulster Union Club, at anti-conscription rally in Belfast. *The Irish Press*, May 26, 1941.

May 27, 1941
Winston Churchill

It [conscription in Northern Ireland] would be more trouble than it was worth to enforce.

Announcing, as Prime Minister, decision to refuse NI Government's offer of conscription in face of widespread Nationalist protests. Dwyer, Thomas Lyle, *Irish Neutrality and the USA 1939-1947*, Rowman and Littlefield & Gill and Macmillan, 1977, p. 127.

June 2, 1941
Right Rev. J. B. Woodburn

I have been working 19 years in Belfast and I never saw the like of them before – wretched people, very undersized and underfed down-and-out-looking men and women. They had been bombed out of their homes . . . We have got to see that there is more talk of justice; we have got to see it enacted, and the work will have to begin immediately. If something is not done now to remedy this rank inequality there will be a revolution after the war.

In sermon as retiring Moderator of Presbyterian Assembly. Bardon, Jonathan, *Belfast*, Blackstaff, 1983, p. 248.

August 21, 1941
President Roosevelt

If factories close in Ireland and there is a great deal more suffering there, there will be less general sympathy in the United States than if it happened six months ago. People are, frankly, getting pretty fed up with my old friend Dev.

Writing to US Ambassador in Dublin on growing lack of sympathy in America for economic disadvantages suffered by Ireland because of British cut-backs on war-time exports. Dwyer, Thomas Lyle, *Irish Neutrality and the USA 1939-1947*, Rowman and Littlefield & Gill and Macmillan, 1977, p. 134.

December 1, 1941
Winston Churchill

The straits to which we are being reduced by Irish action compel a reconsideration of the subsidies . . . let me know how these subsidies could be terminated . . . observing that we are not afraid of their cutting off their food [to Britain].

In directive to British Chancellor of Exchequer. The subsidies were in fact paid by Free State. Meenan, James F., *Ireland in the War Years and After*, Gill and Macmillan, 1969, pp. 33-34.

December 8, 1941
Winston Churchill

MOST IMMEDIATE. PRIME MINISTER TO MR DE VALERA. PERSONAL, PRIVATE AND SECRET. NOW IS YOUR CHANCE. NOW OR NEVER. 'A NATION ONCE AGAIN'. AM VERY READY TO MEET YOU AT ANY TIME. ENDS.

Telegram, sent after Japanese bombing of Pearl Harbour, suggesting end of partition for Irish participation in war, which resulted in inconclusive meeting in Dublin between de Valera and Dominions Secretary Lord Cranborne. Fisk, Robert, *In Time of War*, Paladin, 1985, p. 323.

December 14, 1941
Eamon de Valera

We can only be a friendly neutral. From the moment this war began, there was for this State only one possible policy – neutrality. Our circumstances, our history, the incompleteness of our national freedom through the partition of our country, made any other policy impracticable. Any other policy would have divided our people, and for a divided nation to fling itself into this war would be to commit suicide.

Speaking in Cork after Pearl Harbour. Moynihan, Maurice, *Speeches and Statements by Eamon de Valera 1917-1973*, Gill and Macmillan, 1980, p. 462.

January, 1942
George Gavan Duffy

The question is whether Mrs Schlegel has unreasonably refused her consent [to take in Mr Gros as a lodger]. Like her husband she was Irish and a Catholic. On ascertaining that Mr Gros was a Jew, she refused consent explaining: 'Their principles are not ours; they are anti-Christian and I could not have an anti-Christian living in the house where I live.'

As justice, upholding in court right of landlady to refuse tenancy to Jewish dentist. Carroll, Joseph T., *Ireland in the War Years*, David & Charles, 1975, p. 137.

February 10, 1942
James Dillon

Whatever the sacrifice, whatever America may want from us to protect her from her enemies, she will get it for the asking.

Addressing Fine Gael Árd Fheis, as deputy leader. This departure from party support for neutrality forced Dillon's resignation from Fine Gael. Fisk, Robert, *In Time of War*, Paladin, 1985, p. 332.

August, 1942
Tom Williams

Well may England quake, Ireland's awake, Ireland's awake. After twenty years of slumber our nation will once again strike, please God, at the despoilers who have infringed the nation's liberty, freedom, and murdered her sons, her daughters, who have given us a foreign tongue ... Better would be that the heavens would open and send fire to destroy Erin, than to accept another Treaty like it [the Treaty of 1921].

In letter from Crumlin Road Prison, Belfast, before his execution on September 2, 1942, for shooting policeman in Belfast, written to Hugh McAteer, IRA Chief of Staff. Coogan, Tim Pat, *The IRA*, Fontana, 1980, pp. 234-35.

August 27, 1942
David Gray

Governments, especially in war time, do not like to be coerced, and fear that clemency exercised under pressure will be interpreted as weakness ... Ireland does not seem to appreciate what the war means, the gravity of the situation and the danger of rocking the boat at such a time.

In letter to Eamon de Valera warning against pressure on UK and Stormont Governments to reprieve six men sentenced to death in Belfast for murder of RUC man. Five were reprieved. Coogan, Tim Pat, *The IRA*, Fontana, 1980, p. 233.

September 27, 1942
Cardinal MacRory

When I read day after day in the press that this war is being fought for the rights and liberties of small nations and then think of my own corner of our country overrun by British and United States soldiers against the will of the nation, I confess I sometimes find it exceedingly hard to be patient.

In statement attacking arrival in Northern Ireland of American troops to fight in Europe. Dwyer, Thomas Lyle, *Irish Neutrality and the USA 1939-1947*, Rowman and Littlefield & Gill and Macmillan, 1977, p. 152.

October, 1942
United States Army

Éire's neutrality is a real danger to the Allied cause. There, just across the Irish Channel from embattled England, and not too far from your own billets in Ulster, the Axis nations maintain large legations and staffs. These Axis agents send out weather reports, find out by espionage what is going on in Ulster.

Statement in *Pocket Guide to Northern Ireland*, issued to each American soldier stationed there. Despite Irish Government protests it was never retracted. Dwyer, Thomas Lyle, *Irish Neutrality and the USA 1939-1947*, Rowman and Littlefield & Gill and Macmillan, 1977, pp. 155-56.

November 4, 1942
T. J. Campbell

He [Campbell] went [to take his seat at Stormont] from duty and not from desire. They [Catholics] had no representative at Westminster or Dublin. Were they to be the only community of white ones with no representation anywhere?

Explaining, as reported to *Irish News*, why he was
taking his seat as Nationalist MP at Stormont
despite Nationalist abstentionist policy. Farrell,
Michael, *Northern Ireland: The Orange State*, Pluto,
1983, p. 171.

February 25, 1943
John Maffey
[The US Ambassador in Dublin, David Gray]
had the temerity to make it plain to Irish
Nationalists that they were no longer the
darling Playboy of the Western World, and to
point out that the audience were bored.

In report, as British Ambassador, sent to Dominions
Office in London on unpopularity of US
Ambassador in Dublin. Dwyer, Thomas Lyle, *Irish
Neutrality and the USA 1939-1947*, Rowman and
Littlefield & Gill and Macmillan, 1977, p. 216.

March 17, 1943
Eamon de Valera
Let us turn aside for a moment to that ideal
Ireland that we would have. That Ireland
which we dreamed of would be the home of a
people who valued material wealth only as the
basis of right living, of a people who were
satisfied with frugal comfort and devoted their
leisure to the things of the spirit – a land whose
countryside would be bright with cosy
homesteads, whose fields and villages would
be joyous with the sounds of industry, with the
romping of sturdy children, the contests of
athletic youths and the laughter of comely
maidens, whose firesides would be forums for
the wisdom of serene old age. It would, in a
word, be the home of a people living the life
that God desires that man should live.

In St Patrick's Day radio broadcast. Moynihan,
Maurice, *Speeches and Statements by Eamon de
Valera 1917-1973*, Gill and Macmillan, 1980, p. 466.

April 24, 1943
The IRA
This cinema has been commandeered by the
Irish Republican Army for the purpose of
holding an Easter commemoration for the
dead who died for Ireland.

Message flashed on screen of Broadway cinema,
Falls Road, Belfast, after it had been taken over by
IRA. Coogan, Tim Pat, *The IRA*, Fontana, 1980,
p. 241.

July 9, 1943
Oliver J. Flanagan
How is it that we do not see any of these
[Emergency] Acts directed against the Jews
who crucified Our Saviour nineteen hundred
years ago and who are crucifying us every day
of the week? How is that we do not see them
directed against the Masonic Order? How is it
that the IRA is considered an illegal
organisation while the Masonic Order is not
considered an illegal organisation? There is
one thing that Germany did and that was to
rout the Jews out of their country. Until we
rout the Jews out of this country it does not
matter a hair's breadth what Orders you make.
Where the bees are there is the honey and
where the Jews are there is the money.

Speaking in Dáil, as Fine Gael TD. *DÉ*, Vol. 91,
Col. 569.

February 20, 1944
Dr McQuaid, Archbishop of Dublin
No Catholic may enter the Protestant
University of Trinity College without the
previous permission of the Ordinary of the
Diocese. Any Catholic who disobeys this law is
guilty of mortal sin and while he persists in
disobedience is unworthy to receive the
sacraments.

Reiterating Catholic Church ban on Trinity College
enrolment, without special permission. Whyte, J.
H., *Church & State in Modern Ireland*, Gill and
Macmillan, 1980, p. 306.

February 21, 1944
United States Government
Despite the declared desire of the Irish
Government that its neutrality should not
operate in favour of either of the belligerents,
it has in fact operated and continues to operate
in favour of the Axis powers ... Axis agents
enjoy almost unrestricted opportunity for
bringing military information of vital
importance from Great Britain and Northern
Ireland and from there transmitting it by
various routes and methods to Germany ...
We request therefore that the Irish
Government take appropriate steps for the
recall of German and Japanese representatives
in Ireland.

In formal note presented to Taoiseach Eamon de
Valera by American Ambassador David Gray.

Dwyer, Thomas Lyle, *Irish Neutrality and the USA 1939-1947*, Rowman and Littlefield & Gill and Macmillan, 1977, p. 183-84.

February 21, 1944
Eamon de Valera

As long as I am here, Éire will not grant this request [to expel German and Japanese diplomatic representatives]; we have done everything to prevent Axis espionage, going beyond what we might reasonably be expected to do, and I am satisfied that there are no leaks from this country ... the German Minister, I am satisfied, has behaved very correctly and decently and as a neutral we will not send him away.

Commenting, as Taoiseach, to US Ambassador after being handed US Government request to expel German and Japanese diplomatic representatives. Dwyer, Thomas Lyle, *Irish Neutrality and the USA 1939-1947*, Rowman and Littlefield & Gill and Macmillan, 1977, p. 185.

February 27, 1944
Eamon de Valera

It is a time of extreme danger ... No words which I can use would be strong enough to express my conviction of the necessity of maintaining [Irish] forces at their maximum strength and efficiency.

In speech at Cavan after putting army on alert in anticipation of Allied military action against Free State because of rejection of US demand for closure of German and Japanese diplomatic posts in Dublin. Dwyer, Thomas Lyle, *Irish Neutrality and the USA 1939-1947*, Rowman and Littlefield & Gill and Macmillan, 1977, p. 189.

March 14, 1944
Winston Churchill

If a catastrophe were to occur to the Allied armies which could be traced to the retention of the German and Japanese representatives in Dublin, a gulf would be opened between Britain on the one hand and Southern Ireland on the other which even generations could not bridge ... [Our policy is] to isolate Southern Ireland from the outer world during the critical period which is now approaching.

Speaking in Commons following refusal by Irish Government of American request to expel German and Japanese representatives in Dublin. Carroll, Joseph T., *Ireland in the War Years*, David & Charles, 1975, p. 150.

March 31, 1944
George Bernard Shaw

I tried hard before the United States entered the war to get de Valera to abandon neutrality and join in. I told him he would not get away with it ... but de Valera did get away with it ... Howbeit, that powerless little cabbage garden called Ireland wins in the teeth of all the mighty powers. Erin go Bragh!

The Irish Press, March 31, 1944.

April 27, 1944
Basil Brooke

Before 1939, Ulster was too often in the position of reminding Great Britain that she also was one of the great family of the British Commonwealth and Empire. During this war Great Britain and the Allies have had reason to be grateful for our insistence on remaining in the family group.

Speaking, as NI Prime Minister, in Guildhall, Derry. Fisk, Robert, *In Time of War*, Paladin, 1985, p. 474.

November 7, 1944
Dr Griffin, Catholic Archbishop of Westminster

Today Roman Catholics are being persecuted in Germany and Poland – and I need hardly mention the persecution that is going on even at the present day in Northern Ireland.

Speaking to meeting of Christians and Jews in London. Fisk, Robert, *In Time of War*, Paladin, 1985, p. 469.

May 2, 1945
Eamon de Valera

I have noted that my call on the German Minister on the announcement of Hitler's death was played up to the utmost. I expected this. I could have had a diplomatic illness but, as you know, I would scorn that sort of thing ... So long as we retained our diplomatic relations with Germany, to have failed to call upon the German representative would have been an act of unpardonable discourtesy to the German nation and to Dr Hempel himself. During the whole of the war, Dr Hempel's conduct was irreproachable. He was always friendly and invariably correct – in marked contrast with Gray [the United States

Ambassador]. I certainly was not going to add to his humiliation in the hour of defeat.

In note to Robert Brennan, Irish Ambassador to Washington, after criticism of his visit to German legation in Dublin two days after Hitler died on April 30, 1945. Longford and O'Neill, *Eamon de Valera*, Arrow, 1974, p. 411.

May 13, 1945
Winston Churchill

Owing to the action of Mr de Valera, so much at variance with the temper and instinct of thousands of southern Irishmen, who hastened to the battle-front to prove their ancient valour, the approaches which the southern Irish ports and airfields could so easily have guarded were closed by the hostile aircraft and U-boats.

This was indeed a deadly moment in our life, and if it had not been for the loyalty and friendship of Northern Ireland, we should have been forced to come to close quarters with Mr de Valera, or perish forever from the earth. However, with a restraint and poise, to which I venture to say, history will find few parallels, His Majesty's Government never laid a violent hand upon them, though at times it would have been quite easy and quite natural, and we left the de Valera Government to frolic with the German and later with the Japanese representatives to their heart's content.

From victory broadcast, as British Prime Minister, at end of war. *Eamon de Valera*, The Irish Times Ltd., 1976, p. 110.

May 16, 1945
Eamon de Valera

It is, indeed, hard for the strong to be just to the weak, but acting justly always has its rewards. By resisting his temptation in this instance, Mr Churchill, instead of adding another horrid chapter to the already blood-stained record of the relations between England and this country, has advanced the cause of international morality an important step ...

Mr Churchill is proud of Britain's stand alone, after France had fallen and before America entered the war. Could he not find in his heart the generosity to acknowledge that there is a small nation that stood alone, not for one year or two, but for several hundred years against aggression; that endured spoliations, famines, massacres in endless succession; that was clubbed many times into insensibility, but that each time, on returning consciousness, took up the fight anew; a small nation that could never be got to accept defeat and has never surrendered her soul?

From radio broadcast, replying, as Taoiseach, to attack on Irish neutrality in victory broadcast of British Prime Minister Winston Churchill. Moynihan, Maurice, *Speeches and Statements by Eamon de Valera 1917-1973*, Gill and Macmillan, 1980, pp. 475-76.

May 21, 1945
John Maffey

There was balm for every Irishman in this, and with the Irish people today, Mr de Valera is as great a hero as is the Irishman who scores the winning try at Twickenham ... This temperamental country needs quiet treatment and a patient, consistent policy. But how are you to control Ministerial incursions into your china shop? Phrases make history here.

Report of British Ambassador in Dublin on outcome of Churchill-de Valera radio exchanges. Fisk, Robert, *In Time of War*, Paladin, 1985, pp. 540-41.

July 17, 1945
Eamon de Valera

Deputy Dillon ... asked was this State a republic ... When I told him that we were a republic his surprise was, as a friend remarked, like that of Molière's Bourgeois Gentilhomme when he learned that he had been speaking prose all his life ... look up any standard text on political theory, look up any standard book of reference and get from any of them any definition of a republic or any description of what a republic is and judge whether our State does not possess every characteristic mark by which a republic can be distinguished or recognised ... We are an independent republic, associated as a matter of our external policy with the States of the British Commonwealth.

As Taoiseach in Dáil in 'Dictionary Republic' speech claiming Free State had become Republic in everything but name. Chubb, Basil, *Source Book of Irish Government*, Institute of Public Administration, 1983, pp. 16-17.

1947
Dr Walsh, Bishop of Tuam, Dr Dignan, Bishop of Clonfert and Dr Browne, Bishop of Galway

It has been contended ... that Catholic farmers ought to admit over their lands whatever person the hunt committee may select as Master. Such a contention shows gross ignorance or contempt for the religious convictions and feelings of a Catholic people.

Joint statement endorsing refusal by farmers to allow Galway Blazers to hunt over their lands because hunt master was divorced Protestant. Whyte, J. H., *Church & State in Modern Ireland*, Gill and Macmillan, 1980, p. 172.

September 27, 1947
Harry Midgley

I have been greatly perturbed by the repeated attacks being made on Ulster's constitutional position ... I have now reached the conclusion that there is no room for division among those ... who are anxious to preserve the constitutional life and spiritual heritage of our people.

In letter written as leader of Commonwealth Labour Party of Northern Ireland to NI Prime Minister applying to join Unionist Party. Farrell, Michael, *Northern Ireland: The Orange State*, Pluto, 1983, p. 192.

November 17, 1947
Andrei Vishinsky

It is impossible to recognise as peace-loving such states as Ireland and Portugal which supported fascism in its struggle against peace and peace-loving peoples and against the United Nations, and which are even now maintaining particularly friendly relations with Franco Spain.

As Soviet Foreign Minister, giving reasons to United Nations in New York for Soviet veto on Ireland joining UN. *The Irish Times*, January 3, 1981.

April 13, 1948
E. C. Ferguson

The Nationalist majority in the county Fermanagh ... stands at 3,604 ... I would ask the meeting to authorise their executive to adopt whatever plans and take whatever steps, however drastic, to wipe out this Nationalist majority.

As Unionist MP, addressing annual Unionist convention in Enniskillen. Farrell, Michael, *Northern Ireland: The Orange State*, Pluto, 1983, pp. 88-89.

July 20, 1948
Sean MacBride

Our sympathies lie clearly with Western Europe, but the continuance of Partition precludes us from taking our rightful place in the affairs of Europe.

Speaking, as Minister for External Affairs, on why Free State could not join new European military alliance which became NATO in 1949. Mansergh, Nicholas, *Ireland in the War Years and After*, Gill and Macmillan, 1969, pp. 136-37.

September 7, 1948
John A. Costello

There was no reason why Éire should not continue in association with Britain but not as a formal member of the British Commonwealth ... the External Relations Act was full of inaccuracies and infirmities and the only thing to do was to scrap it.

As Taoiseach, announcing decision to declare Republic, during press conference in Ottawa, Canada. *The Irish Times*, September 8, 1948.

September 7, 1948
John A. Costello

Partition must end before Éire will consider entering into a defence pact with the Western European countries.

Announcing, as Taoiseach, at press conference in Ottawa, Cabinet decision which kept Republic out of NATO. *The Irish Times*, September 8, 1948.

September 11, 1948
John A. Costello

As you will know, I very nearly, if not actually, 'declared' the Republic – in Ottawa above all places. I will explain when I return why I decided to state publicly that we intended to repeal the External Relations Act. It was really the article in the *Sunday Independent* [predicting this course] that decided me.

In letter from Canada, which he was visiting as Taoiseach, to Labour Party leader William Norton, then Tánaiste in inter-party Government. *The Irish Times*, January 3, 1979.

November 24, 1948
John A. Costello
This Bill will end, and end forever in a simple, clear and unequivocal way, this country's long and tragic association with the institution of the British Crown and will make it manifest beyond equivocation or subtlety that the national and international status of this country is that of an independent Republic.

... No people can be expected willingly and permanently to accept as part of their political institutions the symbol of the British Crown, when fidelity to the Catholic faith, the faith of the vast majority of our Irish people, was throughout the years regarded as disaffection and disloyalty to the British Crown, when love of country became treason to the British Crown.

As Taoiseach, introducing Bill to repeal External Relations Act and proclaim Republic. *Dáil Debates:* Vol. CXIII: Cols. 347-390.

November 25, 1948
Clement Attlee
The Government regret that Éire will ... no longer be a member of the Commonwealth. The Éire Government have, however, stated that they recognise the existence of a specially close relationship between Éire and the Commonwealth countries and desire that this relationship should be maintained ...

Accordingly, the United Kingdom Government will not regard the enactment of this legislation by Éire as placing Éire in the category of foreign countries or Éire citizens in the category of foreigners.

Speaking, as British Labour Prime Minister, in Commons on Irish Government decision to declare Republic. Chubb, Basil, *Source Book of Irish Government*, Institute of Public Administration, 1983, pp. 19-20.

April 9, 1949
Northern Ireland Labour Party
[The party pledges itself] to maintain unbroken the connection between Great Britain and Northern Ireland as a part of the Commonwealth and to ... seek the closest possible means of co-operation with the British Labour Party.

In declaration of partitionist policy, in response to South leaving Commonwealth, and to attract

Unionist votes. Moody, Martin, Byrne (Eds.), *A New History of Ireland*, Vol. VIII, Oxford, 1982, p. 432.

May 3, 1949
Clement Attlee
It is hereby declared that Northern Ireland remains part of Her Majesty's Dominions of the United Kingdom and it is hereby affirmed that in no event will Northern Ireland or any part thereof cease to be part of Her Majesty's Dominions and the United Kingdom without the consent of the Parliament of Northern Ireland.

Provision in Ireland Act introduced in Commons by Attlee, as Prime Minister, in response to declaration of Republic by Government in Dublin. Coogan, Tim Pat, *The IRA*, Fontana, 1980, p. 324.

May 9, 1949
John A. Costello
[We] protest against the introduction by the British Parliament of legislation purporting to endorse and continue the existing partition of Ireland ... and the present occupation of our Six North Eastern Counties.

As Taoiseach, replying in Dáil to introduction in Commons by Attlee of Ireland Act affirming British support for partition. Coogan, Tim Pat, *The IRA*, Fontana, 1980, p. 324.

1950
Eddie McAteer
The mighty spirit of the late Mahatma Gandhi pointed a ... road [of] non-co-operation [and] non-violence ... Increased cost and difficulty in administration here will quickly make itself felt in Whitehall. Should it happen that you have the leisure to go to the department, act stupid, demand explanations, object, anything at all that will clog the departmental machinery.

From pamphlet *Irish Action* published by McAteer as vice chairman of Anti-Partition League in response to police action during riots in Derry. Farrell, Michael, *Northern Ireland: The Orange State*, Pluto, 1980, pp. 203-4.

June 20, 1950
Catholic Hierarchy
The opening of public houses, by reason of the drunkenness and other sins and temporal evils to which it is calculated to lead, would be

particularly repugnant to the sanctity of the Lord's Day. Accordingly, where there has been no existing and longstanding custom, to open public houses on Sundays even for a few hours would be a serious violation of this ecclesiastical law [Canon Law 1248] ... it would be sinful to agitate for their opening.

In statement successfully opposing proposed legislation to allow pubs to open on Sunday. Whyte, J. H., *Church & State in Modern Ireland,* Gill and Macmillan, 1980, p. 178.

October 10, 1950
Catholic Hierarchy

The powers taken by the State in the proposed Mother and Child Health Service are in direct opposition to the rights of the family and of the individual and are liable to very great abuse ... If adopted in law, they would constitute a ready-made instrument for future totalitarian aggression ... The Bishops desire that your Government should give careful consideration to the dangers inherent.

Letter to Taoiseach John A. Costello after consultation about proposed free health scheme. *The Irish Times,* April 12, 1951.

February 13, 1951
Charles Casey

How can any Catholic logically demand or permit any legislation which would endanger the soul of a single child? ... Let me take the case of a Catholic girl who takes this step [legal adoption] and hands her child over to kindly people not of her faith. When that mother has rehabilitated herself and become more normal, she will know that she has done wrong according to the belief of her faith, yet she is powerless to bring her child up in what she knows is the true faith ... legislation has denied her the opportunity to discharge the rights and duties of the natural mother imposed on her by the law of God.

In statement, as Attorney General, defending refusal of Government to introduce legal adoption. Whyte, J. H., *Church & State in Modern Ireland,* Gill and Macmillan, 1980, pp. 189-90.

April 5, 1951
Catholic Hierarchy

The Hierarchy cannot approve of any scheme which, in its general tendency, must foster undue control by the State in a sphere so delicate and so intimately concerned with morals as that which deals with gynaecology or obstetrics and with the relations between doctor and patient. Neither can the bishops approve of any scheme which must have for practical result the undue lessening of the proper initiative of individuals and associations and the undermining of self reliance.

From private letter to Taoiseach John A. Costello on Health Minister Noel Browne's proposed Mother and Child health scheme. Whyte, J. H., *Church & State in Modern Ireland,* Gill and Macmillan, 1980, p. 446.

April 9, 1951
John A. Costello

That decision [to withdraw the Mother and Child health scheme] expresses the complete willingness of the Government to defer to the judgement so given by the Hierarchy.

In letter, as Taoiseach, notifying bishops that Government would drop Health Minister Noel Browne's scheme for limited health service in view of Hierarchy's opinion that it was opposed to Catholic social teaching. Whyte, J. H., *Church & State on Modern Ireland,* Gill and Macmillan, 1980, p. 232.

April 10, 1951
Sean MacBride

The creation of a situation where it is made to appear that a conflict exists between the spiritual and temporal authorities is always undesirable; in the case of Ireland, it is highly damaging to the cause of national unity ... I feel that I owe to the nation, to the Government, and to the Clann [na Poblachta], the duty of ensuring that any minister for whom I am responsible discharges his duties with that high standard of conduct which is required in Government.

In letter, as leader of Clann na Poblachta (one of parties in Coalition Government), requesting resignation of party colleague and Health Minister, Noel Browne, from Government following his conflict with Catholic Hierarchy over proposed Mother and Child health scheme. *The Irish Times,* April 12, 1951.

April 10, 1951
Noel Browne

Your letter is a model of the two-faced hypocrisy and humbug so characteristic of you. Your references to a conflict between the spiritual and temporal authorities will occasion a smile among the many people who remember the earlier version of your kaleidoscopic self. On the other side is your envenomed attack on me at the executive meeting last Sunday because ... I had allowed myself to be photographed with the Protestant Archbishop of Dublin. This puerile bigotry is scarcely calculated to assist the cause of national reunification which you profess to have at heart.

In reply to letter of same date from Sean MacBride requesting his resignation from Government. *The Irish Times,* April 12, 1951.

April 12, 1951
The Irish Times
The most serious revelation, however, is that the Roman Catholic Church would seem to be the effective government of this country.

In editorial on disclosure of role of Hierarchy in opposing Mother and Child health scheme. *The Irish Times,* April 12, 1951.

April 12, 1951
John A. Costello
I as a Catholic obey my Church authorities and will continue to do so, in spite of *The Irish Times* or anything else. Deputy Dr Browne was not competent or capable to fulfil the duties of the Department of Health. He was incapable of negotiation; he was obstinate at times and vacillating at other times.

As Taoiseach, in Dáil debate following Noel Browne's resignation. Whyte, J. H., *Church & State in Modern Ireland,* Gill and Macmillan, 1980, p. 232.

April 12, 1951
Noel Browne
I as a Catholic accept unequivocally and unreservedly the views of the Hierarchy on this matter.

In resignation speech to Dáil, emphasising his complaint was because of treatment by Government colleagues. Whyte, J. H., *Church & State in Modern Ireland,* Gill and Macmillan, 1980, p. 233.

April 12, 1951
Sean MacBride
For the last year, in my view, the Minister for Health has not been normal.

Speaking in Dáil, as leader of Clann na Poblachta, after requesting resignation of party colleague, Noel Browne, from Government. Whyte, J. H., *Church & State in Modern Ireland,* Gill and Macmillan, 1980, p. 229.

April 12, 1951
Eamon de Valera
I think we have heard enough.

Only contribution, as Fianna Fáil leader in Opposition, to Dáil debate on controversy over Mother and Child scheme. Murphy, John A., in *De Valera and His Times,* Cork University Press, 1983, p. 8.

April 17, 1951
Dr Farren, Bishop of Derry
The power and the spirit behind practically all social legislation at the present time is taken from the worst principles of both Nazi and Russian materialism.

Defending Hierarchy's opposition to provision of limited health service in Noel Browne's Mother and Child health scheme. *The Irish Press,* April 18, 1951.

April 30, 1951
Dr Browne, Bishop of Galway
The establishment of this scheme [Mother and Child] would soon eliminate the free medical practitioner and create a monopoly of socialised medical services under complete State control – a terrible weapon to put into the hands of men who might not have received instruction in Catholic principles, or who might repudiate such principles.

Outlining reasons for Hierarchy's opposition to Mother and Child health scheme. *The Irish Times,* May 1, 1951.

June 1, 1951
Seán Ó Faoláin
In practice, the Hierarchy does much more than 'comment' or 'advise'. It commands ... when the Catholic Church, through its representatives, speaks, he[the Taoiseach] realises, and the Roman Catholic public realises, that if they disobey, they may draw on themselves this weapon whose touch means death.

Commenting, as Irish author, on Government decision to drop Mother and Child health scheme after opposition expressed by Catholic Hierarchy. O'Faolain, Sean, 'The Dáil and the Bishops', in *The Bell,* Vol. XVII 3, June 1951.

November 21, 1953
Liam Kelly
I do not believe in constitutional methods. I believe in the use of force; the more the better, the sooner the better.

Speaking as successful abstentionist candidate for mid-Tyrone in Stormont election, at time when he was also leader of militant Republican group, Saor Uladh ('Free Ulster'). Farrell, Michael, *Northern Ireland: The Orange State,* Pluto, 1983, p. 205.

April 16, 1954
G. B. Hanna
Were I to ban a Republican ... procession or meeting in one part of the country and, not only to permit an Orange procession in a Nationalist district, but to provide police protection for that procession, I would be holding up our entire administration up (*sic*) to ridicule and contempt.

Announcing, as Stormont Minister of Home Affairs, ban on Orange parade along Longstone Road, Co. Down, which he lifted the following year allowing parade led by Brian Faulkner. Farrell, Michael, *Northern Ireland: The Orange State,* Pluto, 1983, p. 208.

October, 1954
The IRA
Volunteers are strictly forbidden to take any militant action against 26-County Forces under any circumstances whatsoever.

From Standing Order Number Eight, incorporated into IRA's 'General Army Orders' after raid on Omagh barracks, and remaining nominally in force ever since. Coogan, Tim Pat, *The IRA,* Fontana, 1980, p. 328.

April 12, 1955
Dr Lucey, Bishop of Cork and Ross
When the bishops in this country took a stand not so long ago on the health bill ... their position was that they were the final arbiters of right and wrong, even in political matters.

Commenting on role of Hierarchy in forcing Government to abandon Mother and Child health scheme in 1951. *The Irish Times,* April 13, 1955.

October 14, 1955
Rev. Fr O'Reagan
[Dr McQuaid, Archbishop of Dublin] had heard with regret that the match [between Republic and Yugoslavia] had been arranged ... it was regretted that the [Football]

Association [of Ireland] had not had the courtesy to obtain the views of the Archbishop on the proposed game as it had done when the Yugoslavs had wanted a game in Dublin in 1952. He hoped that even at this stage, the Association might reconsider its decision and abandon the match.

In telephone call, as spokesman for Dr McQuaid, to Football Association of Ireland, in unsuccessful attempt to have Ireland-Yugoslavia match in Dublin called off because Yugoslavia was a communist country. *The Irish Times,* October 17, 1955.

November 27, 1955
Thomas Leonard
There is no name [on the death certificate]. I could not say if the man was married or single, what occupation he had. In the age column I wrote 'about 30', that was all.

Describing how, as coroner for North East Monaghan, he had signed death certificate for Connie Green, killed during raid on Rosslea RUC barracks across Border in Co. Fermanagh. Green was buried secretly, by agreement with members of Government. Coogan, Tim Pat, *The IRA,* Fontana, 1980, p. 364.

November 30, 1955
Basil Brooke (Lord Brookeborough)
It is unbelievable that any civilised country which has outlawed the IRA is yet afraid to take action which any civilised country would take to prevent blackguards and scoundrels coming here to commit murder and create antagonism among the people.

Speaking at Stormont, as NI Prime Minister, after cross-border raid on Rosslea RUC barracks. Coogan, Tim Pat, *The IRA,* Fontana, 1980, p. 365.

November 30, 1955
John A. Costello
We are bound to ensure that unlawful activities of a military character shall cease, and we are resolved to use if necessary all the powers and forces at our disposal ... there can be no question of our handing over, either to the British or to the Six-County authorities, persons whom they may accuse of armed political activities in Britain or in the Six Counties.

Speaking, as Taoiseach, in Dáil after cross-border raid on Rosslea RUC barracks. Coogan, Tim Pat, *The IRA,* Fontana, 1980, p. 367.

January 18, 1956
Catholic Hierarchy

We declare that it is a mortal sin for a Catholic to become or remain a member of an organisation or society, which arrogates to itself the right to bear arms or to use them against its own or another state; that it is also sinful for a Catholic to co-operate with, express approval of, or otherwise assist any such organisation or society, and that if the co-operation or assistance be notable, the sin committed is mortal.

Statement issued as IRA prepared for Border campaign. Whyte, J. H., *Church & State in Modern Ireland,* Gill and Macmillan, 1980, p. 321.

July 7, 1956
Liam Cosgrave

The Republic was not and could not be neutral in the issue between communism and democracy, usually described as the struggle between East and West ... if the unnatural political division of our island were removed ... the main obstacle to fuller collaboration with the West would also be removed.

Speaking, as Minister for External Affairs, at Queen's University, Belfast, shortly before Republic took its place in United Nations. *The Irish Times,* July 9, 1956.

December 17, 1956
Nat Minford

We Protestants are running this country, and are going to run it. We want to live in a country where peace will prevail. If we find that these attacks are going to continue, then we Protestants ourselves will have to determine what the future will be.

Speaking at Stormont from Unionist benches about IRA campaign. Coogan, Tim Pat, *The IRA,* Fontana, 1980, p. 389.

December 19, 1956
Anthony Eden

In the Ireland Act 1949 the Parliament of Westminster declared Northern Ireland to be an integral part of the United Kingdom. This is a declaration which all parties in this House are pledged to support. The safety of Northern Ireland and its inhabitants is therefore a direct responsibility of Her Majesty's Government which they will, of course, discharge.

Speaking in Commons, as Prime Minister, after IRA launched Border campaign. *HC Debates:* Vol. 562: Col. 1270.

December 29, 1956
Pravda

The Irish patriots cannot agree with Britain transforming the Six Counties into one of its main military bases in the Atlantic pact.

Explaining IRA Border campaign to readers. Coogan, Tim Pat, *The IRA,* Fontana, 1980, p. 387.

January 6, 1957
John A. Costello

Neither appeals for sympathy with young men who had put themselves in danger, nor natural sorrow for tragic deaths, should be allowed to betray anybody into an appearance of encouraging these actions ... Three young Irishmen had been killed ... two of them were from the Republic and the third was a [Northern Ireland] policeman.

As Taoiseach, speaking on radio after death of Fergal O'Hanlon and Sean South in IRA attack on Brookeborough RUC barracks and large turn-out at their funerals in Republic. *The Irish Times,* January 7, 1957.

January 6, 1957
Eamon de Valera

I am entirely in agreement with what the Taoiseach said. The problem of Partition cannot be solved by force ... To allow any military body not subject to Dáil Éireann to be enrolled, organised and equipped is to pave the way to anarchy and ruin.

Responding, as Fianna Fáil leader, to plea from Taoiseach John A. Costello to Irish people not to sympathise with IRA after death of Sean South and Fergal O'Hanlon in IRA raid on Brookeborough RUC barracks. *The Irish Times,* January 7, 1957.

January 6, 1957
Brian Maginnis

I hope that Mr Costello's well-reviewed, courageous and statesman-like speech, particularly those parts which asked for discouragement of any signs of sympathy with men of violence, will have good effect on everybody.

As NI Attorney General, reacting to radio broadcast by Taoiseach John A. Costello following IRA attack on RUC barracks in Brookeborough. *The Irish Times,* January 7, 1957.

January 23, 1957
Judge Michael Lennon
This proclamation does not end with the words 'God save the King' ... I remember proclamations of this kind made in relation to myself [before 1922] and they always ended with the words 'God save the King'.

Ironic remark – which cost him his office – to prosecutor about proclamation bringing in Offences Against the State Act, during trial of alleged IRA members in Dublin. Coogan, Tim Pat, *The IRA*, Fontana, 1980, p. 381.

February 15, 1957
Harry Midgley
All the minority are traitors and have always been traitors to the Government of Northern Ireland.

Speaking in Portadown Orange Hall as NI Minister of Education. Farrell, Michael, *Northern Ireland: The Orange State*, Pluto, 1983, p. 221.

June 30, 1957
Dr Browne, Bishop of Galway
There seems to be a concerted campaign to entice or kidnap Catholic children and deprive them of their faith ... [the boycott is] a peaceful and moderate protest.

Preaching, at Wexford congress, on boycott of Protestant businesses in Fethard-on-Sea, Co. Wexford, after local Protestant woman left her Catholic husband following disagreement over education of their children whom she took to Belfast. Whyte, J. H., *Church & State in Modern Ireland*, Gill and Macmillan, 1980, p. 323.

July 4, 1957
Eamon de Valera
I can only say, from what has appeared in public, that I regard this boycott as ill-conceived, ill-considered and futile for the achievement of the purpose for which it seems to have been intended; that I regard it as unjust and cruel to confound the innocent with the guilty; that I repudiate any suggestion that this boycott is typical of the attitude or conduct of our people; that I am convinced that ninety per cent of them look on this matter as I do; and that I beg of all who have regard for the fair name, good repute and well-being of our nation to use their influence to bring this deplorable affair to a speedy end.

I would like to appeal also to any who might have influence with the absent wife to urge on her to respect her troth and her promise and to return with her children to her husband and her home.

Speaking, as Taoiseach, in Dáil about boycott of Protestant businesses in Fethard-on-Sea after Protestant woman left her Catholic husband and took her children to Belfast. (The woman returned home some months later.) Moynihan, Maurice, *Speeches and Statements by Eamon de Valera 1917-1973*, Gill and Macmillan, 1980, p. 580.

March 6, 1959
Harold Macmillan
Your Ministers have told me of their grave concern over the action of the Government of the Irish Republic in releasing the IRA terrorists they had interned in the Curragh. I may say at once that I fully share that concern. Indeed I have already instructed the British Ambassador in Dublin [Alexander Clutterbuck] to express to the Irish Republican Government the disquiet of Her Majesty's Government at these releases.

Speaking, as British Prime Minister, at annual luncheon of Northern Ireland Unionist Council in Belfast. Moynihan, Maurice, *Speeches and Statements by Eamon de Valera 1917-1973*, Gill and Macmillan, 1980, p. 595.

March 6, 1959
Eamon de Valera
I regard Mr Macmillan's statement as ill-advised and uncalled-for ... the use or non-use of detention ... is a matter for the Irish Government alone.

In statement, as Taoiseach, responding to speech of British Prime Minister Harold Macmillan in Belfast, criticising de Valera's release of internees from Curragh. Moynihan, Maurice, *Speeches and Statements by Eamon de Valera 1917-1973*, Gill and Macmillan, 1980, p. 595.

March 7, 1959
Harold Macmillan
I did not wish to intrude in the internal affairs of the Republic. [I supported partition in Ireland but rejected it as a solution in Cyprus because] there is no Greek or Turkish area in Cyprus. The villages are intermingled. It would have been quite impossible to make territorial partition work there without mass or forced emigration.

Responding to questions at press conference before leaving Belfast where he had made speech criticising Republic. Moynihan, Maurice, *Speeches and Statements by Eamon de Valera 1917-1973*, Gill and Macmillan, 1980, p. 595.

March 8, 1959
Eamon de Valera
The British Prime Minister ... explained why partition would not work in Cyprus ... It is necessary therefore to point out ... that in about one half of the area of the Six Counties there is a nationalist majority ... If the considerations which weighed with Mr Macmillan in arriving at the decision not to partition Cyprus would only be taken into account in the case of Ireland, a satisfactory solution could be arrived at ... Instead Mr Macmillan foolishly tells us that partition must stay.

Speaking at Fianna Fáil convention in Ennis in response to remarks made by Macmillan in Belfast. Moynihan, Maurice, *Speeches and Statements by Eamon de Valera 1917-1973*, Gill and Macmillan, 1980, pp. 596-97.

April 30, 1959
The BBC
Strong feelings were aroused in Northern Ireland by the political statements made by Miss Siobhan McKenna ... the Corporation has no wish to add to these feelings.

On cancellation of second part of programme 'Small World' after actress had expressed sympathy for IRA and described Harold Macmillan as 'impertinent' for criticism of de Valera. *The Irish Times*, May 1, 1959.

November 10, 1959
George Clark
It is difficult to see how a Catholic with the vast differences in our religious outlook, could be either acceptable within the Unionist Party as a member, or for that matter, bring himself unconditionally to support its ideals.

Replying, as Orange Grand Master and Unionist senator, to suggestion from Northern Ireland industrialist, Clarence Graham, that Catholics be permitted to join Unionist Party. Farrell, Michael, *Northern Ireland: The Orange State*, Pluto, 1983, p. 223.

November 12, 1959
Sean Lemass
The agreement ... provides that the thirty-nine Lane pictures will be divided into two groups which will be lent in turn [by trustees of National Gallery, London], for public exhibition in Dublin, for successive periods of five years, over a period of twenty years.

As Taoiseach, announcing compromise over disputed Lane pictures between Commissioners of Public Works in Ireland and trustees of National Gallery in London. *The Irish Times*, November 13, 1959.

July 12, 1960
Brian Faulkner
When we in the Unionist Party defend ourselves against the political attacks of the Nationalist Party, we are perforce defending ourselves against the Roman Catholic hierarchy ... until the hierarchy renounces its influence in politics, the Orange Order cannot renounce its influence in the Unionist Party.

Speaking, as Unionist politician, at Twelfth of July demonstration at Comber, Co. Down. Boyd, Andrew, *Brian Faulkner and the Crisis in Ulster Unionism*, Anvil, 1972, pp. 35-36.

August 3, 1961
Basil Brooke (Lord Brookeborough)
Ulster has only room for one party ... recent economic issues should not divide Protestants.

As NI Prime Minister, speaking against Protestant support for the NI Labour Party because of unemployment. Arthur, Paul, *Government & Politics of Northern Ireland*, Longman, 1984, p. 78.

December 31, 1961
Eamon de Valera
It is you, the people, who will ultimately determine what the programmes are to be. If you insist on having presented to you the good, the true and the beautiful you will get this, and I for one will find it hard to believe, for example, that a person who views the grandeurs of the heavens, or the wonders of this marvellous, mysterious world ... will not find more pleasure in that than in viewing some squalid, domestic brawl or a street quarrel.

In televised address on occasion of inauguration of RTE television, speaking as President of Republic. *The Irish Times*, January 1, 1962.

December 31, 1961
Eamonn Andrews
Fortunately [RTE television] had come into being under a Minister [M. J. Hilliard] who refused to be stampeded [into] the final betrayal of Kathleen Ni Houlihan by depriving her of the classic 36-24-36, and containing her Celtic charms in a 14 inch or a 17 inch – or for the landed gentry – in a 24-inch glass[screen] so that she was in danger of becoming Cathode Ni Houlihan.

As Chairman of RTE Authority, launching State's first television service at ceremony in Shelbourne Hotel, Dublin. *The Irish Times*, January 1, 1962.

January 14, 1962
Sean Lemass
In this situation [EEC membership] partition will become so obviously an anachronism that all sensible people will want to bring it to an end.

As Taoiseach, on renewed negotiations for EEC membership for UK and Ireland. *The Irish Times*, June 15, 1962.

February 26, 1962
Irish Republican Publicity Bureau
The leadership of the Resistance Movement has ordered the termination of 'The Campaign of Resistance to British Occupation' ... Foremost among the factors responsible for the ending of the campaign has been the attitude of the general public whose minds have been deliberately distracted from the supreme issue facing Irish people – the unity and freedom of Ireland.

Statement issued to press to announce end of IRA campaign. Coogan, Tim Pat, *The IRA*, Fontana, 1980, p. 418.

June 27, 1963
President Kennedy
No country in the world, in the history of the world, has endured the haemorrhage which this island endured over a period of a few years for so many of its sons and daughters. These sons and daughters are scattered throughout the world and they give this small island a family of million upon millions ... in a sense, all of them who visit Ireland come home.

On arrival at Dublin airport for three-day visit to Republic. *The Irish Times*, June 28, 1963.

June 27, 1963
Eamon de Valera
We welcome you ... as the representative of that great country in which our people sought refuge when driven by the tyrant's laws from their motherland, sought refuge and found themselves and their dependants a home in which they prospered, won renown and gave distinguished service in return.

Welcoming, as President of Ireland, US President John F. Kennedy on three-day visit to Republic. *The Irish Times*, June 28, 1963.

June 28, 1963
President Kennedy
If this nation had achieved its present political and economic stature a century or so ago, my great-grandfather might never have left New Ross, and I might, if fortunate, be sitting down there with you. Of course, if your own President had never left Brooklyn, he might be standing up here instead of me.

Addressing joint session of Oireachtas during visit to Ireland. *The Irish Times*, June 29, 1963.

October 18, 1963
Terence O'Neill
Let there be an end to public statements either in Ireland or abroad about 'ultimate unification of our country', the 'evil of partition', the 'Six-County area' ... only in mutual respect ... can any real progress be made. Talk will not of itself change things. There is more to the wind of change than hot air.

Speaking, as NI Prime Minister, at Newcastle on new era in relations with Republic. *The Irish Times*, January 15, 1965.

October 20, 1963
Sean Lemass
We now see our task as reuniting the Irish people as well as reuniting the Irish territory.

In speech in Boston, responding, as Taoiseach, to call for 'mutual respect' by NI Prime Minister Terence O'Neill on October 18, 1963. *The Irish Times*, January 15, 1965.

February 14, 1964
Terence O'Neill
The people of Londonderry and the people of Ulster would do very ill to exchange their

hope of prosperity for a tattered green banner and a snatch of old song, carried away by the wind.

Speaking, as NI Prime Minister, in Derry. *The Irish Times,* January 15, 1965.

April 12, 1964
Sean Lemass

There is among them [NI people] a growing desire to change the present image of that area from a place where time never seemed to move, where old animosities are carefully fostered, and where bigotry and intolerance seem to be preserved as a way of life, to one in closer conformity to the spirit of the age.

Speaking, as Taoiseach, in Arklow. *The Irish Times,* January 15, 1965.

May 26, 1964
Fine Gael

The social and economic thought of the Fine Gael Party has been informed and moulded by the social doctrines contained in the papal encyclicals. Most people in public life will state their acceptance of the teachings contained in the papal encyclicals. But two dangers exist. Firstly, such acceptance may amount merely to lip service, and secondly, these principles may be used as an excuse for inaction.

Announcing acceptance of modified version of Declan Costello's 'just society' proposals as party policy, involving economic and social planning to achieve progress. *Fine Gael: Winning through to a Just Society,* Fine Gael Party (undated), p. 3.

September 27, 1964
Rev. Ian Paisley

If that flag is not removed tomorrow, I will organise a march and remove it myself.

In Ulster Hall address on day before RUC removed Irish tricolour from Republican Party headquarters in Divis Street, Belfast. Marrinan, Patrick, *Paisley, Man of Wrath,* Anvil, 1973, p. 82.

September 28, 1964
James Kilfedder

REMOVE TRICOLOUR IN DIVIS STREET WHICH IS AIMED TO PROVOKE AND INSULT LOYALISTS OF BELFAST.

Telegram sent by West Belfast Unionist election candidate to Brian McConnell, Minister of Home Affairs at Stormont. Police removed tricolour and

rioting followed. Bardon, Jonathan, *Belfast,* Blackstaff, 1983, p. 271.

October 8, 1964
Patrick Smith

When we are faced, as we are now, with not only a tyranny, but a dishonest incompetent one, matters become much more serious for the country. I say dishonest because of the utter disregard by the unions and their alleged leaders of the National Wage Agreement, incompetent because of the complete indiscipline of their union members and their own utter lack of leadership ... [they] could not lead their own grandmother.

On resigning as Fianna Fáil Minister for Agriculture in protest at attitude of trade unions in pay bargaining, thus becoming first minister to resign voluntarily since 1924. *The Irish Times,* October 9, 1964.

January 14, 1965
Sean Lemass

I shall get into terrible trouble for this.

Terence O'Neill

No, Mr Lemass, it is I who will get into trouble for this.

Exchange between two premiers in Stormont lavatory after Lemass had arrived to visit O'Neill as first Taoiseach to come to Stormont. O'Neill, Terence, *The Autobiography of Terence O'Neill,* Rupert Hart-Davis, 1972, p. 72.

January 14, 1965
Terence O'Neill

We both share the same rivers, the same mountains, and some of the same problems, and therefore I think it is reasonable that the two premiers should meet and discuss matters of mutual interest, and that is actually what we did today.

From television interview after meeting Lemass at Stormont. Bardon, Jonathan, *Belfast,* Blackstaff, 1983, p. 273.

January 14, 1965
George Clark

One country lives beside another, and it is surely common sense that the two leaders meet to discuss ways of expanding their economies.

Reacting, as Grand Master of Orange Order, to Lemass-O'Neill meeting at Stormont. *The Irish Times,* January 15, 1965.

January 14, 1965
Sean Lemass
I think I can say a roadblock has been removed.

At interview by press after meeting O'Neill at Stormont. Bardon, Jonathan, *Belfast*, Blackstaff, 1983, p. 273.

January 15, 1965
Rev. Ian Paisley
We as Protestant Unionists are not prepared to sit idly by and have our heritage bartered by you or anyone else. We declare that we ... will act as the Ulster Volunteers acted to defend our rights.

As Protestant activist, in protest letter handed into NI Prime Minister's residence at Stormont after Lemass-O'Neill meeting. *The Irish Times*, January 16, 1965.

January 30, 1965
Sean Lemass
I can think of nothing which would work more strikingly the great changes of our times, or the strengthening of our Republican self-respect, than to see a member of the British royal family coming to Ireland on a private visit, travelling freely round Ireland, without anyone paying special attention.

Commenting, as Taoiseach, on demonstrations against visit to Republic by Princess Margaret which led to demonstrations and baton charges in Portlaoise during subsequent court hearings. *The Irish Times* ('This Week They Said'), January 30, 1965.

February 2, 1965
Nationalist Party
It is essential to enter into official Opposition at Stormont to ensure that existing parliamentary machinery operates for the common good ... our fidelity to the united Ireland ideal remains unaltered by this decision.

In statement announcing that Party would become official Opposition at Stormont in improved climate after Lemass-O'Neill meetings. *The Irish Times*, February 3, 1965.

February 2, 1965
Sinn Féin
The puppet regime [Stormont] is now accepted as permanent, and the object of a 32-

County Republic is further away than ever, if not completely abandoned.

In statement on Nationalist Party accepting role of official Opposition at Stormont. *The Irish Times*, February 3, 1965.

February 12, 1965
John Hume
Many people in Northern Ireland have not yet realised the depth of feeling and anger in this city at the Government's decision [to site second NI university at Coleraine rather than Derry]. On Thursday they will see a whole city stand outside Parliament Buildings while the [Unionist] mayor [A. W. Anderson] hands the city's claim to the Prime Minister. We are not asking for favours for Derry. We want justice.

Speaking, as chairman of University for Derry Action Committee, on NI Government's acceptance of Lockwood Committee recommendation on future of higher education. *The Irish Times*, February 13, 1965.

February 12, 1965
Eddie McAteer
The Government might be able to slap down the men of Derry. They might even be able to slap down the men of Londonderry. But they cannot slap down the united men of Derry and Londonderry.

Speaking, as Nationalist MP, on united Derry rejection of Government decision to accept recommendation of Lockwood Committee and site second NI university in Coleraine rather than Derry. *The Irish Times*, February 13, 1965.

February 18, 1965
A. W. Anderson
We are demonstrating the unanimous feeling in this city and in County Tyrone and I believe, in County Fermanagh, behind this claim [that Derry should get second NI university]. Derry has a flourishing university college. It should be developed immediately.

Speaking, as Unionist Mayor of Derry, before joint Unionist-Nationalist demonstration at Stormont, accompanied by Nationalist Party MP Eddie McAteer and John Hume. *The Irish Times, February 19, 1965.*

December 10, 1965
Dr McQuaid, Archbishop of Dublin
You may have been worried by much talk of changes to come. Allow me to reassure you. No change will worry the tranquility of your Christian lives.

Preaching in Dublin on return from Second Vatican Council in Rome. *The Irish Times,* April 17, 1973.

February 13, 1966
Dr Ryan, Bishop of Clonfert
I regret having to commence my sermon today with a vigorous protest against the contents of the Late Late Show ... I am referring to certain morally – or rather immorally – suggestive parts of the show which were completely unworthy of Irish television, unworthy of Irish producers, unworthy of Irish audiences for whom the programme was destined, unworthy of a public service which is being maintained by public monies.

Commenting on couple being asked on television the colour of nightdress worn by woman on their wedding night. McLoone, M., and MacMahon, J. *Television and Irish Society,* RTE/IFI, 1984, pp. 109-10.

February 16, 1966
Stephen Barrett
I understand that part of the entertainment offered to viewers of the Late Late Show on Saturday night consisted of questioning a husband and wife, in the absence of each other, about the colour of the nightdress worn by the lady on her honeymoon ... In many homes, such a discussion is not usually engaged in and to have it thrust into the middle of family and friends can, to some of us at all events, appear to be in utter bad taste.

As TD, in letter to *The Irish Press,* February 16, 1966.

May 21, 1966
Ulster Volunteer Force
From this day on, we declare war against the IRA and its splinter groups.

Statement signifying re-emergence after some fifty years as paramilitary force. Deutch and Magowan, *Northern Ireland, 1968-1973, A Chronology of Events,* Vol. 1, Blackstaff, 1973, p. 4.

June 7, 1966
Gerry Fitt
The only sensible thing was to have him [Rev. Ian Paisley] certified as a person insane. There could be no doubt in any person's mind that Mr Paisley was insane and an absolute lunatic.

Speaking at Stormont, as Republican Labour MP, after riots in Belfast's Cromac Square when Paisley supporters marched through Nationalist area carrying anti-Catholic slogans. *The Irish Times,* June 8, 1966.

June 15, 1966
Terence O'Neill
To those of us who remember the Thirties, the pattern is horribly familiar. The contempt for established authority; the crude and unthinking intolerance; the emphasis upon monster processions and rallies; the appeal to a perverted form of patriotism – each and every one of these things has its parallel in the rise of the Nazis to power.

In address, as NI Prime Minister, on Paisleyism to Stormont Parliament. Marrinan, Patrick, *Paisley, Man of Wrath,* Anvil, 1973, p. 109.

June 26, 1966
Richard Leppington
I don't know why these men shot at us. We were doing nothing political.

Belfast Catholic, after surviving shooting by UVF of four barmen in Malvern Street, one of whom, Peter Ward, died, in first sectarian shooting of present troubles. *The Irish Times,* June 27, 1966.

June 26, 1966
Paul Rose
Following this killing there could be retaliation and a spread of violence. Action must be taken before this happens. The situation is very dangerous.

As Labour MP and Chairman of Campaign for Democracy in Ireland, on UVF attack on Catholic barmen in Malvern Street, Belfast, on June 25, 1966. *The Irish Times,* June 27, 1966.

June 28, 1966
Hugh Arnold McLean
I am ashamed of myself. I am sorry I ever heard tell of that man Paisley or decided to follow him.

On being charged with murder of Peter Ward in shootings in Malvern Street, Belfast. Marrinan, Patrick, *Paisley, Man of Wrath,* Anvil, 1973, p. 114.

June 28, 1966
Terence O'Neill
This evil thing in our midst [Ulster Volunteer Force] ... now takes its proper place alongside the IRA in the schedule of illegal bodies.

Announcing at Stormont regulations to proscribe UVF. Deutch and Magowan, *Northern Ireland, 1968-1973, A Chronology of Events*, Vol. 1, Blackstaff, 1973, p. 5.

September 10, 1966
Donogh O'Malley
I propose from the coming school year, beginning in September of next year, to introduce a scheme whereby up to the completion of the Intermediate Certificate course, the opportunity for free post-primary education will be available to all families.

Announcing, as Education Minister, in speech in Dun Laoghaire, radical new education policy involving extensive Government expenditure, without prior consultation with Finance Minister Jack Lynch, who was out of the country. Farrell, Brian, *Sean Lemass*, Gill and Macmillan, 1983, pp. 106-7.

October 12, 1966
Sean Lemass
Radio Telefís Éireann was set up by legislation as an instrument of public policy and as such is responsible to the Government.

Speaking in Dáil, as Taoiseach, in debate on complaint by Agriculture Minister Charles Haughey that RTE news was not giving his statements more weight that those from Irish Farmers' Association. McLoone, M. and MacMahon, J., *Television and Irish Society*, RTE/IFI, 1984, p. 6.

February 9, 1967
Donogh O'Malley
No one is going to stop me introducing my scheme [for free secondary education] next September. I know I am up against opposition, and serious organised opposition, but they are not going to defeat me on this.

Speaking, as Education Minister, in Seanad on scheme which he announced five months earlier without consulting Cabinet, and succeeded in implementing. *The Irish Times*, February 10, 1967.

April, 1967
George Colley
Do not be dispirited if at some time people in high places appear to have low standards.

As Fianna Fáil Minister, in comment to youth gathering in Galway, widely interpreted as veiled attack on cabinet colleague, Charles Haughey. *The Irish Times*, May 11, 1967.

April, 1967
Protestant Telegraph
These Protestant robbers and brutes, these unbelievers of our faith, will be driven like the swine they are into the sea by fire, the knife or by poison cup until we of the Catholic Faith and avowed supporters of all Sinn Féin action and principles, clear these heretics from our land.

Alleged version of Sinn Féin oath circulated among Orange lodges in Northern Ireland. Coogan, Tim Pat, *The IRA*, Fontana, 1980, p. 322.

April 13, 1967
Frank Aiken
RTE [is] a semi-state body, and if they sent a team to [North and South] Vietnam, it would not be believed that they had done this without the approval of the Government ... the television camera [is] still a very crude instrument to describe and illustrate a highly complicated political and social situation ... people wishing to report objectively should go out there and learn the language and then describe the situation. For a camera team it would [otherwise] be a conducted tour.

Speaking in Dáil, as Minister for External Affairs, on Government ban on RTE sending film crew to North Vietnam. *The Irish Times*, April 14, 1967.

April 26, 1967
Terence O'Neill
The standards governing the conduct of Ministers are, and must be, more stringent than those which cover the conduct of private people. They must stand above suspicion. They must not place themselves in the way of adverse comment.

As NI Prime Minister, dismissing Agriculture Minister Harry West for urging Government to reopen St Angelo airport near Enniskillen in which he had undeclared interest. *The Irish Times*, April 27, 1967.

April 27, 1967
Paddy Harte
Which member of this Cabinet was going to go 'West'? The lobbies and corridors of the

House were seething with rumours of corruption on housing in Dublin city, of men who had become very rich at the expense of the local authorities and the poor.

Speaking in Dáil as opposition Fine Gael TD, after sacking of Harry West from NI Government on previous day. *The Irish Times,* April 28, 1967.

May 9, 1967
Liam Cosgrave
When, as happened recently, a Government Minister considers it necessary to refer publicly to the apparently low standards of integrity of those in high places, it is clear that we are faced with something more than normal, irresponsible rumour-mongering. The only people in high places are Fianna Fáil.

Addressing Fine Gael Árd Fheis, as party leader, referring to remark in April 1967 of George Colley, Fianna Fáil Minister, about low standards in high places. *The Irish Times,* May 10, 1967.

June 23, 1968
Austin Currie
If we cannot obtain justice through normal channels, then we should do so through the only other effective means at our disposal. There was no danger of violence. Indeed, civil disobedience was a safety valve.

Speaking at Nationalist Party conference after squatting in council house in Caledon, Co. Tyrone, to highlight case of discrimination in favour of nineteen-year-old single Protestant girl. *The Irish Times,* June 24, 1968.

October 5, 1968
Gerry Fitt
Blood began to flow but as I felt all right I uttered a prayer of thanks as the blood spilled over my face and on to my shirt ... I knew that at last Northern Ireland as she really was would be seen before the world.

As Republican Labour MP, after being batoned by RUC at Civil Rights march in Derry. *The Irish Times,* November 23, 1979.

October 7, 1968
Terence O'Neill
We might get back to the situation of 1912 when a Liberal Government tried to interfere in Irish affairs [and Unionists threatened rebellion].

As NI Prime Minister, warning of consequences of British Government intervening in North after Derry riots of October 5, 1968. *The Irish Times,* October 8, 1968.

October 15, 1968
Nationalist Party
Being disappointed by Captain O'Neill's Government's failure to deal effectively with the root causes of unrest afflicting our society, we cease to function as official Opposition until such time as the Government gives further concrete evidence of a sincere desire to remedy the situation.

Announcing withdrawal as official Opposition at Stormont in protest against both slow pace of reform and police action in Derry on October 5, 1968. *The Irish Times,* October 16, 1968.

October 16, 1968
William Craig
I believe the Londonderry disorder has brought the guns a step nearer.

Speaking, as Home Affairs Minister, in Stormont debate on events of October 5, 1968, in Derry. *The Irish Times,* October 17, 1968.

October 21, 1968
Harold Wilson
I do not think anyone in this House is satisfied with what has been done and in particular the feeling that he [Terence O'Neill] is being blackmailed by thugs who are putting pressure on him is something this House cannot accept.

Speaking in Commons, as British Prime Minister, about Unionist opposition in Northern Ireland to O'Neill reform programme. Deutch and Magowan, *Northern Ireland, 1968-1973, A Chronology of Events,* Vol. 1, Blackstaff, 1973, p. 11.

October 30, 1968
Basil Brooke (Lord Brookeborough)
How can you give somebody who is your enemy a higher position in order to allow him to come to destroy you?

In interview in *The Irish Times* when asked why Catholics did not attain higher positions in Northern Ireland life. *The Irish Times,* October 30, 1968.

November 28, 1968
William Craig
We face a reality: where you have a Roman Catholic majority you have a lower standard of democracy ... you remember when Dr [Noel] Browne [Republic's Minister for Health] brought in a small measure of social reform, the Mother and Child Bill [in 1951], it was accepted by the Cabinet and Parliament but the Church authorities said this was not a matter for the people to decide because it was a matter of faith and morals ... In the Republic [democracy] is subject to an overriding authority.

Speaking, as NI Home Affairs Minister, in address at Loyalist Ulster Hall rally, later criticised for its anti-Catholic tone by NI Prime Minister Terence O'Neill. *The Irish Times*, November 29, 1968.

November 30, 1968
County Inspector Sam Sherrard
It would be quite unsafe to allow you people to go any further ... I have spared no effort in trying to keep your route clear ... I must assure you of my sincerity.

As senior RUC officer, stopping six thousand Civil Rights marchers going through Armagh city because of presence of Paisley-led counter-demonstrators. *The Irish Times*, December 2, 1968.

December 9, 1968
Terence O'Neill
Ulster stands at the crossroads ... There are, I know, today some so-called Loyalists who talk of independence from Britain – who seem to want a kind of Protestant Sinn Féin ... Rhodesia, in defying Britain, at least has an air force and an army of her own. Where are the Ulster armoured divisions and the Ulster jet planes? ... Unionism armed with justice will be a stronger cause than Unionism armed merely with strength ... What kind of Ulster do you want? A happy and respected province in good standing with the rest of the United Kingdom? Or a place continually torn apart by riots and demonstrations?

In appeal, as NI Prime Minister, on television as tension increased over Civil Rights agitation. *The Irish Times*, December 10, 1968.

December 10, 1968
William Craig
I will resist any effort by any Government in Great Britain ... to interfere with the proper jurisdiction of the Government of Northern Ireland.

In speech, as Home Affairs Minister, to Bloomfield Unionists, widely interpreted as support for NI independence. *The Irish Times*, December 11, 1968.

December 11, 1968
Terence O'Neill
I have known for some time that you [William Craig] were attracted by ideas of a UDI [Unilateral Declaration of Independence] nature ... clearly you cannot propose such views and remain in the Government.

As NI Prime Minister, in letter to William Craig, Home Affairs Minister, demanding his resignation. *The Irish Times*, December 12, 1968.

December 19, 1968
Conor Cruise O'Brien
Ireland puts the portrait of that great enemy of imperialism, James Connolly, on its postage stamps, but in practice, in the routine conduct of its foreign policy, daily betrays everything that he, Connolly, stood for. This hypocrisy does not make us respected.

In speech at Liberty Hall, Dublin, on joining Irish Labour Party. *The Irish Times*, December 20, 1968.

1969
Michael O'Morain
Left-wing political queers from Trinity College and Telefís Éireann.

Describing, as Minister for Justice, people running Labour Party. Browne, Vincent, *The Magill Book of Irish Politics*, Magill, 1981, p. 284.

January 3, 1969
Ronald Bunting
I have given a request to the loyal citizens of Ulster and, thank God, they have responded, to hinder and harry it, and I think they've hindered it and, I think you will agree, to a certain extent they have harried it.

As loyalist leader, on attacks by loyalists on People's Democracy march from Belfast to Derry, which culminated following day in ambush at Burntollet Bridge, Co. Derry. Marrinan, Patrick, *Paisley, Man of Wrath*, Anvil, 1973, p. 162.

January 4, 1969
Bernadette Devlin

It is impossible to describe the atmosphere, but it must have been like that on V-Day; the war was over and we had won; we hadn't lifted a finger but we'd won.

On arrival in Derry of People's Democracy march after ambush at Burntollet Bridge by loyalists. Devlin, Bernadette, *The Price of my Soul*, Pan, 1969, p. 143.

January 23, 1969
Brian Faulkner

I have been unhappy about the setting up of the [Cameron] Commission [into disturbances]. It is, in my opinion, a political manoeuvre and to some extent an abdication of authority, and it is misleading to the Parliamentary Party. The Government is better qualified to decide for itself what is to be done ... I have remained throughout successive crises when resignation might have further disrupted the Party. And for the same reasons I have hesitated now.

In letter of resignation as NI Minister of Commerce. Boyd, Andrew, *Brian Faulkner and the Crisis in Ulster Unionism*, Anvil, 1972, p. 60.

January 24, 1969
Terence O'Neill

I am bound to say that if, instead of passively 'remaining' you had on occasions given me that loyalty and support which a Prime Minister has the right to expect from his Deputy, some of these so-called crises might never have arisen ... If ... you took issue with me on some vital point of principle, you should surely have resigned. Alternatively you should have been to the fore in defending the administration. But you did neither; as you yourself so accurately put it you 'remained'.

As NI Prime Minister, replying to letter of resignation from Faulkner. Boyd, Andrew, *Brian Faulkner and the Crisis in Ulster Unionism*, Anvil, 1972, pp. 61-62.

January 24, 1969
Brendan Corish

I am against coalition. In the present context we shall never be accepted as equal partners ... if [the Labour Party] Conference should in future decide by democratic choice to change its mind [and agree to coalition] I will ...

accpet that decision. But the Party must appreciate that to me, this is a matter of conscience and that in such an eventuality, my continued support for socialism will be from the backbenches.

Addressing Labour Party Conference, as party leader, four years before becoming Tánaiste (deputy Taoiseach) in Coalition Government. *The Irish Times*, January 25, 1969.

January 25, 1969
Conor Cruise O'Brien

We should support the Civil Rights campaign in the North ... the [Irish] unity we desire is one of free consent among Irishmen and must be agreed to by a majority of Catholics and Protestants in the North. There is a majority there that wants unity with Britain and we must respect that, but at the same time we must reject their right to oppress the minority.

Addressing Labour Party Conference after joining party. *The Irish Times*, January 27, 1969.

January 30, 1969
Terence O'Neill

I understand there are some in my Party who have stated they want a change of leadership. What they truly seek is a change of policy. I will not back down. I will not trim my sails. I will do my duty.

Reacting to defection of twelve Unionist MPs to 'O'Neill must go' faction. Deutch and Magowan, *Northern Ireland, 1968-1973, A Chronology of Events*, Vol. 1. Blackstaff, 1973, p. 19.

March 4, 1969
Jeremy Thorpe

Northern Ireland is still at the crossroads and the sky is overcast.

Speaking in Belfast, as Liberal leader. Deutch and Magowan, *Northern Ireland, 1968-1973, A Chronology of Events*, Vol. 1. Blackstaff, 1973, p. 21.

April 24, 1969
William Craig

The people of Ulster will not surrender their Parliament without a fight. What we see today on the streets of our Province – the disorders – will look like a Sunday school picnic if Westminster tries to take our Parliament away.

Speaking at Stewartstown. Deutch and Magowan, *Northern Ireland, 1968-1973, A Chronology of Events*, Vol. 1. Blackstaff, 1973, p. 25.

April 28, 1969
Terence O'Neill

Ours is called a Christian country. We could have enriched our politics with our Christianity, but far too often we have debased our Christianity with our politics.

On resigning as Prime Minister of Northern Ireland. Marrinan, Patrick, *Paisley, Man of Wrath*, Anvil, 1973, p. 178.

May 10, 1969
Terence O'Neill

It is frightfully hard to explain to Protestants that if you give Roman Catholics a good job and a good house, they will live like Protestants, because they will see neighbours with cars and television sets. They will refuse to have eighteen children, but if a Roman Catholic is jobless and lives in a most ghastly hovel, he will rear eighteen children on National Assistance. If you treat Roman Catholics with due consideration and kindness, they will live like Protestants in spite of the authoritative nature of their Church.

In interview in *Belfast Telegraph*, after resigning as NI Prime Minister. *Belfast Telegraph*, May 10, 1969.

June 16, 1969
Roy Bradford

Ask any of the thousands of visitors now enjoying the wonderful colours of June and they will tell you that the North of Ireland is essentially a peaceful place. The tourist has just about as much chance of being molested as he has of being knocked over by a runaway camel.

Speaking in London as NI Minister of Commerce. Deutch and Magowan, *Northern Ireland, 1968-1973, A Chronology of Events*, Vol. 1, Blackstaff, 1973, p. 30.

July 8, 1969
Louis Boyle

I was due to address a Young Unionist meeting but it did not materialise because they held their meetings in the local Orange halls and were told they could not use it if I were to attend.

On resigning as Catholic from Unionist Party on grounds it could not break away from sectarian roots. *The Irish Times*, July 9, 1969.

July 12, 1969
James Chichester-Clark

We have deeply resented the ambivalent and malicious picture of the Province which has been presented to the world. What we cannot accept is the way in which the British people themselves have been misled. Do they not understand even now who are the true friends of Britain in these islands?

Speaking at Twelfth demonstration at Moneymore. *The Irish Times*, July 14, 1969.

July 13, 1969
Rev. Ian Paisley

I hate the system of Roman Catholicism, but, God being my judge, I love the poor dupes who are ground down under that system. Particularly I feel for their Catholic mothers who have to go and prostitute themselves before old bachelor priests.

In speech at Loughall, Co. Armagh. Marrinan, Patrick, *Paisley, Man of Wrath*, Anvil, 1973, p. 184.

July 14, 1969
Eddie McAteer

Unless we [Unionists and Nationalists] get together, there will be no city left for us to quarrel over.

Commenting, as Nationalist Party leader, on rioting in Derry. *The Irish Times*. July 15, 1969.

July 15, 1969
Charles Haughey

This is something completely new in this country and indeed so far as I am aware in the world. We are entering a field in which there is no precedence of experience to guide us.

Speaking in Dáil on introduction in Finance Bill of provision to exempt from income tax writers, sculptors and painters. *The Irish Times*, July 16, 1969.

July 31, 1969
Sean Bourke

I will have a few pints, and after that I will have a few more pints, and then I will have a jolly good booze-up and go for a holiday somewhere.

Speaking after Supreme Court in Dublin had refused his extradition to Britain on charge of helping Soviet spy, George Blake, escape from Wormwood Scrubs Prison, England, in October 1966. *The Irish Times,* August 1, 1969.

August 6, 1969
Harold Wolsely

I would say the question of using troops here is very remote. After all, the RUC have this situation absolutely taped. We're in full control.

Interviewed, as Belfast Commissioner of Police, after serious rioting in city. *The Irish Times,* August 7, 1969.

August 6, 1969
Oliver J. Flanagan

Too much of our land has fallen into German hands. We have no room in this country for Nazis and we are not going to entertain them here. We have no liking for Nazis and there is no room in this country for Germans.

Speaking, as Fine Gael delegate, at Agriculture Committee meeting in Dublin about purchase of Irish property by Germans. *The Irish Times,* August 7, 1969.

August 12, 1969
Vincent McDowell

We urgently request that the [Irish] Government take immediate action to have a United Nations peacekeeping force sent to Derry ... pending the arrival of a United Nations force we urge the immediate suspension of the Six-County Parliament and the partisan RUC and B Specials and their temporary replacement by joint peace-keeping patrols of Irish and British troops.

In statement, as vice-chairman of NI Civil Rights Association, after severe rioting in Derry. *The Irish Times,* August 13, 1969.

August 13, 1969
Northern Ireland Civil Rights Association

The Executive would like to make clear that at no time did it call for the intervention of Irish troops in Derry. This report was not authorised by the Executive and we expressly disassociate ourselves from this statement.

Statement issued after NICRA vice-chairman called for joint British-Irish patrols. *The Irish Times,* August 14, 1969.

August 13, 1969
Jack Lynch

It is clear now that the present situation cannot be allowed to continue. It is evident that the Stormont Government is no longer in control of the situation. Indeed the present situation is the inevitable outcome of the policies pursued for decades by successive Stormont Governments. It is clear also that the Irish Government can no longer stand* by and see innocent people injured and perhaps worse.

In television broadcast in response to continuous rioting between police and Nationalists in Derry in which, as Taoiseach, he also announced that army field hospitals would be set up near Border. (*His script said 'stand idly by' but 'idly' was omitted from teleprompter transcription.) *The Irish Times,* August 14, 1969.

August 13, 1969
James Chichester-Clark

I must hold Mr Lynch personally responsible for any worsening of feeling which these inflammatory and ill-considered remarks may cause.

Responding, as NI Prime Minister, to broadcast by Taoiseach on Derry rioting. *The Irish Times,* August 14, 1969.

August 13, 1969
Eddie McAteer

I believe there must be intervention from somewhere. I would welcome a move from the United Nations or failing that from the Irish Republic. We must have protection.

Speaking, as Nationalist Party leader, during Derry riots. *The Irish Times,* August 14, 1969.

August 14, 1969
Cardinal Conway

I cannot understand why a parade, lasting five or six hours, and accompanied by dancing women singing party songs and firing off imitation cannon was allowed to take place in a city which was tinder-dry for an explosion.

Commenting on Apprentice Boys' parade which preceded rioting in Derry. *The Irish Times,* August 15, 1969.

August 14, 1969
British Home Office
The Government of Northern Ireland has informed the United Kingdom Government that as a result of the severe and prolonged rioting in Londonderry, it has no alternative but to ask for the assistance of troops at present stationed in Northern Ireland to prevent a breakdown of law and order ... troops will be withdrawn as soon as this is accomplished.

From statement issued in London announcing use of British Army for first time since outbreak of present troubles. *The Irish Times,* August 15, 1969.

August 14, 1969
James Callaghan
By God, it is enjoyable being a minister. This is what I like doing, taking decisions, and I had to take the decision to put the troops in while I was in the plane on the way back from Cornwall.

Remarking, as Home Secretary, on how he took decision to send troops into Derry. Crossman, Richard, *The Diaries of a Cabinet Minister,* Vol. 3, Hamilton and Cape, 1977, p. 619.

August 14, 1969
James Chichester-Clark
We must, and we will, treat the Government which seeks to wound us in our darkest hour as an unfriendly and implacable Government, determined to overthrow by any means the state which enjoys the support of a majority of our electorate.

Speaking, as Prime Minister, at Stormort. Deutch and Magowan, *Northern Ireland 1968-1973, A Chronology of Events,* Vol. 1, Blackstaff, 1973, p. 39.

August 15, 1969
Frank Gogarty
For Christ's sake tell someone to intervene. Tell someone in Dublin. There will be another four hours of murder here.

Speaking, as chairman of NICRA, at 2.00 am in Belfast after rioting had claimed five lives. *The Irish Times,* August 15, 1969.

August 15, 1969
Tomás MacGiolla
Now is the time for action. The only units in a position to make any defence last night in Belfast were the units of the IRA ... The weapons are in this country. The weapons are in the FCA and in the Free State army – if you [Irish Government] are not prepared to use them will you give them to us?

Speaking at meeting at GPO in Dublin about Northern Ireland riots, before leading march to Collins barracks. *The Irish Times,* August 16, 1969.

August 16, 1969
Paddy Devlin
We need money to feed and house people, but as we stand here talking there are people being shot down. The only way we can defend ourselves is with guns and we haven't got them. We need them.

Speaking, as NI Labour representative, at meeting at GPO in Dublin about Northern Ireland riots. *The Irish Times,* August 18, 1969.

August 17, 1969
Richard Crossman
I fear that once the Catholics and Protestants get used to our presence they will hate us more than they will hate each other.

Reflecting on introduction of troops into Northern Ireland conflict. Crossman, Richard, *The Diaries of a Cabinet Minister,* Vol. 3, Hamilton and Cape, 1977, p. 620.

August 18, 1969
Lieutenant-General Sir Ian Freeland
Honeymoons can be very short-lived.

Commenting, as GOC, British Army, Northern Ireland, on reception given to troops brought in to stop rioting. *The Irish Times,* August 19, 1969.

August 18, 1969
Cathal Goulding
In response to urgent çalls for help from an almost defenceless people ... the [IRA] army council has placed all volunteers on full alert and has already sent a number of fully equipped units to the aid of their comrades in the Six Counties.

Speaking, as IRA leader, in interview in Dublin. *The Irish Times,* August 19, 1969.

August 18, 1969
Pravda
English imperialism is ready to use the powers of its bayonets to hold on to the Six Counties

of Ulster which it tore by force from their native Ireland.

Commenting on events in Northern Ireland. *The Irish Times*, August 19, 1969.

August 19, 1969
Jack Lynch
No group has any authority to speak or act for the Irish people except the lawful Government of Ireland.

Responding to statement by Cathal Goulding on August 18. *The Irish Times*, August 20, 1969.

August 19, 1969
Harold Wilson
We now want to see the B Specials phased out. Their disarming is entirely a matter for the GOC [General Freeland].

Speaking, as British Prime Minister, in television interview during break in meeting in London with Northern Ireland ministers. *The Irish Times*, August 20, 1969.

August 20, 1969
Brian Faulkner
There is absolutely no suggestion that the USC [B Specials] will be disbanded. Let me make that crystal clear.

Interview following meeting in London between British and Northern Ireland Cabinet ministers. Deutch and Magowan, *Northern Ireland, 1968-1973, A Chronology of Events*, Vol. 1, Blackstaff, 1973, p. 40.

August 20, 1969
Brian Faulkner
Mr [Harold] Wilson was *not* talking about standing them down.

Responding at press conference to question about future of B Specials and referring to Wilson's statement of August 19, 1969. *The Irish Times*, August 21, 1969.

August 20, 1969
Rev. Ian Paisley
If you want to destroy a government you pull its teeth ... Faulkner should tell the truth. The B Specials will be destroyed and our line of defence with it.

The Irish Times, August 21, 1969.

August 24, 1969
Raymond Wolseley
We are going to have another Cuba in Ireland in two months' time ... There are dark strangers from Europe in the Bogside.

Referring to foreign students, after leading delegation to Stormont as founder of Derry Chamber of Commerce. *The Irish Times*, August 25, 1969.

August 28, 1969
James Callaghan
I am not neutral. I am on the side of all people who are deprived of justice.

Addressing Bogsiders through megaphone from upstairs window of terraced house, on visit to Northern Ireland as Home Secretary. *The Irish Times*, August 29, 1969.

August 28, 1969
James Callaghan
You know, Mr Paisley, we are all the children of God.

Rev. Ian Paisley
No, we are not, Mr Callaghan. We are all the children of wrath.

Exchange between Paisley and Home Secretary at meeting in Conway Hotel, Belfast. Callaghan, James, *A House Divided*, Collins, 1973, p. 82.

September 11, 1969
Cameron Commission
Mr Gerry Fitt, MP, sought publicity for himself and his political views and must clearly have envisaged the possibility of a violent clash with the police as providing the publicity he so ardently sought. His conduct in our judgement was reckless and wholly irresponsible in a person occupying his public position.

From official report on disturbances in North, referring to Civil Rights march in Derry on October 5, 1968. *The Irish Times*, September 12, 1969.

September 19, 1969
Denis Healey
The honeymoon period [is] coming to an end, but it has not ended in divorce or a stand-up fight between husband and wife. The troops have been accepted by both communities and a happy, comfortable married life [is] under way.

On visit to Northern Ireland, as British Minister for Defence. *The Irish Times,* September 20, 1969.

September 20, 1969
Jack Lynch

It was and has been the Government's policy to seek the reunification of the country by peaceful means ... Let me make it clear too that in seeking reunification, our aim is not to extend the domination of Dublin. We have many times down the years expressed our willingness to seek a solution on federal lines.

Speaking, as Taoiseach, at Tralee. Lynch, John, *Speeches and Statements, August 1969-October 1971,* Government Information Bureau, 1971, pp. 10-11.

September 22, 1969
Cardinal Conway

I personally would not shed a tear if the relevant sub-sections of Article 44 were to disappear.

Speaking about Article in Constitution recognising special position of Catholic Church. *The Irish Times,* September 23, 1969.

October 8, 1969
Quentin Hogg

They [loyalists] were going to a religious service which was to be held in a place I hear is called the Martyrs' Memorial. They weren't in a very religious frame of mind. And they weren't obeying the law. And they weren't being very loyal. And they weren't being very peaceful.

Describing to Conservative Party conference in Brighton scenes he witnessed in Belfast when Paisley supporters staged illegal march. *The Irish Times,* October 10, 1969.

October 10, 1969
Lord Hunt

The protection of the Border and the State against armed attacks is not a role which should have to be undertaken by the police, whether they be regular or special.

A locally-recruited part-time force under the control of the GOC Northern Ireland should be raised as soon as possible for such duties as may be laid upon it. The force, together with the police volunteer reserve, should replace the Ulster Special Constabulary.

From *Hunt Report* on RUC, set up by British Government, announcing disbandment of B Specials. *The Irish Times,* October 11, 1969.

October 12, 1969
James Callaghan

Citizens of Bogside! I said I'd return. I have brought the new Inspector-General to see you ... you'll have to look after him (applause).

Introducing, as Home Secretary, new RUC Inspector-General Sir Arthur Young to crowd in Derry. *The Irish Times,* October 13, 1969.

October 19, 1969
Harry Sheehan

If the drink ban [in Belfast] was introduced to prevent drunkenness, then it was a complete flop. It had in fact the opposite effect. Publicans had to deal with more drunks than for many a long day.

Commenting, as general secretary of Belfast Licensed Vintners' Association, on Saturday-night ban on serving drink after 7.00 pm because of rioting. *The Irish Times,* October 20, 1969.

November 4, 1969
Rev. Ian Paisley

I have information that the Government is planning to have me certified by psychiatrists. This is abominable and savours of the corruption of the present regime.

The Irish Times, November 5, 1969.

November 18, 1969
Austin Currie

Some of the Opposition members showed political courage in saying that members of the minority should join the new force [UDR] ... members of the minority should join the forces [UDR and RUC reserve].

Advising Catholics to join new security forces, as Nationalist MP at Stormont, in debate on disbandment of B Specials. *The Irish Times,* November 19, 1969.

November 19, 1969
Michael O'Morain

All [the interviewees] ... were offered money ... Some of the people concerned have, I understand, criminal records ... their statements are at best valueless evidence and

... according to themselves, now nothing more than a tissue of lies.

Speaking in Dáil, as Minister for Justice, on RTE 'Seven Days' programme alleging widespread illegal money-lending in Dublin. *The Irish Times,* November 20, 1969.

November 19, 1969
RTE
Those taking part [in the programme] were treated and paid in the normal way of such programmes. There is no question of the participants being paid fees to say something impliedly desired by RTE.

In defence of money-lending programme criticised by Minister for Justice Michael O'Morain. *The Irish Times,* November 20, 1969.

November 20, 1969
Bernadette Devlin
For half a century it [Unionist Party Government] has misgoverned us, but it is on the way out. Now we are witnessing its dying convulsions. And with traditional Irish mercy, when we've got it down, we will kick it into the ground.

As MP and Civil Rights leader, concluding her autobiography. Devlin, Bernadette, *The Price of my Soul,* Pan, 1969, p. 206.

November 23, 1969
Eddie McAteer
Let those who seek to dance on our graves dance lightly lest they waken the corpse ... Be not troubled by the strange epithets which are flung at this [Nationalist] party. Green Tory appears to be a Roman Catholic who works for his living. As for some of the paper working-class leaders, I would do more work in the while of a morning than they have done in their whole embittered lives.

Speaking at Derry conference of Nationalist Party after being elected President. *The Irish Times,* November 24, 1969.

November 25, 1969
Tom O'Higgins
I viewed with astonishment a spectacle I saw with my own eyes in the High Court in Galway three weeks ago of the Minister for Justice [Michael O'Morain] ... instructing counsel and getting witnesses together.

Michael O'Morain
That is not true ... I was in the bar room talking to some of my friends ...

Dáil exchange when shadow Finance Minister charged Minister for Justice with carrying on his practice as solicitor. *The Irish Times,* November 26, 1969.

November 26, 1969
Michael O'Morain
A participant states that ... he was well-jarred when he was making his statement to RTE ... The people in this programme ... were faced with the choice of saying what they said and getting a fee, or not saying it and not getting a fee.

In further attack in Dáil on RTE money-lending programme, into which, as Minister for Justice, he then set up a sworn inquiry. *The Irish Times,* November 27, 1969.

December 8, 1969
Neil Blaney
If a situation were to arise in the Six Counties in which the people who do not succumb to the Unionist regime were under sustained and murderous assault, then, as the Taoiseach said on August 13th, we 'cannot stand idly by' ... The Fianna Fáil Party has never taken a decision to rule out the use of force if the circumstances of the Six Counties so demand.

Speaking, as Minister in Fianna Fáil Government, at Donegal dinner. *The Irish Times,* December 9, 1969.

December 9, 1969
John Hume
The border is a sectarian border. To attempt to use force to break it down would lead not only to civil war but to a religious war. There are hostages in Derry and hostages in Belfast. We are the ones who would suffer.

Commenting on speech of Neil Blaney of December 8, 1969, in Donegal in which he said Fianna Fáil had not ruled out use of force. *The Irish Times,* December 10, 1969.

December 28, 1969
IRA Provisional Army Council
In view of the decision by a majority of delegates at an unrepresentative convention of the IRA to recognise the British, Six-County and 26-County Parliaments, we, the minority

of delegates at that convention ... do hereby repudiate that compromising decision and reaffirm the fundamental Republican position ... The adoption of the compromising policy referred to is a logical outcome of an obsession in recent years with parliamentary politics with the consequent undermining of the basic military role of the Irish Republican Army. The failure to provide the maximum defence possible of our people in Belfast is ample evidence of this neglect.

In statement signalling birth of Provisional IRA. *The Irish Times*, December 29, 1985.

February 17, 1970
Samuel Stevenson

I explained to them [alleged accomplices] it was to be done on behalf of the Big Man – the Rev. Ian Paisley. When they heard that they were much more enthusiastic about doing it.

Giving evidence in court as self-confessed leader of UVF about how explosion at Dunadry in 1969 was carried out to topple NI Prime Minister O'Neill and secure release of Paisley from prison. *The Irish Times*, February 18, 1970.

February 18, 1970
Enoch Powell

Your Stormont Parliament and your special form of local administration in Northern Ireland ... are the fragments of a structure of which the remainder never came into existence ... A part of the process [to peace] could well include the closer constitutional and administrative identification of these counties with the rest of the United Kingdom.

Speaking, as Conservative MP, at Unionist meeting in Enniskillen. *The Irish Times*, February 8, 1970.

March 11, 1970
Kevin Boland

I can understand that the consortium of belted earls and their ladies and left-wing intellectuals who can afford the time to stand and contemplate in ecstasy the unparalleled man-made beauty of the two corners of Hume Street and St. Stephen's Green may well feel that the amateurish efforts of Mother Nature in the Wicklow Mountains are unworthy of their attention. Indeed it may be that the

Guinness nobility who pull the strings to which the Georgians dance may feel that as long as the private mountain amenities of Lough Tay and Lough Dan are preserved free from the intrusions of the local peasantry and the uncultured mob it is all right to permit an architect closely associated with a prominent An Taisce personality to intrude a man-made building in an unspoiled area like Glenmalure.

Speaking in Dáil, as Minister for Local Government, on planning decisions which had brought Government and An Taisce into conflict over preservation of Georgian Dublin. *The Irish Times*, March 12, 1970.

March 12, 1970
Stephen Coughlan

Limerick has always been known for its Christian outlook, its charity, but anyone in Limerick could have seen this trouble coming. The Maoist bookshop had been a deliberate provocation. The people of this city abhor the introduction of these people who are completely opposed to our Christian tradition.

Commenting, as Labour Mayor of Limerick, on gun attack on The Little Red Bookshop, Castle Parade, Limerick. *The Irish Times*, March 13, 1970.

March 25, 1970
John Hume

We have opted out of Northern Ireland for the last 50 years and we must involve ourselves now. Many people would not like to join the UDR because it was against their traditions but Catholics must move in to make it a neutral force and prevent it being taken over by the B Specials.

Speaking at Labour Party meeting in Birmingham. *The Irish Times*, March 26, 1970.

April 18, 1970
Stephen Coughlan

I remember when I was a very young boy ... the problem of the Jews in Limerick. A Father Creagh, in his courageous way, declared war on the Jews at Killooney Street which is now Wolfe Tone Street. The Jews at that time, who are now gone, were extortionists ... I remember an unfortunate woman was having a baby and they came getting their five shillings a week ... scourging her ... they took the bed from under her.

In speech, as Labour Mayor of Limerick, to Credit
Union League of Ireland which immediately voted
unanimously to disassociate itself from his remarks.
The Irish Times, April 20, 1970.

April 19, 1970
Gerald Goldberg
Gentle Jesus, meek and mild, was absent
[from Limerick] from January to July 1904,
and as far as I can see, He has never bothered
to return.

Commenting, as Cork City alderman, on remarks
about alleged Jewish extortion in Limerick in 1904
by Limerick Mayor, Stephen Coughlan. *The Irish
Times,* April 25, 1970.

April 20, 1970
Peter Berry
I have come into knowledge of matters of
national concern. I am afraid that if I follow
the normal course the information might not
reach the Government. Does my duty end
with informing my Minister or am I
responsible to the Government by whom I am
appointed?

Own account, as secretary of Department of Justice,
of his request for advice to President de Valera when
his minister, Michael O'Morain, did not pass on to
Taoiseach Jack Lynch information Berry had given
him about arms plot involving other ministers. De
Valera advised him to speak to Lynch. Walsh, Dick,
The Party, Gill and Macmillan, 1986, p. 108.

April 25, 1970
Ben Briscoe
He [Stephen Coughlan, Mayor of Limerick] is
not and never has been anti-semitic ... I wish
to express to the people of Limerick my own
deep personal sorrow for the manner in which
they have been made the scapegoat by
Alderman Goldberg, a man with a very large
chip on his shoulder.

In statement from Jewish Fianna Fáil TD for
Dublin South Central on controversy over
Coughlan's remarks about Jews and extortion in
Limerick in 1904. *The Irish Times,* April 27, 1970.

May 6, 1970
Sean Flanagan
There is no crisis in Fianna Fáil, never was,
and never will be.

Commenting, as Fianna Fáil Minister for Lands, on
rumours of Government crisis. *The Irish Times*
('This Week They Said'), May 9, 1970.

May 7, 1970
Jack Lynch
I have requested the resignations as members
of the Government of Mr Neil Blaney,
Minister for Agriculture and Fisheries, and
Mr Charles J. Haughey, Minister for Finance,
because I am satisfied that they do not
subscribe fully to Government policy in
relation to the present situation in the Six
Counties.

Statement issued by Taoiseach from Government
Information Service at 2.50 a.m. *The Irish Times,*
May 7, 1970.

May 7, 1970
Jack Lynch
I told them both that I had information which
purported to connect them with an alleged
attempt to unlawfully import arms, on the
basis of which information I felt it was my
duty to request their resignations.

Explaining in Dáil resignation from Government of
Neil Blaney and Charles Haughey. *The Irish Times,*
May 8, 1970.

May 8, 1970
Charles Haughey
I now categorically state that at no time have I
taken part in any illegal importation or
attempted importation of arms into this
country.

In statement on arms crisis, after resigning from
Government at request of Taoiseach, issued from
his home where he was recovering after fall from
horse. *The Irish Times,* May 9, 1970.

May 8, 1970
Neil Blaney
I have run no guns; I have procured no guns;
I have paid for no guns, and I have provided
money to pay for no guns.

Speaking in Dáil debate on arms crisis, after
resigning from Government at request of Taoiseach.
The Irish Times, May 9, 1970.

May 8, 1970
James Gibbons
I wish to deny emphatically any such
knowledge or consent [concerning the role of
Captain James Kelly in arms crisis]. In recent
times [I] formed the opinion that Captain

Kelly was becoming unsuitable for the type of work [intelligence] which he was employed at.

Speaking in Dáil as Minister for Defence, after disclosure that Captain Kelly of Irish Army had been attempting to procure arms for defence groups in Northern Ireland without proper legal authority. *The Irish Times*, May 9, 1970.

May 8, 1970
Captain James Kelly

Under privilege of the Dáil, Mr Gibbons has attacked me. The Army work which I did was brought to the knowledge of Mr Gibbons at any and every opportunity.

Reacting to disclaimer by Minister for Defence of any knowledge of role of Captain Kelly in arms crisis. *The Irish Times*, May 9, 1970.

May 8, 1970
Eddie McAteer

The screeching dove might well remember that Neil Blaney stood beside us in our hour of need ... and if the midnight knock comes to our door, would not the gentlest of us love the feeling of security that a pike in the thatch can give?

Reacting, as President of Nationalist Party, to arms crisis resignations. *The Irish Times*, May 9, 1970.

May 11, 1970
Sinn Féin

Republicans in many areas throughout the Six Counties were approached with offers of aid [by Irish Army intelligence officers] on two conditions, that they break with the Republican leadership in Dublin and set up a separate Republican movement for the North ... there was intense Fianna Fáil activity in the Six Counties.

Statement on arms crisis. *The Irish Times*, May 12, 1970.

May 23, 1970
Charles Haughey

Every TD from the youngest or newest in the House dreams of being Taoiseach.

In interview after resigning from Government. *The Irish Times*, May 23, 1970.

May 28, 1970
Kevin Boland

This [the arrest by gardaí of John Kelly, chairman of Belfast Citizen's Defence Committee] ... constitutes felon-setting by the leader of the Irish Government ... the greatest treachery of which an Irishman could be guilty.

Commenting on arrest on arms charges of Kelly and others, including Haughey and Blaney, with whom Boland had resigned from Government in sympathy. (Boland was expelled from Fianna Fáil Parliamentary Party for refusing to withdraw this treachery charge against Lynch and resigned from Fianna Fáil on June 22). *The Irish Times*, May 29, 1970.

June 25, 1970
Cardinal Conway

Nobody wanted to rake up old sores but ... the bishops would like to stress their belief that [although] it had been amply justified in the past ... account now had to be taken of changed circumstances.

In press conference at Maynooth announcing end of ban on Catholics attending Trinity College (where several hundred Catholics had in fact enrolled). *The Irish Times*, June 26, 1970.

July 1, 1970
Reginald Maudling

For God's sake bring me a large Scotch. What a bloody awful country.

Comment made on flight back to London after first visit to Northern Ireland as Conservative Home Secretary. The Sunday Times Insight Team, *Ulster*, Penguin, 1972, p. 213.

July 3, 1970
General Sir Ian Freeland

All civilians in this locality are to get into their houses and stay there. After the military occupy the area, anyone found in the street will be arrested.

Proclamation of curfew on Falls Road after arms search led to rioting and gun battles. *The Irish Times*, July 4, 1970.

July 6, 1970
Patrick Hillery

It would be an awful thing if we had to regard a visit by me to Northern Ireland as something to be embarrassed about. After all they [Unionists] come to the Horse Show and we say nothing about it.

At Dublin press conference after clandestine visit as Minister for Foreign Affairs to Falls Road area to see effects of arms searches by British Army. *The Irish Times,* July 7, 1970.

July 7, 1970
Alec Douglas-Home
I should have expected him [Hillery] to have consulted Her Majesty's Government in advance if he wished to make a visit. Not to have done so, particularly in present circumstances, is a serious diplomatic discourtesy.

Speaking, as Foreign Secretary, in Commons, about clandestine visit to Belfast of Minister for Foreign Affairs. *The Irish Times,* July 8, 1970.

July 11, 1970
Peadar O'Donnell
The Protestant Ascendancy ... has been overrun in part of Ireland, but a tricky, backward, largely papist middle-class took its place ... Thus we have two Irelands where only the working class has a real interest in unity. The middle-class for which Jack Lynch speaks and the feudal remnant carried over from the 17th century for which the Orange Order is a weapon and for which Chichester-Clark speaks could arrive at a careful accommodation, but the men napping stones North and South will still nap stones.

Commenting, as 1920s and 1930s left-wing Republican leader, on troubles in North. *The Irish Times,* July 11, 1970.

July 23, 1970
James Anthony Roche
How do you like that, you bastards? Now you know what it's like in Belfast.

Shouted while throwing two cannisters of CS gas into chamber of House of Commons from public gallery. *The Irish Times,* July 24, 1970.

August 9, 1970
Tom Barry
There has never been so much love-talk with British imperialism as of late, never so much sloppy talk and sloppy actions – particularly to the effect that Ireland can only be united by peaceful means.

At commemoration of Kilmichael ambush (in war of independence) which he organised and led. *The Irish Times,* August 10, 1970.

August 12, 1970
Conor Cruise O'Brien
I was spotted by a young man who asked me why I did not clap one of the speakers. I told him I did not clap because I did not agree with him. I thought for a moment perhaps I ought to have clapped but then I felt I was going to be beaten up anyway and it would have been annoying if I had been beaten up and had clapped.

Interviewed after being assaulted by crowd of forty youths while attending Apprentice Boys' Rally in Derry as observer. *The Irish Times,* August 13, 1970.

September 16, 1970
Eamonn McCann
[Responding to cry from audience, 'What about non-violence?'] Non-violence, my arse. Tell that to the imperialists. Anyone who thinks that the events in Northern Ireland are a matter of laughter is a hypocrite.

Tomás MacAnna
[To audience] All we can say is to echo the words of Byron: if we laugh at any mortal thing it is that we may not weep.

Exchange in Dublin's Peacock Theatre after McCann and others jumped on stage in protest at portrayal of Northern Ireland in premier of satirical revue *A State of Chassis* by John D. Stewart, Tomás MacAnna and Eugene Walters. *The Irish Times,* September 17, 1970.

October 5, 1970
President Nixon
I think politics are hard in our country, but in Ireland where you have to run against somebody who is Irish all the time, it must be impossible.

In speech at State luncheon in Dublin Castle, during three-day visit to Ireland. *The Irish Times,* October 6, 1970.

October 15, 1970
Roy Bradford
When it comes to asserting the integrity of this Province against attack, moderation must go hand in hand with the mailed fist.

Remark made as NI Minister of Commerce. *The Irish Times,* October 16, 1970.

October 23, 1970
Justice Henchy
There was a flat contradiction between Mr Haughey's version [of conversation] and Mr Gibbons's version, and the difference seemed to be irreconcilable.

In summing up for jury at end of arms trial. *The Irish Times,* October 24, 1970.

October 23, 1970
Charles Haughey
I think those that were responsible for this debacle [arms trial] have no alternative but to take the honourable course [to resign] that is open to them.

At press conference after being found not guilty in arms trial. *The Irish Times,* October 24, 1970.

October 24, 1970
Jack Lynch
No one can deny that there was this attempt to import arms illegally. Blaney was involved too.

As Taoiseach, at press conference in New York after hearing of not guilty verdicts in arms trial. *The Irish Times,* October 26, 1970.

November 3, 1970
Garret FitzGerald
Either Mr Gibbons or Mr Haughey had perjured themselves in court. The judge had made that clear . . . How could the House have confidence in a Government which was kept in office by the vote of Deputy Haughey, one of the possible perjurers, or Mr Gibbons?

Speaking in Dáil in confidence debate after arms trial. *The Irish Times,* November 4, 1970.

November 7, 1970
Neil Blaney
I feel a greater kinship with a Protestant from Antrim than I do with a Catholic from Cork . . . I don't necessarily mean Jack Lynch.

In interview, as Minister forced to resign by Taoiseach Jack Lynch, in *Spectator. The Irish Times,* November 7, 1970.

December 4, 1970
Jack Lynch and Des O'Malley
A secret armed conspiracy exists in the country . . . the Government have given instructions that places of detention be prepared immediately, and the Secretary General of the Council of Europe is now being informed . . . as these proposals will involve certain derogations from the European Convention on Human Rights.

In statement, as Taoiseach and Minister for Justice, to political correspondents on basis of information from gardaí. *The Irish Times,* December 5, 1970.

December 4, 1970
Eddie McAteer
Dear God, have they gone back to this? Only near insurrection could justify such destruction of civil rights.

Reacting to threat of internment in Republic. *The Irish Times,* December 5, 1970.

December 5, 1970
Gerry Collins
The Labour Party is like the Widow Macree's dog who will go a piece of the road with anyone.

As Fianna Fáil frontbencher on possibility of Labour adopting coalition policy. *The Irish Times,* December 5, 1970.

February 4, 1971
General Farrar-Hockley
Battle has been joined with the IRA. It is not war, but it is definitely battle.

Director of Land Operations, British Army, after severe rioting in Catholic areas of Belfast. *The Irish Times,* February 5, 1971.

February 4, 1971
John Taylor
We are going to shoot it out with them [IRA]. It is as simple as that.

In interview as junior Home Affairs Minister about tougher action against IRA. *The Times,* February 4, 1971.

February 20, 1971
Patrick Hillery
Fianna Fáil will survive. You can have Boland but you can't have Fianna Fáil.

Shouting to hecklers supporting former Cabinet colleague, Kevin Boland, over arms crisis divisions, at Fianna Fáil Árd Fheis. *The Irish Times,* February 22, 1971.

February 20, 1971
Jack Lynch
Where it can be shown that attitudes embodied in our laws and Constitution give offence to liberty of conscience, then we are prepared to see what can be done to harmonise our views so that, without detracting from genuine values, a new kind of Irish society may be created equally agreeable to North and South ... We wish to extend an olive branch to the North.

In speech to Fianna Fáil Árd Fheis. Lynch, John, *Speeches and Statements, August 1969–October 1971*, Government Information Bureau, 1971, p. 47.

March 9, 1971
Patrick Hillery
Legislators in a plural society should guard against considering matters solely from the standpoint of their personal religious practices.

As Minister for Foreign Affairs, signalling Fianna Fáil Government thinking in debate on legalising contraception. *The Irish Times*, March 11, 1971.

March 10, 1971
Oliver J. Flanagan
It is popular in . . . Europe to talk of sex, divorce and drugs. These things are foreign in Ireland and to Ireland and we want them kept foreign.

Speaking in Dáil in debate on possible EEC membership. *The Irish Times*, March 11, 1971.

March 11, 1971
Catholic Hierarchy
The bishops fully share the disquiet ... regarding pressures being exerted on public opinion on questions concerning the civil law on divorce, contraception and abortion ... Civil law on these matters should respect the wishes of the people who elected the legislators and the bishops confidently hope that the legislators themselves will respect this important principle.

Statement after Maynooth meeting which considered growing public pressure to legalise contraception. *The Irish Times*, March 12, 1971.

March 21, 1971
James Chichester-Clark
I have decided to resign [as Prime Minister of Northern Ireland] because I see no other way

of bringing home to all concerned the realities of the present constitutional, political and security situation ... it would be misleading the Northern Ireland community to suggest that we are faced with anything but a long haul.

In resignation statement, after it became clear he no longer had support of majority of his MPs. *The Irish Times*, March 22, 1971.

March 25, 1971
Stephen Coughlan
With regard to contraception, abortion and all those nonsensical things, the Minister should put his two feet on top of them – if we wanted a healthy nation this was what the Minister should be doing or considering – not the ridiculous suggestion that if you do not give up smoking you will die of cancer.

Speaking from Labour benches in Dáil. *The Irish Times*, March 26, 1971.

March 28, 1971
Dr McQuaid, Archbishop of Dublin
Any such contraceptive act is always wrong in itself. To speak then ... of a right to contraception on the part of an individual, be he Christian or non-Christian or atheist, or on the part of a minority or a majority, is to speak of a right that cannot even exist. [Legalising contraceptives] would be an insult to our Faith ... a curse upon our country.

In pastoral letter read in Dublin churches. Some people walked out in protest, shouting, 'Rubbish'. *The Irish Times*, March 29, 1971.

April 23, 1971
Noel Browne
Consciously or unconsciously many of them [bishops, archbishops and cardinals] have chosen their celibate lives because they find the whole subject of sex and heterosexual relationships threatening and embarrassing. Their judgement then cannot be trusted on these issues.

In speech at Tramore, later disowned by his colleagues in Labour Parliamentary Party. *The Irish Times*, April 24, 1971.

May 1, 1971
Dr Lucey, Bishop of Cork and Ross
The people before us didn't rat on their children for the sake of Protestant schooling,

land or soup. Surely we won't for the sake of easy sex.

In sermon on contraception controversy. *The Irish Times* ('This Week They Said'), May 1, 1971.

May 15, 1971
Rev. Fr Denis Faul
Celibacy is now being quoted by some doctors as a disease, and I am now waiting for some TDs or maybe senators to propose a law against it.

Responding to remarks on clerical celibacy made by Noel Browne on April 23, 1971. *The Irish Times,* May 16, 1971.

May 22, 1971
June Levine
It was when Mary [Kenny] started to blow up condoms that I restrained her. She could blow them up to a huge balloon size and collapse with laughter as she let go of the end and the thing went shooting round the carriage. 'Mary, come on, what would your mother say?' I pleaded, and off she'd go again, blowing the condom up and holding it well out of reach.

Describing, as member of women's liberation movement, scene on Belfast-Dublin train when dozens of women challenged law by openly bringing contraceptives into Republic. Levine, June, *Sisters,* Ward River, 1982, p. 179.

May 23, 1971
Jack Lynch
I would not like to leave contraception on the long finger too long.

Commenting, as Taoiseach, on plans for legislative reform. *The Irish Times* ('This Week They Said'), May 23, 1971.

July 2, 1971
Bernadette Devlin
My morals are a private matter ... There are no illegitimate children, only illegitimate parents, if the term is to be used at all.

In interview with Mary Cummins about news that she was expecting a baby. *The Irish Times,* July 2, 1971.

July 3, 1971
Joanna Collins
I feel terribly upset about Arthur Griffith's being ignored. It's alright for Michael. He's a

sort of hero. But poor Mr Griffith has been ignored.

Speaking, at age of ninety-one, about her brother Michael Collins and Arthur Griffith, both signatories of 1921 Treaty. *The Irish Times* ('This Week They Said'), July 3, 1971.

July 9, 1971
Cathal Goulding
When their [the forces of imperialism] answer to the just demand of the people are the lock-out, the strike-breaking, evictions, coercions, the prison cell, intimidation or the gallows, then our duty is to reply in the language that brings these vultures to their senses most effectively, the language of the bomb and the bullet.

Speaking, as Chief of Staff of Official IRA, at graveside oration in Cork. *The Irish Times,* July 10, 1971.

July 11, 1971
Maire Drumm
The people of Derry are up now off their bended knees. For Christ's sake stay up. [People] should not shout 'up the IRA', they should join the IRA.

Addressing Derry rally, as Belfast Executive member of Sinn Féin, after shooting of two Derry men during rioting. *The Irish Times,* July 12, 1971.

July 11, 1971
John Hume
Their [British Army's] impartial role has now clearly ended ... we cannot continue to give our consent to a continuation of the present situation ... if our demand [for an inquiry] is not met by Thursday next we will withdraw immediately from Parliament.

Speaking after SDLP meeting following shooting by British Army of two Derry men during rioting. *The Irish Times,* July 12, 1971.

July 12, 1971
Lord Balniel
I am satisfied from inquiries I have made there is no misconduct to be inquired into.

Rejecting, on behalf of British Government, demands for inquiry from SDLP into shooting by British Army of two Derry men. *The Irish Times,* July 13, 1971.

July 17, 1971
Noel Browne
The courts are open to anyone – like the Ritz.

Commenting, as Labour TD, on legal system. *The Irish Times* ('This Week They Said'), July 17, 1971.

July 18, 1971
John Taylor
I would defend without hesitation the action taken by the Army authorities in Derry against subversives during the past week or so when it was necessary in the end to shoot to kill. I feel that it may be necessary to shoot even more in the forthcoming months in Northern Ireland.

Interviewed on radio, as NI Minister of State for Home Affairs, following shooting of two Derry men. *The Irish Times,* July 19, 1971.

July 29, 1971
Lieutenant-General Sir Harry Tuzo
I have always attributed to the IRA a certain mild romance as patriots of a rather poetic and unusual nature, and Brady [Ruairi Ó Brádaigh, President of Sinn Féin] has effectively removed any starry-eyed attitude which I and others could have. These Provisionals [are] simply a straightforward gang of murderers, extortionists, intimidators, people of the worst possible kind.

Speaking, as GOC British Army NI, at press conference about increasing violence between Provisional IRA and British Army. *The Irish Times,* July 30, 1971.

August 5, 1971
Reginald Maudling
Lift some Protestants if you can.

Remark to Stormont Prime Minister Brian Faulkner when discussing, in private, introduction of internment. Faulkner, Brian, *Memoirs of a Statesman,* Weidenfeld and Nicolson, 1978, p. 119.

August 6, 1971
John Bryans
We have no right to go into the EEC. We were never part of Europe and we never will be.

Interviewed as Grand Master of Grand Orange Lodge. *The Irish Times,* August 8, 1971.

August 9, 1971
Brian Faulkner
I have decided . . . to exercise where necessary . . . the powers of detention and internment . . . We, quite simply, are at war with the terrorist . . . I want to say a word directly to my Catholic fellow-countrymen . . . we are now acting to remove the shadow of fear which hangs over too many of you.

In statement, as NI Prime Minister, announcing introduction of internment without trial after several hundred arrests that morning. *The Irish Times,* August 10, 1971.

August 11, 1971
Charles Haughey
The cynical experiment of partitioning Ireland has ended in total, tragic failure . . . The Irish nation must now mobilise all its moral and physical resources, it must manifest without equivocation its concern for the people of the North.

Commenting on internment and subsequent violence in North. *The Irish Times,* August 12, 1971.

August 12, 1971
Jack Lynch
The Stormont regime, which has consistently repressed the non-Unionist population and bears responsibility for recurring violence in the Northern community, must be brought to an end.

In statement on introduction of internment. Lynch, John, *Speeches and Statements, August 1969-October 1971,* Government Information Bureau, 1971, p. 76.

August 13, 1971
Brigadier Marston Tickell
Operations by the security forces have virtually defeated the hard core of these gunmen . . . of course isolated gunmen remain and we must expect isolated attacks to continue and the people of the Province must not get over-excited if they do.

At press conference in Belfast as British Army Chief of Staff on aftermath of internment. *The Irish Times,* August 14, 1971.

August 13, 1971
Joe Cahill
The battle of the British Army hasn't been won, the losses of the IRA have been very

slight ... somewhere in the region of 30 men [two killed, the rest interned]. This is only a pinprick of the strength here.

At press conference in Belfast, as spokesman for Provisional IRA, on aftermath of internment. *The Irish Times,* August 14, 1971.

August 14, 1971
Brian Faulkner
Internment has flushed out the gunmen.

Commenting on internment policy for which, as NI Prime Minister, he was responsible. *The Irish Times* ('This Week They Said'), August 14, 1971.

August 19, 1971
Austin Currie
[I am] no longer, because of [British] Army action and the policy of the British Government, prepared to say to Catholics that they should join the UDR.

In interview after addressing meeting of thirty-one Catholic members of the Ulster Defence Regiment in Belfast, twenty-four of whom stated afterwards they would resign because of internment. *The Irish Times,* August 20, 1971.

August 19, 1971
Jack Lynch
The events since the introduction of internment without trial on Monday, 9th August, clearly indicate the failure of internment and of current military operations as a solution to the problems of Northern Ireland ... I intend to support the policy of passive resistance now being pursued by the non-Unionist population ... I am prepared to come to a meeting of all the interested parties designed to find ways and means of promoting the economic, social and political wellbeing of all the Irish people, north and south, without prejudice to the aspiration of the great majority of the Irish people to the re-unification of Ireland.

In telegram to British Prime Minister Edward Heath. Lynch, John, *Speeches and Statements, August 1969-October 1971,* Government Information Bureau, 1971, pp. 77-78.

August 20, 1971
Edward Heath
Your telegram of today is unjustifiable in its contents, unacceptable in its attempt to interfere in the affairs of the United Kingdom

and can in no way contribute to the solution of the problems of Northern Ireland ...

The military operations to which you refer are designed solely for the defence of the people against armed terrorists whose activities, many of which originate in or are supported from the Republic, I hope you would deplore and join me in suppressing ... I cannot accept that anyone outside the United Kingdom can participate in meetings to promote the political development of any part of the United Kingdom. I find your reference to supporting the policy of passive resistance now being pursued by certain elements in Northern Ireland calculated to do maximum damage to the co-operation between the communities in Northern Ireland which it is our purpose, and I would hope would be your purpose, to achieve.

In telegram replying to telegram from Taoiseach Jack Lynch. Lynch, John, *Speeches and Statements, August 1969-October 1971,* Government Information Bureau, 1971, pp. 78-79.

August 20, 1971
Jack Lynch
Mr Heath's assertion that what is happening in Northern Ireland is no concern of mine is not acceptable. The division of Ireland has never been, and is not now, acceptable to the great majority of the Irish people who were not consulted in the matter when that division was made fifty years ago.

In statement in response to telegram from British Prime Minister Edward Heath. Lynch, John, *Speeches and Statements, August 1969-October 1971,* Government Information Bureau, 1971, p. 81.

September 12, 1971
Cardinal Conway
Who wanted to bomb a million Protestants into a United Ireland?

In statement, issued with six other Catholic bishops, condemning IRA. Deutch and Magowan, *Northern Ireland, 1968-1973, A Chronology of Events,* Vol. 1, Blackstaff, 1973, p. 126.

September 28, 1971
Jack Lynch, Edward Heath and Brian Faulkner
It is our common purpose to seek to bring violence and internment and all other emergency measures to an end without delay

... Our discussions in the last two days have helped to create an atmosphere of greater understanding and it is our hope that the process of political reconciliation may go forward to a successful outcome.

From joint statement, as Taoiseach, and British and NI Prime Ministers, issued after meeting at Chequers. Lynch, John, *Speeches and Statements, August 1969-October 1971*, Government Information Bureau, 1971, pp. 84-85.

October 1, 1971
Gerry Collins
[RTE should] refrain from broadcasting any matter calculated to promote the aims or activities of any organisation which engaged in, promotes, encourages or advocates the attaining of any political objective by violent means.

Directive issued, as Minister for Posts and Telegraphs, under Section 31 of Broadcasting Act, effectively banning interviews on Irish radio or television with Provisional IRA or Sinn Féin representatives (still in effect). *The Irish Times*, October 2, 1971.

October 6, 1971
Eamonn McCann
I am not certain how many of our speakers mesmerised the masses. Certainly the masses mesmerised the speakers.

In *Irish Times* interview, as leader of Derry Labour Party, on events in the city since 1968. *The Irish Times*, October 6, 1971.

October 16, 1971
Edward Heath
If our troops were withdrawn and our efforts relaxed, we would be condemning the whole of Ireland to civil war and slaughter on a scale far beyond anything we have seen in recent years.

Responding, as British Prime Minister, to demands for British withdrawal as violence worsened in Northern Ireland. *The Irish Times*, October 18, 1971.

October 20, 1971
Senator Edward Kennedy
[Northern Ireland] is becoming Britain's Vietnam ... The Government of Ulster rules by bayonet and bloodshed ... if only the cruel and constant irritation of the British military

presence is withdrawn, Ireland can be whole again.

Speaking to US Congress as violence worsened in Northern Ireland. *The Irish Times*, October 21, 1971.

November 16, 1971
Edmund Compton
Our investigations have not led us to conclude that any of the grouped or individual complainants suffered physical brutality, as we understand the term.

In official report, as chairman, into allegations, mainly in *Sunday Times* and *Irish Times*, of brutality against detainees in North. *The Irish Times*, November 17, 1971.

November 21, 1971
Cardinal Conway
We condemn this treatment [interrogation 'in depth'] as immoral and inhuman. It is unworthy of the British people. It is the test of a civilised people that the methods of its elected government remain civilised, even under extreme provocation.

Reacting to disclosure in *Compton Report* of use by police and army of five techniques of interrogation 'in depth', i.e. hooding, wall-standing, use of constant ('white') noise and deprivation of food and sleep. *The Irish Times*, November 22, 1971.

November 21, 1971
Neil Blaney
Give shelter to those who come to you, give them aid and money and anything else that might be useful to them. Let the people who are carrying on the struggle in the Six Counties know you are with them.

Speaking to crowd at Letterkenny after being expelled from Fianna Fáil parliamentary party for refusing to support Taoiseach Jack Lynch in vote of confidence. *The Irish Times*, November 22, 1971.

November 25, 1971
Harold Wilson
I believe the situation has now gone so far that it is impossible to conceive of an effective long-term solution in which the agenda does not at least include consideration ... of progress towards a united Ireland.

Outlining, as British Labour leader, in Commons, 'blueprint' for united Ireland. *The Irish Times*, November 26, 1971.

November 26, 1971
Graham Greene

'Deep interrogation' – a bureaucratic phrase which takes the place of the simpler word 'torture' and is worthy of Orwell's 1984 – is on a different level of immorality than hysterical sadism or the indiscriminate bomb of urban guerrillas. It is something organised with imagination, and a knowledge of psychology, calculated and cold-blooded, and it is only half-condemned by the Compton investigation.

In letter to *Times* on finding of Compton inquiry into alleged brutality in Northern Ireland interrogations. *The Times*, November 26, 1971.

December 11, 1971
Senator Edward Kennedy

The Alice-in-Wonderland logic of the *Compton Report* [on allegations of brutality against detainees] and the British Government's defence of it in Parliament would be laughable, were the implications of its cruel hypocrisy not so ominous for the prospects of peace in Ulster.

In statement on *Compton Report* claiming no brutality used in interrogation of detainees. *The Irish Times* ('This Week They Said'), December 11, 1971.

December 13, 1971
Official IRA

On entering the house the officer in charge informed Senator Barnhill that his house was to be destroyed ... he [Senator Barnhill] then attacked the raiding party and in the ensuing struggled received wounds from which he died ... The officer in charge knelt down beside the Senator to ascertain if he needed any assistance. At no time was there any desire to physically harm ... the Senator.

In statement on killing of Unionist senator near Strabane. *The Irish Times*, December 14, 1971.

December 13, 1971
Bernadette Devlin

Senator Barnhill was a bigot of first class order but he did not represent British imperialism and was not a threat to the IRA.

Speaking, as Independent MP for Mid-Ulster, on Official IRA killing of Unionist senator, at Official Sinn Féin meeting in Dublin. *The Irish Times*, December 14, 1971.

December 15, 1971
Reginald Maudling

I don't think one can speak of defeating the IRA, of eliminating them completely, but it is the design of the security forces to reduce their level of violence to something like an acceptable level.

In statement, at end of visit as Home Secretary to Northern Ireland, which gave rise to phrase used against him in future – the 'acceptable level of violence'. *The Irish Times* ('This Week They Said'), December 18, 1971.

December 16, 1971
David Thornley

If the present Dáil carried any flavour at all it was the smell of death and corruption in every sense of the word since the events of May 1970 [arms crisis]. So low is the status of politics that if every one of us [in the Dáil] was led off to internment in the Blasket Islands, in the words of Cromwell, not a dog would bark.

As Labour TD, speaking in Dáil. *The Irish Times*, December 17, 1971.

December 20, 1971
Lieutenant-General Sir Harry Tuzo

The IRA campaign has caused us to direct our energies in their [Catholics'] direction and inevitably this has caused us to collide from time to time with the Roman Catholic communities ... I say to the Catholics of Northern Ireland ... you have nothing to fear from the Army.

Speaking at press conference as GOC British Army (NI). *The Irish Times*, December 21, 1971.

January 28, 1972
Garret FitzGerald

The diminishing importance of London as a centre of decisions affecting Northern Ireland, many of which would in future be taken in Brussels, might reduce northern Unionists' sensitivities on the issue of whether the remaining powers were exercised in Westminster or in Dublin ... The sense of common Irishness ... would be heightened.

Speaking, as Fine Gael frontbencher, in favour of EEC membership. *The Irish Times*, January 29, 1972.

January 30, 1972
John Hume
Their action was nothing short of cold-blooded mass murder – another Sharpeville and another Bloody Sunday.

Reacting, as Derry MP, to shooting by British Army of thirteen people at anti-internment rally. *The Irish Times*, January 31, 1972.

January 31, 1972
Bernadette Devlin
I have a right to ask a question of that murdering hypocrite [Reginald Maudling] ... if I am not allowed to inform the House of what I know, I'll inform Mr Maudling of what I feel. [Later] I am just sorry I didn't go for his throat.

Speaking in Commons on killing of thirteen civilians by British Army in Derry; she then ran across floor, pulled Home Secretary Maudling's hair and slapped his face. *The Irish Times*, February 1, 1972.

January 31, 1972
John Hume
Many people down there [in the Bogside] feel now that it's a united Ireland or nothing.

In RTE interview on Derry walls after killing of thirteen civilians by British Army. Political opponents later attributed to Hume the statement, 'It's a united Ireland or nothing'. White, Barry, *John Hume, Statesman of the Troubles*, Blackstaff, 1984, p. 120.

January 31, 1972
Derry priests
We accuse the Commander of Land Forces [British Army] of being an accessory after the fact. We accuse the soldiers of firing indiscriminately into a fleeing crowd, of gloating over casualties ... these men are trained criminals. They differ from terrorists only in the veneer of respectability that a uniform gives them.

In statement on Bloody Sunday killings, signed by seven priests: Edward Daly, Anthony Mulvey, George McLaughlin, Joseph Carolan, Michael McIvor, Denis Bradley and Tom O'Gara. *The Irish Times*, February 1, 1972.

February 1, 1972
Patrick Hillery
If Ireland received no help from the West, it might turn to the East. My orders are to seek help wherever I can get it ... From now on my aim is to get Britain out of Ireland.

At press conference at Kennedy airport on arrival as Foreign Minister to speak at United Nations on Bloody Sunday killings. *The Irish Times*, February 2, 1972.

February 1, 1972
Lord Balniel
In each case soldiers fired aimed shots at men identified as gunmen or bombers, in self defence or in defence of comrades who were threatened.

Speaking, in Commons, as junior Defence Minister, about Bloody Sunday killings in Derry. *The Irish Times*, February 2, 1972.

February 6, 1972
John McKeague
The troops did not shoot enough of them [on Bloody Sunday].

Commenting, as Belfast loyalist leader, during 'David Frost Show' on ITV, on Bloody Sunday killings in Derry. *The Irish Times*, February 7, 1972.

February 7, 1972
Lord Kilbracken
The time comes when one has to stand up and be counted ... I don't want to retain the symbolic souvenir of my service in British uniform.

On returning his war medals from his home in Co. Leitrim to British Government in protest against Bloody Sunday shootings. *The Irish Times*, February 8, 1972.

February 9, 1972
Maurice Hayes
The effect of the present security policy [is] alienating the whole Catholic community while at the same time failing to produce peace and security for any section of the population.

On resigning as Community Relations Commissioner in Northern Ireland, following Bloody Sunday shootings. *The Irish Times*, February 10, 1972.

February 12, 1972
William Craig
We are determined to preserve our British traditions and way of life, and God help those, ladies and gentlemen, who get in our way.

Speaking, as leader of new loyalist group, Vanguard, at paramilitary rally in Lisburn. *The Irish Times,* February 14, 1972.

February 28, 1972
Senator Edward Kennedy

Today the British troops in Ulster have become an army of occupation ... Stormont is now defunct in all but name and it is time for Britain to deliver the coup de grace ... the goal of reunification is now too close for Ireland to turn back.

Speaking at US Congress hearing on Northern Ireland. *The Irish Times,* February 29, 1972.

March 2, 1972
Lord Parker

We have come to the conclusion that there is no reason to rule out these techniques [hooding, wall-standing, use of constant noise and deprivation of food and sleep] on moral grounds and that it is possible to operate them in a manner consistent with the highest standards in our society.

From *Parker Commission Report* on 'in-depth' interrogations in North, commissioned by British Government. *The Irish Times,* March 3, 1972.

March 2, 1972
Lord Gardiner

The blame for this sorry story [use of 'in-depth' interrogation techniques] ... must lie with those who many years ago decided that in emergency conditions in colonial-type situations, we should abandon our legal, well-tried and highly-successful wartime interrogation methods and replace them by procedures which were secret, illegal, not morally justifiable and alien to the traditions of the greatest democracy in the world.

As dissenting member of Parker Commission whose minority report was accepted by British Government as basis for banning 'in-depth' interrogations in Northern Ireland. *The Irish Times,* March 3, 1972.

March 13, 1972
Harold Wilson

The [Provisional] IRA truce had shown that they had a disciplined, tightly-knit organisation.

After meeting IRA secretly on visit to Dublin as leader of British Labour Party. *The Irish Times,* March 14, 1972.

March 18, 1972
William Craig

We must build up a dossier of the men and women who are a menace to this country because, if and when the politicians fail us, it may be our job to liquidate the enemy.

Speaking, as leader of Vanguard, at Belfast rally of sixty thousand loyalists. *The Irish Times,* March 20, 1972.

March 24, 1972
Brian Faulkner

Such a transfer [of security powers to London] is not justifiable and cannot be supported or accepted by us. It would wholly undermine the powers, authority and standing of this Government.

In letter, as NI Prime Minister, to British Prime Minister Edward Heath, refusing demand that law and order powers be handed over to London, and announcing resignation of NI Government. *The Irish Times,* March 25, 1972.

March 24, 1972
Edward Heath

The transfer of security powers [to London] is an indispensable condition for progress in finding a practical solution in Northern Ireland. The Northern Ireland Government's decision [to refuse the transfer] therefore leaves us with no alternative to assuming full and direct responsibility for the administration of Northern Ireland.

As British Prime Minister, announcing, to Commons, prorogation of Stormont. *The Irish Times,* March 25, 1972.

March 24, 1972
Eddie McAteer

This is a day of sadness. I find no joy in being ruled from the remote, insensitive smokerooms of Westminster. Faced with the choice, I would in principle prefer to be ruled by a Protestant Irishman rather than by an Englishman.

Commenting, as Nationalist Party President, on end of Stormont. Boyd, Andrew, *Brian Faulkner and the Crisis in Ulster Unionism,* Anvil, 1972, pp. 114-15.

March 25, 1972
William Whitelaw

One must be careful not to prejudge the past.

Referring to Irish politics, on being appointed Secretary of State for Northern Ireland after abolition of Stormont Government. (Author's recollection.)

March 27, 1972
Brian Faulkner

Northern Ireland is not a coconut colony and no coconut commission will be able to muster any credibility or standing.

As Unionist leader in speech to Ulster Unionist Council on British suggestion to set up advisory commission after fall of Stormont. *The Irish Times,* March 28, 1972.

April 2, 1972
Seán Mac Stiofáin

If we become hesitant, the fight of this generation is lost. Concessions bedamned. We want freedom.

Speaking, as Provisional IRA Chief of Staff, at Derry meeting on prorogation of Stormont. *The Irish Times,* April 3, 1972.

April 2, 1972
Cardinal Conway

I have taken soundings of feelings of the Catholic community ... Never before have I experienced the voice of the people coming through so loud and clear [for peace].

In RTE interview on prorogation of Stormont. *The Irish Times,* April 3, 1972.

April 3, 1972
Ruairi Ó Brádaigh

In his excursion into politics, all the influence the Cardinal can command is being thrown behind Direct British Rule, just as his predecessors had urged successfully the acceptance of the disastrous treaty of surrender of 1921.

In RTE radio interview, as President of Provisional Sinn Féin, in response to Cardinal Conway's call for end to violence. *The Irish Times,* April 4, 1972.

April 19, 1972
Lord Widgery

There would have been no deaths in Londonderry on January 30th if those who organised the illegal march had not thereby created a highly dangerous situation ... Some soldiers showed a high degree of restraint in opening fire, the firing of others bordered on the reckless.

Official report on Bloody Sunday in Derry when thirteen civilians were shot dead by British Army. *The Irish Times,* April 20, 1972.

April 19, 1972
Eddie McAteer

This is a political judgement by a British officer and British judge upon his darling British Army. I suppose we are lucky he didn't also find that the thirteen committed suicide.

As Derry Nationalist leader, on *Widgery Report* clearing British Army of criminal charges concerning Bloody Sunday. *The Irish Times,* April 20, 1972.

April 20, 1972
Peter O'Toole

There is a war going on [in Northern Ireland]. There is a war that's been going on for years and years and years and can only and will only end when the British leave Ireland.

In interview in Rome where he was filming *Man of La Mancha. The Irish Times,* April 21, 1972.

May 5, 1972
Jack Lynch

The choice is between taking part in the great new renaissance of Europe or opting for economic, social and cultural sterilisation. It is like that faced by Robinson Crusoe when the ship came to bring him back into the world again.

Speaking as Taoiseach, in support of joining EEC, at rally in Cork. *The Irish Times,* May 6, 1972.

May 5, 1972
Brendan Corish

We are not sharing our sovereignty [by entering the EEC], we are surrendering it. We are not at this moment ... fit to compete. We are too small and our tiny voice in the organs of government of the EEC can and will be drowned out.

Speaking, as Labour leader, at anti-EEC rally in Cork. *The Irish Times,* May 6, 1972.

May 7, 1972

Charles Haughey

I cannot understand how any patriotic Irishman or woman can oppose our going into Europe ... I can understand a Northern Unionist who wishes to keep Ireland divided hoping that Britain and the Six Counties of Northern Ireland will go into Europe while the Republic stays out so that the Border may thereby be permanently entrenched.

As Fianna Fáil spokesman, at Edenmore. *The Irish Times*, May 8, 1972.

May 20, 1972

Liam Cosgrave

I don't know whether some of you do any hunting or not but some of these commentators and critics are now like mongrel foxes, they are gone to ground (applause) and I'll dig them out and the pack will chop them when they get them.

As leader of Fine Gael, departing from script in speech at party's Árd Fheis to take issue with critics of his leadership in Fine Gael. RTE archives.

May 21, 1972

Official IRA

Regardless of the calls for peace from slobbering moderates, while British gunmen are on the streets of the Six Counties the IRA will take action against them – in particular a British soldier from the Derry area who could remain in such a force after a massacre of 13 Derrymen by the British Army.

Statement issued after Official IRA had killed Ranger William Best (aged nineteen) of Derry, at home on leave. *The Irish Times*, May 22, 1972.

May 29, 1972

Official Sinn Féin

The overwhelming desire of all the people of the North is for an end to military action by all sides.

Announcing ceasefire, on behalf of Official IRA, a week after its members had assassinated Ranger William Best of Derry, provoking outcry among local people. *The Irish Times*, May 30, 1972.

May 31, 1972

Joseph Cairns

Ulster has been cynically betrayed [and] relegated to the status of a fuzzy wuzzy colony.

In speech about fall of Stormont on retiring as Belfast's Lord Mayor. Deutch and Magowan, *Northern Ireland 1968-1973, A Chronology of Events*, Vol. 2, Blackstaff, 1974, p. 181.

June 5, 1972

William Whitelaw

There can be no question of negotiations with people who are shooting at British troops. I cannot foresee negotiations with them even after the violence has stopped.

As NI Secretary, commenting on possibility of his meeting Provisional IRA. *The Irish Times*, June 6, 1972.

June 11, 1972

Colonel Gadafy

We support the Irish revolutionaries who are fighting Britain ... we have strong ties with the revolutionaries to whom we have supplied arms.

Speaking at rally in Tripoli. *The Irish Times*, June 12, 1972.

June 22, 1972

Provisional IRA

The IRA will suspend offensive operations as and from midnight on Monday, June 26, 1972, providing that a public reciprocal response is forthcoming from the armed forces of the British Crown.

In statement offering ceasefire. *The Irish Times*, June 23, 1972.

June 22, 1972

William Whitelaw

As the purpose of Her Majesty's forces in Northern Ireland is to keep the peace, if offensive operations by the IRA cease on Monday night, Her Majesty's forces will obviously reciprocate.

Responding in Commons, as NI Secretary, to IRA offer of ceasefire. *The Irish Times*, June 23, 1972.

July 6, 1972

Professor Alwyn Williams

In terms of its educational system, Northern Ireland, to put it bluntly, is the Alabama of Europe.

Commenting, as pro-Vice Chancellor of Queen's University, Belfast, on segregated education in city. Deutch and Magowan, *Northern Ireland 1968-1973, A Chronology of Events*, Vol. 2, Blackstaff, 1974, p. 193.

July 7, 1972
Provisional IRA
(1) A public declaration by the British Government that it is the right of all the people of Ireland acting as a unit to decide the future of Ireland.
(2) A declaration of intent to withdraw British forces from Irish soil by January 1, 1975.
(3) A general amnesty

Demands at meeting of IRA and British ministers in London, as outlined in Commons by NI Secretary William Whitelaw. *The Irish Times*, July 11, 1972.

July 8, 1972
Provisional IRA
The truce between the Irish Republican Army and the British occupation forces was broken without warning by British forces at approximately 5.00 pm today at Lenadoon Estate, Belfast. Accordingly, all IRA units have been instructed to resume offensive action.

Statement on breakdown of truce over housing allocations in Lenadoon in Belfast, resulting in gun battle in which six people died. *The Irish Times*, July 10, 1972.

July 10, 1972
William Whitelaw
I arranged to see them [the IRA] because I have ... discussed these grievous problems with representatives of many shades of opinion. Any action that I could honourably take that would save lives or avoid further damage to property seemed to me should be taken.

Explaining to Commons why he had secretly met IRA delegation in London with other British ministers to try, unsuccessfully, to secure indefinite ceasefire. *The Irish Times*, July 11, 1972.

July 18, 1972
Governor Ronald Reagan
It was unseemly for an American legislator [Senator Kennedy] to make proposals, as I understand it, that the United States should suddenly interject itself and become the arbitration board for settling this dispute. [My policy?] California does not have a foreign policy.

Speaking during visit to Dublin as Governor of California about call by Senator Edward Kennedy for British withdrawal. *The Irish Times*, July 19, 1972.

July 20, 1972
Paddy Devlin
If Mr Whitelaw [NI Secretary] thinks that Army behaviour will lead to our rejection of the Provisional IRA ... he has grossly miscalculated. Military excesses create the need for a Provisional IRA.

In statement, as SDLP chief whip, after his Andersonstown home came under fire from British Army. *The Irish Times*, July 21, 1972.

July 21, 1972
Northern Ireland Office spokesman
It looks like Bloody Friday.

Giving name to Friday, July 21, 1972, when IRA bombs in Belfast killed nine people and injured 130. *The Irish Times*, July 22, 1972.

July 23, 1972
Dr Philbin, Bishop of Down and Connor
[Irish] ministers in Asia and Africa are being told to go home and make Christians of their fellow countrymen.

In sermon at Muckamore. *The Irish Times*, July 24, 1972.

August 24, 1972
John Taylor
If we were not allowed to have our own parliament, then we must have an independent British Ulster.

As Unionist MP, in first public speech since being shot six months previously. *The Irish Times*, August 25, 1972.

September 2, 1972
Bob Cooper
Not since the worst excesses of Hitler and Stalin have so many suffered so much for the madness of so few.

Speaking, as joint leader of Alliance Party. *The Irish Times* ('This Week They Said'), September 2, 1972.

October 7, 1972
Rev. Martin Smyth
Integration [with Britain] would be a stepping stone to a United Ireland.

Commenting, as leading Orangeman, on need for devolution. *The Irish Times* ('This Week They Said'), October 7, 1972.

October 19, 1972
William Craig

We are prepared to come out and shoot and kill. I am prepared to come out and shoot and kill. Let us put the bluff aside. I am prepared to kill, and those behind me will have my full support.

Addressing Monday Club meeting in Commons, as Vanguard leader, in what became known as his 'shoot to kill' speech. *The Irish Times*, October 20, 1972.

October 20, 1972
William Craig

All I drink is an occasional glass of wine with a meal.

Denying to reporters that he was drunk when, as Vanguard leader, he said at London meeting that he was prepared to shoot and kill. *The Irish Times*, October 21, 1972.

October 22, 1972
Rev. Ian Paisley

Let me make it perfectly clear that I and the Democratic Unionist Party are still dedicated to achieving total integration with Great Britain ... legislative union must be absolute. On this as a party there can be no going back.

In statement, as DUP leader, prior to visiting British Prime Minister Edward Heath. *The Irish Times*, October 23, 1972.

October 25, 1972
Henry Kelly

If the referendum [to remove special position of Catholic Church from Irish Constitution] were a success for the Government, people would say, 'We've done our bit for the Protestants. If that does not bring them in [to a united Ireland] nothing will'. Suppose one day Mr Whitelaw were to say to Mr Lynch, 'It's all yours', what would happen? Where is the preparation for unity here?

Speaking as *Irish Times* Northern Editor at Dublin debate organised by Solicitors' Apprentices Society in Four Courts. *The Irish Times*, October 26, 1972.

November 2, 1972
Jack Lynch

The specific list of Churches [in the Constitution] was neither desirable nor necessary and should be deleted ... the proposed change would contribute to Irish unity.

As Taoiseach, speaking on Bill to amend Constitution to remove special position of Catholic Church. *The Irish Times*, November 3, 1972.

November 2, 1972
Joseph Leneghan

Why should they change the Constitution to suit a crowd of thugs in the North of Ireland? God grant that we shall never see that crowd of thugs come in here. We have enough as we are without taking the risk of crossing the breed.

Speaking in Dáil, as independent TD, on Bill to amend Constitution to remove special position of Catholic Church. *The Irish Times*, November 3, 1972.

November 2, 1972
Conor Cruise O'Brien

The Bill was too little and too late. If this is an olive branch [to the Unionists] it is being extended with a very languid hand, almost contemptuous.

Speaking in Dáil, as Labour TD, on Bill to amend Constitution to remove special position of Catholic Church. *The Irish Times*, November 3, 1972.

November 16, 1972
Edward Heath

To those who urge that Northern Ireland should seize its own unilateral independence, I must say that not only would such an attempt bring about a blood bath, but that were it to succeed, the British Government would not pay one penny of the £200 million a year now provided.

Referring to statements from leading Unionists about possibility of independent Northern Ireland, during visit to Belfast. *The Irish Times*, November 17, 1972.

November 19, 1972
Kevin O'Kelly

Mr Seán Mac Stiofáin said, 'We believe that by armed struggle alone can we achieve our objectives'.

As RTE interviewer, in account on radio of conversation with IRA leader, outcome of which was jailing of O'Kelly and sacking of RTE Authority on grounds that Government's directive under Section 31 had been defied. *The Irish Times*, November 20, 1972.

November 23, 1972
Conor Cruise O'Brien
Surely it was more dangerous to leave these people [IRA] in the shadows? ... In a modern democracy, the autonomy of radio or television was as vital as the freedom of the press or of Parliament.

Commenting in Dáil, as Labour TD, on row over RTE interview with Provisional IRA leader Seán Mac Stiofáin. *The Irish Times*, November 24, 1972.

November 23, 1972
Garret FitzGerald
The Government was now using that interview as an excuse to destroy the independence of the [RTE] Authority and that was something that was totally unacceptable ... The real threat to the country was not the IRA but the threat to freedom of speech.

Commenting in Dáil, as Fine Gael Opposition TD, on row over RTE interview with Provisional IRA leader Seán Mac Stiofáin. *The Irish Times*, November 24, 1972.

November 26, 1972
Seán Mac Stiofáin
I will be dead in six days. Live with that.

In Dublin's Special Criminal Court, after declaring his intention to go on hunger strike after being sentenced to six months for IRA membership (the hunger strike lasted fifty-seven days before being called off). *The Irish Times*, November 27, 1972.

November 29, 1972
Paddy Cooney
How can [the Minister for Justice] come into this Parliament and ask it to support a Bill the like of which can only be found on the statute books of South Africa?

As Fine Gael spokesman on justice, opposing the Offences Against the State (Amendment) Bill, allowing wide Government powers against subversives – but which he continued to operate in Government later. Browne, Vincent, *The Magill Book of Irish Politics*, Magill, 1981, p. 266.

December 1, 1972
Neil Blaney
Not only did circumstances bring the freedom fighters into existence but so did the promised support of help not just by me but by a lot of other people as well. The blame lies on me and a whole lot of others.

On his role as Fianna Fáil minister in creation of Provisional IRA. *DÉ:* Vol. 264: Col. 668.

December 1, 1972
Patrick Cooney
We have decided to put the nation before party and accordingly we withdraw the amendment.

Announcing in Dáil withdrawal of Fine Gael opposition to anti-IRA legislation (Offences against the State Act), which threatened to bring down Government, after bombs in centre of Dublin killed two people. *The Irish Times*, December 2, 1972.

December 9, 1972
John D. Stewart
Northern Ireland is like one of her great sons, George Best – on the transfer list but no rash of offers.

Northern writer and columnist on effect of troubles. *The Irish Times* ('This Week They Said'), December 9, 1972.

December 18, 1972
Noel Browne
Yeats's 'terrible beauty' ... has become a sick and sectarian, angry and repressive old crone.

Writing, as Labour TD, in British left-wing weekly, *Tribune. The Irish Times*, December 19, 1972.

January 13, 1973
Captain James Kelly
The two bombs which exploded in Dublin at precisely the right time to bring a recalcitrant Opposition to heel were on a par with the burning of the Reichstag, used by Hitler in the 1930s to bring his Nazi party to power.

Commenting, as former army officer involved in arms crisis, on Fine Gael withdrawal of opposition to new anti-IRA measures after explosions in Dublin. *The Irish Times* ('This Week They Said'), January 13, 1973.

February 6, 1973
Rev. Ian Paisley
I utterly deplore the action of those leaders in

Northern Ireland who are calling on people to jeopardise the whole economy of Ulster.

Opposing United Loyalist Council strike against internment of loyalists. *The Irish Times,* February 7, 1983.

February 15, 1973
John Peck

I do not see what political interests would suffer if there were a single national orchestra [for the whole of Ireland], school of drama, school of ballet etc., just as there is a single rugby fifteen.

On retiring as British Ambassador to Dublin. *The Irish Times,* February 15, 1973.

February 17, 1973
William Craig

Much though we wish to maintain the union [with Great Britain] we should all be seriously thinking of an independent dominion of Ulster . . . if ever there is to be unification of Ireland . . . it is only neighbourly relations that can bring it about.

As loyalist Vanguard leader, speaking in Ulster Hall, Belfast. *The Irish Times* ('This Week They Said'), February 17, 1973.

February 17, 1973
Gerry Fitt

The tired old rafters of the Ulster Hall must have been on the verge of collapse when Mr Craig enunciated breaking the link with Britain.

As SDLP leader, commenting on William Craig's Ulster Hall speech on possible break with Britain. *The Irish Times* ('This Week They Said'), February 17, 1973.

March 20, 1973
William Whitelaw

Her Majesty's Government believe that these proposals offer a reasonable deal for reasonable people and as such should be accepted.

Speaking, as NI Secretary, in Commons on White Paper to provide both power-sharing in North and Council of Ireland. *The Irish Times,* March 21, 1973.

March 24, 1973
Frankfurter Rundschan

Summing it all up and considering what has happened, the Catholic side has won.

West German journal's comment on British Government proposals for power-sharing and Council of Ireland. *The Irish Times* ('This Week They Said'), March 24, 1973.

March 29, 1973
Patrick Donegan

She'll get a boot up the transom and be told to get out of our waters fast.

As Minister for Defence in new Coalition Government, on action against Cypriot coaster, *Claudia,* apprehended off Helvick Head with arms for IRA. *The Irish Times,* March 30, 1973.

April 1, 1973
Rev. Fr Michael McGreil

It is time that the Republic replaced its National Anthem with something more worthy of a civilised people, which would express sentiments of peace, justice and brotherhood, instead of the gun and the *bearna baoil* [gap of danger].

In talk as lecturer in sociology at Maynooth. *The Irish Times,* April 2, 1973.

April 23, 1973
Pope Paul VI

May the official [British] proposals [on Northern Ireland] offer a favourable basis for . . . true reconciliation in justice and charity . . . Let the voice of violence become silent and let there be heard instead the voice of wisdom and guidance.

Expressing support for British White Paper proposing power-sharing in Northern Ireland, during Easter message from balcony of St Peter's in Rome. *The Irish Times,* April 23, 1973.

May 8, 1973
Brian Faulkner

We are not opposed to power-sharing in Government, but we will not be prepared to participate in Government with any whose primary aim is to break the union with Great Britain.

Carefully-worded policy statement which enabled Unionist Party to later share power with SDLP, on grounds primary aim of SDLP was peace. *The Irish Times,* May 9, 1973.

May 23, 1973
Liam Ahern

More guns we want, bags of guns.

Interjecting, as Fianna Fáil TD, in debate on *Claudia* gun-running in Dáil. *The Irish Times*, May 24, 1973.

June 8, 1973
Conor Cruise O'Brien

I intend to take out Section 31 of the Broadcasting Act and remove altogether, and deprive any future Minister of, the power to issue the kind of directions that we have.

Speaking, as Minister for Posts and Telegraphs, at ITGWU conference on legislation allowing Government to instruct RTE not to interview members of certain organisations. *The Irish Times*, June 9, 1973.

June 8, 1973
Rev. Robin J. Williamson

In Ulster we have failed Christ miserably.

In sermon as outgoing Moderator of Non-Subscribing Presbyterian Church in Belfast. *The Irish Times*, June 9, 1973.

June 8, 1973
Justice Breathnach

Why are you dressed up in those ridiculous garments? ... I could sentence you for contempt wearing a scarf like that ... I can warn you, you were lucky not to have been assaulted by a crowd. Any decent Irishman would object to this carry-on ... my only regret [is] that I cannot have you locked up.

Addressing five members of Hare Krishna religious sect in Dublin District Court when they appeared charged with using musical instruments in street and obstructing traffic by marching in single file along road. *The Irish Times*, June 9, 1973.

July 10, 1973
Dr (Cahal) Daly, Bishop of Ardagh and Clonmacnoise

Men still speak today of completing the unfinished business of 1916-1922. There is, after 50 years, much unfinished business still to do for Ireland. But the weapons of its completion are no longer rifles and grenades. Violence ... puts in gravest peril all that has been achieved ... The tools of Irish patriotism now are not the drill of war but the politics and economics of social justice and the structures of inter-community peace.

Speaking during requiem mass at funeral of Lieutenant-General Sean Mac Eoin, member of old

IRA and former Justice Minister, at Ballinalee, Co. Longford. *The Irish Times*, July 11, 1973.

July 15, 1973
George Colley

Some of the national newspapers right through the election campaign adopted a really outright campaign of vilification and distortion against us [Fianna Fáil] ... there are journalists in some of the newspapers today writing regularly who are closely associated with ... illegal organisations.

Speaking as former Fianna Fáil minister on defeat in election. *The Irish Times*, July 16, 1973.

July 15, 1973
Erskine Childers

The violence in the North has postponed the day of reunification.

In interview, as President, on ABC network in New York. *The Irish Times*, July 16, 1973.

August 6, 1973
British Ministry of Defence

[Kenneth] Littlejohn was told that if he had or obtained information about the activities of the IRA, the British Government was prepared to receive it ... The British Government was not authorising or implicitly condoning the commission of criminal offences in pursuance of such information.

In statement following controversy over disclosure by Littlejohn, during trial in Dublin when he was sentenced to twenty years for armed robbery, that some of his actions stemmed from meeting, before going to Ireland, with British Junior Defence Minister Geoffrey Johnson Smith. *The Irish Times*, August 7, 1973.

August 7, 1973
Lord Carrington

This man [Kenneth Littlejohn] said he had information about the source of arms. He would only give that information to a Minister whose face he recognised. Would I have gone back and slept happily in my bed knowing that there might be information which I was refusing to get which would save the lives of British soldiers in Ireland? I would never hold up my head again.

Explaining in radio interview, as British Defence Minister, why a junior minister met Littlejohn before he went to Ireland where he was convicted of armed robbery. *The Irish Times*, August 8, 1973.

August 7, 1973
Marcus Lipton
There is little doubt that the [British] Government made a hard and fast deal with criminals.

As British Labour MP, commenting on meeting between junior minister and Kenneth Littlejohn who offered to spy in Republic and was later convicted of armed robbery in Dublin. *The Irish Times*, August 8, 1973.

August 8, 1973
Kenneth Littlejohn
One of my main functions was to assassinate Shamus (*sic*) Costello who was the effective Number 1 of the Officials [Official Republicans] and who had been trained in Moscow. I was also to assassinate another high-up member in the Officials, Sean Patrick Garland, who I believe was trained in Cuba ... I was also told to assassinate Seán Mac Stiofáin.

Statement published in London magazine, *Time Out*, on his conviction in Dublin of armed robbery allegedly carried out as British agent in Ireland. *The Irish Times*, August 9, 1973.

August 10, 1973
Irish Government
It was made clear to the British Government that intelligence activities on their part in the Republic are unacceptable and counter-productive.

In statement on admission by British Government that junior minister had met Kenneth Littlejohn and discussed intelligence-gathering in Ireland, where Littlejohn was imprisoned later for armed robbery. *The Irish Times*, August 11, 1973.

August 11, 1973
Jack Lynch
The IRA had accepted responsibility publicly for almost all the explosions it had caused. In the absence of such a claim [for bombs which influenced Dáil vote on anti-IRA legislation], many people in Ireland believe that these explosions were the work of British intelligence agents.

As former Taoiseach, commenting on disclosure that Kenneth Littlejohn, convicted of armed robbery in Dublin, had met junior minister before coming to Ireland. *The Irish Times*, August 13, 1973.

August 13, 1973
Jack Lynch
I want to admit frankly that when I made my statement last week to the effect that the first contact that we, the then Irish Government, had with the British Government about their involvement with the Littlejohn affair was the request for an affidavit . . . in connection with the extradition proceedings . . . I want to admit that I did not recall Mr McCann's [Secretary, Department of Foreign Affairs] visit to me and I would like to thank the Minister [Garret FitzGerald, Minister for Foreign Affairs] for his courtesy in asking Mr McCann to remind me.

Admission by Fianna Fáil leader – who offered to resign as a consequence – that he forgot being informed seven months previously by Irish Ambassador in London of British Government's admission of involvement in Littlejohn affair. On August 31 Lynch said he would stay on as Fianna Fáil leader. *The Irish Times*, August 14, 1973.

August 21, 1973
Major Hubert O'Neill
It strikes me that the [British] Army ran amok that day [Bloody Sunday] and shot without thinking what they were doing. They were shooting innocent people. These people may have been taking part in a march that was banned, but that does not justify the troops coming in and firing live rounds indiscriminately. I would say without hesitation that it was sheer unadulterated murder. It was murder.

Finding, as Derry City Coroner (and former British Army officer), on cause of death at inquest in Derry courthouse on thirteen victims of Bloody Sunday shootings on January 30, 1972. *The Irish Times*, August 22, 1973.

August 28, 1973
Dr Butler, Bishop of Connor (Church of Ireland)
He [Lord Brookeborough] was convinced that Roman Catholics should be excluded from responsibility and participation in Government . . . Lord Brookeborough was not a political visionary. He was not a man who thought in terms of long-term solutions to our problems. It can be argued that if he had thought differently, if he had acted differently,

Northern Ireland would not be in its present unhappy state.

In eulogy for Lord Brookeborough at memorial service after his death in Belfast's St Anne's Cathedral, attended by British Prime Minister Edward Heath. *The Irish Times*, August 29, 1973.

September 5, 1973
Rt Rev. G. W. Tickle

If [British] soldiers have killed, it has been in their own self-defence or in defence of the civilian population, or in the belief that in no other way could terrorists be prevented from doing their evil work ... [Major Hubert O'Neill, Derry City Coroner] was out of order. Roman Catholics would do well to reflect that a significant proportion of these soldiers are Roman Catholics themselves ... I am proud to be associated with an army which shows such restraint and compassion.

Speaking, as Bishop in Ordinary to Catholic chaplains in British Army, during press conference in Lisburn, when asked about coroner's finding of murder against British soldiers on Bloody Sunday. *The Irish Times*, September 6, 1973.

September 18, 1973
Edward Heath

If an Executive is not formed [from the NI Assembly] and functioning by the date laid down by the Act [March 1, 1974] there will be a situation of the utmost gravity. We cannot fall back on Direct Rule again ... There are those who favour ... total integration ... Northern Ireland could no doubt be run fairly and efficiently under such a scheme.

In London speech as Prime Minister, criticised for its support for integration of Northern Ireland with Britain, which he withdrew following day. *The Irish Times*, September 19, 1973.

September 29, 1973
Major Hubert O'Neill

It was sheer, unadulterated, cold, calculated and fiendish murder.

Finding as Derry City Coroner on cause of death at inquest on six people killed by IRA car bombs in Claudy. *The Irish Times* ('This Week They Said'), September 29, 1973.

October 13, 1973
William Whitelaw

I have met more clergy of all denominations in the past eighteen months than in the whole of

my previous life. Time will tell if it has done me any good.

On term of office as NI Secretary. *The Irish Times* ('This Week They Said'), October 13, 1973.

October 15, 1973
Brian Faulkner

A win is a win. The first past the post is the victor.

As Unionist Party leader, after anti-power-sharing motion rejected by 132 votes to 105 at meeting of Unionist Standing Committee, allowing Faulkner to continue negotiations on power-sharing with SDLP and Alliance. *The Irish Times*, October 24, 1973.

October 30, 1973
Rona Fields

The analogy with the Nazis is real. The operating systems which have historically resulted in the destruction of a people are in operation in Northern Ireland.

Speaking in Dublin as American sociologist and author of book on Northern Ireland – *Society on the Run*. *The Irish Times*, November 1, 1973.

November 20, 1973
Brian Faulkner

Any time I had a horse running in a race, I was very content if he won by a neck. Mr Whitelaw will recognise a winner.

As Unionist leader, after anti-power-sharing motion rejected by 374 votes to 362 at meeting of Ulster Unionist Council, again allowing Faulkner to continue negotiations with SDLP and Alliance on power-sharing. *The Irish Times*, November 21, 1973.

November 22, 1973
John Hume

For the first time in any part of Ireland, Protestant, Catholic and Dissenter will be working together to build a new society.

Speaking as SDLP deputy leader at press conference on power-sharing agreement. *The Irish Times*, November 23, 1973.

November 22, 1973
Brian Faulkner

I know enough of Mr [Gerry] Fitt and his colleagues to believe them to be men of their word, and I think he knows enough about me and my colleagues to believe us also to be men of our word ... we will make a fairly formidable combination in Ulster.

Speaking as Unionist leader at press conference on power-sharing agreement. *The Irish Times,* November 23, 1973.

November 22, 1973
Rev. Ian Paisley

The so-called settlement is nothing less than the first instalment and down payment on an eventual united Ireland scheme. That scheme will fail for the Unionist people are determined that they will never submit their necks to the heel of a Southern Parliament.

In interview at Bob Jones University on power-sharing agreement in North and on support from Dublin for Council of Ireland. *The Irish Times,* November 23, 1973.

November 22, 1973
Bernadette McAliskey (Devlin)

Paddy Devlin as Minister for Health? ... Was this the same Paddy Devlin who stood ... in the streets of Northern Ireland asking people not to pay rent, rates and other payments? Does the Government expect Mr Devlin to retain an ounce of credibility with his own community when he plays the debt collector of the Tory Government?

Attack in Commons on SDLP members of power-sharing Executive. *The Irish Times,* November 23, 1973.

November 22, 1973
Gerry Fitt

Mr [Paddy] Devlin has helped more people ... in one day than she [Bernadette Devlin] would ever do in her lifetime. The days of the charisma of Bernadette Devlin are gone. We have found out what the little girl is capable of doing.

As SDLP leader in Commons, replying to attack on SDLP members joining power-sharing Executive. *The Irish Times,* November 23, 1973.

November 25, 1973
Catholic Hierarchy

No change in State law can make the use of contraceptives morally right ... It does not follow of course that the State is bound to prohibit the importation and sale of contraceptives.

In statement following publication of private Bill to legalise sale of contraceptives, tabled in Seanad by Labour member, Mary Robinson. *The Irish Times.* November 26, 1973.

December 1, 1973
Rev. Ian Paisley

I have reason to believe that the fowl pest outbreaks are the work of the IRA.

The Irish Times ('This Week They Said'), December 1, 1973.

December 2, 1973
Conor Cruise O'Brien

If the [contraceptive] Bill is defeated, Northern Ireland will point to it as final proof that Home Rule does indeed mean Rome Rule ... Few things have done more damage to the cause of better relations between the two communities on this island than the atmosphere of pussy-footing or hugger-mugging that has prevailed in the Republic on such an issue.

As Coalition Government minister, speaking at Irish Humanist Association in Dublin. *The Irish Times,* December 3, 1973.

December 2, 1973
Cardinal Conway

It [legalising sale of contraceptives] would affect marital fidelity and mean a general extension of promiscuity ... There is a contagion in these things. The effect seems to spread.

Interviewed on RTE. *The Irish Times,* December 3, 1973.

December 9, 1973
Sunningdale Communiqué

The Irish Government fully accepted and solemnly declared that there could be no change in the status of Northern Ireland until a majority of the people of Northern Ireland desired a change in that status.
The British Government solemnly declared that ... if in the future, the majority of the people of Northern Ireland should indicate a wish to become part of a united Ireland, the British Government would support that wish. The Conference agreed that a Council of Ireland would be set up [which] could take executive decisions.

From text of agreement signed by British and Irish Governments and three NI power-sharing parties at Sunningdale. *The Irish Times,* December 10, 1973.

December 9, 1973
Rev. Martin Smyth
I think the negotiators will get a welcome home in Northern Ireland similar to that given to Chamberlain when he returned from Munich.

As Grand Master of Orange Order, commenting on Sunningdale Agreement setting up Council of Ireland (assuming, wrongly, that Chamberlain had been given cold reception). *The Irish Times,* December 10, 1973.

December 12, 1973
Brian Faulkner
I come here to speak in the Assembly and I find that this crowd of disloyalist wreckers, led by a demon doctor who goes round the country preaching sedition, are preventing me. It is diabolical ... the Unionist, SDLP and Alliance coalition will get good government going here.

Commenting after Assembly sitting adjourned after two minutes because of loyalist protests against Sunningdale Agreement. *The Irish Times,* December 13, 1973.

December 12, 1973
Roy Bradford
I am totally convinced that the Sunningdale Agreement will be recorded in the history books as the first realistic and workable response to the Irish question mark which has hung like a sword of Nemesis over Anglo-Irish relations.

Speaking as Unionist member of NI Executive to Unionists at Ballyholme. *The Irish Times,* December 13, 1973.

December 15, 1973
Ulster Defence Association
Brian Faulkner, despite his acknowledged shrewdness, has been conned, just as Michael Collins was conned in the formulation of the Anglo-Irish Treaty in 1921.

Commenting on Unionist leader's agreement on Council of Ireland at Sunningdale conference. *The Irish Times* ('This Week They Said'), December 15, 1973.

December 15, 1973
Tomás Mac Giolla
Mr Cosgrave has lived to confirm the work of his father, W. T. Cosgrave, who signed the partition Treaty of 1921 and the boundary agreement of 1925.

Commenting, as Official Sinn Féin President, on role of Taoiseach in signing Sunningdale Agreement with British Government. *The Irish Times* ('This Week They Said'), December 15, 1973.

December 27, 1973
Oliver Napier
Do you [people of Republic] really want a Council of Ireland? ... The Council of Ireland hangs by a thread ... if you do nothing in the next few weeks, history will judge you and its judgement will be harsh and unforgiving.

In open letter, as Alliance Party leader in North, to people of Republic, urging that concessions be made to Unionists on extradition, constitutional reform and security co-operation. *The Irish Times,* December 28, 1973.

January 2, 1974
Paddy Devlin
As far as I am concerned, sectarianism in Government employment [in Northern Ireland] is dead.

In interview, as SDLP Minister in NI Executive. *The Irish Times,* January 3, 1974.

January 7, 1974
Desmond Boal
Britain is in the process of disengaging ... the connection is in the process of being broken no matter how many hypocritical screams of horror come from people who have been blind to recent history ... I would now consider a federal Irish parliament ... with a provincial parliament possessing the powers recently held by Stormont.

In article as one of founders of Democratic Unionist Party of Rev. Ian Paisley who disassociated himself from views expressed. *The Irish Times,* January 8, 1974.

January 8, 1974
Ruairi Ó Brádaigh
The proposal [by Desmond Boal for a federal Ireland] was a giant step ... very courageous. He said that Protestants were concerned to preserve their heritage. Very good. This is the type of solution that would satisfy the Republican movement.

Responding, as Provisional Sinn Féin President, to proposal from colleague of Paisley for return of

Stormont within federal Ireland. *The Irish Times,* January 9, 1974.

January 16, 1974
Justice Murnaghan
[The acknowledgement] that Northern Ireland could not be reintegrated into the national territory until and unless a majority of the people of Northern Ireland indicated a wish to become part of a united Ireland [was] no more than a statement of policy.

Ruling in Dublin High Court that Irish Government statement on North in Sunningdale Agreement was not repugnant to Constitution, as claimed by Kevin Boland, former Fianna Fáil minister. *The Irish Times,* January 17, 1974.

January 16, 1974
Hugh Logue
[The Council of Ireland is] the vehicle which would trundle the North into a united Ireland.

From speech prepared by SLDP member for debate at Trinity College. (John Hume, SDLP leader asked him not to deliver this sentence as it would be seized upon by loyalists, but script had already been circulated to newspapers.) White, Barry, *John Hume, Statesman of the Troubles,* Blackstaff, 1984, p. 156.

February 1, 1974
United Ulster Unionist Coalition
Dublin is only a Sunningdale away.

Slogan pasted up all over Northern Ireland in general election by Unionist candidates opposed to Council of Ireland, who won eleven of twelve seats. (Author's recollection.)

February 16, 1974
Harry West
Our newly elected members at Westminster must insist on the suppression, defeat and elimination of the Terrorists ... so that we may return to an Éire of peace, security and prosperity.

Daily Telegraph transcription of remark by leader of Unionists opposed to power-sharing, confusing words 'Éire' and 'era'. *The Irish Times* ('This Week They Said'), February 16, 1974.

February 21, 1974
Mary Robinson
We will be hypocrites with no right to the respect of the people of Northern Ireland or to self respect if we move a declaratory section

[from Constitution] giving a particular Church a privileged position while retaining the denominational moral outlook of that Church which is in conflict with the outlook of other Churches in the State.

Proposing, as Labour member of Seanad, private Bill to legalise sale of contraceptives. *The Irish Times,* February 22, 1974.

February 27, 1974
Liam Cosgrave
The Council of Ireland would not be a threat to the interests or loyalties of the majority in Northern Ireland who now oppose any change in the status of the area. It is not a way of achieving unity by stealth.

In statement to Dáil, as Taoiseach, after meeting with Unionist leader, Brian Faulkner. *The Irish Times,* February 27, 1974.

March 2, 1974
Kevin Boland
Redmondism ... has become rampant. The one-time Republican Party [Fianna Fáil] still dithers about openly embracing it ... but the Coalition parties [Fine Gael and Labour] have grasped the nettle with both hands ... Venal politicians with a vested interest in the status quo ... have blasphemed the cause that dead generations of Ireland served ... The primary national need now, as it was in Tone's day, is to break the connection with England. When it is done, the rest will follow by peaceful evolution.

As former Fianna Fáil minister, addressing Árd Fheis of his new party, Aontacht Éireann. *The Irish Times,* March 4, 1974.

March 9, 1974
Rev. Fr Denis Faul
Is it the Irish ideal for a bridegroom to fly out to Majorca with new wife and a pocketful of contraceptives, removing all the romance out of marriage?

Opposing legalisation of sale of contraceptives in Republic. *The Irish Times* ('This Week They Said'), March 9, 1974.

March 9, 1974
Rev. Fr James Healy, SJ
I am proud to say I know happy, healthy couples, in love with each other, who have

abstained from sexual intercourse for over twenty years.

Speaking, as professor of moral theology and President of Milltown Institute, Dublin, against legalisation of sale of contraceptives. *The Irish Times* ('This Week They Said'), November 9, 1974.

March 13, 1974
Liam Cosgrave
The factual position of Northern Ireland is that it is within the United Kingdom and my government accepts this fact. I now solemnly reaffirm that the factual position of Northern Ireland within the United Kingdom cannot be changed except by a decision of a majority of the people of Northern Ireland.

As Taoiseach, in further attempt to reassure Unionists about status of North under Sunningdale. *The Irish Times*, March 14, 1974.

March 13, 1974
Major Vivion de Valera
[Mr Cosgrave came] perilously near recognising without qualification a de jure right of a section of the Irish people to maintain partition.

As Fianna Fáil TD, responding to declaration on status of Northern Ireland by Taoiseach. *The Irish Times*, March 14, 1974.

March 13, 1974
Brian Faulkner
For the first time a Government of the Republic has made a solemn declaration which accepts our right to remain part of the United Kingdom for as long as that is the wish of a majority of our people.

Responding, as leader of NI Executive, to Dáil declaration of March 13 by Taoiseach on status of Northern Ireland. *The Irish Times*, March 14, 1974.

March 13, 1974
John Laird
Instead of being a step forward, it was more like a half-inch shuffle.

As Unionist Assembly member opposed to Faulkner, on Dáil declaration by Taoiseach on status of Northern Ireland. *The Irish Times*, March 14, 1974.

March 17, 1974
John Kelly
Once upon a time the mention of Irishman suggested the pig in the parlour. We resented

this ignorant smear . . . but it was at least better than the 'bomb in the boot' image that is now being wished on us by our own people.

As Fine Gael TD, addressing Irish Universities Club in London. *The Irish Times*, March 18, 1974.

March 25, 1974
Willy John McBride
I'm a rugby player, not a politician and as an Irishman I'm proof that rugby and politics are divorced.

As Irish international, justifying acceptance of captaincy of Lions team to tour South Africa. *The Irish Times*, March 26, 1974.

March 30, 1974
Joseph B. Murray
I have received pledges from 2,000 people and two Protestants.

Comment by President of League of Decency. *The Irish Times* ('This Week They Said'), March 25, 1974.

March 30, 1974
James Downey
We have got the pigs out of the parlour but we have not yet shifted the bishops out of the bedroom.

As *Irish Times* political correspondent, referring to John Kelly's comments of March 17, 1974. *The Irish Times*, March 30, 1974.

April 1, 1974
Garret FitzGerald
It is South Africa which has brought politics into sport . . . the question which we as Irish people have to consider is whether we want to encourage this process of human degradation by involving ourselves in it.

As Minister for Foreign Affairs, appealing to Irish Rugby Football Union over selection of seven Irish players for Lions tour of South Africa. *The Irish Times*, April 2, 1974.

April 13, 1974
P. C. Henry
To give the BBC the free run of Ireland, as suggested by the Minister of Posts and Telegraphs [Conor Cruise O'Brien] is tantamount to reconquest.

Commenting, as Professor of Old and Medieval English at UCG, on controversy over moves to relay BBC broadcasts throughout Republic. *The Irish Times* ('This Week They Said'), April 13, 1974.

April 24, 1974
Roy Mason
Pressure is mounting on the mainland to pull out the troops; equally, demands are being made to set a date for withdrawal.

Speaking as British Defence Secretary at Staffordshire. *The Irish Times*, April 25, 1974.

April 25, 1974
Conor Cruise O'Brien
I am allowing the directive issued by my predecessor to stand [forbidding representatives of paramilitary groups to broadcast on RTE] ... I am determined to ensure as far as I can that while armed conspiracies continue to exist in this country, their agents shall not be allowed to use the State broadcasting system for a systematic propaganda effort.

As Minister for Posts and Telegraphs, replying to NUJ criticism of his retention of directive issued under Section 31 of Broadcasting Act. *The Irish Times*, April 26, 1974.

May 13, 1974
Harold Wilson
These documents reveal a specific and calculated plan on the part of the IRA by means of ruthless and indiscriminate violence to foment inter-sectarian hatred and a degree of chaos, with the object of enabling the IRA ... to occupy and control certain predesignated and densely-populated areas in the centre of Belfast ... their intentions would have been to carry out a scorched-earth policy of burning the houses of the ordinary people as they were compelled to withdraw.

As Prime Minister, informing Commons of contents of IRA documents found in house at Myrtlefield Park, Belfast. *The Irish Times*, May 14, 1974.

May 14, 1974
Ulster Workers' Council
This strike has been organised by the Ulster Workers' Council as a result of the decision by the Assembly to support the Sunningdale Agreement.

Announcing start of loyalist strike against power-sharing Executive after Assembly had voted forty-four to twenty-eight to ratify Sunningdale Agreement setting up Council of Ireland. *The Irish Times*, May 15, 1974.

May 15, 1974
Brian Faulkner
The Northern Ireland public is again being made the target of irresponsible extremists who abuse the freedom of the press and television to make the most reckless pronouncements to the public without regard for the consequences. Where do they come from? Who elected them? What is their authority?

As leader of power-sharing Executive on statements from Ulster Workers' Council about their intention to bring it down by stoppages. Fisk, Robert, *The Point of No Return*, Deutsch, 1975, p. 62.

May 16, 1974
Harry Murray
If that parrot beside you doesn't stop nodding, his head will fall off.

As chairman of Ulster Workers' Council, at Stormont Castle meeting, addressing junior Minister Stanley Orme and referring to NIO Permanent Secretary Frank Cooper who showed vigorous approval of what Orme was saying. *The Irish Times*, March 20, 1976.

May 17, 1974
Sammy Smyth
I am very happy about the bombings in Dublin. There is a war with the Free State and now we are laughing at them.

As UDA press officer, after UDA car bombs had killed twenty-three people in centre of Dublin. *The Irish Times*, May 18, 1974.

May 17, 1974
Harry West
Loyalist workers are prepared to plunge the country into chaos.

Commenting, as leader of Official Unionist Party, on determination of loyalist strikers to bring down NI power-sharing Executive. *The Irish Times*, May 18, 1974.

May 19, 1974
Roy Bradford
If the strikers ... are saying that the Council of Ireland should not be implemented until the people have a chance to give their verdict at the poles, there is solid sympathy for this view among pro-Assembly Unionists ... the Secretary of State should be encouraged to reopen lines of communication with the Ulster

Workers' Council before the province is allowed to slide into chaos.

As Unionist Environment Minister in NI power-sharing Executive, in statement which ran counter to declared policy of power-sharing parties not to negotiate with loyalist strikers. *The Irish Times,* May 20, 1974.

May 21, 1974
Seamus Mallon

I must remind this man [pointing to Roy Bradford] that political treachery is not forgotten, no less than other forms of treachery. It is reprehensible for this man to act the Pontius Pilate on his colleagues.

As SDLP member in NI Assembly, directing his remarks to Environment Minister in power-sharing Executive who had suggested negotiations with loyalist strikers. *The Irish Times,* May 22, 1974.

May 21, 1974
Len Murray

It is not a strike. It is a stoppage of work imposed by an unrepresentative group of people on the vast mass of people in Northern Ireland who want to go to work today and tomorrow and next week and all the time.

As TUC General Secretary, during unsuccessful attempt to lead shipyard employees back to work during loyalist strike. Fisk, Robert, *The Point of No Return,* Deutsch, 1975, p. 109.

May 22, 1974
Brian Faulkner

We do recognise that for a long time there have been fears among a fairly large number of people on this matter of a Council of Ireland . . . we have called for a test of opinion at the next election.

Announcing, as Chief Minister of NI power-sharing Executive, decision to postpone giving any powers to a Council of Ireland, due to be set up under Sunningdale Agreement of December 9, 1973. *The Irish Times,* May 23, 1974.

May 22, 1974
Rev. Ian Paisley

The Faulkner Unionists . . . are now preparing to force the people of Northern Ireland to swallow Sunningdale in two spoonfuls instead of one.

In statement, as DUP leader, on decision of power-sharing Executive to delay transferring any powers

to a Council of Ireland. *The Irish Times,* May 23, 1974.

May 25, 1974
Harold Wilson

The people on this side of the water . . . see property destroyed [in NI] by evil violence and are asked to pick up the bill for rebuilding it. Yet people who benefit from all this now viciously defy Westminster, purporting to act as though they were an elected government; people who spend their lives sponging on Westminster and British democracy and then systematically assault democratic methods. Who do these people think they are?

In televised broadcast from London, as British Prime Minister, to people of Northern Ireland restating support for power-sharing Executive in face of loyalist strike. *The Irish Times,* May 27, 1974.

May 25, 1974
Brian Faulkner

Today, I fear, we are the despair of our friends and the mockery of our enemies. Let us not plunge this country, which all of us love in our different ways, into a deepening and potentially disastrous conflict.

Appealing on television, as Chief Minister in NI power-sharing Executive, for end of loyalist strike against his administration. *The Irish Times,* May 27, 1974.

May 27, 1974
Merlyn Rees

I have this morning authorised British troops to take control of the distribution of petroleum products to essential users in the province . . . No parliamentary democracy . . . can accept that a gang of men, self appointed and answerable to no one, should decide when and where and to whom the essentials of life should be distributed . . . Let us all work together . . . Give peace a chance.

As NI Secretary, in 5am statement announcing Government decision to use troops to take over petrol depots. *The Irish Times,* May 28, 1974.

May 27, 1974
Hugo Patterson

The mind simply boggles at the thought of a whole community without electricity. Absolutely nothing will move . . . there'll be absolute chaos whenever we have this final shutdown. There's no question about that whatever.

Warning, as spokesman for NI Electricity Service, on day before threatened shut-down of power by loyalist strikers. Fisk, Robert, *The Point of No Return*, Deutsch, 1975, p. 182.

May 28, 1974
Lord Hailsham
It's no good being or calling yourself Loyalist if you don't obey the law, and this [Ulster Workers' Strike] is a conspiracy against the State. There is no doubt about it – in previous times, judges would have had no difficulty in describing it as high treason because it's an attempt to overthrow the authority of the Queen in Parliament.

In radio interview in London, as Lord Chancellor. Fisk, Robert, *The Point of No Return*, Deutsch, 1975, p. 223.

May 28, 1974
Department of the Environment, Stormont
The water and sewage situation is deteriorating. Workers are now leaving the plants. Even without a power supply, water could have been maintained for two or three days, but without workers this cannot be maintained. Supplies may now cease almost at once in some areas.

News release, issued by NI Executive. Office of Information Services, NI Executive, May 28, 1974.

May 28, 1974
John Hume
I'll sit here [Stormont] until there is shit flowing up Royal Avenue and then the people will realise what these people [loyalist strikers] are about.

As SDLP deputy leader, speaking to colleagues on power-sharing Executive before it fell with resignation of Unionist leader, Brian Faulkner. White, Barry, *John Hume, Statesman of the Troubles*, Blackstaff, 1984, p. 170.

May 28, 1974
Brian Faulkner
It is ... apparent to us, from the extent of support for the present stoppage, that the degree of consent needed to sustain the Executive does not at present exist. Nor, as Ulstermen, are we prepared to see our country

undergo, for any political reason, the catastrophe which now confronts it.

Announcement of resignation, as Unionist member of power-sharing Executive, because of effects of loyalist strike. Office of Information Services, NI Executive, May 28, 1974.

May 30, 1974
Lord Arran
I loathe and detest the miserable bastards ... savage murderous thugs. May the Irish, all of them, rot in hell.

Columnist writing in *London Evening News* on recent violence in Ireland. *The Irish Times*, May 31, 1974.

May 31, 1974
Merlyn Rees
There is a strong feeling of Ulster nationalism growing which will have to be taken into account and which it would be foolish to ignore.

At Stormont press conference, as NI Secretary, on success of loyalist strike in bringing down power-sharing Executive. *The Irish Times*, June 1, 1974.

June 2, 1974
Paddy Devlin
There [was] massive concealed resistance within the [Northern Ireland] civil service [to power-sharing] ... There had been a civil service revolt during the strike as part of the middle-class Protestant swing behind the loyalists in its last few days.

Commenting, as former minister in NI Executive, on success of loyalist strike in bringing it down. *The Irish Times*, June 3, 1974.

June 3, 1974
Reginald Maudling
Withdrawal of troops was a repugnant thought but there comes a time when one must consider any possibility no matter how repugnant.

Speaking in Commons as former Home Secretary on success of loyalist strike against power-sharing Executive. *The Irish Times*, June 4, 1974.

June 3, 1974
Merlyn Rees
It was not like the miners' strike. Speaking as a son of a miner, we never used guns. I refused to be bombed to the conference table

by the Provos, so I have been adamant that a sectarian strike by so-called loyalists, backed by paramilitary forces, would not force me to such a conference table.

Speaking in Commons, as NI Secretary, on loyalist strike against power-sharing executive. *The Irish Times,* June 4, 1974.

June 4, 1974
Harold Wilson

I noticed that yesterday [Mr Paisley] was wearing a small piece of sponge as a political symbol ... all the sponges in the ocean are not capable of washing away the things for which he has been responsible in Ulster over these past weeks.

As Prime Minister, in Commons debate, on Ulster Workers' Strike. *HC Debates:* Vol. 874: Col. 1045.

June 4, 1974
Edward Heath

We are facing the most ruthless group of urban guerrillas the Western world has ever seen.

Speaking, as Conservative leader, in Commons, about IRA. *The Irish Times,* June 5, 1974.

June 8, 1974
Rev. Fr Michael Connolly

This is a fitting tribute to a great man. The price of freedom has always been very high and Irishmen have always been prepared to pay it in full.

As Wolverhampton priest at paramilitary parade in London for IRA hunger striker, Michael Gaughan, in speech for which he was later disciplined by Church authorities. *The Irish Times,* June 11, 1974.

June 9, 1974
Rev. Fr Michael Keane

England is always seen as our enemy. But we may think how good a country it has been to us in the past, giving us work, opportunity and money. It is a pleasant land and it is a sad thing to see the fighting going on and on. Can we not sit down and talk?

In sermon at requiem Mass in Ballina for IRA hunger striker, Michael Gaughan, which prompted walk-out from church by Republican leader, Daithi Ó Conaill, and others. *The Irish Times,* June 10, 1974.

June 9, 1974
Earl of Donoughmore

We did not talk politics with them but they know a lot more about racing now.

On being released after being kidnapped by IRA from Clonmel home and held as hostage for lives of Price sisters, who came off hunger strike day before he was set free. *The Irish Times,* June 10, 1974.

June 13, 1974
Liam Cosgrave

They [people in the Republic] are expressing more and more, and I mention this simply as a matter of record without comment, one way or the other, the idea that unity or close association with a people so deeply imbued with violence and its effects is not what they want. Violence ... is killing the desire for unity.

As Taoiseach, referring to North, in Dáil. *The Irish Times,* June 14, 1974.

June 22, 1974
Micheál Mac Liammóir

What a paradise Ireland would be if it had as much affection and respect for the living as it has for the dead.

The Irish Times ('This Week They Said'), June 22, 1974.

June 25, 1974
Bridget Rose Dugdale

I stand proudly here as the perpetrator of a calm political act to change the corporate conscience of a Cabinet. If 'guilty' has come to describe one who takes up arms to defend the people of Ireland against the British tyrant, who would deprive the people of their land and their wealth, then I am guilty, proudly and incorruptibly guilty.

Plea in Special Criminal Court on charge of receiving nineteen paintings stolen from Alfred Beit, for which she received nine-year sentence. *The Irish Times,* June 26, 1974.

July 1, 1974
Harry West

There are more ways, Dr FitzGerald, of killing a dog than stuffing its mouth with butter.

Remark, as Unionist leader, to Minister for Foreign Affairs at meeting in Belfast, referring to Irish attempts to placate Unionists. *The Irish Times*, July 6, 1974.

July 11, 1974
Michael Kitt
He [Michael Kitt] never thought he'd live to see the day when he'd be asked in an Irish Parliament to betray that society which the great Mr de Valera extolled in his celebration of the delights and serenity of the peasant society of comely maidens and athletic young men on the village green.

Fianna Fáil TD from Galway speaking in Dáil on Bill to make contraceptives available. *The Irish Times*, July 12, 1974.

July 11, 1974
Oliver J. Flanagan
It is a vote against filth and dirt ... coupled with the chaotic drinking we have, the singing bars, lounge bars, the side-shows and all-night shows, the availability of contraceptives will, in my opinion, add more serious consequences to those already there. You do not quench a fire by sprinkling it with petrol.

Fine Gael TD from Laois/Offaly, speaking in Dáil on Bill to make contraceptives available. *The Irish Times*, July 12, 1974.

July 11, 1974
Michael Kennedy
If in a small town or village one chemist applied for a licence to sell contraceptives and another did not, did the Minister not think that this would give rise to a reaction within the community that so and so is the man who handles the quare things?

As Fianna Fáil frontbench spokesman, speaking in Dáil on Bill to make contraceptives available. *The Irish Times*, July 12, 1974.

July 20, 1974
David Thornley
The Taoiseach has behaved like an idiot, but one thing he has succeeded in doing is getting himself into the Guinness Book of Records.

Commenting, as Labour TD, on decision of Taoiseach Liam Cosgrave to vote against his own Government's Contraception Bill, helping to defeat it by seventy-five votes to sixty-one. *The Irish Times* ('This Week They Said'), July 20, 1974.

July 31, 1974
Harold Wilson
We now understand that the Conservative leadership are entering into discussions with the Unionist extremists with whom they wouldn't be seen dead when they were in Government ... It is outrageous and squalid.

As British Prime Minister, on speculation that Tory Party was preparing to offer Unionists extra NI seats in return for Commons support (as Labour did some years later). *The Irish Times*, August 5, 1974.

August 8, 1974
Lieutenant-General Sir Frank King
If you get a very large section of the population which is bent on a particular course, then it is a difficult thing to stop them taking that course ... you can't go round shooting people because they want to do a certain thing.

Interviewed, as General Officer Commanding (NI), on why British Army felt it could not stop loyalist strike that brought down power-sharing Executive. Fisk, Robert, *The Point of No Return*, Deutsch, 1975, p. 152.

September 25, 1974
Conor Cruise O'Brien
In the event of a British withdrawal ... it is virtually certain civil war would break out in Northern Ireland ... It is reliably estimated that with its present effective size it [the Irish Army] could, if called upon, hold one Border town, e.g. Newry ... Dublin's present policy is aimed mainly at doing everything in our power that might help to avert the emergence of a Loyalist majority in the [NI] Convention elections.

In confidential document written as member of Coalition Government and circulated to Labour Party Administrative Council, and leaked to *Irish Times*. *The Irish Times*, September 25, 1974.

October 3, 1974
Brian Faulkner
We ask the electors ... to support candidates who: (one) accept the wishes of the majority of our citizens to stay in the United Kingdom; (two) are ready to get together to work in Government.

In election call as leader of Unionist Party of Northern Ireland (UPNI) widely interpreted as support for SDLP in his own constituency of South

Down where SDLP was only power-sharing party.
The Irish Times, October 4, 1974.

October 14, 1974
Ivan Cooper
[Broadcasting the Angelus on RTE] was
essentially for Catholics and excluded a
section of the population ... if people south of
the Border wanted to move towards unity,
they would have to get rid of it.

In interview on RTE as Protestant SDLP Assembly
member. *The Irish Times*, October 15, 1974.

October 18, 1974
Garret FitzGerald
The society that we have created here in the
Republic is one which is unattractive not
merely to bigoted Loyalists but indeed to
moderate and liberal Protestants in Northern
Ireland ... we must have ... the courage to
make ... changes.

As Minister for Foreign Affairs, at Dublin meeting.
The Irish Times, October 19, 1974.

October 28, 1974
Rev. Joseph Parker
I would be very concerned for the future of
Christianity in Ireland because I think there is
a grave danger that institutionalised Churches
have been a hindrance towards reconciliation
... [I leave as] a sad, lonely and disillusioned
man.

Church of Ireland founder member of Witness for
Peace movement, started when son Stephen killed
on Bloody Friday, announcing he was leaving North
with no plans ever to return. *The Irish Times*,
October 29, 1974.

November 17, 1974
Daithi Ó Conaill
The consequences of war are not going to be
kept solely in Ireland, they are going to be felt
on the mainland of Britain.

In statement, as Republican leader, four days before
nineteen people killed in Birmingham bombings.
The Irish Times, November 23, 1974.

November 25, 1974
Roy Jenkins
These powers are draconian. In combination,
they are unprecedented in peacetime. I believe
they are fully justified to meet the clear and
present danger.

As Home Secretary, introducing Prevention of
Terrorism Act, allowing detention for seven days
without charge and expulsion from UK, after
Birmingham bombings of November 21, which
killed nineteen people. *The Irish Times*, November
26, 1974.

November 28, 1974
Kevin McNamara
We in this House have a duty not only to pass
this legislation to protect our own people but
also to pause and think why it is that such a
dreadful massacre as took place in
Birmingham would suddenly precipitate a
debate about Northern Ireland in this House
this week.

As British Labour MP, in Commons debate on
Prevention of Terrorism Act introduced after
Birmingham bombings. *The Irish Times*, November
29, 1974.

December 1, 1974
Rita Childers
On the very evening ... of the burial of
President Childers, I was shocked when it was
reported that the hackles were up over ...
seating at the funeral services. The nation and
my family had only just said goodbye to him
at Derrylossary when this almost unbelievable
degradation of the Presidency began in
Dublin. Only two days later my name was
printed ... as a favoured candidate ... some
reports asserted that I was merely being used
as a 'ruse' ... I saw how once again a woman
in Ireland can be regarded as a mere baggage.

Commenting on unsuccessful manoeuvring in
Leinster House to force Fianna Fáil to accept her as
Presidential nominee to succeed her husband,
Erskine Childers. *The Irish Times*, December 2,
1974.

December 11, 1974
Daithi Ó Conaill
The national leadership of the IRA did not
order that attack [Birmingham bombings]. To
the contrary, we condemn it. An attack like
the one in Birmingham is murder.

In interview as Republican leader in German
magazine, *Stern*. *The Irish Times*, December 12,
1974.

December 12, 1974
Dr Butler, Bishop of Connor (Church of Ireland)
We were all most impressed with their attitude, with their fairmindedness, and we were so pleased to find that they were talking seriously and deeply and with great conviction and had listened very carefully to what we had to say.

Commenting, as member of delegation of Protestant churchmen, on December 10 meeting with leaders of IRA at Feakle, as result of which IRA called ceasefire on December 22. *The Irish Times*, December 13, 1974.

January 1, 1975
William Shannon
Once again there is the shadow of the gunman and the crack of the sniper's rifle, once again Irish freedom fighters are interned without trial.

In article in 1975 *Annual of American Historical Society*, used to embarrass him when appointed US Ambassador to Ireland four years later. *The Irish Times*, September 23, 1980.

January 16, 1975
The IRA
Principally due to a total lack of response to our peace proposals by the British Government, the Army Council cannot in conscience renew the order suspending offensive military actions.

Announcing end of ceasefire called after talks with Protestant churchmen at Feakle on December 10, 1974. *The Irish Times*, January 17, 1975.

January 30, 1975
Jack Lynch
Mr Haughey had given a personal undertaking that he fully supported and was committed to the party's policy on Northern Ireland as enunciated by me as party leader.

On restoring Charles Haughey to Fianna Fáil front bench for first time since 1970 arms trial. *The Irish Times*, January 31, 1975.

January 30, 1975
Charles Haughey
In the sense that it's open to anybody at any time to put themselves forward to be leader of a party, there is always a perennial challenge to any leader of any political party. But at the moment the leadership of the party is not an issue.

On being restored to Fianna Fáil frontbench for first time since 1970 arms trial. *The Irish Times*, January 31, 1975.

February 6, 1975
Justice McGonigle
What appears before me today under the name of the UDA is gang law, a vicious and brutalising organisation. This is not an association of decent hard-working respectable people that is represented before me.

Passing judgement in Belfast City Commission in 'Romper-room' (name taken from children's TV programme and applied to any room where sectarian victims were beaten to death) killing by Ulster Defence Association members of Ann Ogilby. *The Irish Times*, February 7, 1975.

February 9, 1975
The IRA
In the light of discussions which have taken place between representatives of the Republican movement and British officials on effective arrangements to ensure that there is no breakdown of a new truce, the Army Council of Óglaigh na hÉireann have renewed the order suspending military action.

Announcing renewed ceasefire after meeting British officials. *The Irish Times*, February 10, 1975.

February 9, 1975
Merlyn Rees
A genuine and sustained cessation of violence can be the basis for a more constructive and peaceful future for Northern Ireland.

As NI Secretary, on renewal of IRA ceasefire, using for first time phrase about violence which he repeated many times in subsequent statements directed at IRA. *The Irish Times*, February 10, 1975.

February 24, 1975
Seamus Costello
It had never been true, despite press and other rumours, that [the IRSP] had a military wing.

As Irish Republican Socialist Party leader at Belfast funeral of IRSP member shot by Official IRA. *The Irish Times*, February 25, 1975.

February 27, 1975
Cathal Goulding

By God, the threats of a few misguided and confused malcontents will not stop us now.

As Official IRA leader at Belfast funeral of IRA member shot in 'war' with IRSP. *The Irish Times,* February 28, 1975.

April 12, 1975
Lieutenant-General Sir Frank King

The [British] Army was making such good progress that in another two or three months we would have brought the IRA to the point where they would have had enough ... If the ceasefire had not been agreed ... the campaign would have been over in two months.

Speaking, as General Officer Commanding (NI), at meeting in Nottingham on ceasefire agreed between IRA and Government officials. *The Irish Times,* April 14, 1975.

April 14, 1975
Merlyn Rees

The General has expressed his regrets to me. The Government's actions with regard to the role of the Army ... will be ... directly related to a genuine and sustained cessation of violence.

As NI Secretary, informing Commons of outcome of meeting with General Sir Frank King, GOC (NI), about King's criticism on April 12 of IRA ceasefire arrangement. *The Irish Times,* April 15, 1975.

May 8, 1975
Harry West

We in the United Ulster Unionist Coalition will not use our position to kick the minority around ... we will work in partnership in many matters ... with those who hold sentiments and hopes of a united Ireland [but] we are not going to be responsible for allowing the hand of such a person to be laid on the actual steering wheel of state.

As Unionist leader, on opening of NI Convention in which loyalists gained majority of fourteen seats. *The Irish Times,* May 9, 1975.

May 21, 1975
Dean Victor Griffin

Any society pledged to uphold democracy and freedom must be prepared to tolerate different views and practices in relation to moral questions ... as a pluralist society [which] will keep its legislation on controversial moral matters to the minimum necessary to safeguard society from abuses and moral anarchy.

Addressing Church of Ireland Synod in Dublin, as Dean of St Patrick's Cathedral. *The Irish Times,* May 22, 1975.

May 23, 1975
Dr Casey, Bishop of Kerry

We have never asked as a Church that our moral law be reflected in the civil law.

At Maynooth press conference, responding to questions about call by Church of Ireland Synod for more pluralist society and change in divorce and contraception laws. *The Irish Times,* May 24, 1975.

May 25, 1975
Rev. William Arlow

The British ... made a firm commitment [to the IRA] to withdraw ... If the Convention failed to produce a structure of government for Northern Ireland, they [the British] would begin a programme of withdrawal ... they would do what the Americans call a Vietnam; they would pull out.

Interviewed on RTE as Church of Ireland minister in touch with both IRA and British officials. *The Irish Times,* May 26, 1975.

May 27, 1975
Merlyn Rees

There will be no sell-out. A genuine and sustained cessation of violence would create a new situation.

Responding, as NI Secretary, to claim by Rev. William Arlow on May 25 that Britain had given commitment to withdraw. *The Irish Times,* May 28, 1975.

June 7, 1975
Oliver Napier

Europe needs us as much as we need Europe.

Alliance Party leader on EEC membership. *The Irish Times* ('This Week They Said'), June 7, 1975.

June 17, 1975
Rev. Ian Paisley

No one in the SDLP was going to become a United Unionist and no one believed [I myself] was going to join the SDLP. But could we not have a united Ulster in which each . . . would be justly proud?

In first major Convention debate, as one of three Unionist leaders. *The Irish Times,* June 18, 1975.

June 19, 1975
John Hume

An approach which seeks to exclude other traditions leads only to the grave, destruction, death and conflict. It may satisfy the bugles in the blood, it may satisfy the atavism in everyone, we may feel proud of it, but it will not succeed.

In first major Convention debate, as SDLP deputy leader. *The Irish Times,* June 20, 1975.

June 24, 1975
William Craig

Violence created violence. Sectarian killings . . . illustrated just how true that was and how depraved people had become . . . they [politicians] must see to it that this sort of conduct could no longer be perpetuated.

In first major Convention debate, as one of three Unionist leaders. *The Irish Times,* June 25, 1975.

July 7, 1975
Robert Molloy

I wish to make it clear that I acted in good faith in making these allegations and that I also acted in good faith in the subsequent withdrawal and in the public apology which I gave. I am however conscious that my action in this matter in present circumstances may be of some embarrassment to the Fianna Fáil party.

On resigning from Fianna Fáil frontbench after making and then withdrawing allegation against Minister for Local Government James Tully that he had improper association with businessman. *The Irish Times,* July 8, 1975.

July 11, 1975
James Tully

Less than two years ago I opened the first fifty-one houses on this estate for Bobby Farrell . . . It is great to see him making such progress and I hope that firms like his will keep building good, cheap houses. Good luck, Bobby, and to hell with the begrudgers.

As Minister for local Government, at launch of housing development in Kells, before celebration

dinner and dance to mark withdrawal of allegations by colleague Molloy that he had improper business association with Bobby Farrell. *The Irish Times,* July 12, 1975.

September 9, 1975
William Craig

We [Unionists] have been less than wholehearted in our endeavours . . . it is no argument to say we were about to breach our undertaking on power-sharing . . . Coalition government . . . cannot be equated with the ill-named concept of power-sharing.

On resigning as leader of Vanguard Unionist Party because members failed to support his suggestion of coalition with SDLP in future government. *The Irish Times,* September 10, 1975.

October 2, 1975
Altiero Spinelli

Ireland had isolated itself. [I wonder] if it might not be a question of Catholic solidarity.

As EEC Commissioner, commenting on Ireland, alone among EEC countries, refusing to withdraw Ambassador from Madrid in protest at execution of five Basque separatists by Franco Government. *The Irish Times,* October 3, 1975.

October 6, 1975
Patrick Cooney

The payment of a ransom would be a private matter for Ferenka . . . but if it were to free Dr Herrema, the Government certainly would not disapprove of its being paid.

As Minister for Justice, on kidnapping of Dutch industrialist, Tiede Herrema, in attempt to free Republican prisoners. *The Irish Times,* October 7, 1975.

October 29, 1975
Fianna Fáil

Fianna Fáil calls on the British Government to encourage the unity of Ireland by agreement, in independence and in a harmonious relationship between the two islands, and to this end to declare Britain's commitment to implement an ordered withdrawal from her involvement in the Six Counties of Northern Ireland.

In new policy statement issued in Dublin. *The Irish Times,* October 30, 1975.

November 2, 1975
Gerry Fitt
Mr Lynch, whether he himself would agree or not, had put himself into the Provisional IRA camp in asking for a declaration from the British of their intention to withdraw from Northern Ireland.

Speaking on RTE, as SDLP leader, on call for British withdrawal by Fianna Fáil under leadership of Jack Lynch. *The Irish Times,* November 3, 1975.

November 8, 1975
Tiede Herrema
I have children of the same age and I see them [kidnappers] as children with a lot of problems. I must say that if they were my children I would do my utmost to help them.

At press conference held by Dutch industrialist after release by kidnappers, Eddie Gallagher and Marion Coyle, from house in Monasterevin. *The Irish Times,* November 10, 1975.

November 9, 1975
Colonel Gadafy
We always support people fighting for their freedom no matter where. We are backing Ireland which is fighting for its independence and not a religious war. We shall continue to assist until Ireland gains the final victory. But we shall never for any reason get involved in internal quarrels.

In interview in Italian journal *Il Tempo,* generally seen as indication that Libyan leader was re-thinking support for IRA. *The Irish Times,* November 10, 1975.

November 11, 1975
IRA gunman
Christ, I'm in the wrong house.

After shooting dead Belfast man in front of his family during Republican feud in which victim was not involved. *The Irish Times,* November 12, 1975.

November 12, 1975
Rev. Fr Denis Faul
If Senator Mary Robinson's Bill [legalising sale of contraceptives] was passed, fornication, adultery and abortion would be on the rates.

Speaking in TCD debate on Mary Robinson's Bill then before Seanad. *The Irish Times,* November 13, 1975.

January 5, 1976
Merlyn Rees
Unless someone in their right senses stops it, it will go on. This is not political violence. It is not concerned with what I may or may not say in political terms. It is straight gangsterism ... Something has got to emerge in the community to stop it. Extra soldiers, extra police by themselves just will not do it.

Commenting, as NI Secretary, on sectarian killing of five Catholics and ten Protestants in Co. Armagh. *The Irish Times,* January 6, 1976.

January 5, 1976
Cardinal Conway
Those who take a life for a life are spitting in the face of Christ.

Commenting on sectarian killing of five Catholics and ten Protestants in Co. Armagh. *The Irish Times,* January 6, 1976.

January 8, 1976
Rev. Robert Nixon
They were Unionists to a man and some were Orangemen, but as I knew them they would not hurt anyone; they would not even hurt those who took them out of that minibus ... I hope my grief does not distress anyone in the church. If they had all been rolled into one big man, they would not have had it in them to have hurt anyone ... but ... those responsible for the murder of five Catholics in the families of Reavy's and O'Dowd's might as well have stopped the minibus at Kingsmills themselves ... Those who murdered in those households sealed the fate of the ten who died on Monday.

Presbyterian minister at service for victims of massacre of ten Protestants at Kingsmills, Co. Armagh, after assassination of five Catholics on previous day. *The Irish Times,* January 9, 1976.

January 12, 1976
Edward Heath
What I find intensely depressing ... is that after six years of the most appalling civil strife, continuous bloodshed, and now one of the most brutal massacres of all, the parties in Northern Ireland are not able to come together ... it is this feeling that is bringing a majority of British people to say 'pull our

forces out' and there comes a point where no political party can withstand that feeling.

As former Conservative Prime Minister, speaking in Commons after sectarian killing of five Catholics and ten Protestants in Co. Armagh. *The Irish Times*, January 13, 1976.

January 12, 1976
Airey Neave

We must stand firm, resist voices of defeat, and not be intimidated, or beguiled into retiring to our tents to sulk.

As Conservative NI spokesman, replying in Commons to Edward Heath's warning of withdrawal of troops. *The Irish Times*, January 13, 1976.

February 1, 1976
Maire Drumm

If they send Frank Stagg home in a coffin, I would expect the fighting men of Crossmaglen would send the SAS home in boxes.

As Sinn Féin Vice President, at Derry meeting in support of Frank Stagg, Republican prisoner on hunger strike in Wakefield Prison, England. *The Irish Times*, February 6, 1976.

February 21, 1976
Governor George Wallace

It is of course none of my business. My folks have been here from Northern Ireland and Scotland — it's so long ago now it's now a foreign country in a sense — but we feel that we are kin ... I side with the side of peace in the hope that it will come not only to Catholic but to Protestant as well. I'm gonna pray for you all in Northern Ireland, Catholic and Protestant.

Commenting on events in Ireland in interview with *Irish Times* in Montgomery, Alabama. *The Irish Times*, February 21, 1976.

February 22, 1976
Joe Cahill

I pledge that we will assemble here again in the near future when we have taken your body from where it lies. Let there be no mistake about it, we will take it, Frank, and we will leave it resting side by side with your great comrade, Michael Gaughan.

Speaking, as Belfast Republican, at Sinn Féin service in Leigue cemetery, Ballina, after hunger striker, Frank Stagg, was buried by State on previous day to prevent IRA funeral. (The body was reburied secretly some months later). *The Irish Times*, February 23, 1976.

March 18, 1976
Merlyn Rees

Because of the divided community in the North and the fact that one section of the population did not favour increased links with London, such a change [increasing number of NI seats at Westminster] would not be feasible.

As NI Secretary, speaking during Commons exchanges on why Labour Party opposed giving NI extra Commons seats. *The Irish Times*, March 19, 1976.

March 25, 1976
Merlyn Rees

[I am] examining the action and resources required for the next few years to maintain law and order, to achieve the primacy of the police, and how there could be a progressive reduction of armed forces.

Announcing policy of putting RUC in front line against IRA, during Commons debate. *The Irish Times*, March 26, 1976.

April 1, 1976
Merlyn Rees

Mrs Maire Drumm ... boasted of sending British soldiers home in their coffins. She is rather like the women at the guillotine during the French revolution - she is knitting and enjoying what is going on.

Interviewed on radio, as NI Secretary, about remarks of Sinn Féin Vice President on February 1, 1976. *The Irish Times*, April 2, 1976.

April 11, 1976
A. J. P. Taylor

It is the British presence in Ireland that has created the past Irish problems and is helping to continue the present problem ... Every day the British stay is likely to increase the number of those who will be killed in the end ... I don't accept that withdrawal will necessarily lead in the end to a very bloody civil war ... the general tendency in these national conflicts is that the extremists are proven in the end to have taken the right line.

Interviewed, as British historian, on RTE. *The Irish Times*, April 12, 1976.

April 28, 1976
David Thornley
My presence [on the Sinn Féin platform] was directed by my desire to defend free speech. If there are prosecutions, they will have to start with me.

As Labour TD, after appearing on Sinn Féin platform at GPO, Dublin, where banned meeting was held. He was later fined. *The Irish Times,* April 29, 1971.

May 5, 1976
Dr Lucey, Bishop of Cork and Ross
If democratic rule means anything, it means majority rule, and if that majority is Catholic it means Catholic rule; if it is Protestant it means Protestant rule; if it is Muslim, it means Muslim rule ... if there is a dispute as to whether some particular thing such as divorce is a natural right or a religious right ... if the minority demanding it is a religious one and a sizeable one, the State may provide it for that particular group.

In sermon at Ovens, Co. Cork, on renewed debate on secularism in Irish society. *The Irish Times,* May 6, 1976.

May 6, 1976
Thomas Passmore
Éire is more Romish than Rome itself. It would make no difference to us if birth pills were sold over the counter by the bucketful and Bills for divorce were available at ten minutes' notice. How dare he [Dr Lucey, Bishop of Cork] offer crumbs of civil rights to Protestants as though they were something less than human beings.

Reacting, as Belfast Orange Grand Master, to suggestion of Dr Lucey on May 5, 1976, that divorce should be allowed to religious minorities. *The Irish Times,* May 7, 1976.

August 9, 1976
Maire Drumm
When the first boy or girl is sentenced after the first of March, will you march after us until we pull the town down? ... by God if it is necessary it will come down stone by stone, and if it is necessary other towns will come down, and some in England too.

Speaking, as Sinn Féin Vice President, at Belfast rally about British Government proposal to refuse special category status to IRA prisoners after March 1, 1977. *The Irish Times,* October 29, 1976.

August 9, 1976
Gerry Fitt
I don't think I will ever be as close to death until it actually happens. For a few seconds I was faced with a crowd who were actually in my bedroom. I had a revolver in my hand and I pointed it at them ... The thoughts that went through my head at that time all in the space of a few seconds were 'Gerry, this is how you die'; secondly, 'I hope to God you don't get my wife and young daughter', and thirdly, 'I hope to God I don't have to pull this trigger and kill someone myself.'

SDLP leader describing how he forced pro-IRA crowd out of his house in Antrim Road, Belfast, at gunpoint. *The Irish Times,* August 10, 1976.

August 29, 1976
Mairead Corrigan
[I] always thought that the people of the Falls and the people of the Shankill were just the same. Now I know ... we will get our peace with God and the Northern Irish people.

At rally as leader of Peace People after march up Shankill Road, Belfast, in first major demonstration following death on August 10 in Andersonstown of her sister's children when hijacked car crashed into them after driver shot dead by soldier. *The Irish Times,* August 30, 1976.

August 31, 1976
Liam Cosgrave
The Government believes the extent of violent crime by irregular, subversive, terrorist bodies ... and the further threat to the institutions of the State implied by [recent] events constitute a national emergency affecting the vital interests of the State.

As Taoiseach, proposing Declaration of Emergency which replaced that declared during Second World War in 1939. *The Irish Times,* September 1, 1976.

September 2, 1976
European Commission of Human Rights
They [interrogation techniques] constitute a breach of Article 3 of the [European] Convention [on Human Rights] in the form, not only of inhuman and degrading treatment but also of torture.

Finding in case brought by Republic on five techniques of interrogation used in 1971 on IRA suspects: hooding, wall-standing, use of 'white' noise and deprivation of food and sleep. *The Irish Times,* September 3, 1976.

September 2, 1976
Merlyn Rees
We regret the Irish Government's persistence in their raking over the events of five years ago ... the only people who can derive any satisfaction from all this are the terrorists.

Reacting on behalf of British Government to finding of European Commission of Human Rights in case brought by Republic that Britain had been guilty of torture in Northern Ireland. *The Irish Times,* September 3, 1976.

September 7, 1976
Paddy Donegan
The Government will never accept an acceptable level of violence.

As Defence Minister in Dáil, on Criminal Law Bill. *The Irish Times,* September 8, 1976.

September 26, 1976
Dr (Edward) Daly, Bishop of Derry
There is an open door. The politicians have only to push it. Realistically, you can hardly expect the bishops to advocate a law legalising contraception, but I assure you, the door is open.

Commenting on debate in Republic on reform of contraceptive legislation. *The Observer,* September 26, 1976.

October 18, 1976
Paddy Donegan
It was amazing when the President sent the Emergency Powers Bill to the Supreme Court. He did not send the powers of the Army [contained in Criminal Law Act] to the Supreme Court. He did not send the seven years maximum penalty for membership [of the IRA, also in Criminal Law Act]. He did not send the ten years maximum penalty for inciting people to join the IRA [also in Criminal Law Act] to the Supreme Court.

In my opinion he is a thundering disgrace. The fact is that the Army must stand behind the State.

Speaking as Defence Minister to army officers at Columb Barracks, Mullingar, on decision of

President Cearbhall Ó Dálaigh to refer Emergency Powers Bill to Supreme Court (as reported by Don Lavery, only reporter present). *The Irish Times,* October 19, 1976.

October 18, 1976
Joe Dowling
I consider today's remarks of the Minister for Defence to be a flagrant breach of both the spirit and the letter of the Constitution, compounded by the fact that they were delivered publicly before members of the Irish Army of whom the President is Commander in Chief.

As shadow Defence Minister, calling in Dáil for resignation as Defence Minister of Paddy Donegan for referring to President as 'thundering disgrace'. *The Irish Times,* October 19, 1976.

October 19, 1976
Cearbhall Ó Dálaigh
A special relationship exists between the President and the Minister for Defence. That relationship has been irreparably breached not only by what you said yesterday but also because of the place where, and the persons before whom, you chose to make your outrageous criticism. I adopt the term from today's leading article in *The Irish Times.* The gravamen of your utterance is 'In my opinion, he (the President) is a thundering disgrace'. These words, I find, are followed by the sentence 'The fact is that the Army must stand behind the State'. Can this sequence be construed by ordinary people otherwise than as an insinuation that the President does not stand behind the State? Have you any conception of your responsibilities as a Minister of State and in particular as Minister for Defence?

As President, responding in letter to Paddy Donegan's speech to army officers in Mullingar on October 18, 1976. *The Irish Times,* October 23, 1976.

October 19, 1976
Paddy Donegan
As you did not find it possible to accede to my request for an appointment, I hasten to make my apologies to you, sincerely and humbly, in this letter ... I wish to tender to you my very deep regret for my use of the words 'thundering disgrace' in relation to you.

As Defence Minister, in letter to President
Ó Dálaigh concerning his speech of October 18,
1976. *The Irish Times,* October 23, 1976.

October 21, 1976
Liam Cosgrave
I regret that the Minister should have made
any remarks which slighted the President . . .
The Minister for Defence did not attack our
institutions, he made what he and I regard as a
serious comment on what the President did in
a disrespectful way . . . the extent of his
apology demonstrates his regret.

As Taoiseach, making clear to Dáil that Defence
Minister Paddy Donegan would not be required to
resign because of his description of President as
'thundering disgrace'. *The Irish Times,* October 22,
1976.

October 22, 1976
Cearbhall Ó Dálaigh
The only way now open to me to assert
publicly my personal integrity and
independence as President of Ireland and – a
matter of much greater importance for every
citizen – to endeavour to protect the dignity
and independence of the Presidency as an
institution is . . . to resign.

As President, following Dáil vote by sixty-three to
fifty-eight not to force resignation of Defence
Minister Paddy Donegan for referring to President
as 'thundering disgrace' on October 18, 1976. *The
Irish Times,* October 23, 1976.

October 27, 1976
Jimmy Carter
It was a mistake for the United States
Government to stand quiet in the struggle of
the Irish for peace, for the respect of human
rights, and for unifying Ireland.

As Democratic presidential candidate, in speech in
Pittsburg to Irish Americans which he later said was
'misrepresented'. *The Irish Times,* October 29, 1976.

October 28, 1976
Betty Williams
When I am abroad, I have my two feet firmly
planted in Northern Ireland.

Replying, as leader of Peace People, when in
Germany, to criticism of her frequent trips abroad.
The Irish Times, October 29, 1976.

November 4, 1976
Paddy Devlin
The diminution of support for the [peace]
movement has been caused by the leaders and
the latest wave of political rejects who have
imposed themselves on the Peace People [who
are] carrying on a campaign of denigration of
established politicians.

As SDLP Assembly member. *The Irish Times,*
November 5, 1976.

November 9, 1976
Edward du Cann
It is a matter of fury that the Government
should have been saved by an MP who does
not believe in the United Kingdom.

Commenting on vote in Commons of Independent
MP for Fermanagh and South Tyrone, Frank
Maguire, which prevented defeat of Labour
Government in guillotine motion. *The Irish Times,*
November 10, 1976.

November 24, 1976
Bernadette McAliskey (Devlin)
You will be marching to the cheers of
reactionaries the length and breadth of
Britain. When you marched in the United
States, you were . . . a rebel against Authority.
On Saturday you would be marching with
Authority against the rebels.

As socialist leader, in message to American singer,
Joan Baez, who had announced intention of joining
Peace People march in London, planned for
November 27, 1976. *The Irish Times,* November 25,
1976.

November 27, 1976
Jane Ewart-Biggs
In Ireland I learned of its beauty and its
sorrow, and its sorrow became my sorrow.

Addressing London Peace People rally as widow of
former British Ambassador to Ireland, Christopher
Ewart-Biggs, assassinated by IRA in July, 1976. *The
Irish Times,* November 29, 1976.

December 2, 1976
John Pardoe
A date should now be set for withdrawal and
Northern Ireland politicians brought together
in a constitutional conference and told that in
two years the last British soldier and the last
British subsidy will be gone.

As Liberal MP, in interview in London. *The Irish
Times,* December 3, 1976.

December 6, 1976
Joan Baez
Bernadette [McAliskey] has accused me of interfering in things I know nothing of. All I can say is that it would take her a long time to understand anything about my kind of politics.

Speaking after Peace People rally at Boyne River about criticism from Bernadette McAliskey for associating with Peace People on grounds that they were doing work of establishment. *The Irish Times*, December 7, 1976.

January 1, 1977
Dr (Cahal) Daly, Bishop of Ardagh and Clonmacnoise
One has repeatedly denounced the IRA for mindless militarism, for their total lack of credible political thinking. But official policy in the North begins itself to look more and more like a replica of this . . . Northern Ireland threatens to become one of Britain's great historical failures . . . the political vacuum which Britain is leaving today is unpardonable and disastrous.

Commenting, in New Year's Day message, on British policy under NI Secretary Roy Mason. *The Irish Times*, January 1 and 3, 1977.

January 6, 1977
Peace People
There is little or nothing that political parties can do to solve our problems at this stage.

In policy document urging members to exercise community control. *The Irish Times*, January 10, 1977.

January 6, 1977
Roy Mason
[The BBC] was disloyal, supported the rebels, purveyed their propaganda and refused to accept the advice of the Northern Ireland Office on what views to carry.

Report of private remarks made by NI Secretary at dinner party in North for BBC governors. *The Irish Times*, January 7, 1977.

January 9, 1977
Garret FitzGerald
If the provisions for mixed marriages were more generously operated in other countries, why had nothing been done [in Ireland]? Everyone had responsibility. Not solely the

British Government was to blame for everything . . . the Churches had not fully undertaken their responsibilities. We must examine our record and our consciences.

As member of Coalition Government, addressing Dr Daly, Bishop of Ardagh and Clonmacnoise, in RTE exchanges over bishop's New Year message. *The Irish Times*, January 10, 1977.

January 9, 1977
Rev. Fr Des Wilson
I am blazingly angry when I see people traipsing up streets and over bridges. They had the opportunity to make changes in the [Catholic] Church but refused. What they want is peace without change.

Commenting, as Belfast priest, on Catholic Church leaders who supported Peace People marches but not Church reform. *The Irish Times*, January 10, 1977.

January 23, 1977
Sean Garland
We have dismissed from our ranks, too often with bitter, even deadly consequences for ourselves, those who subscribed to militarism, opportunism and attitudes that tended towards sectarian conflict and the destruction of our class.

Speaking, as national organiser at Official Sinn Féin Ard Fheis, in Dublin. *The Irish Times*, January 24, 1977.

January 27, 1977
Conor Cruise O'Brien
A new Constitution should be put before the people, omitting the present Articles 2 and 3 and freely declaring itself to be what it was . . . a Constitution for our actual present State consisting of 26 Counties.

Speaking as member of Coalition Government. *The Irish Times*, January 28, 1977.

January 30, 1977
Kieran McKeown
Miss Corrigan to visit Australia for five weeks . . . Mrs Williams to spend the month of March in the United States and Canada . . . other Peace leaders are to visit various European countries.

As leader of Peace People, outlining travel plans for his colleagues, at one-day peace conference in Belfast. *The Irish Times*, January 31, 1977.

February 8, 1977
Sam Silkin
I am authorised to give, in relation to the five techniques [of interrogation], the following unqualified undertaking, and I measure my words with care ... the five techniques will not in any circumstances be reintroduced as an aid to interrogation.

As British Attorney General, during hearing of Irish Government case against Britain in European Court of Human Rights at Strasbourg, concerning use of wall-standing, use of 'white' noise, hooding and deprivation of food and sleep in NI interrogations. *The Irish Times,* February 9, 1977.

February 10, 1977
Roy Mason
Britain had recognised it was guilty of ill-treating fourteen persons. We admitted it and we have paid these fourteen compensation. I would think that was a first-class example of a mature democracy. Only the IRA can gain by this continuing.

As NI Secretary, referring in Commons to Irish torture case against Britain before European Court of Human Rights. *The Irish Times,* February 11, 1977.

February 14, 1977
Joe Joyce, Don Buckley and Renagh Holohan
The heavy gang, as the group has been nicknamed within the force, physically assaults and applies severe psychological pressure on suspects.

Exposing, as reporting team in *The Irish Times,* existence of garda 'heavy gang', later confirmed in Amnesty report, which led to inquiry into garda methods. *The Irish Times,* February 14, 1977.

March 5, 1977
Charles Curran
I can see the reason for Section 31 [of the Broadcasting Act]. A Minister in Dublin told me once 'We in Ireland still have the whiff of gunpowder in our nostrils. That's why we have this Section'. We don't have the smell of gunpowder in Britain. That's why we don't have a Section 31 here.

In *Irish Times* interview, as Director General of BBC. *The Irish Times,* March 5, 1977.

March 7, 1977
John M. Lawson
[We] crossed the Border due to a map-reading error.

Describing to Dublin court how he and seven other armed SAS men found themselves in Co. Louth. *The Irish Times,* November 8, 1977.

March 9, 1977
William Whitelaw
I shall admit that I was very wrong and that I made a major mistake when I was in Northern Ireland.

As former NI Secretary, on his decision to allow special category status to paramilitary prisoners. *The Irish Times,* March 12, 1977.

March 17, 1977
Tip O'Neill, Edward Kennedy, Daniel Moynihan and Hugh Carey
Renounce any action that promotes the current violence or provides support or encouragement for organisations engaged in violence.

First joint anti-IRA statement from leading Irish American politicians who became known as 'Four Horsemen'. *The Irish Times,* March 31, 1977.

May 2, 1977
Fred Mulley
We cannot let Northern Ireland just feel they can do what the hell they like and the British Army will always bail them out.

Speaking, as British Defence Minister, on RTE about new loyalist strike. *The Irish Times,* May 14, 1977.

May 3, 1977
Rev. Ian Paisley
When I consider the drunkenness, lewdness, immorality and filthy language of many of those Members [of Parliament], I care absolutely nothing for their opinion. Ulster Protestants are not interested in gaining the goodwill of these reprobates.

As leader of Ulster Action Council strike, in response to call from NI Secretary Roy Mason to condemn activities of his followers. *The Irish Times,* May 4, 1977.

May 4, 1977
James Molyneaux
There is evidence that some people on the Action Council have a provisional government [for Northern Ireland] in mind, and are moving in that direction.

As Unionist leader at Westminster, announcing end of loyalist coalition with Paisley because of his organisation of loyalist strike. *The Irish Times*, May 5, 1977.

May 21, 1977
Liam Cosgrave
Not for the first time has this party stood between the people of this country and anarchy. And remember, those people who comment so freely and write so freely – some of them aren't even Irish – no doubt many of you are familiar with an expression in some parts of the country where an outsider is described as a blow-in. Some of these are blow-ins. Now as far as we're concerned they can blow out or blow up.

As Fine Gael leader, at party's Árd Fheis, departing from prepared speech to attack political commentators. *The Irish Times*, May 23, 1977.

June 5, 1977
Dr. Lucey, Bishop of Cork and Ross
They [partners in mixed marriage] have to agree that the children will be brought up as Catholics. That's the second part – first they have to agree what is going to happen to their children. Then, only if their agreement is that the children will be brought up as Catholics, will they get a dispensation [to marry].

In interview on strict conditions imposed in Cork to obtain Church dispensation for mixed marriages. *The Sunday Press*, June 5, 1977.

June 8, 1977
Robert Muldoon
Normal immigration requirements [are] being waived for people recommended by the Peace Movement. We are thinking of the people on the fringe, like the person who drove a car two years ago and now finds he can't get out of the organisation. Half the population of Northern Ireland have written to me asking 'why can't I come, I've done nothing', but it's important to give the Peace People moral support for their work. ·

As New Zealand Prime Minister, interviewed in London on his agreement to allow 'converted terrorists' from Northern Ireland to settle in New Zealand. *The Irish Times*, June 9, 1977.

June 23, 1977
Airey Neave
Could not TV give our children more of the routine of danger experienced by the RUC? Is it not possible to create a series showing a Belfast Starsky and Hutch?

Speaking, as shadow NI Secretary, at Media Society dinner in London. *The Irish Times*, June 24, 1977.

July 5, 1977
Garret FitzGerald
My greatest pride is a remark by a Northern politician that our [Coalition] Government had won more respect from both sections in the North than any previous Government had won from either.

In first speech to Dáil after becoming Fine Gael leader following Fianna Fáil election victory. *The Irish Times*, July 6, 1977.

July 6, 1977
Jack Lynch
Our position is that we desire unification of the Irish people and that the Irish people will manage their own affairs within this island without foreign and outside interference. (Requiring a British declaration of intent to withdraw?) No, I never said that.

As Taoiseach, at press conference following Fianna Fáil election victory. *The Irish Times*, July 7, 1977.

July 6, 1977
James Molyneaux
They [Unionist MPs] have agreed to a parliamentary pact with the [Labour] Government under which they would not vote to bring it down, in return for progress on administrative devolution for Northern Ireland and an increase in the number of Northern Ireland seats at Westminster.

As leader of Unionist MPs, speaking at press conference at Westminster on proposals put to them by minority Labour Government to stay in power. *The Irish Times*, July 7, 1977.

July 31, 1977
Senator Edward Kennedy
It is important for Irish Americans in the United States to do what we can to reassure the Protestants in Northern Ireland that they have nothing to fear from the Irish American community and that we are as concerned to reach a settlement that respects their basic rights as we are to secure the basic rights of the members of the Catholic community.

Speaking at Library of Congress in Washington. *The Irish Times*, August 1, 1977.

August 7, 1977
Aindrias O'Callaghan
We're telling Betty and we're telling Mairead, 'by all means go and sip champagne on the *Britannia*, but just tell Lizzie that as long as there's one British soldier in any part of Ireland, there will be always people who will struggle.'

As Sinn Féin Árd Comhairle member, speaking at Belfast rally about invitation from Queen Elizabeth to Peace People leaders, Betty Williams and Mairead Corrigan, to visit her on royal yacht *Britannia* during royal visit to Northern Ireland. *The Irish Times*, August 8, 1977.

August 11, 1977
Queen Elizabeth
If this community is to survive and prosper, they must live and work together in friendship and forgiveness. There is no place here for old fears and attitudes born of history, no place for blame for what is past.

In speech at New University of Ulster. *The Irish Times*, August 12, 1977.

August 11, 1977
Mairead Corrigan
The SDLP ... lost a lot of Catholic support by not going to meet Queen Elizabeth ... Many Catholics had not minded the Queen's visit ... They had let down many people on the Catholic side.

Replying, as leader of Peace People, to criticisms of their decision to meet Queen Elizabeth during NI tour. *The Irish Times*, August 12, 1977.

August 22, 1977
Dr Ó Fiaich, Archbishop of Armagh
I believe that the day will come when Ulster Protestants will see that the best way to fulfil

their aspirations and achieve happiness will be in the full Irish context.

On being appointed Archbishop of Armagh to succeed Cardinal Conway. *The Irish Times*, August 22, 1977.

Augut 30, 1977
President Carter
The United States wholeheartedly supports peaceful means for finding a just solution that involves both parts of the community of Northern Ireland ... a solution that the people in Northern Ireland as well as the Governments of Great Britain and Ireland can support ... In the event of such a settlement, the United States Government would be prepared to join with others to see how additional job-creating investment could be encouraged to the benefit of all the people of Northern Ireland.

In statement issued in Washington on US policy on North. *The Irish Times*, August 31, 1977.

August 30, 1977
Senator Edward Kennedy
My hope is that once a peaceful settlement is reached, the United States would undertake a Marshall-type programme of assistance to heal the wounds of the present conflict.

Commenting on President Carter's policy statement on North. *The Irish Times*, August 31, 1977.

September 13, 1977
Roy Mason
Her Majesty's Government has not made any pact or secret deal with Unionists at Westminster.

Denying, as NI Secretary, Unionist claims that number of NI seats would be increased as part of deal to keep minority Labour Government in office. *The Irish Times*, September 14, 1977.

September 17, 1977
Conor Cruise O'Brien
It is mischievous in its effects for the Government of the Republic to seek unity ... There is in fact more support for Irish unity in Britain than in [the whole of] Ireland ... Goodwill to an imaginary Ireland is dangerous to people living in Ireland.

Speaking as Labour Party member at Oxford conference, following which, in face of criticism from colleagues, he resigned party whip. *The Irish Times,* September 19, 1977.

September 28, 1977
Jack Lynch
I got a positive statement from the Prime Minister that there was not a scintilla of movement in that direction.

Referring to prospect of integration of NI with Britain, after summit meeting with British Prime Minister James Callaghan. *The Irish Times,* September 29, 1977.

October 3, 1977
Senator George McGovern
A united Ireland can neither be secured nor sustained short of bloody civil conflict because Northern Ireland Protestants genuinely fear Catholicism and its influence on the Dublin Government.

US presidential candidate, in report on Ireland published in Washington. *The Irish Times,* October 4, 1977.

October 8, 1977
Irish Independence Party
We hear much talk about the use of violence to coerce a million Unionists into a united Ireland. We hear too little talk about the use of force to compel half a million non-Unionists to remain within a united British kingdom.

From statement announcing launch of new NI political party, led by Fergus McAteer and Frank McManus. *The Irish Times,* October 9, 1977.

October 10, 1977
Betty Williams
The prize money would not belong to Mairead and me as some people will say. The Peace People have two and a half million pounds of projects on the table and this still would not be enough for what we have to do.

As leader of Peace People, on being told she and Mairead Corrigan had won Nobel Peace Prize, worth £80,000, which they later decided to keep for themselves. *The Irish Times,* October 11, 1977.

October 10, 1977
Mairead Corrigan
I accept the award on behalf of those people of the world, particularly in Northern Ireland, who have worked, and are working, so desperately for peace.

As leader of Peace People, on being told she and Betty Williams had won Nobel Peace Prize, worth £80,000. *The Irish Times,* October 11, 1977.

October 14, 1977
Margaret Thatcher
What happens in Ulster touches us all. It is a part of our country, our United Kingdom. Let the people of Ulster be assured of this – the Conservative Party stands rock firm for the Union of Great Britain and Northern Ireland.

Addressing Conservative Party rally in Blackpool, as party leader. *The Irish Times,* October 15, 1977.

October 14, 1977
Amnesty International
Maltreatment of persons detained in police stations [in the Republic] appears to have occurred in a number of cases ... Amnesty International is concerned that despite widespread allegations made public in Ireland earlier this year that persons under arrest have been maltreated, the Government of the time saw no necessity to instigate an impartial inquiry.

Report on activities of garda 'heavy gang'. *The Irish Times,* October 15, 1977.

October 19, 1977
Democratic Unionist Party
Save Ulster from Sodomy.

From advertisement in *Belfast News Letter* placed by party of Rev. Ian Paisley to oppose reform of homosexual legislation. *The Irish Times,* October 20, 1977.

November 8, 1977
Garret FitzGerald
It is hard to see precisely what is meant by the idea of divorce being a civil right. A right must surely be more clearly defined than would appear to be the case in this instance.

As Fine Gael leader, in speech at Kings Inns, Dublin. *The Irish Times,* November 9, 1977.

November 10, 1977
Canon Keith Walker
The crimes of Britain in Ireland during past centuries teach us that the moral justification of our presence in Ireland cannot be assumed, it can only be argued. We have taken from Ireland more than we have given.

In speech by Chichester clergyman to Church of England annual synod in London. *The Irish Times,* November 11, 1977.

November 14, 1977
William van Straubenzee

The Republic of Ireland is a haven for terrorists and takes its place proudly alongside states like Libya who also do not recognise the obligations of civilisation.

In article, as former Tory Minister of State for Northern Ireland, on Republic's refusal to sign European Convention on Suppression of Terrorism. *The Irish Times,* November 15, 1977.

November 24, 1977
Roy Mason

Every terrorist would rig a complaint when in jail. If he didn't, his mates would want to know why not ... prisoners were deliberately injuring themselves ... even if they had been 'taken on', TV reporters didn't mind as long as it was good copy.

As NI Secretary, commenting in Commons on Thames Television programme alleging brutality against prisoners by RUC. *The Irish Times,* November 25, 1977.

January 4, 1978
John McAuley

Pandering to the whim of those who wish to keep Ballymena's swimming pool open on Sundays would open the gates for a flood of godlessness such as Ulster has never seen.

As DUP Mayor of Ballymena, after using casting vote to close swimming pool on Sundays. *The Irish Times,* June 5, 1978.

January 8, 1978
Jack Lynch

I think it [the time for British declaration of intent to withdraw] has [come], yes. If the British Government indicated that they would like to see the Irish people coming together and not continue to subsidise a small corner of Ireland, I believe the people of the North would be realistic and hard-headed enough to reach accommodation with the minority there and with ourselves.

[As for the possibility of an amnesty in the future], naturally enough, if peace came and there was a complete ceasefire, we would look at the situation again.

Interviewed, as Taoiseach, on RTE. *The Irish Times,* January 9, 1978.

January 8, 1978
Eddie McAteer

Molaim thú. Your voice is the true voice of Ireland. One more heave and we can all get some real peace.

In telegram, as former Nationalist Party leader, to Taoiseach Jack Lynch, after Taoiseach called for British declaration of intent to withdraw from North. *The Irish Times,* January 9, 1978.

January 9, 1978
Roy Mason

I am surprised and disappointed by the unhelpful comments made by Mr Lynch ... Talk of an amnesty for those convicted on carefully-gathered evidence can do nothing but give succour to law-breakers.

As NI Secretary, responding to comments of Taoiseach on January 8. *The Irish Times,* January 10, 1978.

January 15, 1978
John Robb

What we need in the Ireland of the '80s is a Westminster withdrawal ... if the Protestants of Northern Ireland waited long enough they would either be spurned by Britain or out-voted by their Catholic fellow-Ulstermen into something they did not want. If they seized their opportunity while it still existed, they might even yet rise to become the architects of a new federal Ireland forged on the anvil of negotiated independence for Northern Ireland.

As Presbyterian leader of New Ireland Movement, from Co. Antrim, addressing Fianna Fáil youth conference in Cork. *The Irish Times,* January 16, 1978.

January 16, 1978
Dr Ó Fiaich, Archbishop of Armagh

I believe the British should withdraw from Ireland. I think it's the only thing that will get things moving.

In interview in *The Irish Press,* January 16, 1978.

January 16, 1978
Rev. Ian Paisley

[Dr Ó Fiaich] now could rightly be called the IRA's bishop from Crossmaglen.

Commenting on Archbishop's call for British withdrawal. *The Irish Times,* January 17, 1978.

January 18, 1978
European Court of Human Rights
[The five interrogation techniques] did not occasion suffering of the particular intensity and cruelty implied by the word torture as so understood.

In ruling delivered by European Court judges in Strasbourg, rejecting word 'torture' used by European Commission of Human Rights when finding in 1976 against Britain on use of wall-standing, 'white' noise, hooding and deprivation of food and sleep in interrogation of IRA suspects. *The Irish Times,* January 19, 1978.

January 18, 1978
Michael Flannery
It's my experience from being in jail and on the [IRA flying] column in Tipperary that morale could be seriously affected by men worrying about their wives and children. If we help these people it will help the IRA to have contented men. My intention is to help the IRA but not break the law here.

In *Irish Times* interview in Brooklyn, as leader of pro-IRA fund-raising body, NORAID. *The Irish Times,* January 19, 1978.

January 22, 1978
Airey Neave
These actions of a neighbouring State are becoming intolerable. I invite ... the Foreign Secretary to inform the Irish Government that we are no longer going to bear these insults with a stiff upper lip.

Speaking at Abingdon, as Conservative NI spokesman, on recent statements by Taoiseach Jack Lynch and others calling for British declaration of intent to withdraw. *The Irish Times,* January 23, 1978.

February 11, 1978
Garret FitzGerald
If I were a Northern Protestant, and I'm half a Northern Protestant, I wouldn't be happy about unification with people who haven't shown themselves to be open-minded. We need to shake people here out of their loyalty to the State to a wider loyalty to the Irish nation. This is so partitionist a State that Northern Protestants would be bloody fools to join it.

Speaking in Dublin, as Fine Gael leader. *The Irish Times,* February 13, 1978.

February 18, 1978
Betty Williams
[The Taoiseach, Jack Lynch] has given the Provisional IRA the go-ahead to continue their campaign.

Referring at Peace People rally in Dublin to Lynch's comments on possible future amnesty. *The Irish Times,* February 21, 1978.

February 19, 1978
The IRA
The IRA admits responsibility for the bombing operation in La Mon House in which twelve innocent people died ... We accept condemnation and criticism ... from the relatives and friends and from our supporters who have rightly and severely criticised us.

In statement acknowledging fire-bombing of La Mon House in Co. Down. *The Irish Times,* February 20, 1978.

February 19, 1978
Jack Lynch
I have it from the highest authority, from the British authorities themselves, that only two per cent of all the violence in Northern Ireland is generated from this side of the Border.

Speaking, as Taoiseach, on RTE. *The Irish Times,* February 20, 1978.

February 20, 1978
Roy Mason
I disagree absolutely and fundamentally with the statement [by Taoiseach Jack Lynch] that only two per cent of incidents affect the Border. There has been a high attrition rate against terrorists last year and now people are using the Border to operate from.

As NI Secretary, in Commons. *The Irish Times,* February 21, 1978.

February 20, 1978
Mairin Lynch
For a Peace leader to suggest that Jack Lynch ... could or would encourage murderous violence to promote the legitimate aspirations of [Fianna Fáil] ... is certainly not advancing

the cause of the Peace Movement on this island. The peace that obtains in the southern part of our country has been dearly bought. My husband has worked hard and unceasingly to maintain that peace.

As wife of Taoiseach, in letter to *The Irish Times* responding to comments of Betty Williams on February 18, 1978. *The Irish Times,* February 20, 1978.

March 9, 1978
Jack Lynch
I want to say forthrightly that my Government have never considered amnesty and have no intention of considering amnesty and certainly as far as the kind of violent crimes that have been committed in the North, we wouldn't contemplate amnesty for these kind of crimes.

As Taoiseach, in interview for television programme about his remarks of January 8, 1978, about possible future amnesty. *The Irish Times,* March 15, 1978.

April 4, 1978
Catholic Hierarchy
No change in State law can make the use of contraceptives morally right . . . it does not necessarily follow from this that the State is bound to prohibit the distribution and sale of contraceptives.

In statement before meeting Minister for Health Charles Haughey to discuss change in legislation on contraceptives. *The Irish Times,* April 5, 1978.

April 27, 1978
Harry West
Look at the birth rate. A majority of Roman Catholics will come in Northern Ireland. Not in my lifetime, but it will come. And it's inevitable that that majority will want to come into a united Ireland. It's inevitable that it will happen sometime.

Interviewed, as Unionist leader, by Olivia O'Leary in *The Irish Times,* April 27, 1978.

April 28, 1978
Paddy Duffy
Would I inform if I knew a murder had been committed? I'd never inform. I have to live around here you know. At least, I couldn't tell you exactly what I'd do. I'd be very cagey. I'd want to be one hundred per cent sure – and

that's almost impossible – before I'd put a boy in the hands of the RUC.

Interviewed, as leading SDLP member and Dungannon solicitor, by Olivia O'Leary in *The Irish Times,* April 28, 1978.

May 10, 1978
Tip O'Neill
The Protestants in Northern Ireland today have every right to be regarded as Irishmen. After all, if that were not the case, my family would not be entitled to call themselves Americans – for we have been in this country a far shorter time than those Protestants have been in Northern Ireland.

As Speaker of US House of Representatives, at Ireland Fund dinner in New York. *The Irish Times,* May 23, 1978.

May 28, 1978
Josie Airey
It's a strange thing that they [Irish Government] could take Britain to the European Court on torture charges, while their laws have been torturing me for years.

Cork woman, commenting on ruling of European Human Rights Commission that she had been denied proper access to Irish courts to obtain legal separation, because of lack of legal aid. *The Irish Times,* May 29, 1978.

June 4, 1978
Amnesty International
On the basis of the information available to it, Amnesty International believes that maltreatment of suspected terrorists by the RUC has taken place with sufficient frequency to warrant the establishment of a public inquiry to investigate it.

In finding on interrogations at Castlereagh police holding centre in Belfast. *The Irish Times,* June 5, 1978.

June 18, 1978
Rev. Ian Paisley
It certainly does not become the Protestant cause, or anybody claiming to be Protestant, to act in the same way the IRA has acted, and I would appeal to those responsible to return this gentleman to his home in peace and quietness and in safety.

Appealing, successfully, for release of Co. Antrim priest, Rev. Fr Hugh Murphy, kidnapped by loyalists after RUC constable, William Turbitt, had been abducted by IRA (and subsequently killed). *The Irish Times*, June 19, 1978.

June 19, 1978
Louis Hasrouni
If any Irish or other United Nations troops come in [to our area] we will defend ourselves and shoot if necessary – unless of course they telephoned us first and let us know they are coming.

Pro-Israeli Lebanese militia leader in *Irish Times* interview on deployment of Irish UN troops in south Lebanon. *The Irish Times*, June 20, 1978.

July 6, 1978
Rev. Ian Paisley
I would like to solemnly protest in the name of the Lord, Jesus Christ, the great King and Head of the Church. You can't reverse 400 years of history. The Mass is a blasphemous fable and a dangerous deceit.

Remarks addressed to Cardinal Hume in Westminster Hall crypt where Mass was being celebrated for first time in four centuries. *The Irish Times*, June 7, 1978.

August 1, 1978
Dr Ó Fiaich, Archbishop of Armagh
No one could look on them as criminals. These boys are determined not to have criminal status imposed on them.

Speaking after visit to Maze Prison, NI, where Republican prisoners were engaged in 'dirty' protest (by fouling cells) in claim for political prisoner status, creating conditions likened by Archbishop to Calcutta sewers. *The Irish Times*, August 2, 1978.

August 14, 1978
Daily Mirror
The *Mirror* believes that there is a policy – and only one – that can be carried through to success. And that is for Britain to announce its unshakable intention to withdraw altogether from Northern Ireland.

In leader, announcing change in editorial policy. *Daily Mirror*, August 14, 1978.

September 12, 1978
Ó Briain Committee
Nothing that we heard gave any ground for suspecting that garda questioning was ever done through sadism or for purposes of graft.

At worst it was suggested that the purpose of questioning was to extract confessions of guilt ... the practice of detaining persons for the purpose of questioning them has no justification in law.

In finding of committee headed by Justice Barra Ó Briain set up to investigate allegations of garda brutality, but most of whose recommendations on treatment of suspects were rejected by Fianna Fáil Government as too liberal. *The Irish Times*, September 13, 1978.

September 22, 1978
Professor Alfred Heijder
There can be no outburst of moral outrage by this Irish Government in the future about police methods in Northern Ireland.

Speaking, as Dutch lawyer and leader of Amnesty International Irish team, at annual Amnesty conference in Cambridge after rejection by Fianna Fáil Government of recommendations of Ó Briain Committee on safeguards for people in custody. *The Irish Times*, September 23, 1978.

September 28, 1978
Mary Kenny
The [Irish] media is now more or less dominated by a liberal elite of people in their thirties and early forties ... If I lived in Ireland all the time, I would hold most of the same opinions. But I don't. I live in the centre of London [where] it is frightening indeed to see what happens to a society when it throws out the entire morality which has shaped its civilisation. I have come to believe that Christian values are extremely important.

Speaking in Dublin, as former leader of Irish women's liberation movement. *The Irish Times*, September 29, 1978.

October 13, 1978
Margaret Thatcher
If you wash your hands of Northern Ireland, you wash them in blood.

Speaking, as Conservative leader, at annual party conference in Brighton, on renewed calls for British withdrawal. *The Irish Times*, October 14, 1978.

December 15, 1978
Jack Lynch
The decision we have taken today [that Republic should join European Monetary System] ... will add a further dimension to

partition, although the ultimate benefits of membership of the system could outweigh the problems.

Commenting, as Taoiseach, in Dáil on decision which meant Irish pound would break with sterling, as UK did not join same system, and Border would, in future, separate two currency systems. *The Irish Times*, December 16, 1978.

January 18, 1979
Rev. Ian Paisley
These [cross-border EEC projects] are worked out by the Irish Government, our traditional enemy, and the British Government, which doesn't understand Ulster. No elected representative in Northern Ireland has any say. It gets our hackles up. We want to know what's going on.

Speaking during first visit to EEC headquarters in Brussels, as head of delegation from DUP, described on EEC sign erected for occasion as 'Democratic Unionist Party of Ireland'. *The Irish Times*, January 19, 1979.

February 28, 1979
Charles Haughey
An Irish solution to an Irish problem [which will] meet the wishes of the great majority of sensible, responsible citizens.

Describing, as Taoiseach, Health (Family Planning) Bill allowing availability of contraceptives only on doctor's prescription. *Irish Independent*, March 3, 1979.

March 14, 1979
Robert Irwin
In my capacity as Forensic Medical Officer in this city [Belfast] I have seen more bodies and parts of bodies in explosions and murder by knife and bullet than any other doctor ... I support no terrorist organisation. I abhor them ... I have the records of 160 patients [in custody] ... who have injuries I would not say were self-inflicted.

Confirming ill-treatment of IRA and other suspects in Castlereagh Detention Centre by RUC, detailed by *Bennet Report* issued two days later. *The Irish Independent*, March 15, 1979.

March 16, 1979
Bennet Report
There can – whatever the precise explanation – be no doubt that the injuries were not self-

inflicted and were sustained during the period of police detention at a police office.

Official report rejecting Northern Ireland Office claims that injuries received by prisoners at Castlereagh Detention Centre in Belfast were self-inflicted. *Irish Independent*, March 17, 1979.

March 16, 1979
Roy Mason
I am not aware of any ill-treatment at Castlereagh.

Reacting, as NI Secretary, to *Bennet Report* confirming that some 160 people had been ill-treated, mainly at Castlereagh RUC Detention Centre. *Irish Independent*, March 17, 1979.

March 28, 1979
Gerry Fitt
Because of what you have done in the last five years – disregarded the minority and appeased the blackmailers of the Northern Ireland Unionist majority – I cannot go into your lobby tonight.

Speaking in Commons, as independent socialist MP, on why he could not use vote to keep Labour in office, as result of which Government fell by vote of 311 to 310. *Irish Independent*, March 29, 1979.

March 28, 1979
Frank Maguire
You could say I came over to London to abstain in person.

Comment after travelling to London, as independent Fermanagh/South Tyrone MP, and refusing to vote to keep Labour in Government in confidence vote which Government lost by 311 votes to 310, because ministers would not make sufficient commitments on improving conditions for Irish prisoners. (In conversation with author, March 28, 1979.)

March 30, 1979
Airey Neave
He [Neave] would hold a most searching inquiry into these allegations [of RUC ill-treatment of suspects] and if he found any persons were responsible they would meet the full fury of his wrath, because he, as a prisoner of war, had suffered interrogation at the hands of the Gestapo – Gerry, it leaves its mark on you.

Comment to MP, Gerry Fitt, forty minutes before being killed by INLA bomb in Commons car-park ramp, as recounted by Gerry Fitt. *Irish Independent*, March 31, 1979.

April 19, 1979
Tip O'Neill
We [American politicians] have been concerned that the problem [of Northern Ireland] has been treated as a political football in London.

Comment, as guest at Dublin Castle dinner, for which he was criticised by British politicians. *The Irish Press,* April 20, 1979.

May 11, 1979
British Army
The Provisional IRA (PIRA) has the dedication and the sinews of war to raise violence intermittently to at least the level of early 1978, certainly for the foreseeable future ... there is a strata of intelligent, astute and experienced terrorists who provide the backbone of the organisation ... our evidence of rank and file terrorists does not support the view that they are mindless hooligans.

Analysis of Provisional IRA contained in British Army document Number 37 which was obtained by IRA, and published in *Republican News. The Irish Press,* May 11, 1979.

July 18, 1979
Rev. Ian Paisley
In the name of Ulster's dead, I indict you for harbouring their murderers.

Shouted remark when withdrawing from European Parliament when Taoiseach Jack Lynch began his address as incoming President of EEC Council with few words in Irish language. *The Irish Press,* July 19, 1979.

July 18, 1979
John Taylor
[Mr Lynch] started babbling away in Irish which is not even an official EEC language.

Explaining, as Unionist member, why he followed Paisley out of European Parliament chamber when Taoiseach Jack Lynch spoke in Irish. *The Irish Times,* July 19, 1979.

July 22, 1979
Rev. Ian Paisley
[Speaking] as leader of the Northern Ireland people, this visit is not on – full stop. [The Pope] is anti-Christ, the man of sin in the Church. Pope Benedict blessed the 1916 rebels ... from that has flowed the IRA.

Comment, as recently elected Member of European Parliament, on prospect of Pope visiting Northern Ireland. *The Irish Press,* July 23, 1979.

August 29, 1979
Rev. Fr Romeo Panciroli
With deep regret, due to the dreadful murders of recent days, it has now been decided not to include a venue in Northern Ireland in the papal itinerary.

As Director of Vatican Press Office, announcing that IRA killing of Lord Mountbatten and eighteen British soldiers had caused cancellation of papal visit to North. *The Irish Times,* August 30, 1979.

August 30, 1979
John Taylor
If the leadership of the Loyalist paramilitaries find it absolutely impossible to refrain from renewed action on the ground, then in no way can that action occur on Ulster's soil. It should be directed to targets within the Republic of Ireland.

In statement, as Unionist MP, after killing by IRA of Lord Mountbatten and eighteen British soldiers. *The Irish Times,* August 31, 1979.

September 1, 1979
The IRA
We will tear out their sentimental, imperialist heart.

In statement, referring to British establishment, issued after assassination of Lord Mountbatten when bomb destroyed his launch off Mullaghmore. *The Republican News,* September 1, 1979.

September 2, 1979
Samuel Duddy
It's people like John Taylor ... who have egged on loyalists with inflammatory speeches and then stepped back to allow the rank and file to take the rap.

Commenting, as spokesman for paramilitary Ulster Defence Regiment, on remarks of Unionist MP John Taylor on August 30, 1979, on possible loyalist paramilitary action south of Border. *The Irish Times,* September 3, 1979.

September 9, 1979
Sile de Valera
If our political leaders are not seen to be furthering our republican aspirations through constitutional means, the idealistic young members of our community will become

disillusioned ... and turn to violence to achieve their aims ... I look to our party, and particularly our leader, to demonstrate his republicanism, and bring these beliefs to fruition in our people.

As Fianna Fáil TD and grand-daughter of Eamon de Valera, in speech at Liam Lynch commemoration at Fermoy seen as challenge to leadership of Jack Lynch. *The Irish Times,* September 10, 1979.

September 23, 1979
Jack Lynch

We favour a process of discussion and negotiation between those concerned in Northern Ireland and the Irish and British Governments leading to consent and agreement on appropriate structures of government ... We recognise that in the present atmosphere there is little immediate prospect of progress along these lines. We are reconciled to this and for our part have no wish to pressurise our Northern fellow-countrymen to take steps they are not ready for.

As Taoiseach, in speech at Waterville replying to comments of Sile de Valera of September 9, 1979. *The Irish Times,* September 24, 1979.

September 26, 1979
Martin Smyth and Walter Williams

While you [Pope John Paul II] and your predecessors have called for peace and justice, the reality is that your followers continue to destroy peace and deny the very basic right to life, and call forth counter atrocities from people who have suffered grievously. The full rites of the Roman Catholic sacramental system have been given to the IRA.

Writing, as Grand Master and Grand Secretary of Orange Order of Ireland, in open letter to Pope on his forthcoming visit to Ireland. *The Irish Times,* September 27, 1979.

September 29, 1979
Pope John Paul II

To all of you who are listening, I say: do not believe in violence; do not support violence. It is not the Christian way. It is not the way of the Catholic Church. Believe in peace and forgiveness and love; for they are of Christ. On my knees I beg of you to turn away from the paths of violence and to return to the ways

of peace. You may claim to seek justice. I too believe in justice and seek justice. But violence only delays the day of justice. Violence destroys the work of justice ... do not follow any leaders who train you in the ways of inflicting death.

Those who resort to violence always claim that only violence brings about change. You [those with political responsibility] must show that there is a political, peaceful way to justice.

Speaking at Drogheda in major address to Irish people on two-day visit to Republic. *The Irish Times,* October 1, 1979.

October 2, 1979
The IRA

In all conscience we believe that force is by far the only means of removing the evil of the British presence in Ireland ... we know also that upon victory, the [Catholic] Church would have no difficulty in recognising us.

Responding to Pope's appeal for peace at Drogheda. *The Irish Times,* October 3, 1979.

October 3, 1979
Patrick Hillery

It has come to my attention that there were rumours circulating as to the possibility of my resigning as President ... I am not resigning ... There is not a problem. There are difficulties for people living in public life but thank God we have a happy family life.

Speaking, as President of Republic, to political reporters summoned to Áras an Uachtaráin to hear denial of rumours of domestic difficulties which might have led to his resignation. *The Irish Times,* October 4, 1979.

October 13, 1979
Princess Margaret

The Irish, they're pigs. Oh, oh! You're Irish!

Comment at Chicago dinner after discussion about death of Lord Mountbatten (later denied by Princess Margaret and Chicago Mayor Jane Byrne, to whom it was allegedly made, but confirmed by hostess of dinner). *The Irish Times,* October 17, 1979.

October 20, 1979
Governor Ronald Reagan

It's tragic that so much is being done in the name of God [in Ireland] and it's the same God.

In interview with *The Irish Times* in Baltimore when running for Republican presidential nomination. *The Irish Times*, October 20, 1979.

November 9, 1979
Jack Lynch
Since 1952 we have had the Military Aircraft Overflying Agreement under which the military aircraft of any other country can fly over [Irish territory] to a limited extent . . . we have decided to improve this situation very, very slightly. There is no question of a free [air] corridor.

As Taoiseach, explaining at press conference in United States , new agreement with Britain on helicopter overflights along Border, details of which he had refused to give to TDs in Dáil. *The Irish Times*, November 10, 1979.

November 10, 1979
Charles Haughey
[Padraic] Pearse saw the British presence in Ireland as a source of conflict and a barrier to progress . . . Pearse's enemies claim that the Rising of 1916 denies him the right to be called a democrat. He is reviled as a militarist, a man who glorified in war. The truth however is that Pearse sought freedom in arms only because there was no other way open to him in the circumstances of the time.

As Fianna Fáil Government minister, in speech regarded as challenge to leadership of Taoiseach Jack Lynch, because of its 'Republican' tone compared with moderate policies of Lynch. *The Irish Times*, November 12, 1979.

November 11, 1979
Jack Lynch
We are concerned with the moral, cultural and material well-being of the Irish people, and that can be advanced not by killing, not by death or hatred or destruction but by life. The paradox of Pearse's message for the Irish nation is that we must work and live for Ireland, not die, and most certainly not kill for it.

As Taoiseach, when visiting Boston, in passage inserted into speech after hearing reports of address endorsing Pearse by party colleague Charles Haughey in Dublin. *The Irish Times*, November 12, 1979.

November 13, 1979
Bill Loughnane
He [Taoiseach Jack Lynch] hid the thing from us [details of agreement with Britain on cross-border helicopter flights] at the parliamentary party meeting. He said there was going to be no infringement of our sovereignty . . . you can tell the truth some place and lie in the other place.

In comment for which he was threatened with withdrawal of Fianna Fáil party whip as TD until he withdrew statement next day, but which was also seen as first serious challenge to Lynch leadership of Fianna Fáil. *The Irish Times*, November 14, 1979.

November 14, 1979
Conor Cruise O'Brien
He [Padraic Pearse] was a manic, mystic nationalist with a cult of blood sacrifice and a strong personal motivation towards death. A nation which takes a personality of that type as its mentor is headed towards disaster.

As former Labour minister, in Dublin debate on occasion of Pearse centenary. *The Irish Times*, November 15, 1979.

November 22, 1979
Gerry Fitt
I regard myself as representing the voice of sanity, the voice of concern, the voice that believes in political dialogue.

At Westminster press conference, on resigning as SDLP leader on grounds that party had become too 'Republican'. *The Irish Times*, November 23, 1979.

December 11, 1979
Garret FitzGerald
Deputy Haughey presents himself here [in the Dáil], seeking to be invested in office as the seventh in this line [of Irish Government Heads of State], but he comes with a flawed pedigree. His motives can be judged ultimately only by God but we cannot ignore the fact that he differs from his predecessors in that these motives have been and are widely impugned, most notably but by no means exclusively by people within his own party . . . They and others . . . have attributed to him an overweening ambition . . . a wish to dominate, even to own, the State.

Speaking in Dáil, as Fine Gael leader, on assumption of Fianna Fáil leadership and office of

Taoiseach by Charles Haughey, after resignation of Jack Lynch. *The Irish Times,* January 14, 1979.

December 20, 1979
George Colley

In my speech to the party meeting, I referred to Mr Haughey's ability, capacity and flair and I wished him well in the enormous task he was taking on. I did not however use the words 'loyalty' and 'support' which he ... attributed to me.

In speech at Fianna Fáil function at Baldoyle on conditions under which he accepted post of Tánaiste (deputy Taoiseach) under Haughey. *The Irish Times,* December 21, 1979.

December 21, 1979
Charles Haughey

I confirm that before he [George Colley] agreed to join the Government, the Tánaiste expressed to me the views which he has now expressed publicly. Following our discussions he has assured me of his full support and loyalty in his office as Tánaiste.

In statement, as Taoiseach, after meeting with his deputy Taoiseach who had expressed conditional loyalty on December 20, 1979. *The Irish Times,* December 22, 1979.

January 11, 1980
Yasser Arafat

I could challenge the Israelis or any British source for one single proof of an IRA connection [with PLO]. It is a big lie.

As PLO leader, speaking to Irish TDs in Beirut. *The Irish Times,* January 12, 1980.

February 16, 1980
Charles Haughey

The situation [in Northern Ireland] is pretty desperate. It has gone on for too long. I believe the time has come for a major effort directed towards a solution ... I am inviting the British Government to join with us in bringing forward a final and lasting solution.

Speaking, as Taoiseach, at Fianna Fáil Árd Fheis. *The Irish Times,* February 18, 1980.

April 10, 1980
Vladimir Guncherov

We have a class approach. We do not hide the fact that our sympathies are with the oppressed people of Afghanistan, just as they

are with the oppressed Catholic people of Northern Ireland.

In interview in Moscow, as foreign editor of Soviet foreign news agency, TASS. *The Irish Times,* April 11, 1980.

April 11, 1980
Patrick Cooney

The vast majority of Fine Gael TDs and Senators are opposed to any change in our laws [forbidding] divorce. Consequently, any suggestion of an all-party committee to look at the subject is pointless ... it could be used by some parliamentarians as the thin edge of a wedge to produce a debate and thereby pressure for change ... The time and resources of Parliament would be better spent devising ways and means to prepare young people for marriage and its obligations.

Speaking, as frontbench member of Fine Gael, at Tullamore. *The Irish Times,* April 12, 1980.

April 28, 1980
Saad Haddad

The hostile attitude of the Irish Prime Minister is serving the PLO. The Irish behaviour is endangering the life of the [Irish] soldiers and deteriorating the situation. Whoever will look at Mr Haughey's past will find that the man himself was a gunrunner for the IRA and is known for his good relations with terrorists in Europe and the Middle East.

In interview, as leader of pro-Israeli militia in south Lebanon, after fatal clashes with Irish soldiers in UN force, and criticism of Haddad's forces by Taoiseach Charles Haughey. *The Irish Times,* April 29, 1980.

May 1, 1980
John Hume

The cynicism and dismissiveness of the Irish style – Churchill's Dunkirk exhortation 'The situation is serious but not desperate' is said to have evoked a somewhat bleary comment from an Irish listener 'Over here the situation is always desperate but never serious' – often [conceals] as the readers of Joyce and Swift will know a quite serious desperation ... It is beyond high time the British and Irish took each other – and our common crisis – seriously. There is, I believe, urgent need for the friends of Britain and Ireland to do likewise.

As SDLP leader, writing in US journal *Foreign Affairs. The Irish Times,* May 21, 1980.

May 20, 1980
Margaret Thatcher

[The constitutional affairs of Northern Ireland are] a matter for the people of Northern Ireland, this government and this parliament and no one else.

Speaking, as Prime Minister, in Commons before summit meeting in Downing Street with Taoiseach Charles Haughey. *The Irish Times,* May 21, 1980.

June 9, 1980
Charles Haughey

If there is a prospect of moving to unity, to some new arrangement, then we have no doubt whatever that the wishes of the northern Unionists, particularly the Protestant people of Northern Ireland, can be provided for both in regard to divorce, contraception or any of these other things about which they have strong feelings.

Interviewed, as Taoiseach, on BBC programme 'Panorama' after meeting with British Prime Minister Margaret Thatcher. *The Irish Times,* June 10, 1980.

June 25, 1980
US Democratic Party

The solution offering the greatest promise of permanent peace is to end the division of the Irish people.

In resolution adopted for Democratic Convention, endorsing policies of leading Irish-American politicians – Edward Kennedy, Tip O'Neill, Daniel Moynihan and Hugh Carey. *The Irish Times,* June 26, 1980.

June 26, 1980
Brian Lenihan

The commentators, our good friends on the press benches, lobby correspondents, and ourselves tend to get into this incestuous dance in a gold-fish bowl. The people outside are not interested ... The 18-year-olds who were eight years of age in 1970 are not interested ... let history judge.

Remark, as member of Fianna Fáil Government, during Dáil row over revelations in *Magill* magazine about role of Fianna Fáil ministers in arms crisis of 1970. *The Irish Times,* June 26, 1980.

July 7, 1980
Neil Blaney

His [Sean Donlon's] performance out there [Washington] was such that he was doing us no favours because of his attitude towards those who were trying to bring to the notice of the public the state of affairs in Ireland.

As former Fianna Fáil member, commenting on reports that Taoiseach Charles Haughey planned to transfer Donlon from his post as Irish Ambassador in Washington as part of deal whereby Blaney would return to Fianna Fáil. *The Irish Times,* July 8, 1980.

July 8, 1980
Daniel Moynihan

Sean Donlon is an outstanding ambassador. He is knowledgable, thoughtful and responsible. No one has done more for Irish-American relations.

As US senator, commenting on reports that Taoiseach Charles Haughey planned to move Irish Ambassador in Washington, Sean Donlon; similar tributes were paid by other Irish-American leaders when it was announced Donlon would not be moved. *The Irish Times,* July 9, 1980.

July 27, 1980
Charles Haughey

There is a clear and conclusive evidence available to the Government here from security and other sources that NORAID has provided support for the campaign of violence ... on the basis of these activities, it stands condemned.

In statement clarifying policy towards Irish-American organisations sympathetic to IRA, on being challenged to do so by Fine Gael leader, Garret FitzGerald. *The Irish Times,* July 28, 1980.

July 27, 1980
Jim Gibbons

You can't go on indefinitely living with a lie. If you attempt it you will be a miserable person.

In comment addressed to Taoiseach Charles Haughey in RTE interview as one of leading figures with Haughey in arms crisis of 1970 concerning which they gave conflicting evidence in court. *The Irish Times,* July 28, 1980.

October 28, 1980
Margaret Thatcher

There will be no concessions to those on hunger strike. None at all.

Speaking, as Prime Minister, in Commons on IRA hunger strike in Maze Prison for political status. *The Irish Times,* October 29, 1980.

November 2, 1980
Sile de Valera
As a woman, I am deeply shocked by Mrs Thatcher's lack of compassion on the issue of H Blocks ... if ... the situation is allowed to continue and deteriorate, the British Government must shoulder responsibility for further deaths, whether it be in H Blocks or the streets or elsewhere throughout the Six Counties.

As Fianna Fáil TD, in remarks at by-election meeting in Letterkenny from which Fianna Fáil disassociated itself because of apparent endorsement of protest activity on H Blocks and support for hunger strikers. *The Irish Times,* November 3, 1980.

November 11, 1980
Gerry Fitt
In 1972, I went to Willie Whitelaw [then NI Secretary], to every corridor, to every tea-room in the House of Commons and pleaded time after time to grant political or special category status [to IRA prisoners] because I believed it would in some way bring to an end the terrible situation which had been brought about by the introduction of internment ... I was wrong. It is a tragedy to have to admit it.

As West Belfast independent socialist MP, on hunger strike by IRA prisoners for political status, interviewed on RTE. *The Irish Times,* November 12, 1980.

November 16, 1980
Garret FitzGerald
We have always in this State rejected the demand for political status. We cannot urge another government to do what the Irish Government did not do.

As Fine Gael leader, speaking on RTE about hunger strike by IRA prisoners in North for political status. *The Irish Times,* November 15, 1980.

November 20, 1980
Margaret Thatcher
I want this to be utterly clear. There can be no political justification for murder or any other crime. Her Majesty's Government will never concede political status to the hunger strikers, or to any others convicted of criminal offences in the Province.

Speaking, as Prime Minister, in Commons on hunger strike by IRA prisoners for political status in North. *The Irish Times,* November 21, 1980.

November 25, 1980
Charles Haughey
The Government believe that if some adjustments could be made in the prison rules themselves, or in their interpretation, or in their application, a solution would be possible.

As Taoiseach, outlining policy in Dáil debate on hunger strike by IRA prisoners in North for political status. *The Irish Times,* November 26, 1980.

December 8, 1980
Charles Haughey and Margaret Thatcher
They [Haughey and Thatcher] accepted the need to bring forward policies and proposals to achieve peace, reconciliation and stability ... the best prospects of attaining these objectives was the further development of the unique relationship between the two countries. They accordingly decided to devote their next meeting in London during the coming year to special consideration of the totality of relationships within these islands. For this purpose they had commissioned joint studies covering a range of issues including possible new institutional structures.

In joint communiqué after summit meeting at Dublin Castle between Taoiseach and British Prime Minister. *The Irish Times,* December 9, 1980.

December 8, 1980
Charles Haughey
[I am] hopeful [we are] are in the middle of a historic breakthrough.·

As Taoiseach, at press conference after meeting British Prime Minister Margaret Thatcher at Dublin Castle on same day. *The Irish Times,* December 9, 1980.

December 12, 1980
Brian Lenihan
As far as we are concerned, everything is on the table.

Commenting in BBC interview, as Minister for Foreign Affairs, on new situation after summit meeting on December 8 at Dublin Castle to discuss North. *The Irish Times,* December 13, 1980.

December 18, 1980
Republican prisoners
In ending our hunger strike, we make it clear that failure by the British Government to act in a responsible manner towards ending the conditions which forced us to a hunger strike will lead to inevitable and continual strife within H Blocks.

In statement from Maze Prison after fifty-three days on hunger strike, ended on appeal from Cardinal Ó Fiaich and with apparent prospect of movement towards political prisoner status. *The Irish Times*, December 19, 1980.

December 25, 1980
Robin Berrington
Ireland [is] pretty small potatoes compared to the other countries of Europe ... no great issues burn up the wires between Dublin and Washington ... the high cost of goods, their unavailability, the dreary urbanscapes, the constant strikes and the long, dank and damp winters combine to gnaw away at one's enthusiasm for being here.

As US embassy Cultural Affairs Officer, in circular letter to friends in Washington which was leaked to *Irish Times*, as a result of which he was given forty-eight hours by US Ambassador to return to America. *The Irish Times*, January 28, 1981.

January 8, 1981
Enoch Powell
[Rev. Ian Paisley is] the most resourceful, inveterate and dangerous enemy of Unionism ... a greater threat to the Union than the Foreign Office and the Provisional IRA rolled into one.

As Unionist MP, on call by Democratic Unionist Party leader Paisley for UK referendum on status of Northern Ireland, and for devolution. *The Irish Times*, January 9, 1981.

February 1, 1981
Andy Tyrie
The only way to beat terrorists is to terrorise them.

In interview, as leader of paramilitary Ulster Defence Association, on BBC. *The Irish Times*, February 2, 1981.

February 4, 1981
Yuri Ustimenko
If a person [in Ireland] goes to bed late, he is a Catholic, if early, a Protestant. Moreover, the Irish possess the astonishing ability of being able to determine the religion of people unknown to them from a first glance.

Writing, as first correspondent in Ireland for Soviet foreign news agency, TASS, in book, *Ireland*, published in Moscow. *The Irish Times*, February 4, 1981.

February 5, 1981
Republican prisoners
Our last hunger strikers were morally blackmailed ... Where is the peace in the prisons which, like a promise, was held before dying men's eyes?

In statement from Maze and Armagh prisons warning of further hunger strike. *The Irish Times*, February 6, 1981.

February 6, 1981
Rev. Ian Paisley
As elected leader of the Protestant people, I have entered into a compact with these men ... with the help of God they and I ... will yet defeat the most nefarious conspiracy that has ever been hatched against a free people.

As DUP leader, at midnight show of strength with five hundred men brandishing firearms certificates on Co. Antrim hillside, in protest against Thatcher-Haughey communiqué of December 8, 1980. *The Irish Times*, February 7, 1981.

February 9, 1981
Rev. Ian Paisley
All they [IRA] want to do is kill, kill, kill Protestants ... All they had to do is to go to their priest and get a pardon. Isn't it remarkable that all the worst crimes of Republican violence have been committed immediately after Mass?

In sermon, as leader of Free Presbyterian Church, in Belfast. *The Irish Times*, February 10, 1981.

March 1, 1981
Dr (Edward) Daly, Bishop of Derry
I do not believe that it is morally justified to endanger health or life by hunger strike in the present circumstances.

Comment made on day Republican prisoner, Bobby Sands, went on hunger strike for special category or political prisoner status. *The Irish Times*, March 2, 1981.

March 4, 1981
Bobby Sands
If I die, God will understand.

As IRA hunger striker, in prison interview, rejecting view that hunger strike had no moral justification. *The Irish Times,* March 5, 1981.

March 5, 1981
Margaret Thatcher
There is no such thing as political murder, political bombing or political violence. There is only criminal murder, criminal bombing and criminal violence. We will not compromise on this. There will be no political status.

Speaking, as British Prime Minister, during visit to Belfast, on hunger strike by Republican prisoners for special status. *The Irish Times,* March 6, 1981.

March 6, 1981
Dr Hurley, Archbishop of Durban
Be quite clear about it, both the white South Africans and the oppressed majority of the people of South Africa clearly interpret the [Irish rugby] tour as an acceptance of apartheid.

Commenting from South Africa on proposed Irish Rugby Football Union tour of South Africa. *The Irish Times,* March 7, 1981.

March 11, 1981
Charles Haughey
In a world in which the threat of war looms and recedes, a solution to the situation in Northern Ireland becomes increasingly urgent. When a satisfactory political solution is arrived at, we would of course have to review what would be the most appropriate defence arrangements for the island as a whole.

Speaking, as Taoiseach, in Dáil after accusations that he was prepared to sell out neutrality in negotiations with Britain over North. *The Irish Times,* March 12, 1981.

March 11, 1981
Frank Cluskey
The Government ... must not fall into the trap of trading our neutrality for some imagined settlement of the Northern problem. Mr de Valera avoided that trap in 1941 ... To us in the Labour Party, neutrality is not a tradable commodity.

Speaking in Dáil, as Labour leader, in row over Government's attitude towards neutrality in talks with UK. *The Irish Times,* March 12, 1981.

April 20, 1981
Neil Blaney
I got the impression very strongly that he [Bobby Sands] would prefer to die of hunger rather than go back to the prison conditions he and his fellow-prisoners have endured for four and a half years. In the light of that I felt that to try in any way to press him to give up his hunger strike would be futile. I do not think that this kind of torture should be added to his condition.

Commenting, as one of three TDs allowed to visit Sands on hunger strike, after Sands had been elected MP in Fermanagh/South Tyrone by-election on April 10. *The Irish Times,* April 21, 1981.

April 21, 1981
Margaret Thatcher
We are not prepared to consider special category status for certain groups of people serving sentences for crime. Crime is crime is crime: it is not political.

As British Prime Minister, when asked at press conference in Saudi Arabia about hunger strikers in Maze Prison. *The Irish Times,* April 22, 1981.

April 27, 1981
Gerry Adams
Attempts to justify the British Government's ghoulish preoccupation with killing Bobby Sands flies in the face of all logic — either moral or factual. The H Blocks crisis did not have to come to death ... efforts to project the political prisoners as criminal have foundered upon the rocks of the five years of passive protest by 400 Republican prisoners.

In statement, as Vice President of Provisional Sinn Féin, on hunger strike by Bobby Sands. *The Irish Times,* April 28, 1981.

April 28, 1981
Humphrey Atkins
If Mr Sands persisted in his wish to commit suicide, that was his choice. The Government would not force medical treatment upon him.

As NI Secretary, on IRA hunger strike in Maze Prison. *The Irish Times,* April 29, 1981.

April 30, 1981
Cardinal Hume
Any hunger strike to death that includes within it the intention to die is suicide.

Commenting, as Archbishop of Westminster on IRA hunger strikes. *The Irish Times,* May 1, 1981.

April 30, 1981
Rev. Fr John Magee
All life is sacred and must be preserved as a gift from God. I therefore appealed, in the name of Christ and his vicar on earth, saying that violence of all kinds must be condemned in the clearest terms as being against the law of God.

Speaking, as envoy of Pope, after three visits to Bobby Sands to ask him to give up hunger strike. *The Irish Times,* May 1, 1981.

April 30, 1981
Humphrey Atkins
Don't play the IRA's game or anyone else's. Don't listen to the Provisionals. Don't believe lies and rumours. Do listen to your local clergymen ... We will be making it our business to ensure that the news media gets the facts so listen to that too. Observe the law ... keep away from trouble.

Appealing, as NI Secretary, to people of North as IRA hunger striker, Bobby Sands, slipped into coma. *The Irish Times,* May 1, 1981.

May 5, 1981
Margaret Thatcher
Mr Sands was a convicted criminal. He chose to take his own life, a choice that his organisation did not allow to many of their victims.

Speaking, as Prime Minister, in Commons after death of Bobby Sands from hunger strike to obtain political prisoner status. *The Irish Times,* May 6, 1981.

May 6, 1981
Republican prisoners
You have got your pound of flesh, now give us our rights. Do not for one minute think that we are going to allow you to rob us of our principles. There are more Bobby Sands in these Blocks and we will continue to die if need be to safeguard these principles.

Statement directed to Margaret Thatcher after death of Bobby Sands in hunger strike for political status. *The Irish Times,* May 7, 1981.

May 10, 1981
Dr (Edward) Daly, Bishop of Derry
I would not describe Bobby Sands's death as suicide. I could not accept that. I don't think he intended to bring about his own death.

Commenting, in RTE interview, on Cardinal Hume's statement of April 30 on hunger strike deaths. *The Irish Times,* May 11, 1981.

May 15, 1981
Margaret Thatcher
Yielding to coercion would provoke further coercion and encourage more young people to follow the path of violence.

Commenting, as Prime Minister, on death of second IRA hunger striker, Francis Hughes. *The Irish Times,* May 16, 1981.

May 15, 1981
Edward Kennedy
Unfeeling inflexibility will achieve nothing but more deaths.

Commenting, as US senator, on death of second IRA hunger striker, Francis Hughes, on May 12. *The Irish Times,* May 16, 1981.

June 3, 1981
Alexander Haig
If there were not Great Britain playing the role that it's playing there today, we might even have to create one to prevent a blood bath.

Commenting, as US Secretary of State, to newspaper editors in Washington on need for British presence in Northern Ireland. *The Irish Times,* June 4, 1981.

June 4, 1981
Garret FitzGerald
We are on the brink of a unique breakthrough in Irish politics, that is, the emergence of Fine Gael as the largest single party in the State ... Should this assessment be correct, and should we require additional support in the Dáil, we are prepared to discuss with the Labour Party the formation of a strong alternative Government.

Speaking, as Fine Gael leader, at Newbridge during general election campaign. *The Irish Times,* June 5, 1981.

June 24, 1981
Charles Haughey
I invite all members of Dáil Éireann who seek a Government that will last and give effective leadership, to support us on the basis of our programme for the '80s . . . A shaky and uncertain coalition Government would be a sure recipe for a prolonged period of political instability.

Appealing, unsuccessfully, for support of independent TDs to enable Fianna Fáil to remain in office after general election. *The Irish Times,* June 25, 1981.

July 6, 1981
Mother Teresa
We have no right to destroy the beautiful gift of God's life, so any way of destroying that gift is a violence. I see many people dying of hunger because they don't have a decent chance to eat. I see people who are hungry because they haven't got food, but I've never dealt with people who are hungry because they chose to be hungry.

Speaking about Republican hunger strike while on visit to Corrymeela, Co. Antrim. *The Irish Times,* June 7, 1981.

August 10, 1981
Rev. Fr Michael Flanagan
[It was] disappointing when those who called the hunger strike did not end it when they achieved particular political-electoral victories in both North and South, and thus spare their own members and families and communities continued suffering.

Speaking, as parish priest of Bellaghy, at funeral service for hunger striker, Thomas McElwee, which prompted walk-out by several women, including Bernadette McAliskey, in protest. *The Irish Times,* August 11, 1981.

August 10, 1981
Bernadette McAliskey (Devlin)
What he [Father Flanagan] was saying to those of us who have been trying to save the prisoners was that we've been playing with these young men's lives for electoral gain in Free State elections. The hunger strike was never called to achieve any electoral victory.

Replying, as leading supporter of hunger strikers, to remarks of Bellaghy parish priest at funeral service for hunger striker, Thomas McElwee. *The Irish Times,* August 11, 1981.

August 22, 1981
John Kelly
[The State] is lying, panting, exhausted by her own weight, and being rent by a farrow of cannibal piglets.

In comment, as leading member of Fine Gael, on need to curb public expenditure which was causing strains in Coalition. It was included in script of speech at Claremorris and published in press but speech was not delivered. *The Irish Times,* August 22, 1981.

August 26, 1981
Owen Carron
Dr FitzGerald's father was a gunman and nobody inquired into the legitimacy of that. So if a thing is legitimate in 1920, I don't see what makes it illegitimate in 1981. Dr FitzGerald's father and his comrades shot RIC policemen. That is how they came to power, through the shooting of Catholic RIC policemen who were propping up the British State in Ireland.

Interviewed on support for violence by *The Irish Times* after winning Fermanagh/South Tyrone by-election as independent, after death of Bobby Sands who had won seat as hunger striker. *The Irish Times,* August 27, 1981.

August 30, 1981
Ken Livingstone
What I would say to everybody who's got arms and is carrying arms in Northern Ireland, whether they are in the British Army or the IRA, is to put those arms down and go back to your home . . . I think that there would be no greater move for peace than if the British forces just packed up and went home.

Speaking, as leader of Greater London Council, on British Forces Broadcasting Service. *The Irish Times,* August 31, 1981.

September 6, 1981
Dr (Cahal) Daly, Bishop of Down and Connor
Your capacity for endurance, however misguided, is not so common in this materialistic age that Ireland can afford to be deprived of it.

Appealing to Republican prisoners to call off hunger strike. *The Irish Times,* September 7, 1981.

September 19, 1981
Fidel Castro
The Irish patriots are in the process of writing one of the most heroic pages in human history.

Commenting, as President of Cuba, on Republican hunger strike. *The Irish Times,* ('This Week They Said'), September 19, 1981.

September 26, 1981
Edward Koch
If enough of us spoke out and urged the English to get out and let the Irish settle their differences, the English would return to England, as they should.

Speaking, as Mayor of New York, about Republican hunger strike and violence in Northern Ireland. *The Irish Times* ('This Week They Said'), September 26, 1981.

September 27, 1981
Garret FitzGerald
What I want to do is to lead a crusade — a Republican crusade — to make this a genuine Republic on the principles of [Wolfe] Tone and [Thomas] Davis ... I believe we could have the basis then on which many Protestants in Northern Ireland would be willing to consider a relationship with us ... If I was a Northern Protestant today, I can't see how I could aspire to getting involved in a state which is itself sectarian ... if the people of this State want to remain fundamentally a 26-County State, based on a majority ethos and are not prepared to work with the people of Northern Ireland towards unity ... well then, I will accept defeat and leave politics at that stage, if necessary.

In interview, as Taoiseach, on RTE. *The Irish Times,* September 28, 1980.

September 28, 1981
Rev. Ian Paisley
Dr FitzGerald does not have a pup's chance of bringing in reform.

Commenting on desire expressed by Taoiseach Garret FitzGerald to make South a 'genuine Republic' in interview on September 27. *The Irish Times* ('This Week They Said'), October 3, 1981.

September 28, 1981
Charles Haughey
[Thomas] Davis had said 'A free people can

afford to be generous. A struggling people cannot and should not be so' ... I cannot accept this self-abasement – this suggestion that we in the Republic have something to be ashamed of because of Partition.

As Fianna Fáil leader, in RTE interview responding to desire expressed by Taoiseach Garret FitzGerald on September 27 to lead crusade for Republic on principles of Thomas Davis and Wolfe Tone. *The Irish Times,* September 29, 1981.

October 4, 1981
Republican prisoners
Mounting pressure and cleric-inspired demoralisation led to [family] interventions and five [hunger] strikers have been taken off their fast. We accept that it is a physical and psychological impossibility to recommence a hunger strike after intervention ... a considerable majority of the present hunger strikers' families have indicated that they will intervene and under these circumstances, we feel that the hunger strike must, for tactical reasons, be suspended.

In statement from Maze Prison calling off hunger strike for political status. *The Irish Times,* October 5, 1981.

October 10, 1981
Rev. Fr Denis Faul
It takes two glasses of whiskey to bring an Englishman up to the functional level of an Irishman.

Comment by Dungannon priest on dealings with British officials. *The Irish Times* ('This Week They Said'), October 10, 1981.

October 11, 1981
Charles Haughey
Eamon de Valera and his comrades had at all times to fight against the remnants of that colonial mentality that still linger on in Irish life ... we can see emerging once more in modern Ireland that mentality. Once again we are asked to accept a jaundiced view of ourselves ... we will not apologise to anyone for being what we are.

Speaking, as Fianna Fáil leader, at unveiling of de Valera memorial at Ennis, shortly after call by Fine Gael leader Garret FitzGerald for reform of 'sectarian' Republic. *The Irish Times,* October 12, 1981.

October 11, 1981
Dr Empey (Church of Ireland), Bishop of Limerick

I happen to believe that on the whole we have a very fine constitution. I for one would be loath to use the emotive description of 'sectarian' in reference to it ... It would I believe be a sad mistake to use any change [in the Constitution] as a means of wooing the Northern Unionist ... he will not be slow to see through it.

Commenting at Church of Ireland Synod in Tralee on call by Fine Gael leader Garret FitzGerald for reform of 'sectarian' state. *The Irish Times*, October 12, 1981.

October 31, 1981
Danny Morrison

Who here really believes we can win the war through the ballot box? But will anyone here object if, with a ballot paper in this hand, and an armalite in this hand, we take power in Ireland?

Speaking, as Provisional Sinn Féin Director of Publicity, at Sinn Féin Árd Fheis in Dublin, on desirability of Provisional Republicans standing in elections. *The Irish Times*, November 2, 1981.

October 31, 1981
Jimmy Drumm

Wreck the system from without as the lads are doing. You'll never wreck it from within.

Advice, as member from Belfast of Provisional Sinn Féin Árd Comhairle, to Sinn Féin Árd Fheis in Dublin. *The Irish Times*, November 2, 1981.

November 6, 1981
Garret FitzGerald and Margaret Thatcher

Recognising the unique character of the relationship between the two countries, the Prime Minister and the Taoiseach have decided to establish an Anglo-Irish inter-governmental council, through which institutional expression can be given to that relationship. This will involve regular meetings between the two Governments.

From communiqué after meeting between two leaders at Downing Street to begin new Anglo-Irish dialogue. *The Irish Times*, November 7, 1981.

November 10, 1981
Charles Haughey

Britain will now proceed to deal with Northern Ireland as if it were an internal British problem [and] turn to the world and say all is well between her and Ireland.

Speaking, as Fianna Fáil leader, in Dáil debate on Anglo-Irish communiqué of November 6, 1981. *The Irish Times*, November 11, 1981.

November 10, 1981
Margaret Thatcher

Northern Ireland is part of the United Kingdom – as much as my constituency [Finchley] is.

As Prime Minister, in Commons reply to Unionist MP Harold McCusker, often misquoted as 'Northern Ireland is as British as Finchley'. *HC Debates:* Sixth Series: Vol. 12: Col. 427.

November 10, 1981
Rev. Ian Paisley

On behalf of the people of Ulster, I brand you [Margaret Thatcher] a traitor and a liar.

Addressing Thatcher in Commons after her assurances that agreement of November 6 with Garret FitzGerald did not affect Union. (He was later suspended from House.) *The Irish Times*, November 12, 1981.

November 14, 1981
The IRA

Armchair generals who whip up anti-nationalist murder gangs ... cannot expect to remain forever immune from the effects of their evil work.

Statement issued after killing in Belfast by IRA gunmen of Unionist MP, Rev. Robert Bradford. *The Irish Times*, November 21, 1981.

November 22, 1981
Cardinal Ó Fiaich

Most of the murders have been committed by the IRA ... participation in [their] evil deeds ... murder, wounding, intimidation, kidnapping, destruction of property or any other form of violence is a mortal sin.

In statement after IRA killings, including Rev. Robert Bradford, MP. *The Irish Times*, November 28, 1981.

November 22, 1981
Dr (Edward) Daly, Bishop of Derry
No member of our [Catholic] Church can
remain a member, and at the same time
remain a member of any organisation that
decides of its own accord to perpetuate cold-
blooded murder ... whatever the motive,
whatever the ideal.

In statement after IRA killings, including Rev.
Robert Bradford, MP. *The Irish Times*, November
28, 1981.

December 27, 1981
Charles McCreevy
There is a considerable number of the Fianna
Fáil parliamentary party ... who are less than
satisfied with the direction of Fianna Fáil in
opposition ... The Irish people need some
leadership and it is not being supplied.

In statement, as Kildare Fianna Fáil TD, signalling
opposition to leader Charles Haughey in party, for
which he was expelled from parliamentary party.
Sunday Tribune, December 27, 1981.

January 11, 1982
Fred O'Donovan
Death on demand is what we are talking
about.

As RTE chairman, referring to abortion in remarks
which prompted calls for his resignation by Anti-
Amendment Campaign, which opposed change in
Constitution to outlaw abortion. *The Irish Times*,
January 14, 1983.

January 13, 1982
Lord Gowrie
The Border is an economic nonsense. Just
look at the agriculture system – anyone with
initiative can laugh all the way to the bank by
fiddling.

In interview, as NI Office Minister of State, in
Belfast Telegraph. *Belfast Telegraph*, January 13,
1982.

January 27, 1982
Jim Kemmy
They took me for granted. That was the
mistake they made last night. It might seem
pompous for me to say it, but I feel I was
entitled to influence the Government more
than I did.

As independent TD, on withdrawal of support from
Coalition Government because of budget measures,

resulting in defeat by eighty-two votes to eighty-one
and general election. *The Irish Times*, January 28,
1982.

February 2, 1982
Lieutenant-General Carl O'Sullivan
We are not equipped to face even a minimum
attack from outside. We haven't the ships, the
planes, the artillery, the armour ...
Sovereignty is the ability to defend ourselves
or to be defended. The 26-County State
would do well to grow to such mature
sovereignty before we think about other areas
of sovereignty like Northern Ireland.

In interview after retiring as Chief of Staff of army.
The Irish Times, February 2, 1982.

March 8, 1982
Graham Greene
It seemed to me that the new, Provisional,
IRA was closer to the Chicago gangster than
to the idealism of the men like Erskine
Childers, and my friend, Ernie O'Malley.

In interview after visit to Belfast in French
magazine, *Etudes Irlandaises*. *The Irish Times*,
March 8, 1982.

March 9, 1982
Mark Killilea
I caught them by the seat of the trousers and
pushed them towards the press area and told
them: 'In, quick, hard to your left, up on top
of the Irish box, and jump for your lives'.

Describing, as Fianna Fáil supporter, how he got
the three Sinn Féin the Workers Party TDs into
Dáil chamber after they had been locked out of
division on who would form Government, which
Fianna Fáil leader Charles Haughey won with their
help by eighty-six votes to seventy-nine. *The Irish
Times*, March 10, 1982.

March 13, 1982
James Prior
Let's face it, it's the Catholics who have
suffered more from the violence.

Comment made as NI Secretary of State. *The Irish
Times* ('This Week They Said'), March 13, 1982.

March 30, 1982
Charles Haughey
I have decided to take the unusual course of
asking a member of the Opposition, in the

national interest, to accept the appointment [as Ireland's EEC Commissioner].

As Taoiseach, on his offer of post as EEC Commissioner to Fine Gael TD, Dick Burke, thus creating by-election which could have resulted in gain for his party, Fianna Fáil, then in Government without overall majority. (It didn't.) *The Irish Times,* April 2, 1982.

March 30, 1982
Dick Burke
My acceptance was based on my perception of the national interest.

As Fine Gael TD, on his acceptance of offer from Fianna Fáil leader Charles Haughey, then Taoiseach in minority Government, to become EEC Commissioner. *The Irish Times,* April 2, 1982.

May 3, 1982
Paddy Power
We felt that Argentina were the first aggressors. Obviously Britain themselves are very much the aggressors now.

As Fianna Fáil Minister for Defence, commenting on sinking of Argentinian aircraft carrier *Belgrano* by British submarine in Falklands/Malvinas war. *The Irish Times,* May 4, 1982.

May 6, 1982
Charles Haughey
As a neutral nation that has always refrained from military alliances of any kind, we have to take a clear view of any action, economic or otherwise, that would appear supportive of military action.

As Taoiseach, announcing decision to withdraw support for British request for EEC sanctions against Argentina in Falklands/Malvinas war. *The Irish Times,* May 7, 1982.

May 6, 1982
Nicanor Costa Mendez
Ireland has suffered injustice and has had to endure many attacks. So we were somewhat surprised by Ireland's first reaction [not to oppose British request for international sanctions against Argentina in Falklands/Malvinas war]. And now we are very happy with the change in your political position ... We have learned from the Irish spirit of endurance.

As Foreign Minister of Argentina, interviewed during Falklands/Malvinas war in Buenos Aires by

Olivia O'Leary for *The Irish Times. The Irish Times,* May 7, 1982.

May 22, 1982
David Owen
Ireland has behaved with gross impertinence throughout.

As former British Labour Foreign Minister on refusal of Fianna Fáil Government to back British sanctions against Argentina during Falklands/Malvinas war. *The Irish Times,* May 22, 1982.

May 25, 1982
Gerry Fitt
Ireland's stance on sanctions has led to a greater degree of anti-Irish feeling in Britain than at the time of the Birmingham bombings.

As independent socialist MP, on Irish refusal to back British sanctions against Argentina during Falklands/Malvinas war. *The Irish Times,* May 26, 1982.

June 10, 1982
Charles Haughey
Violence, evil in itself and appalling in its consequences, can only postpone the day of Irish unity.

Speaking, as Taoiseach, in New York to Irish Americans: he had been criticised for not condemning violence forcefully on previous visits to America. *The Irish Times,* June 11, 1982.

June 11, 1982
Padraig Flynn
There's one thing we have that they [Fine Gael] can never have, and that's a love of the four green fields of Ireland.

Speaking, as Fianna Fáil Minister for Gaeltacht, at by-election meeting in Galway. *The Irish Times,* June 12, 1982.

June 18, 1982
Lord Gowrie
I don't think much of the 1921 settlement ... Northern Ireland is extremely expensive on the British taxpayer ... if the people of Northern Ireland wished to join with the south of Ireland, no British Government would resist it for twenty minutes.

Speaking, as Minister of State for Northern Ireland, at Irish Club, London. *The Irish Times,* July 19, 1982.

June 21, 1982
Kenneth Walton
There is a common fallacy that the IRA is a bunch of Barry Fitzgerald leprechauns. They aren't. They are killers.

As deputy director of FBI in New York, on discovery of plan to smuggle surface-to-air missiles to IRA. *The Irish Times*, June 22, 1982.

July 8, 1982
Duke of Norfolk
I had the privilege of giving him [Garret FitzGerald] lunch the other day here in your Lordships' House ... he sees this Bill [to set up Northern Ireland Assembly] as being a wonderful step forward.

Speaking in Lords on alleged support of Fine Gael leader for NI Bill, officially opposed by all main parties in Dublin. *The Irish Times*, November 19, 1982.

July 29, 1982
Fianna Fáil Government
Questions ... need to be asked about the recent activities of Dr [Garret] FitzGerald in London where he met the British Secretary of State [for Northern Ireland], Mr Prior, without revealing to the Government or the public what was said. If what Dr FitzGerald told Mr Prior was in line with what he told the Duke of Norfolk ... then [his] activities ... must become a cause of concern.

In statement attacking Fine Gael leader following remarks by Duke of Norfolk in House of Lords on July 8, 1982, about Garret FitzGerald's alleged agreement with British policy on North. *The Irish Times*, July 30, 1982.

July 29, 1982
Margaret Thatcher
No commitment exists for Her Majesty's Government to consult the Irish Government on matters affecting Northern Ireland.

As British Prime Minister, signalling in Commons end of Anglo-Irish negotiations because of bad relations over Irish 'neutrality' in Falklands/Malvinas war. *The Irish Times*, July 30, 1982.

August 15, 1982
James Prior
Mr [Charles] Haughey's relations with the British Government are supposedly not very good. In fact, they are pretty awful at the moment.

As NI Secretary, on effects of Irish 'neutrality' in Falklands/Malvinas war. *The Irish Times*, August 16, 1982.

August 17, 1982
Charles Haughey
[It was] a bizarre happening, an unprecedented situation ... a grotesque situation ... an almost unbelievable mischance.

As Taoiseach, at Dublin press conference on resignation of Attorney General Patrick Connolly after man wanted for murder found at his home. *The Irish Times*, August 18, 1982.

August 24, 1982
Conor Cruise O'Brien
You've got to hand it to the man, you really have. He [Charles Haughey] is grotesque, unbelievable, bizarre and unprecedented.

Writing in *The Irish Times* on remarks of Taoiseach on August 17, 1982, and his use of adjectives, the initials of which came to form word 'GUBU', subsequently used to describe any misfortune to befall Haughey. *The Irish Times*, August 24, 1982.

September 10, 1982
Nuala Fennell
Under Garret FitzGerald's leadership, Fine Gael remains opposed to sectarianism in our Constitution. Under a Fine Gael Government, such a sectarian amendment [to the Constitution] would not pass our constitutional review committee.

Responding, as leading member of Fine Gael Party, to statement from Paddy Power, Fianna Fáil Minister for Defence, that his Government would bring in anti-abortion Constitutional amendment. *The Irish Times*, September 11, 1982.

September 15, 1982
Garret FitzGerald
There is a story being spread around ... It is a form of politics I don't like, something I have not experienced in the past. It is being suggested that I am in favour of abortion ... I have expressed my deep conviction that abortion is wrong.

Speaking, as Fine Gael leader, at Dublin press conference. *The Irish Times*, September 16, 1982.

September 28, 1982
Geraldine Kennedy

It'll break on Saturday morning in one newspaper. It'll be followed up on Sunday ... it'll happen on Wednesday ... There will be a vote, even if it's 50-30 in favour of your man [Charles Haughey] which weakens his position considerably. There will be a vote this time so I think Garret should be warned.

As journalist, predicting in telephone call to Fine Gael press officer, Peter Prendergast, attempt by Fianna Fáil TD Charles McCreevy to have Charles Haughey removed as party leader. Call was monitored by gardaí on orders of Fianna Fáil Minister for Justice Sean Doherty and transcript later published in *Sunday Independent. Sunday Independent,* March 11, 1984.

October 3, 1982
Charles Haughey

I will insist that the Cabinet stand firm behind me with no shilly-shallying ... The situation is going to be dealt with. We are going to bring to an end the simmering dissension and sniping ... I do not contemplate defeat.

As Fianna Fáil leader, on motion of no confidence in his leadership tabled for party meeting by Fianna Fáil TD Charles McCreevy. *The Irish Times,* October 4, 1982.

October 6, 1982
Des O'Malley

You are aware of the reasons and I think in the circumstances it is unavoidable.

In letter of resignation as Minister of Trade Commerce and Tourism to Taoiseach Charles Haughey because of disagreements over policy on North and economy. *The Irish Times,* October 7, 1982.

October 6, 1982
Eoin Ryan

It is a question of the idealism and the integrity of the party ... I am convinced that we are gradually losing the ideals that we had in the past.

Speaking, as Fianna Fáil senator and senior party member, on why he thought Charles Haughey should go as party leader. *The Irish Times,* October 7, 1982.

October 7, 1982
Mary Colley

He [anonymous telephone caller] said they would blow his [George Colley's] head off, and other parts of his body as well ... it was very frightening.

As wife of Fianna Fáil TD George Colley, who opposed Charles Haughey as party leader, on 'night of long telephone calls' which preceded vote of confidence in Haughey by parliamentary party, which he won by fifty-eight votes to twenty-two. *The Irish Times,* October 8, 1982.

October 21, 1982
Ray MacSharry

I really hit the roof when I heard my name mentioned in connection with money ... arising from a conversation with yourself ... and £100,000 being offered.

Martin O'Donoghue

I certainly did not say that ... What was being said was if there was any suggestion of somebody being compromised financially [by Charles Haughey being ousted as Fianna Fáil leader] that it would be sorted out.

Conversation between two leading Fianna Fáil members in Dáil after Fianna Fáil leader Charles Haughey had been weakened by leadership vote which he survived by fifty-eight votes to twenty-two. Conversation was recorded by MacSharry using tape recorder supplied by gardaí, as he was told he might be compromised. Transcript of recording was made public after change of Government. Murtagh and Joyce, *The Boss,* Poolbeg, 1983, pp. 375-76.

October 29, 1982
Provisional Sinn Féin

Candidates in national and local elections must be unambivalent in support of the armed struggle.

Resolution passed at party Árd Fheis in Dublin. *The Irish Times,* November 6, 1982.

November 2, 1982
Michael O'Leary

People appear to be astounded that a politician can say what he means ... the whole vocabulary of politics has been debased ... we have become a nation of alibis, stratagems and veiled means ... I didn't want to be a scarecrow leader.

Explaining his resignation as leader of Labour Party after it had rejected his advice and decided future decisions on coalition with Fine Gael (which O'Leary supported) be left to delegate conference. *The Irish Times*, October 29, 1982.

November 13, 1982
Joan FitzGerald

It was my fault. I'm to blame, but he isn't absent-minded about anything to do with his work. He is very much on the ball.

Commenting on appearance of husband, Fine Gael leader Garret FitzGerald, in general election campaign, wearing odd shoes. *The Irish Times* ('This Week They Said'), November 13, 1982.

November 21, 1982
Fianna Fáil election poster

Thatcher wants Garret. Do you?

Election slogan published by Meath Fianna Fáil on Margaret Thatcher's assumed support for Fine Gael leader Garret FitzGerald in general election. *The Irish Times*, November 22, 1982.

November 23, 1982
Maureen Haughey

He's always Garret the good. Garret has a halo, and Haughey has horns.

Commenting in interview on better press given to Fine Gael leader Garret FitzGerald than to her husband, Fianna Fáil leader Charles Haughey. *The Irish Times*, November 24, 1982.

November 25, 1982
Jim Kemmy

They [election opponents] all played the abortion card.

Explaining, as former independent TD in Limerick, how he believed he lost his seat because he was identified with pro-abortion lobby. *The Irish Times*, November 26, 1982.

December 7, 1982
Chief Justice O'Higgins

The [Supreme] Court is invited to assume that because of the existence of widespread violence ... any charge associated with terrorist activity should be regarded as a charge in respect of a political offence ... I am not prepared to make such an assumption.

In ruling in Supreme Court which opened way for extradition to North for first time of members of Republican paramilitary groups. *The Irish Times*, December 8, 1982.

January 5, 1983
Sean Doherty

The investigation is to cease immediately. It is a source of irritation to the Government.

As Fianna Fáil Minister for Justice, in instruction relayed through senior official to Garda Deputy Commissioner Joe Ainsworth who was investigating allegations of telephone tapping of journalists: as recalled by Ainsworth. *The Irish Times*, March 23, 1984.

January 19, 1983
Charles Haughey

I want to make it crystal clear that the government as such and I as Taoiseach knew absolutely nothing about any activities of this sort ... I think at this stage we're only dealing with unfounded allegations and unsubstantiated statements.

In RTE interview, as former Taoiseach, on report by Peter Murtagh in *The Irish Times* that telephones of two journalists were officially tapped while Fianna Fáil were in Government. *The Irish Times*, January 24, 1983.

January 21, 1983
Sean Doherty

The request to have the phones of two named journalists put under surveillance resulted from discussions between me and garda security chiefs when concern was being expressed that national security was endangered through leaks of highly confidential Government papers ... my actions as referred to were motivated solely by my concern for the security of my country.

On resigning from Opposition Fianna Fáil frontbench after disclosure that as Justice Minister he had had telephones of two journalists writing about internal Fianna Fáil dissension tapped by gardaí. *The Irish Times*, January 22, 1983.

January 23, 1983
Sean Doherty

Mr Haughey did not know that I was tapping those journalists and indeed it was only shortly before Christmas [after *Irish Times* report] that Mr Haughey had a brief discussion with me about the matter.

As former Justice Minister, after incoming Coalition Government had confirmed telephone tapping under Fianna Fáil Government when Charles Haughey was Taoiseach. *The Irish Times*, January 24, 1983.

January 29, 1983
John Hume
As for the Unionists themselves, they have become a petty people.

Addressing SDLP annual conference as party leader on refusal of Unionist leaders to negotiate settlement with SDLP. *The Irish Times*, February 1, 1983.

February 3, 1983
Charles Haughey
Those who bring the party into disrepute, cause dissension or refuse to accept decisions democratically arrived at can no longer remain in the party ... are its policies to be decided for it by alien influences, by political opponents, or worst of all by business interests?

In statement on renewed crisis over his leadership of Fianna Fáil, when forty-one Fianna Fáil TDs called for meeting to discuss issue after revelations about telephone tapping when he was Taoiseach: Haughey survived confidence vote by forty votes to thirty-three. *The Irish Times*, February 4, 1983.

March 17, 1983
Cardinal Cooke
They [British] don't belong there in the first place. I am for a united Ireland for all the people.

Interviewed, as NY cardinal, on steps of St Patrick's Cathedral, New York, after refusing to appear for start of St Patrick's Day parade because it was led by Martin Flannery of NORAID. *The Irish Times*, March 18, 1983.

March 17, 1983
President Reagan
Those [in America] who support violence are no friends of Ireland.

In speech on visit, as US President, to Irish embassy in Washington. *The Irish Times*, March 18, 1983.

March 29, 1983
Catholic Hierarchy
Surely the most defenceless and voiceless in our midst are entitled to the fullest Constitutional protection.

In statement backing referendum to insert anti-abortion amendment into Constitution. *The Irish Times*, March, 30, 1983.

March 29, 1983
Anti-Amendment Campaign
The statement of the Catholic Hierarchy ... reveals ... the determination to enshrine Roman Catholic teaching on issues of private morality in the Constitution.

Responding to Hierarchy's backing for anti-abortion amendment to Constitution. *The Irish Times*, March 30, 1983.

April 4, 1983
Tomás MacGiolla
We are moving back towards a Catholic Constitution for a Catholic people.

As leader of Workers' Party, on statement by Hierarchy of March 29, 1983, backing anti-abortion amendment to Constitution. *The Irish Times*, April 5, 1983.

April 7, 1983
Major Sir Anthony Farrar-Hockley
The Malaysian terrorists were pretty good, but the most efficient terrorists that I have ever fought were the Israelis – the Irgun and Stern Gang ... by God they were good, really good. Compared to them, the IRA are rank amateurs ... they remain just a bunch of murderous thugs really.

In interview, as former British Army Commander of Land Forces in Northern Ireland. *The Irish Times*, April 8, 1983.

April 7, 1983
Constitutional amendment
The State acknowledges the right to life of the unborn, and, with due regard to the equal right to life of the mother, guarantees in its laws to respect and, as far as practicable, by its laws to vindicate and defend that right.

Wording of anti-abortion amendment proposed by Opposition Fianna Fáil Party and passed in Dáil by eighty-seven votes to thirteen. *The Irish Times*, April 28, 1983.

April 9, 1983
Dr Armstrong, Archbishop of Armagh (Church of Ireland)
This is the Mother and Child Act all over again. Can you ... force a moral theology on a whole people which is symptomatic of only one church?

Commenting on Coalition Government plans for anti-abortion referendum. *The Irish Times* ('This Week They Said'), April 9, 1983.

April 27, 1983
Dean Griffin
Can you imagine the old Stormont Parliament carrying through a law or bill against the united wishes of the Roman Catholic Church and people. Would there not be howls of 'sectarianism'?

As Church of Ireland Dean of St Patrick's Cathedral, Dublin, on backing of Catholic Hierarchy for anti-abortion amendment to Constitution. *The Irish Times,* April 28, 1983.

May 4, 1983
Michael Heseltine
Those countries [like the Republic] which don't play a part in NATO should ask themselves why they should take advantage of the umbrella we provide.

As British Defence Minister, in comments made in Belfast following which Government in Dublin lodged official protest. *The Irish Times,* May 6, 1983.

May 5, 1983
Charles Haughey
[It is] unnecessarily restrictive ... people going forward for election should have access to the public.

As Fianna Fáil leader, referring to directive to RTE under Section 31 of Broadcasting Act forbidding interviews with Sinn Féin, which had candidates in general election in North. *The Irish Times,* May 26, 1983.

July 13, 1983
John Hume
If you want the IRA to win, hang them.

Speaking in Commons, as newly-elected SDLP MP, in debate on hanging for terrorists. *The Irish Times,* July 14, 1983.

July 13, 1983
Rev. William McCrea
Give me a thousand dead IRA martyrs rather than a thousand [live] IRA murderers any day.

Speaking, as DUP MP, in Commons in debate on hanging for terrorists. *The Irish Times,* July 14, 1983.

June 19, 1983
Gerry Adams
If Wolfe Tone were alive today ... he would stand firmly with us ... reviled ... as an upstart, a subversive and the 1798 equivalent of the gunman.

Speaking, as Vice-President of Provisional Sinn Féin, at Bodenstown. *The Irish Times,* June 20, 1983.

August 16, 1983
Dr McNamara, Bishop of Kerry
There exists in Ireland a strong pro-abortion lobby, with powerful backing in the media and very substantial support from the international pro-abortion movement under the umbrella of the Anti-Amendment campaign. This group hopes to defeat the [anti-abortion] amendment as a first essential step towards the legalisation of abortion.

In speech at Millstreet, Co. Cork, which Anti-Amendment Campaign claimed was a slur on integrity of their members. *The Irish Times,* August 16, 1983.

August 17, 1983
Justin Keating
The question at issue, as it was in the Mother and Child scheme in 1951 a quarter of a century ago ... is what sort of country we are trying to build. Are we trying to build a 26-County Catholic green Republic? ... The alternative would be to cherish, in the words of the [1916] Proclamation, all the children of the nation equally.

As former Labour minister, speaking at Labour Party meeting to oppose anti-abortion amendment to Constitution. *The Irish Times,* August 18, 1973.

August 22, 1983
Catholic Hierarchy
There are people who are sincerely opposed to abortion and yet who feel that no referendum should take place at all ... we recognise the right of each person to vote according to conscience.

Statement on anti-abortion referendum, welcomed by Anti-Amendment Campaign. *The Irish Times,* August 23, 1983.

August 24, 1983
Malcolm Muggeridge
It is my opinion that the [anti-abortion] amendment as it is worded may in fact open the way to legalised abortion, rather than prevent it.

As English writer and anti-abortion campaigner, on why he decided to cancel plans to come to Ireland to support anti-abortion referendum campaign. *The Irish Times*, August 25, 1983.

August 29, 1983
Dean Griffin
Where there is conflict, the rights of the mother to life and health must take precedence over the unborn child.

As Church of Ireland Dean of St Patrick's Cathedral, Dublin, on anti-abortion referendum. *The Irish Times*, August 30, 1983.

September 5, 1983
Garret FitzGerald
Someone performing an abortion in this country in future *could* do so with less likelihood of being prosecuted and convicted.

As Taoiseach, in television address warning how anti-abortion amendment to Constitution could make prosecutions more difficult because of wording. *The Irish Times*, September 6, 1983.

September 5, 1983
Nell McCafferty
If anyone doubted that the [anti-abortion] amendment was anti-woman, they had only to watch the performance on television of Mr Charles Haughey, who could not bring himself to mention woman, or pregnancy or mothers in the course of his broadcast [on the amendment].

Speaking, as journalist, at press conference held by Women Against the Amendment, in Dublin. *The Irish Times*, September 6, 1983.

September 5, 1983
Louise Asmal
This [anti-abortion] amendment contains within it the concept of revenge against sexually-active women.

As speaker at press conference held by Women Against the Amendment, in Dublin. *The Irish Times*, September 6, 1983.

September 8, 1983
Anti-amendment campaigner
This referendum has been won with a Carmelite in one hand and a ballot box in the other.

Comment to journalist at Dublin counting of votes in referendum, which decided that anti-abortion

amendment be inserted into Constitution. *The Irish Times*, September 9, 1983.

October 22, 1983
Patrick Cahalane
There may be a few [Irish Army officers] who are delighted to participate [in Remembrance Day ceremonies] but there are others who regard it [participation] as a bad decision for the country ... I do not feel the present British Army is a peace-keeping Army.

Replying, as one of a number of retired army officers, to support of Minister for Defence for army participation in British Army Remembrance Day ceremonies in Dublin. *The Irish Times*, October 23, 1983.

October 22, 1983
Patrick Cooney
I think it's wrong to be critical of whatever flag they [Irishmen who fell in battle] were fighting under. I thought we'd all grown up a bit.

As Minister for Defence, stating his support for army participation in British Army Remembrance Day ceremonies in Dublin. *The Irish Times*, October 23, 1983.

November 4, 1983
Maurice Dockrell
He [Maurice Dockrell] told only one lie ever in the Dáil, when, quite unable to resist the temptation, he quipped 'I'm past it but I'm for it' in a debate about contraception.

As Fine Gael TD, in interview on his career. *The Irish Times*, November 5, 1983.

November 10, 1983
James Prior
What on earth would we do? ... it might end with a Cuba off our western coast.

Reported remark at meeting of Conservative MPs in London on prospect of Sinn Féin winning more votes than SDLP in future NI elections. *The Irish Times*, November 11, 1983.

November 26, 1983
Dominic McGlinchey
I am not going to be blackmailed by the grief of children. The only way to end repression in the North is through violence against the security forces and the State itself.

Leader of Irish National Liberation Army, involved by own account in thirty killings in North, in interview with Vincent Browne, editor of *Sunday Tribune,* while on run in Republic. *Sunday Tribune,* November 27, 1983.

November 29, 1983
Rev. Fr Des Wilson

Any solution would have to take into account that the Protestants of Northern Ireland were the best armed and best officially protected minority in Europe ... [but] only Irish Protestants could protect Irish Protestants, and then in company with their fellow Irish citizens of whatever faith.

As Belfast priest, in individual contribution to conference of nationalist parties (Fianna Fáil, Fine Gael, Labour, SDLP) meeting in New Ireland Forum in Dublin to find agreement on way forward regarding Northern Ireland. *The Irish Times,* November 30, 1983.

December 13, 1983
Neils Haagerup

There is no escaping the responsibility of the European Community [for Northern Ireland].

Speaking in Strasbourg on publication of his European Parliament commissioned report on Northern Ireland, recommending power-sharing. *The Irish Times,* December 14, 1983.

December 18, 1983
The IRA

The Harrods bombing was not authorised by the Army Council of the Irish Republican Army. We have taken immediate steps to ensure that there will be no repetition of this type of operation again.

In statement after bomb at Harrods store in London killed five people. *The Irish Times,* December 19, 1983.

December 18, 1983
Denis Thatcher

No damned Irish murderer is going to stop me shopping there.

As husband of British Prime Minister, on IRA bombing of Harrods in London. *The Irish Times,* December 24, 1983.

January 11, 1984
Conor Cruise O'Brien

I asked him [Sean MacEntee] whether the Rising of 1916 might not have been a mistake. He ... replied 'It might have been a mistake, but if so, it's a mistake I'm glad I was in.'

In tribute to father-in-law and former minister Sean MacEntee, who had just died. *The Irish Times,* January 11, 1984.

January 13, 1984
Catholic Hierarchy

Where the offence [in public policy] to the moral principles of the majority of citizens would be disproportionately serious, it is not unreasonable to require sacrifice of the minorities ... Britain for example does not allow polygamy.

In written submission to New Ireland Forum of nationalist parties, meeting in Dublin, outlining Catholic Church views on pluralism. *The Irish Times,* January 14, 1984.

January 15, 1984
Cardinal Ó Fiaich

If a person is convinced that he is joining [Sinn Féin] for these reasons [community activities] and that his positive reasons outweigh any interpretation that may be given his membership as condoning support for violence and crime, he may be morally justified.

In comment on RTE on morality of Sinn Féin membership. *The Irish Times,* January 16, 1984.

January 19, 1984
Sylvia Meehan

A majority of women in the North from both Unionist and Nationalist traditions would not want to endure the present constraints in the South.

As Chairwoman of Employment Equality Agency in Republic, in personal submission to New Ireland Forum of nationalist parties, meeting in Dublin. *The Irish Times,* January 20, 1984.

January 24, 1984
Pastor Eric McComb

We don't need the Sinn Féin Cardinal to be advocating votes for those who are out to murder these men.

Referring, as Superintendent of Elim Pentecostal Churches in Ireland, at funeral of UDR man, to remark of Cardinal Ó Fiaich on January 15, 1984, about morality of Sinn Féin membership. *The Irish Times,* January 25, 1984.

February 9, 1984
Dr (Cahal) Daly, Bishop of Down and Connor

The Catholic Church in Ireland totally rejects the concept of a confessional state. We have not sought, and do not seek, a Catholic state for a Catholic people.

In submission on behalf of Catholic bishops to New Ireland Forum of nationalist parties, meeting in Dublin. *The Irish Times*, February 10, 1984.

April 2, 1984
Jesse Jackson

British troops cannot bring peace to Ireland any more than United States troops can bring peace to Lebanon, Grenada or Vietnam. No one seeking justice can rely on terror and no one seeking peace can tolerate injustice.

As candidate for Democratic nomination for president, in interview in USA. *The Irish Times*, April 3, 1984.

April 13, 1984
Peter Barry

The Government is passionately committed to the proposition that the present situation of the nationalists in Northern Ireland cannot and will not continue.

In speech, as Fine Gael Minister for Foreign Affairs, in Donegal, signalling new emphasis in Government's NI policy. *The Irish Times*, April 14, 1984.

April 24, 1984
Rev. Fr James Shiels

He will be remembered among the saints in heaven. [He was] foremost in the campaign for the preservation of life . . . against abortion in the South.

As priest at funeral of IRA volunteer killed in Derry by own bomb. *The Irish Times*, April 25, 1984.

May 2, 1984
New Ireland Forum

The Forum had identified . . . the desire of nationalists for a united Ireland in the form of a sovereign, independent Irish State . . . in addition, two structural arrangements were examined in detail, a federal/confederal state and joint authority . . . The parties in the Forum also remain open to discuss other

views which may contribute to political development.

Report of New Ireland Forum of nationalist parties, meeting in Dublin. *The Irish Times*, May 3, 1984.

May 2, 1984
Garret FitzGerald

The ideal we would aspire to would be a unitary state . . . but we also recognise that we cannot achieve this ourselves and we have indicated an openness to other views.

As Taoiseach and Fine Gael leader, at end of New Ireland Forum of nationalist parties, meeting in Dublin, making clear he was not tied to report's main recommendations. *The Irish Times*, May 3, 1984.

May 2, 1984
Charles Haughey

It [a unitary state] is not an 'option' – it is the wish of the parties of the Forum . . . Neither of these other two arrangements, federation or joint sovereignty, would bring peace and stability to the North.

Making clear, as Fianna Fáil leader, that he supported only ideal of unitary state, main recommendation of New Ireland Forum of nationalist parties, meeting in Dublin. *The Irish Times*, May 3, 1984.

May 2, 1984
John Hume

To the Unionists of the North with whom we share this piece of earth, Irish nationalism can today repeat de Gaulle's ringing affirmation of reconciliation to the Algerians: '*Je vous ai compris* – we understand your position' . . . we accept that before now we might not have fully understood.

Speaking, as SDLP leader, at closing session of New Ireland Forum of nationalist parties, meeting in Dublin. *The Irish Times*, May 3, 1984.

May 2, 1984
Colonel Gadafy

The Irish cause is a just one [but] in the last few years we've stopped our material support to the IRA in order to establish good relations with Britain.

Comment by Libyan leader on accusations that he supported terrorists. *The Irish Times*, May 3, 1984.

May 26, 1984
P. J. Mara
Uno Duce, una voce.

Commenting, as spokesman for Charles Haughey, leader of Fianna Fáil, on how in the party there was 'one leader, one voice'. *The Irish Times* ('This Year They Said'), December 29, 1984.

May 29, 1984
George Seawright
Fenian scum . . . taxpayers' money would be better spent on an incinerator and burning the whole lot of them. The priests should be thrown in and burned as well.

Remark made as Democratic Unionist councillor at Belfast Education and Library Board referring to Catholics who objected to playing of British national anthem at concerts. (He was later expelled from DUP for refusing to retract.) *The Irish Times*, June 1, 1984.

June 2, 1984
James Prior
The Forum Report outlines three models. One is a unitary state, the second is a form of federation, the third is called joint authority. Now the report makes clear that each is to be achieved by 'agreement and consent' . . . it is a dangerous fallacy to imagine that the Unionist majority in Northern Ireland will agree. It is equally false to imagine that the [British] Government or anyone else can engineer or induce such agreement.

As NI Secretary, giving British Government's response, in Commons, to *Forum Report*. *The Irish Times*, July 3, 1984.

June 2, 1984
Michael D. Higgins
It is wrong that the God of War should be getting a doctorate from the National University of Ireland.

As Chairman of Irish Labour Party, opposing conferring of NUI doctorate on President Reagan. *The Irish Times* ('This Year They Said'), December 29, 1984.

June 3, 1984
President Reagan
I received a paper from Ireland that told me that in the clan to which we belong, those who said 'Regan' and spelt it that way were the professional people and the educators, and

only the common labourers called it 'Reagan'. So meet a common labourer.

Speaking at Ballyporeen, Co. Tipperary, his ancestral home, on three-day visit to Republic. *The Irish Times*, June 4, 1984.

June 4, 1984
President Reagan
My feelings here this morning can best be summarised by the words: 'home, home again' . . . Many of us [Irish-Americans] aren't back in Ireland five minutes before, as the American song has it, we're looking to shake the hand of Uncle Mike and kiss the girl we used to swing down by the garden gate . . . I can perhaps claim to be an Irishman longer than anyone here. I also have some other credentials. I am the great-grandson of a Tipperary man; I am the President of a country with the closest possible ties to Ireland; and I was a friend of Barry Fitzgerald.

Addressing joint houses of Oireachtas on three-day visit to Republic. *The Irish Times*, June 5, 1984.

June 5, 1984
Lord Justice Gibson
I regard each of the accused as absolutely blameless in this matter. That finding should be put in their record along with my own commendation for their courage and determination in bringing the three deceased men to justice, in this case to the final courts of justice.

Delivering written judgement at Belfast Crown Court when acquitting three RUC men of murdering one of three unarmed IRA members at roadblock. *The Irish Times*, June 6, 1984.

June 15, 1984
Cardinal Ó Fiaich
We wish to voice our grave disquiet at the remarks accompanying the judgement delivered recently by Lord Justice Gibson in the case involving certain members of the RUC. Such remarks, made in the context of a considered written judgement, seem to us inexplicable and inexcusable.

In statement also signed by eight other NI Catholic bishops after Lord Justice Gibson praised RUC men for killing unarmed IRA members and sending them to 'final courts of justice'. *The Irish Times*, June 16, 1984.

August 21, 1984
Martin Galvin

If I had a gun at that time, I would have hopefully tried to use it to protect those women and children against the British terrorists.

Commenting on RUC attempts to arrest him in Belfast as banned American representative of NORAID during which Andersonstown man, Sean Downes, was killed by plastic bullet. *The Irish Times*, August 22, 1984.

September 2, 1984
Dr McNamara, Bishop of Kerry

We hear today of proposals to facilitate access to contraceptives for the unmarried and the young in our society . . . if we travel this road . . . we shall be setting the scene for an increase in venereal diseases, teenage pregnancies, illegitimate births and even abortion.

In pastoral letter following reports that Government was planning to liberalise contraceptive legislation making contraceptives available to all people over eighteen. *The Irish Times*, September 3, 1984.

September 13, 1984
Seamus Heaney

Culturally and psychologically, they [Unionists] have to be constantly welcomed on the land. Their collective political machine must, I think, be rebuked and broken if possible. As a power group, they have never collectively yielded a damn thing and they have to learn to be a bit better-mannered towards their Catholic neighbours. But I think that anything that excludes them from being Irish, anything that makes them feel unwanted, is not called for . . . the writers should welcome them and the politicians should punish them.

Interviewed, as Ireland's leading poet, on North, where he was born. *The Irish Times*, September 13, 1984.

October 12, 1984
The IRA

Today, we were unlucky, but remember, we only have to be lucky once – you will have to be lucky always.

Statement directed to British Prime Minister Margaret Thatcher after bombing of Brighton hotel where she was staying. *The Irish Times*, October 13, 1984.

October 14, 1984
Margaret Thatcher

In church on Sunday morning – it was a lovely morning and we haven't had many lovely days – the sun was coming through a stained glass window and falling on some flowers, falling right across the church. It just occurred to me that this was the day I was meant not to see. Then all of a sudden I thought, 'there are some of my dearest friends who are not seeing this day'.

When asked after church service for victims of Brighton bombing about her feelings. *The Spectator*, May 24, 1985.

November 3, 1984
Gerry Adams

The Brighton bombing was an inevitable result of the British presence in this country. Far from being a blow against democracy, it was a blow for democracy.

Addressing Sinn Féin Árd Fheis as President, after attempt by IRA to kill Thatcher and British Cabinet at Brighton. *The Irish Times*, November 5, 1984.

November 8, 1984
Alice Glenn

Legislators would be doing the nation a great disservice if we try to pander to young people who are sexually active. It [making contraceptives more readily available] isn't the basis for any future stable relationship. What man wants to have anything to do with a girl who has been used and abused by any man who comes along with condoms?

Reacting, as Fine Gael TD, to announcement of legislation to make contraceptives available to all people over eighteen years of age. *The Irish Times*, November 9, 1984.

November 18, 1984
Chequers Communiqué

The identities of both the majority and the minority communities in Northern Ireland should be recognised and respected and reflected in the structures and processes of Northern Ireland in ways acceptable to both communities.

From text of joint statement after meeting between Thatcher and FitzGerald at Chequers summit: this phrase provided basis for further talks which led to Anglo-Irish Agreement. *The Irish Times*, November 20, 1984.

November 19, 1984
Margaret Thatcher
I have made it quite clear, and so did Mr Prior when he was Secretary of State for Northern Ireland – that a unified Ireland was one solution. That is out. A second solution was confederation of the two states. That is out. A third solution was joint authority. That is out. That is a derogation from sovereignty.

Statement at televised press conference in London after meeting Taoiseach at Chequers summit, later remembered as her 'out, out, out' dismissal of Forum options. *The Irish Times,* November 23, 1984.

November 20, 1984
Garret FitzGerald
The outcome of this summit is not to be underestimated.

Commenting in Dáil on Chequers meeting with Thatcher. *The Irish Times,* November 21, 1984.

November 20, 1984
Charles Haughey
Mount Everest has never seen such a mad scramble down from a summit as took place at Leinster House today ... To the Taoiseach I say: you have led the country into the greatest humiliation in recent history.

Commenting, as Fianna Fáil leader, in Dáil on aftermath of Chequers summit between FitzGerald and Thatcher. *The Irish Times,* November 21, 1984.

November 20, 1984
Dáil Debates
That is not what the Britshit Prime Minister said.

Misprint in some editions, later withdrawn, of remark attributed to Charles Haughey. *The Irish Times,* November 29, 1984.

November 21, 1984
Garret FitzGerald
[Mrs Thatcher was] gratuitously offensive.

Reported remark at Fine Gael meeting on Thatcher's 'out, out, out' dismissal of Forum options. *The Irish Times,* November 22, 1984.

November 21, 1984
Dr McNamara, Archbishop of Dublin
It would be foolish to try to enforce it [change in contraceptive legislation]. It should be treated as a dead letter.

Referring to plans by Government to introduce legislation to make contraceptives available to all people over eighteen. *The Irish Times* ('This Week They Said'), November 21, 1984.

November 24, 1984
John Biggs-Davison
The search for a solution is part of the problem.

Commenting, as Chairman of Tory NI Backbench Committee, on inadvisability of further Anglo-Irish negotiations. *The Irish Times* ('This Week They Said'), November 24, 1984.

November 24, 1984
James Molyneaux
[It is like] a people walking in the darkness who had suddenly felt the sun in their faces.

Speaking, as party leader, at Official Unionist Conference in Newcastle, Co. Down, referring to Thatcher's rejection of Forum options. *The Irish Times,* November 26, 1984.

November 24, 1984
William Ward
How often I have been irritated as I'm sure you must be by that dreadful pronunciation 'haitch' (laughter). Give me the native Ulster 'h' ... I'd like to point out some of the names that have crept into the BBC and I make no apology, for reading them out.

Speaking, as Gilnahirk-Dundonald delegate, at Official Unionist Party Conference in Newcastle on number of Catholics in BBC, allegedly recognisable by pronunciation of 'h' as 'haitch', and by their names. *The Irish Times,* November 26, 1984.

November 24, 1984
Robert McCartney
Fuck off out of it if you can't observe the niceties.

As Assembly member, at Official Unionist Party Conference in Newcastle, speaking to English reporter who didn't stand when delegates sang British national anthem. *The Irish Times,* November 26, 1984.

November 25, 1984
Dr (Cahal) Daly, Bishop of Down and Connor
Constitutional nationalism has received a humiliating setback. Alienation among

nationalists is now shading over into anger and despair.

In lecture delivered in London following Thatcher's 'out, out, out' dismissal of Forum options. *The Irish Times,* November 26, 1984.

November 25, 1984
John Hume

Not for the first time, the intransigence of Mrs Thatcher has fuelled the anger and bitterness upon which violence in Ireland is fed.

Reacting, as SDLP leader, to Thatcher's 'out, out, out' dismissal of Forum options. *The Irish Times,* November 26, 1984.

November 27, 1984
Rev. Ian Paisley

[Bishop Daly] is the Black Pope of the Republican movement.

Referring to Dr Cahal Daly's remarks on Catholic alienation in Northern Ireland on November 25, 1984. *The Irish Times,* November 24, 1984.

November 29, 1984
Charles Haughey

They'll say something today, and they're totally wrong about it . . . then next day they're back, pontificating the same as ever. That sort of smug know-all commentator – I suppose if anything annoys me, that annoys me . . . I could instance a load of fuckers whose throat I'd cut, and push over the nearest cliff, but there's no percentage in that.

Referring to political commentators in interview in Dublin magazine, *Hot Press,* November 29, 1984.

December 4, 1984
Margaret Thatcher

I am afraid I have a weakness that when people ask me a direct question at a press conference, I give them a direct answer . . . I am anxious to get constructive talks going again.

At press conference in Dublin during EEC summit, answering question about her 'out, out, out' dismissal of Forum options. *The Irish Times,* December 5, 1984.

December 24, 1984
Cardinal Ó Fiaich

No progress would be made in Northern Ireland while Mrs Thatcher remained as Prime Minister . . . she does not have a good

grasp of the complexities of the Northern Ireland system . . . it [supergrass trials] is a system of internment under another name . . . There was never acceptance of the UDR and that has reached rock botton now.

In interview on RTE. *The Irish Times,* December 24, 1984.

January 20, 1985
Douglas Hurd

We [British and Irish Goverments] discuss what happens. If that could be made more methodical, those views could carry greater weight. There could be machinery for this.

Commenting on RTE, as NI Secretary, on possibility of new round of Anglo-Irish negotiations. *The Irish Times,* January 21, 1985.

February 5, 1985
Jack Marrinan

We certainly would not encourage our female members to think that this [pregnancy] is a normal condition for them to get into out of wedlock. We would expect our banghardaí to be moral in every way.

Commenting, as general secretary of Garda Representative Association, on disciplinary proceedings against bangharda because she became pregnant when unmarried. *The Irish Time,* February 6, 1985.

February 12, 1985
Dr Newman, Bishop of Limerick

Let me remind all politicians who profess to be Catholic that they have a duty to follow the guidance of their Church in areas where the interests of Church and State overlap.

In pastoral letter on Bill to liberalise contraceptive legislation. *The Irish Times,* February 13, 1985.

February 13, 1985
John Robb

Are you [members of Oireachtas] going to vote to let us know once and for all that what you want is indeed a Catholic State for a Catholic people?

Commenting, at Dublin press conference, as senator in Oireachtas representing Northern Ireland, on Bill to liberalise contraceptive legislation. *The Irish Times,* February 14, 1985.

February 13, 1985
Dr Cassidy, Bishop of Clonfert
We do not want a Catholic state here for a Catholic people ... we do not advocate a Catholic tyranny. It is not for bishops to decide if the law should be changed. This is a matter for the legislators after conscientious consideration of all the factors involved.

Commenting on RTE on Bill to liberalise contraceptive legislation. *The Irish Times,* January 14, 1985.

February 20, 1985
Des O'Malley
If this Bill [on contraception] is defeated tonight, what is the reaction? What is the effect? The two groups on this island who will rejoice to high heaven will be the Unionists in Northern Ireland and the extreme Roman Catholics in this Republic ... the day of a united Ireland is further away than I had previously believed. But I am certain of one thing: we will never see a 32-county Republic on this island unless we establish a 26-county Republic ... I stand by the Republic and accordingly I will not oppose this Bill.

Announcing to Dáil that he would defy Fianna Fáil whip and abstain rather than vote against Bill to liberalise contraceptive legislation. *The Irish Times,* February 21, 1985.

February 21, 1985
Tip O'Neill
I introduce the Prime Minister of the United Kingdom of Great Britain.

On presenting Margaret Thatcher to joint session of US Congress, deliberately omitting Northern Ireland from full title 'Great Britain and Northern Ireland'. *The Irish Times,* February 22, 1985.

February 21, 1985
Margaret Thatcher
Garret FitzGerald and I ... are united in condemning terrorism ... [we] will continue to consult together in the quest for stability and peace in Northern Ireland.

Addressing joint session of US Congress. *The Irish Times,* February 22, 1985.

February 26, 1985
Pat O'Malley
When I started to do a line with him, Des was terribly worked up about how the politicians

hadn't stood up to the bishops in the Mother and Child scheme ... When the whole issue developed again it was something of major importance to him. If he was now in a position to rectify what happened back in 1951, then he was determined to do it.

Commenting after her husband, Des O'Malley, had been expelled from Fianna Fáil for defying party whip and refusing to vote against contraceptive legislation. *The Irish Times,* February 27, 1985.

March 3, 1985
Peter Barry
It is unfortunate that a row broke out after the last summit ... I criticised Mrs Thatcher strongly at the time. In retrospect I regret this.

Interviewed, as Minister for Foreign Affairs, in *Mail on Sunday,* March 3, 1985.

March 3, 1985
Bob Geldof
It [Dublin] used to be one of the prettiest [cities] in Europe and now it's a shambolical mess ... not only is the city increasingly brutalised but the people in it have lost their old openness and that is a lot to do with the destruction of the city. Please stop destroying Dublin.

Addressing councillors at civic reception in his honour in Mansion House, Dublin. *The Irish Times,* March 4, 1985.

March 8, 1985
Justice Declan Costello
In making their assessment the respondents [Holy Faith secondary school, New Ross] were, it seemed to him, entitled to take into account that her [Ms Eileen Flynn's] association was carried on openly and publicly in a country town of quite a small population ... and that they would regard her conduct as a rejection of the norms of behaviour and the ideals which the school was endeavouring to instil in and set for them.

In judgement ruling that schoolteacher had not been unfairly dismissed from Holy Faith school after going to live with local man whose wife had left him, and becoming pregnant. *The Irish Times,* March 8, 1985.

March 14, 1985
Dr Howard Cromie, Presbyterian Moderator

His [Cardinal Ó Fiaich's] utterances are bound to lead to bitterness and distrust not only among Protestants, but also among many law-abiding Roman Catholics ... To call for a British withdrawal from Northern Ireland can only be regarded as a call for the withdrawal of all those who regard themselves as British ... I hope and pray therefore that we will have no more provocative and coat-trailing statements.

In attack, as Presbyterian Moderator, on Cardinal Ó Fiaich after meeting of church leaders at Dundalk to launch campaign for peace in North. *The Irish Times*, March 15, 1985.

March 22, 1985
Garret FitzGerald

The novel political structure now under discussion ... would also involve such changes in the security forces as would enable both traditions to give their adherence and support to the actions of those forces.

Explaining Anglo-Irish negotiations at London dinner. *The Irish Times*, March 23, 1985.

March 25, 1985
Rev. David Armstrong

In one word – bigotry.

Response when asked what forced him to leave Limavady, Co. Derry, where he had been criticised by members of his Presbyterian congregation for visiting Catholic church. *The Irish Times*, March 26, 1985.

April 21, 1985
Charles McCreevy

Most people are aware of my current domestic situation but they haven't yet heard of the Parnellite lives of people from the top to the bottom in Fianna Fáil.

Remark by Kildare TD after claiming his marital troubles had been used by opponents within Fianna Fáil to prevent his nomination for local government election. *The Irish Times*, April 22, 1985.

May 10, 1985
T. P. McKenna

You have not reflected the anger of the Irish people at that maladroit speech [when Margaret Thatcher said the three Forum options were 'out'].

Peter Barry

Mrs Thatcher's response offended me as well. I can afford to be offended provided I get the end result right.

Exchange between actor and Minister for Foreign Affairs at debate in Tara Hotel, London. *The Irish Times*, May 13, 1985.

May 19, 1985
Garret FitzGerald

The British Government would keep the IRA alive and prevent peace coming to this island [without] radical changes in the structure and method of work of the security forces ... [the UDR] in its present form, in its composition and in its discipline and performance is a force that Nationalists must and do fear. There have been just too many people murdered by the UDR, either on duty or off duty.

In RTE radio interview on weekend of Fine Gael Árd Fheis. *The Irish Times*, May 20, 1985.

June 6, 1985
Joh Bjelke-Petersen

An Irish school wanted a guest speaker and asked the local university to supply a wit. The university replied that they had no one who was a wit but they had two halfwits.

Speaking, as Premier of Queensland, Australia, at lunch in honour of President Hillery, and attended by Irish Ambassador Joe Small who had publicly complained about anti-Irish jokes. *The Irish Times*, June 7, 1985.

June 11, 1985
Pope John Paul II

I ... encourage and support every worthy effort aimed at reconciling opposing sections [in Ireland] and at bringing to an end the tragic suffering that has too long endured. Inevitably there occur discouraging moments in the dialogue for peace but the process must never be abandoned.

In remarks to new British Ambassador to Holy See David Lane, interpreted as support for Anglo-Irish negotiations. *The Irish Times*, June 12, 1985.

June 11, 1985
Rev. Ian Paisley

The Pope would be better off excommunicating those members of his

Church who are butchering the Protestants of Ulster.

Responding to Pope John Paul's support for Anglo-Irish negotiations. *The Irish Times*, June 12, 1985.

June 18, 1985
Garret FitzGerald

Irish people had neither understood nor been able to accept the manner in which Israeli forces and militias, supported, armed and advised by the Israeli army, have harrassed and at times physically attacked the UNIFIL force, including the Irish contingent.

Speaking at luncheon in Dublin in honour of President Herzog of Israel. *The Irish Times*, June 19, 1985.

June 19, 1985
Chaim Herzog

I was informed unequivocally that no Israeli soldiers were there or were involved in any way.

Commenting, during visit to Dublin as President of Israel, on incident involving Irish soldiers in Lebanon when Israeli soldiers shot at Irish UNIFIL troops. *The Irish Times*, June 20, 1985.

June 19, 1985
Peter Barry

My information is that there were . . . members of the Israeli defence forces present.

Commenting, as Minister for Foreign Affairs, on incident involving Irish soldiers in Lebanon. *The Irish Times*, June 20, 1985.

July 12, 1985
Rev. Ian Paisley

If they tried to stop us in Protestant Portadown, what would they do to us if we were ruled from Dublin?

Speaking at Independent Orange Order celebrations in Ballycastle on ban on loyalist parade in Portadown. *The Irish Times*, July 13, 1985.

July 19, 1985
Cardinal Ó Fiaich

I think ninety per cent of religious bigotry [in Northern Ireland] is to be found among Protestants, whereas the bigotry one finds among Catholics is mainly political.

From interview in *Universe*. *The Irish Times*, July 20, 1985.

July 21, 1985
Dr Donal Caird, Archbishop of Dublin (Church of Ireland)

We must record our deep regret and disappointment that such comments should be made . . . Remarks which attribute bigotry primarily to the Protestant community are not only unhelpful but inaccurate.

Commenting in statement, signed also by other Church of Ireland bishops, on Cardinal Ó Fiaich's assertion that ninety per cent of religious bigotry in North was found among Protestants. *The Irish Times*, July 22, 1985.

July 22, 1985
David Steel

I'm a strict Gladstonian. I would rather have seen a united Ireland within a confederal status for the rest of Britain, part of the Commonwealth and all the rest of it. But you can't rewrite history. That all went down the drain, despite Mr Gladstone's attempts.

In *Irish Times* interview as leader of Liberal Party in Britain. *The Irish Times*, July 23, 1985.

August 6, 1985
Dr Tutu, Bishop of Johannesburg

I am really amazed at their commitment, that such young people have been willing to put their money where their mouths are in a very, very real and costly way . . . we must never say 'What can I do?' because here are young people who decided on a matter of principle to do what they thought was right and now they have become celebrities because of their moral stand.

In interview with *Irish Times* in Johannesburg about Dunnes Stores anti-apartheid strikers in Dublin. *The Irish Times*, August 7, 1985.

September 2, 1985
James Prior

The Northern Ireland Office is always regarded as the dustbin.

Commenting, as former NI Secretary, on Cabinet reshuffle in which Tom King replaced Douglas Hurd as NI Secretary. *The Irish Times*, September 3, 1985.

September 3, 1985
Dr (Cahal) Daly, Bishop of Down and Connor

Some Catholics have let the eyes of their souls become so darkened that they no longer recognise sin as sin . . . some people had joined Sinn Féin for idealistic reasons . . . I ask them now to reflect on where that early idealism has left them. They find themselves forced now to carry out or to approve and attempt to condone dreadful deeds and practices.

Preaching at Mass for businessman shot dead by IRA. *The Irish Times,* September 4, 1985.

September 18, 1985
Eugene McCarthy
I could come in and recite 'The Ghost of Roger Casement' . . . that would be better than any testimony, because it was a trial in which forgery and perjury were used. There are foreign policy aspects that relate. I wouldn't want to be extradited to the Republic of Ireland, but I'd rather go there than Northern Ireland.

Giving evidence as former senator and presidential candidate to US Senate Foreign Relations Committee on US-UK extradition treaty. *The Irish Times,* September 19, 1985.

September 30, 1985
Gusty Spence
I am the founder of the UVF. I've spent eighteen and a half years in prison and I am not proud of it. I am ashamed of it. I am against violence. I'd love to take Paisley by the scruff of the neck and rub his face in the blood and brains that have been spilt and make him smell them and taste them.

Speaking at fringe meeting at Labour Party conference in Bournemouth, England. *The Irish Times,* October 1, 1985.

October 1, 1985
John Hewitt
The important thing is never to hope. It is hope that brings turmoil, destruction. Acceptance, resignation, stoicism – yes! But never hope.

Speaking, as Belfast poet, at conference on Northern Ireland troubles at Corrymeela. *The Irish Times,* October 1, 1985.

October 3, 1985
Justice Kevin Lynch
In support of the theory that Joanne Hayes had had twins, the gardaí resorted to unlikely, far-fetched and contradictory theories: first of one different father for the twins, not being Jeremiah Locke, and having blood group 'A'; second, superfecundation, or two separate fathers, one of each baby; thirdly, of Jeremiah Locke being the father of both babies but with bacterial contamination of the Cahirciveen baby's lung specimen . . . causing a true group 'O' to show as a group 'A'; and fourthly, that Joanne Hayes had had twins . . . but the Cahirciveen baby was not one of those twins and accordingly there was a third baby with injuries similar to those of the Cahirciveen baby . . . portions of the garda report display a want of logic.

In summary of findings in inquiry in Kerry Babies case. *The Irish Times,* October 4, 1985.

October 6, 1985
Barry Desmond
The Minister for Health is supposed to do what he is told! The Catholic Hierarchy has found it disturbing that in the last five years, politicians are not afraid to act, whereas up to now there has been an unquestioning acceptance of their [the Hierarchy's] views . . . there was a campaign to get [me] out, and [I have] no doubt that the Catholic Hierarchy are involved at the highest level . . . the campaign had been talked about at polite dinner parties.

Speaking, as Minister for Health, about Church criticisms of his proposed social legislation. *The Irish Times,* October 8, 1985.

October 7, 1985
Catholic Hierarchy
The Hierarchy can only express amazement at the statements attributed to Mr Desmond . . . that they are involved in an alleged campaign aimed at removing him from office. There is no foundation whatever for this.

Response to allegations from Barry Desmond, Minister for Health. *The Irish Times,* October 8, 1985.

October 30, 1985
James Molyneaux
On the day after betrayal by the British Government and Parliament there is no good us saying [to the paramilitaries] 'tut, tut, be good boys and put your guns away'. They would say 'you are yesterday's men'.

As Unionist leader, at London press conference after failing to persuade Margaret Thatcher to break off Anglo-Irish negotiations. *The Irish Times,* October 31, 1985.

November 8, 1985
John Kelly
A referendum [on divorce] now would lead to a [crushing] defeat . . . every Government minister and deputy will be knee deep in cantankerous circulars, petitions, urgings, warnings, political threats and lobbies of all degrees of malignance and unscrupulousness from both sides . . . the last 18 months before a general election is not the moment of to deliberately invite such a thing.

Speaking to Fine Gael meeting in Dublin on Labour proposals for divorce referendum. *The Irish Times,* November 9, 1985.

November 8, 1985
Garret FitzGerald
Our nationalist hopes and aspirations must take second place to providing a stable, peaceful society for those citizens of Europe, of both traditions, in Northern Ireland.

Addressing Young Christian Democrats in Brussels. *The Irish Times,* November 9, 1985.

November 9, 1985
Seamus Mallon
We cannot, will not and must not put this aspiration [United Ireland] on the back-boiler. We cannot make liars of ourselves, we cannot leave it in suspended animation for any length of time, or, like in County Armagh, the boys in the balaclavas will come along and say 'We are the only people pursuing this course'.

Speaking at SDLP conference in Belfast. *The Irish Times,* November 11, 1985.

November 10, 1985
Dr Newman, Bishop of Limerick
I could not but be disappointed at the attitude towards conscience that has been taken recently by some of our politicians . . . one can find Catholics promoting, in the name of a better social scene, ideas and measures that have been opposed by the Church [with] the messianic zeal with which some give themselves up to advancing the cause of contraception, divorce and the like. Unless we

are careful to check this fanatical politics, by the end of the century, genuinely Catholic social expression will have been pushed out of many areas.

In sermon criticising Austin Deasy, Minister for Agriculture, and Barry Desmond, Minister for Health. *The Irish Times,* November 11, 1985.

November 12, 1985
Austin Deasy
To legislate solely as a Roman Catholic for Roman Catholics would amount to political bigotry, and that I will have no part in.

Responding, as member of Government, to criticism of his attitude to social legislation by Bishop Newman of Limerick. *The Irish Times,* November 13, 1985.

November 14, 1985
Enoch Powell
Does the right honourable lady not understand, and if she does not yet she soon will, that the penalty for treachery is to fall into public contempt?

Remark addressed to British Prime Minister Margaret Thatcher in Commons after it became known Dublin and London had finalised Anglo-Irish negotiations. *The Irish Times,* November 15, 1985.

November 15, 1985
Anglo-Irish Agreement
The two Governments . . . affirm that any change in the status of Northern Ireland would only come about with the consent of a majority of the people of Northern Ireland . . .

The United Kingdom Government accept that the Irish Government will put forward views and proposals on matters relating to Northern Ireland . . . in so far as these matters are not the responsibility of a devolved administration in Northern Ireland. In the interests of promoting peace and stability, determined efforts shall be made through the conference to resolve any differences.

From Articles One and Two of Anglo-Irish Agreement signed at Hillsborough by Garret FitzGerald and Margaret Thatcher. *The Irish Times,* November 16, 1985.

November 15, 1985
Garret FitzGerald
Tá sé mar chuspóir againn comh-aitheantas agus comh-urraim a bhaint amach don dá fhéiniúlacht i dTuaisceart Éireann. Féadfaigh náisiúnaithe anois a gceann a ardú agus a fhios acu go bhfuil seasamh acu atá ar comhchéim leis an seasamh atá ag comhaltaí an phobail Aontachtúil agus gur léir don saol go bhfuil an scéal amhlaidh.
As I have just said in Irish, our purpose is to secure equal recognition and respect for the two identities in Northern Ireland. Nationalists can now raise their heads knowing their position is, and is seen to be, on an equal footing with that of members of the Unionist community.

Speaking, as Taoiseach, in Hillsborough Castle after signing of Anglo-Irish Agreement. *The Irish Times,* November 16, 1985.

November 15, 1985
Margaret Thatcher
I went into this Agreement because I was not prepared to tolerate a situation of continuing violence . . . I believe in the union and that it will last as long as the majority so wish.

Speaking in Hillsborough Castle after signing of Anglo-Irish Agreement. *The Irish Times,* November 16, 1985.

November 15, 1985
President Reagan
We applaud its promise of peace and a new dawn for the troubled communities of Northern Ireland.

In statement in Washington on Anglo-Irish Agreement. *The Irish Times,* November 16, 1985.

November 15, 1985
Charles Haughey
I believe that the concept of Irish unity has been dealt a very major blow . . . For the first time ever the legitimacy of the Unionist position, which is contrary to unification, has been recognised by an Irish Government in an international agreement.

Commenting on Anglo-Irish Agreement. *The Irish Times,* November 16, 1985.

November 15, 1985
Gerry Adams
Garret FitzGerald insults the long-suffering nationalist people of the Six Counties when he tells us in gaeilge that we can now raise our heads. It is because we have raised our heads and have struggled and made sacrifices for our civil and national rights that the running sore of British involvement in Ireland has been addressed at all.

Responding, as Sinn Féin President, to remarks of Taoiseach after signing of Anglo-Irish Agreement. *The Irish Times,* November 16, 1985.

November 15, 1985
Ian Gow
I believe that . . . the involvement of a foreign power in a consultative role in the administration of the province will prolong, and not diminish, Ulster's agony.

In letter, as Minister of State, to British Prime Minister on resigning from Government in protest at Anglo-Irish Agreement. *The Irish Times,* November 16, 1985.

November 16, 1985
Peter Robinson
We are on the window ledge of the union.

Speaking, as Democratic Unionist Party deputy leader, in NI Assembly debate on Anglo-Irish Agreement. *The Irish Times,* November 19, 1985.

November 17, 1985
Michael Noonan
In effect we have been given a major and substantial role in the day-to-day running of Northern Ireland.

Commenting, as Irish Minister for Justice, on Anglo-Irish Agreement during American television programme. *The Irish Times,* November 18, 1985.

November 18, 1985
Mary Robinson
I do not believe it [Anglo-Irish Agreement] can achieve its objective of securing peace and stability within Northern Ireland or on the island as a whole.

On resigning from Irish Labour Party in protest at Anglo-Irish Agreement. *The Irish Times,* November 19, 1985.

November 18, 1985
Merlyn Rees
The Orange card will no longer be a trump card . . . the Union is at risk not from this part of the United Kingdom but from within Northern Ireland.

Speaking in Commons, as former Labour NI Secretary, after signing of Anglo-Irish Agreement. *HC Debates:* Vol. 87: No. 9: Col. 24.

November 18, 1985
Harold McCusker

The Prime Minister . . . will have ensured that I shall carry to my grave with ignominy the sense of the injustice that I have done to my constituents down the years – when, in their darkest hours I exhorted them to put their trust in this British House of Commons . . . Is not the reality of this Agreement that they will now be Irish-British hybrids?

Speaking in Commons, as Unionist MP, after signing of Anglo-Irish Agreement. *HC Debates:* Vol. 87: No. 9: Col. 29.

November 19, 1985
Garret FitzGerald

I believe that no sane person would wish to attempt to change the status of Northern Ireland without the consent of a majority of its people. That would be a recipe for disaster and could, I believe, lead only to a civil war.

Speaking, as Taoiseach, in Dáil debate on Anglo-Irish Agreement. *The Irish Times,* November 20, 1985.

November 19, 1985
Charles Haughey

In effect what is proposed in this Agreement is that the Irish Government, accepting British sovereignty over part of Ireland, will involve itself in assisting and advising the British Government to rule that part of Ireland more effectively, to help make it more amenable to the authority of the British Government.

Speaking, as Fianna Fáil Opposition leader, in Dáil debate on Anglo-Irish Agreement. *The Irish Times,* November 20, 1985.

November 20, 1985
Neil Blaney

This [Agreement] is dealing with the restricted violence of the IRA, at the same time ignoring the institutional violence of our occupiers in the North. This agreement will create more violence, not lessen it.

Speaking, as independent TD, in Dáil debate on Anglo-Irish Agreement. *The Irish Times,* November 21, 1985.

November 21, 1985
Des O'Malley

I'm voting for it [Anglo-Irish Agreement] because for this House to reject it would be unthinkable. I shudder to think of the consequences of rejection . . . If Eamon de Valera was a young man and sitting in the House with Frank Aiken, Sean Lemass, Sean MacEntee and the others, and they were asked to make up their minds and vote for this Agreement, does anybody think that they would not support it?

Speaking, as independent TD, in Dáil on Anglo-Irish Agreement. *The Irish Times,* November 22, 1985.

November 26, 1985
Margaret Thatcher

This House represents all the people of the United Kingdom and its decisions are binding on all of them. We shall not give way to threats or to violence from any quarter . . . the agreement enforces the union, and that should bring reassurance and confidence to the Unionist majority . . . As one who believes in the union, I urge the Unionists to take advantage of the chance offered by the agreement.

In speech, as Prime Minister, at start of two-day debate in Commons on Anglo-Irish Agreement signed on November 15, 1985. *HC Debates:* Vol. 87: No. 15: Col. 753.

November 26, 1985
Neil Kinnock

Zephaniah Williams, the Welsh Chartist, said: 'When prejudice blinds the eye of the mind the brightest truth shines in vain.' I do not address the bigots or the wallies on either side of the sectarian divide, when I plead with the majority of non-nationalists not to be blinded by prejudice.

Speaking, as Labour leader, in debate in Commons on Anglo-Irish Agreement. *HC Debates:* Vol. 87: No. 15: Col. 755.

November 26, 1985
James Molyneaux

I have to say honestly and truthfully that in forty years in public life I have never known what I can only describe as a universal cold fury which some of us have thus far managed to contain.

Speaking, as Official Unionist Party leader, in debate in Commons on Anglo-Irish Agreement. *HC Debates:* Vol. 87: No. 15: Col. 769.

November 26, 1985
Clive Soley

The Unionists are not stupid or blind to what is happening. They feel betrayed because they recognise that conditional unionism ... is not a permanent solution for Northern Ireland.

Speaking, as Labour MP, in debate in Commons on Anglo-Irish Agreement. *HC Debates:* Vol. 87: No. 15: Col. 823.

November 26, 1985
Peter Robinson

I wish that the House had a sense of the deep feeling of anger and betrayal in Northern Ireland ... I recall the words of [Rudyard Kipling's] poem 'Ulster 1912':
'The blood our fathers spilt,
Our love, our toils, our pains,
Are counted us for guilt,
And only binds our chains.
Before an Empire's eyes
The traitor claims his price.
What need of further lies?
We are the sacrifice.'

Speaking, as DUP deputy leader, in debate in Commons on Anglo-Irish Agreement. *HC Debates:* Vol. 87: No. 15: Col. 781.

November 26, 1985
John Hume

In 1912 the Ulster Unionists defied the sovereign wish of Parliament to grant home rule ... That taught them a lesson which they have never forgotten – that if one threatens a British Government or British Parliament and produces crowds on the streets from the Orange lodges the British will back down ... a better poet than Kipling, the good, honest voice of the North, Louis MacNeice ... said:
'... castles are out of date,
The tide flows round the children's sandy fancy,
Put up what flag you like, it is too late
To save your soul with bunting.'
It is far too late for the people of Northern Ireland to save their souls with bunting or with flag-waving.

Speaking, as SDLP leader, in debate in Commons on Anglo-Irish Agreement. *HC Debates:* Vol. 87: No. 15: Cols. 786-87.

November 27, 1985
Enoch Powell

When in the coming months the consequences of this understanding work themselves out and the Prime Minister watches with uncomprehending compassion the continued sequence of terrorism, murder and death in Northern Ireland which this Agreement will not prevent but will maintain and foment, let her not send to ask for whom the bell tolls. It tolls for her.

Speaking, as Unionist MP, in debate in Commons on Anglo-Irish Agreement. *HC Debates:* Vol. 87: No. 16: Col. 957.

November 27, 1985
Harold McCusker

The people of Northern Ireland whom I represent would prefer to be governed by a Catholic nationalist in Northern Ireland than a Minister from the Irish Republic who lives in Cork [Irish Foreign Minister Peter Barry] and who did not know where Northern Ireland was until five years ago.

Speaking, as Unionist MP, in debate in Commons on Anglo-Irish Agreement. *HC Debates:* Vol. 87: No. 16: Col. 919.

November 27, 1985
Rev. Ian Paisley

There is a crisis in our land. The only thing that will steady our people is the opportunity to do something ... The House should facilitate those who want this to remain a constitutional battle, not one in the streets of our cities ... [the House] will not hear from me again for some time, and perhaps never again.

Speaking, as DUP leader, in debate in Commons on Anglo-Irish Agreement. *HC Debates:* Vol. 87: No. 16: Cols. 910-13.

November 27, 1985
Edward Heath

I confess that I have always found the Irish, all of them, extremely difficult to understand.

Speaking, as former Tory Prime Minister, in debate in Commons on Anglo-Irish Agreement. *HC Debates:* Vol. 87: No. 16: Col. 900.

November 28, 1985
Mary Harney
Parnell's famous statement on impeding the march of a nation applied to his time, but did not address the realities of 1985. . . . I believe this Agreement copperfastens nothing. I believe it should be seen as a step towards peace and reconciliation.

Speaking after being expelled from Fianna Fáil for defying party whip and voting for Anglo-Irish Agreement. *The Irish Times,* November 28, 1985.

December 3, 1985
Tom King
The Prime Minister of Ireland . . . has in fact accepted that for all practical purposes and into perpetuity there will not be a united Ireland.

Speaking, as NI Secretary, at Brussels dinner. *The Irish Times,* December 4, 1985.

December 4, 1985
Merlyn Rees
Can I bring to the notice of the Secretary of State that wise old Ulster adage which has been put into a poem by Seamus Heaney which is, 'whatever you say, say nothing'.

Speaking in Commons about row which followed Tom King's remark of December 3 in Brussels about Irish unity. *The Irish Times,* December 5, 1985.

January 3, 1986
Pascal O'Hare
The Anglo-Irish Agreement has copperfastened the guarantee to the Unionists.

On resigning from SDLP, as North Belfast Assembly member, in protest at SDLP support for Agreement. *The Irish Times,* January 4, 1986.

January 10, 1986
Tom King
They [the Unionists] cannot go on saying 'no'. They must say 'yes' to something.

Speaking, as NI Secretary, at Oxford conference on Northern Ireland. *The Irish Times,* January 11, 1986.

January 14, 1986
Joint Unionist Election Manifesto
1886 saw the introduction of Gladstone's first Home Rule Bill. One hundred years on, the conspiracy continues to deny the Ulster people the right to self-determination.

Issued by Official and Democratic Unionist Parties prior to by-elections on issue of Anglo-Irish Agreement. *The Irish Times,* January 15, 1986.

January 23, 1986
Joe Burke
Dessie O'Malley [is] a combination of John F. Kennedy, Martin Luther King and Pope John Paul.

County councillor speaking as recruit from Fine Gael at Galway rally for Progressive Democratic Party, founded by Des O'Malley. *The Irish Times,* January 24, 1986.

February 1, 1986
Mairead Corrigan
It was the money that spoilt the whole thing.

As leader of NI Peace People, interviewed on ITV about split between original founders after they decided to keep Nobel Peace Prize money for themselves. *Daily Mirror,* February 1, 1986.

February 1, 1986
Betty Williams
I didn't walk away from Ulster, I ran.

Interviewed on ITV, as former leader of NI Peace People, then living in United States, about break-up of organisation over personality differences and decision to keep Nobel Peace Prize money for themselves. *Daily Mirror,* February 1, 1986.

February 11, 1986
Peter Robinson
There is no point in saying on the Twelfth of July that we are prepared to die for Ulster when the music is in the background, if we are to give in now. Better to languish in jail, be removed from office or face financial penalty than to forsake principle and betray future generations.

At press conference, as DUP deputy leader. *The Irish Times,* February 12, 1986.

February 12, 1986
Gay Byrne
[Ireland] is banjaxed and washed out . . . a man . . . stood up in the audience at the 'Late Late Show' three or four years ago and said that if we had any manners we'd hand the entire island back to the Queen of England at 9 o'clock the following morning and apologise

for its condition ... as every week passes, I think that guy had something.

In *Hot Press* interview, as Ireland's most popular broadcaster. *The Irish Times,* February 13, 1986.

February 14, 1986
Garret FitzGerald
I have today accepted the resignations of ... Michael D'Arcy ... and Donal Creed.

As Taoiseach, detailing Government changes involving removal of two Ministers of State. *The Irish Times,* February 18, 1986.

February 17, 1986
Michael D'Arcy
I did not resign. I was sacked, so to speak.

Commenting on Taoiseach's statement that he had resigned as Minister of State. *The Irish Times,* February 18, 1986.

February 17, 1986
Donal Creed
He did not get any resignation from me. I did not resign, and if I was asked, I would not have done it.

Commenting on Taoiseach's statement that he had resigned as Minister of State. *The Irish Times,* February 18, 1986.

February 18, 1986
Garret FitzGerald
I regret that on Thursday last I informed the House that the two deputies had resigned.

Speaking in Dáil on statement about Government changes of February 14, 1986. *The Irish Times,* February 18, 1986.

February 20, 1986
Charles Haughey
The head of the Government has been shown to be unsound in his judgement, treacherous in his relationships, vacillating in his decisions, incompetent in the management of his party and his Government.

Commenting in Dáil on FitzGerald's handling of dismissal of Ministers of State. *The Irish Times,* February 21, 1986.

February 23, 1986
Harold McCusker
There is nothing that will satisfy the Gaelic, Roman Catholic Republic now on this island other than a total subjugation of the loyalist

nation on this island ... Unionists would have to defeat the threat posed to their position by latter-day Fenians.

Speaking, as Unionist MP, at Ulster Hall rally to mark the centenary of address by Lord Randolph Churchill at same venue against Home Rule. *The Irish Times,* February 24, 1986.

February 25, 1986
James Molyneaux
People will very shortly have concluded that we haven't reached the end of the road, that the elected representatives are still in being, that we still have a role ... the door was not slammed ... we have got away from what I think was anticipated to be a deadlock situation.

At London press conference with Rev. Ian Paisley after he and Molyneaux had met Thatcher to try to persuade her to suspend Anglo-Irish Agreement. (The position on further negotiation was later reversed at Belfast Unionist meeting.) *The Irish Times,* February 26, 1986.

February 25, 1986
Andy Tyrie
I feel if we get into a violent confrontation whether it's with the security forces or with the nationalist community here, it's going to lead to very little future for any of us ... we live here and it's not a matter of surrendering: it's a matter of just compromising for the sake of peace.

Interviewed about possible action against Anglo-Irish Agreement, as leader of paramilitary Ulster Defence Association. *The Irish Times,* February 26, 1986.

February 27, 1986
Margaret Thatcher
A strike ostensibly carried out in the name of the Union is all too likely to lead to erosion of support for the Union in the United Kingdom as a whole.

In letter about planned protest against Anglo-Irish Agreement to Church of Ireland Archbishop of Armagh, Dr Eames. *The Irish Times,* March 1, 1986.

March 3, 1986
Peter Robinson
Marcos Thatcher ... guilty or not guilty? (Cries of 'Guilty'). I would like to have

suggested the electric chair but unfortunately there are power cuts.

DUP deputy leader, addressing loyalist rally in Belfast during day of action against Anglo-Irish Agreement. *The Irish Times,* March 4, 1986.

March 7, 1986
Margaret Thatcher
[Their] importance [incidents at Sellafield nuclear reprocessing plant] has been exaggerated in the media out of all proportion to the real risks to health and safety in an apparent effort to discredit the nuclear industry ... British Nuclear Fuels has substantially reduced its discharges ... further improvements will occur.

In letter to Taoiseach after FitzGerald had complained about leaks from nuclear reprocessing plant. *The Irish Times,* March 8, 1986.

March 12, 1986
House of Commons Environment Committee
The Irish sea is the most radioactive sea in the world.

From report criticising safety standards in British nuclear industry. *The Irish Times,* March 13, 1986.

March 14, 1986
Geoffrey Howe
Let them [Unionists] be in no doubt that the future of the union, so far from being assured, would only be threatened by intransigence, inflexibility and shortsightedness of that kind.

In speech, as British Foreign Secretary, to English Conservatives about unconstitutional loyalist action against Anglo-Irish Agreement. *The Irish Times,* March 15, 1986.

April 14, 1986
Alan Wright
Left on their own after a British pull-out, loyalists would build a Berlin-type wall from Londonderry to Newry, with four border crossings and a 100-yard strip mined and patrolled 24 hours a day. There would be conscription for the 18 to 21-year-olds whose sole duty would be to combat militant nationalism.

Interviewed, as head of Ulster Clubs, formed to resist Anglo-Irish Agreement. *The Irish Times,* April 14, 1986.

April 30, 1986
Seamus Mallon
We could see a new type of fascism emerging ... accompanied by a bible in one hand and a petrol bomb in the other.

Referring to loyalist attacks on homes of Catholics and RUC members in Northern Ireland. *HC Debates:* Vol. 96: No. 104: Col. 978.

May 5, 1986
Dr. Newman, Bishop of Limerick
The [Catholic] Church has the right to tell the people what to do in these matters ... I'm not sure if I'll be telling them how to vote ... but they'll be under no illusions about the way I would like them to vote.

In interview on divorce referendum. *The Irish Times,* May 5, 1986.

May 7, 1986
Eldon Griffiths
It is asking too much to require the police to stand there like sitting ducks while wild men throw petrol bombs at them.

Speaking, as Tory spokesman for Police Federation, in Commons debate on plastic bullets. *HC Debates:* Vol. 97: No. 108: Col. 151.

May 13, 1986
Catholic Hierarchy
We do not ask that Catholic doctrine as such be enshrined in law. Nevertheless we have the responsibility as pastors to offer moral guidance to Catholics ... No Catholic hierarchy anywhere in the world has failed to record its moral objections to the introduction of divorce.

In statement on proposed divorce referendum. *The Irish Times,* May 14, 1986.

May 14, 1986
Alice Glenn
Any woman voting for divorce would be like a turkey voting for Christmas.

Commenting, as Fine Gael TD, on divorce referendum. *The Irish Times,* May 15, 1986.

May 14, 1986
Michael Woods
The Government's proposal [on divorce] could be used as a sledge hammer to crush the rights of the first family which would have lost

its present constitutional protection. Could it be that the Government have unwittingly created a constitutional Frankenstein which may sleep for a while and then rise and stalk the land?

Speaking in Dáil, as Fianna Fáil spokesman on justice, on proposed amendment to Constitution to allow divorce. *The Irish Times,* May 15, 1986.

May 20, 1986
Charles Haughey

It is not reasonable to suggest that there is some form of divorce that could be introduced which would not have many difficult consequences for society and for the stability of the family and for the rights of existing family members.

As Fianna Fáil leader, in Dáil debate on proposed Government amendment to constitution to allow divorce. *The Irish Times,* May 21, 1986.

May 24, 1986
Dr Empey, Bishop of Meath and Kildare (Church of Ireland)

Somehow we will have to nail the lie that permissiveness flows from the Church of Ireland and that morality is the sole possession of one Church in the land.

Commenting on debate on divorce referendum. *The Irish Times* ('This Week They Said'), May 24, 1986.

May 25, 1986
Rev. Fr Pat O'Brien

Victory [for the Catholic Church against divorce] ... may be achieved by pulpit tactics, by insinuation, suggestion, and sometimes downright statements that Catholics have no choice in the matter. That is dishonest, untruthful and ... a form of moral tyranny.

Speaking, as curate at Skehana, during Divorce Action Group meeting in Galway. *The Irish Times,* May 29, 1986.

June 11, 1986
Patrick Magee

Tiocfaidh ár lá (Our day will come).

Called from dock after being sentenced in Old Bailey, London, to life imprisonment as IRA member guilty of bombing hotel in Brighton during Conservative Party conference in 1984, killing five people. BBC report, June 11, 1986.

June 11, 1986
Catholic Hierarchy

We are convinced that the proposed amendment [allowing divorce] would weaken rather than strengthen marriage and the family ... While it would alleviate the pain of some, it would, we believe, release in society a force which would bring pain to a much greater number.

In statement on Government referendum on amendment to Constitution to allow divorce. *The Irish Times,* June 12, 1986.

June 16, 1986
Proposed Constitutional Amendment

Where ... a marriage has failed ... the court may in accordance with law grant a dissolution of the marriage provided ... proper provision ... will be made for any dependent spouse and for any child ...

Wording of amendment to be put to people in referendum, replacing article in Constitution prohibiting divorce. *The Irish Times,* June 16, 1986.

June 24, 1986
Rev. Ian Paisley

You don't come crying to me if your homes are attacked. You will reap what you sow.

To RUC men who were ejecting Paisley and other loyalist politicians from Stormont after British Government had dissolved NI Assembly. *The Irish Times,* June 25, 1986.

June 24, 1986
Rev. Ian Paisley

There could be hand to hand fighting in every street in Northern Ireland. We are on the verge of civil war because when you take away the forum of democracy you don't have anything left.

Speaking after dissolution of NI Assembly because it was not being worked as required by British Parliament. *The Irish Times,* June 25, 1986.

June 25, 1986
John Hume

I hope that the people of the Republic will cast their votes for an Ireland that will respect the rights of conscience of all its people, Protestant, Catholic and dissenter.

As SDLP leader, in message to voters in Republic on eve of referendum on amendment to

Constitution to allow divorce. *The Irish Times,* June 26, 1986.

June 25, 1986
Garret FitzGerald

Ulster says 'no' to its minority. Can we say 'no' to our people whose marriages have failed?

As Taoiseach, in message to voters on eve of referendum on amendment to Constitution to allow divorce. *The Irish Times,* June 26, 1986.

June 29, 1986
Charles Haughey

[The referendum result will] not take away one iota from progress towards a united Ireland ... no matter what we do down here, if we were to elect the head of the Orange Order as President of this Republic, the Unionists would still find we are doing something dishonest, deceitful and totally unacceptable to them.

Commenting, as Fianna Fáil leader, on effect on Unionist attitudes of rejection by electorate in Republic of proposed amendment to constitution allowing divorce. *The Irish Times,* June 30, 1986.

July 1, 1986
Rev. Ian Paisley

It [the referendum result] has brought us back from the brink, because I believe that if it had been a success the British Government would have been pushing us with more vigour down the united Ireland road. I would say that the civil war, which I believed was almost at hand, has receded as a result.

Commenting, as DUP leader, on rejection by electorate in republic of Constitutional amendment to allow divorce. *The Irish Times,* July 2, 1986.

July 8, 1986
Des O'Malley

Just as the 1925 Boundary Commission

reinforced the geographical division of Ireland as negotiated in the 1922 Treaty, the result of the divorce referendum has underpinned the whole concept of partition.

Speaking in Dublin, as leader of Progressive Democrats, on rejection by electorate in Republic of Constitutional amendment to allow divorce. *The Irish Times,* July 9, 1986.

July 16, 1986
Eldon Griffiths

Here is an Irishman speaking about British territory. How dare he do such a thing.

Reacting in Commons, as Conservative MP and Police Federation spokesman, to criticism by Irish Minister for Foreign Affairs Peter Barry to British Government about RUC decision to allow Orange parade through Catholic area of Portadown. *The Irish Times,* July 17, 1986.

August 24, 1986
John Stalker

I am certainly not saying there was a conspiracy, but I think it would be a wise man who could say there was not.

Speaking on RTE, as Deputy Chief Constable of Greater Manchester, on his removal from inquiry into RUC and his three months' suspension on unsubstantiated charges of misconduct. *The Irish Times,* August 25, 1986.

August 24, 1986
Cardinal Ó Fiaich

If we remain the last Catholic country in western Europe, that is because we have been remote, rural and poor: all these things are passing.

In interview in *The Guardian* on aftermath of rejection by electorate in Republic of Constitutional amendment to allow divorce. *The Guardian,* August 25, 1986.

Abbreviations

AOH: Ancient Order of Hibernians, dedicated to Catholic nationalism

BBC: British Broadcasting Corporation

DÉ: Dáil Éireann debates

DUP: Democratic Unionist Party

EEC: European Economic Community

FCA: Fórsa Cosanta Áitiúil (local defence force)

GOC: General Officer Commanding

GPO: General Post Office

HC: House of Commons

IRA: Irish Republican Army

IRSP: Irish Republican Socialist Party

ITGWU: Irish Transport and General Workers Union

ITV: Independent Television

MP: Member of Parliament

NATO: North Atlantic Treaty Organisation

NI: Northern Ireland

NICRA: Northern Ireland Civil Rights Association

NORAID: Irish Northern Aid

NUI: National University of Ireland

OC: Officer Commanding

RIC: Royal Irish Constabulary

RTE: Radio Telefis Éireann

RUC: Royal Ulster Constabulary

SAS: Special Air Service (British Army)

SDLP: Social, Democratic and Labour Party

TD: Teachta Dála, member of Dáil Éireann

TUC: Trades Union Congress

UCG: University College Galway

UDA: Ulster Defence Association

UDR: Ulster Defence Regiment

UK: United Kingdom of Great Britain and Northern Ireland

UNIFIL: United Nations Interim Force in Lebanon

USC: Ulster Special Constabulary (B Specials)

UVF: Ulster Volunteer Force

Apprentice Boys: Protestant organisation to commemorate siege of Derry in 1689

Áras an Uachtaráin: Residence of President of Ireland

Árd Fheis: Annual Conference

Chequers: Country residence of British Prime Minister

Commons: House of Commons, Westminster

Council of Ireland: Cross-border inter-government body, agreed in 1922 and 1973; never set up

Dáil: Dáil Éireann, lower house of Irish Parliament

Fenians: Irish Republican Brotherhood

Irish Party: Pro-Home Rule Irish MPs before independence

Lords: House of Lords, Westminster

Official IRA: Pro-Marxist faction of IRA since 1970

Official Sinn Féin: Political wing of Official IRA

Oireachtas: Irish Parliament

Old IRA: Pre-1922 IRA

Orange Order: Protestant body dedicated to union with Britain

Provisional IRA: Breakaway group from pre-1970 IRA

Provisional Government: Free State Government, between independence in 1922 and first elections

Seanad: Seanad Éireann, upper house of Irish Parliament

Stormont: Northern Ireland Parliament Buildings

Sunningdale: 1973 Agreement to set up power-sharing Executive in Northern Ireland

Tánaiste: Deputy Taoiseach

Taoiseach: Prime Minister

◦৶ Indexes ৶ৎ

INDEX TO SPEAKERS

SUBJECT INDEX

Acknowledgements

Poems of W.B. Yeats pp. 55 and 91 are reproduced by permission of A.P. Watt Ltd., London, and Macmillan Publishing Co. Inc., New York, from *Collected Poems* by W.B. Yeats. Copyright 1912, 1916, 1919, 1924, 1928, 1933, 1934 by Macmillan Publishing Co. Inc. Renewed 1940, 1944, 1947, 1952, 1956, 1961, 1962 by Bertha Georgie Yeats. Copyright 1940 by Georgie Yeats, Michael Butler Yeats and Anne Yeats. Extract p. 64 from *Guerilla Days in Ireland,* Tom Barry, with permission of The Irish Press Ltd.